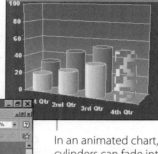

William L. Martin
Product Manager
Twin Cities Operations

Seagate Technology
8053 East Bloomington Freeway
Bloomington, MN 55420
Direct (612) 806-2947
Fax (612) 806-2859
bill_martin@notes.seagate.com

Seagate

PowerPoint's newest templates produce great-looking presentations.

In an animated chart, the cylinders can fade into view one by one.

Place beautiful gradients, textures, and even pictures in the backgrounds of charts and other graphic shapes. See Chapter 10, "Formatting Charts," page 243.

Make charts come alive by animating their bars, lines, and other features. See "Animating Charts," page 396.

Steve Sagman

Steve Sagman is the New York–based author
of more than a dozen computer books,
including *Traveling The Microsoft Network*,
also published by Microsoft Press. His books
have sold more than a half million copies,
and they have been translated into ten
languages.

When he's not writing books, Steve runs a
business called Studioserv, which provides
user documentation, software training, interface
design, and book editing and production.

And when he's not writing or running his
business, Steve plays jazz piano and toils in
the fertile loam of his garden.

Steve welcomes comments and suggestions
about this book at one of the following
addresses:

steves@studioserv.com
570 Mecox Rd., Water Mill, NY 11976
140 Charles St., New York, NY 10014

RUNNING

Microsoft®
PowerPoint® 97

Stephen W. Sagman

PUBLISHED BY
Microsoft Press
A Division of Microsoft Corporation
One Microsoft Way
Redmond, Washington 98052-6399

Library of Congress Cataloging-in-Publication Data
Sagman, Stephen W.
    Running Microsoft PowerPoint 97 / Stephen W. Sagman.
        p.   cm.
    Includes index.
    ISBN 1-57231-324-2
    1. Computer graphics. 2. Microsoft PowerPoint (Computer file)
    3. Business presentations--Data processing.   I. Title.
    T385.S2354 1997
    006.6'869--dc21   96-40954
                                             CIP

Printed and bound in the United States of America.

1 2 3 4 5 6 7 8 9 QFQF 2 1 0 9 8 7

Distributed to the book trade in Canada by Macmillan of Canada, a division of Canada Publishing
Corporation.

A CIP catalogue record for this book is available from the British Library.

Microsoft Press books are available through booksellers and distributors worldwide. For further
information about international editions, contact your local Microsoft Corporation office. Or contact
Microsoft Press International directly at fax (206) 936-7329.

Acquisitions Editors: Lucinda Rowley and Kim Fryer
Project Editors: Lucinda Rowley, Judith Bloch, and Stuart J. Stuple
Technical Editor: Soft-Spec—Pam Toliver
Manuscript Editors: Studio Serv—Tim Leavitt and Devra Hall

Chapters at a Glance

Table of Contents

Acknowledgments

I am deeply grateful to the fine people at Microsoft Press who brought me on board and shepherded this book through three editions, including Lucinda Rowley, Kim Fryer, Judith Bloch, Stuart Stuple, Mary DeJong, Bill Teel, Kim Eggleston, Jim Kramer, Travis Beaven, Peggy McCauley and Ina Chang.

Thanks also to Polly Fox Urban, Deb Fenwick, Christina Dudley, and Ken Sanchez at Online Press, and Mary Deaton and Lynn Van Deventer who revised the previous edition, *Running Microsoft Power-Point for Windows 95*.

For this edition, I'd especially like to thank Pam Toliver and Tim Leavitt for their editing, Christine Solomon for providing Chapter 19, *Automating PowerPoint with Visual Basic for Applications*, which was adapted from her *Developing Business Applications with Microsoft Office* (3rd edition), also published by Microsoft Press, and Devra Hall for stepping in at the eleventh hour and editing, proofing, checking, fixing, revising, and, not least of all, calming.

At Microsoft, Susan Grabau and John Tafoya have generously offered important information about Microsoft PowerPoint.

And finally, as always, a special thanks to Eric and Lola for being there and for being so patient and supportive.

Introduction

Since its introduction in 1987, Microsoft PowerPoint has pioneered new ways of working with presentation graphics. PowerPoint introduced the concept of a presentation as a single entity rather than discrete slides, and it has introduced innovations with each new release.

Microsoft PowerPoint 97 carries on the tradition, adding dozens of features designed to make creating presentations even easier and more intuitive. At the same time, it has become just like its colleagues in the Microsoft Office suite of Windows-based applications, sharing on-screen controls like menus and dialog boxes, chart-making, drawing, document proofing, and techniques like drag and drop. PowerPoint has even mastered the common language of communication that is shared by the Office applications, so you can now effortlessly pass text, numbers, and graphics among the applications using drag and drop.

What's New in PowerPoint 97

Whether you're a new user or a veteran, you'll appreciate Power-Point's many new features. And if you're already familiar with other Microsoft Office 97 applications, such as Microsoft Word 97 or Microsoft Excel 97, you'll recognize many of these innovations. Here is a partial list of the new features in PowerPoint 97:

- Complete integration with the full Microsoft Office 97 suite, including a shared list of commonly misspelled words that PowerPoint can automatically correct as you type, a shared palette of colors from which you can choose, and the ability to add a PowerPoint slide to a binder of other Office documents.

- An expanded and improved AutoContent Wizard, which lets you select a presentation on the basis of both design and content. The wizard also contains more templates—including templates for status or team meetings, information kiosks, certificates, flyers, calendars, and Web home pages—so that you have more presentation designs to choose from.

- New design templates, including templates with preset animations.

- Summary Slide and Expand Slide commands, which automatically summarize slides you select and break crowded slides into multiple slides, respectively.

- Presentation Comments, which you and others in your work-group can add to slides as you collaborate to prepare a presentation. These comments appear like yellow sticky notes, and they can be shown or hidden from view.

- New AutoShapes for drawing graphic objects on slides, including connectors for creating flow charts and schematics. Connectors are lines that connect two shapes and automatically reposition to remain attached when you move the shapes.

- Greatly enhanced drawing tools on the new Drawing toolbar. New tools allow you to add 3-D perspective effects and perspective shadows to objects, and edit the shapes of objects by moving their points. Object alignment and distribution commands enable you to align and evenly space objects on a slide.

- Image adjustment controls so you can modify the brightness and contrast in pictures.

- Slide show improvements, which include custom animations, so you can animate each object on a slide, even the elements within charts.

- Voice narration, music tracks, and enhanced video playback capabilities in slide shows.

- The Clip Gallery now offers sounds, movies, and pictures in addition to clip art graphics.

- Action buttons, action settings, and hyperlinks give you visual controls you can add to slides so the presenter or viewers at a kiosk can navigate the presentation and even jump to other documents, files, addresses on the network and even to Internet addresses.

- A new Save To HTML command, which converts a presentation to Web pages and saves the presentation in standard HTML format.

- View On Two Screens lets you use a direct cable connection between two computers so you can use one computer to control the presentation shown on another computer. The viewing computer shows the presentation as a full-screen slide show. The presenting computer displays the presentation in a window alongside the Slide Navigator, Meeting Minder, and Slide Timer windows.

About This Book

The object of this book is to give you the broadest possible understanding of PowerPoint in the shortest possible time. It serves as a tutorial as you're learning PowerPoint and as a reference for looking up topics. This book assumes that you have a working knowledge of Windows 95 or Windows NT.

The parts and chapters of this book are organized in the order that you're likely to need information as you create presentations in PowerPoint. Part I, which includes Chapters 1 and 2, introduces PowerPoint. You learn the basics of the PowerPoint environment, and you get off on the right footing by learning the essential steps to follow whenever you create a presentation.

Part II, which includes Chapters 3 through 8, provides guidelines for creating the basic elements of a presentation. You learn how to start a presentation and how to work in Outline view and Slide view to enter and organize the text, as well as add graphs, organization charts, and tables.

Part III, which consists of Chapters 9 through 11, offers important information on adapting the basic presentation to your specific needs. You learn how to change the overall presentation design, format the graphs you've created, and use Slide Sorter view to view presentation-wide alterations.

Part IV, which includes Chapters 12 through 14, shows you how to embellish a presentation with text annotations, drawings, clip art, and pictures.

Part V, which consists of Chapters 15, 16, and 17, gives you the information you need to produce the fruits of your labor: printed pages, audience handouts, 35-mm slides, and Web sites. You also learn how to prepare and deliver electronic on-screen presentations called slide shows—complete with transitions, builds, video, sound, and music—both to a "live" audience and over a network as an online conference.

Part VI, which includes Chapters 18, 19, and 20, covers advanced topics such as using PowerPoint with other Windows-based applications, automating PowerPoint with Visual Basic for Applications, and customizing PowerPoint to suit the way you like to work.

Using This Book

In this book, when you see a key combination with a plus sign, like this: Ctrl+Z, it means "Hold down the first key and then press the second key." For example, Ctrl+Z means "Hold down the Ctrl key and then press the Z key."

TIP

> Tips that contain helpful suggestions for getting more out of PowerPoint or for enhancing the visual appeal of your presentations look like this.

NOTE

> Notes about PowerPoint features, commands, or techniques look like this.

WARNING

> Warnings are surrounded by a heavy black border so you will find them quite hard to ignore.

SEE ALSO

Finally, whenever you see the "See Also" icon, you'll find references to other sections in the book that provide additional, related information.

Introducing PowerPoint

Setting the PowerPoint Stage

A word processor prepares the text in your everyday life. A spreadsheet calculates the numbers you need. And a database stores the text and numeric information you've compiled. But to communicate your knowledge, information, and achievements, and to persuade the world at large, you need a powerful presentation processor.

What Is PowerPoint?

PowerPoint is the world's leading, presentation-making program. It takes the text and numbers you've collected and hands back slides and charts with the professional polish that today's sophisticated audiences demand.

PowerPoint follows the premise that because a presentation graphics program might get pulled off the electronic shelf only occasionally, it must always seem familiar and easy to use.

PowerPoint for Microsoft Office 97 is the newest version of Microsoft's presentation graphics software. In many large organizations, Power-Point is the standard-issue presentation graphics software because it takes you by the hand at the very first screen and gently guides you through the process of creating a presentation. It asks for the text and numbers it needs—you can type them in or import them from other applications—and it asks you to select from a palette of designs for the presentation. Then PowerPoint produces the kind of vivid graphics and dazzling images you'd expect from a professional artist.

Once the presentation is complete, PowerPoint can produce pages to hand out at a meeting, bright, crisp slides, speaker notes, or transparencies to use with an overhead projector. And that's not all. More and more people are opting to forego slides and transparencies and show a PowerPoint slide show right onscreen, instead. Electronic presentations like these, with their TV-like special effects, sound, music, animation, and even video clips, are the hottest thing today, and PowerPoint's capabilities for creating and controlling electronic presentations are state-of-the-art.

Best of all, to create professional-quality visuals in PowerPoint, you don't have to be an artist. The program's built-in design templates take care of the presentation's appearance. And you don't have to be a computer expert to use all of PowerPoint's features. There's always an onscreen prompt to lead you to the next task, and often, when you have choices to make, one of PowerPoint's "wizards" appears to guide you through the preliminary decisions. About the only thing

PowerPoint cannot do is help you enunciate while speaking, but the professional quality of the visuals will help give you the confidence to be at your very best.

PowerPoint's special presentation-making features can make your work easier no matter what your presentation needs:

You need quick and easy, high-impact visuals to accompany a talk.

PowerPoint's AutoContent Wizard and templates not only help you design a presentation, but they give you a basic presentation outline to follow. You simply select a theme and design, and watch as PowerPoint generates eye-catching slides that are organized, consistent, and professional.

You need a fact-filled presentation with plenty of graphs and charts.

PowerPoint's Graph, Organization Chart, and Table programs help you create elaborate visuals that depict numeric information, detail the structure of an organization, and make comparisons among ideas.

You need a sophisticated electronic presentation with lots of razzle-dazzle.

PowerPoint's slide shows serve up the most sophisticated special effects you can get, including animated charts, sound, music and audio tracks, embedded video, and those famous, between-slide transitions. Slide shows can also be interactive—you can branch to a subtopic or call up hidden detail to respond to a viewer's question.

You need team-spirit presentations that display your group's logo and colors.

Easily customizable slide backgrounds and color schemes are all part of PowerPoint's repertoire. You can place a logo on the background of every slide or select colors to match your corporate color scheme.

You need to assemble existing text and graphics from other programs.

PowerPoint can easily integrate text, charts, numbers, and diagrams from other Microsoft Office applications (such as Microsoft Word and Microsoft Excel) into presentation materials. You can even edit any of these from within PowerPoint just as though you were working in the original program you used to create them.

You need to deliver your presentation on the road, across the network, or even on the Internet.

PowerPoint's Pack and Go Wizard helps create a disk for taking on the road. Presentation Conferencing lets you share your presentation across a company network or even across the Internet and have colleagues review it with you. And with Stage Manager, Meeting Minder and the Slide Meter, you can preview slides, take notes, read your script, and keep track of the presentation's pace while PowerPoint presents your show to the audience.

PowerPoint Basics (Read This!)

Although PowerPoint is extremely friendly and easy to use, you still need to know just a few basics before you can master the program. The rest of this chapter covers the little bit of groundwork you need. But don't worry; you'll soon start creating an actual presentation.

PowerPoint Views

Unlike early presentation programs, which forced you to create and then save a single slide at a time, PowerPoint creates entire presentations of slides, all similar in appearance and all stored in a single file on your system.

> PowerPoint uses the word *slide* to refer to each page of visuals in a presentation even though you may show the presentation onscreen, or print the presentation on paper or as transparencies rather than create 35-mm slides.

With the early presentation programs and their single slide per file, only one view was necessary. Because PowerPoint can create an entire presentation of slides, it offers not just a view for viewing a single slide, Slide view, but also Outline, Slide Sorter, Notes Page, and Slide Show views. Each view lets you work on a different aspect of the presentation, and the changes you make in one view show up in all the other views as well.

⑦ **SEE ALSO**

For more information about Slide view, see Chapter 5, "Working with Text in Slide View," page 89.

Slide View

In Slide view, you refine and embellish an individual slide in your presentation. You can enter and edit text, and you can add a chart or table to a slide. You can also dress up a slide with drawings, pictures, and text annotations. Figure 1-1 shows a slide in Slide view.

FIGURE 1-1.

Slide view.

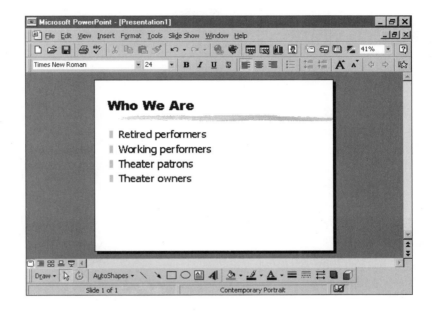

⑦ **SEE ALSO**

For more information about Outline view, see Chapter 4, "Working with Text in Outline View," page 53.

Outline View

In Outline view, PowerPoint displays only the text of the presentation, allowing you to enter text or edit existing text without the distractions you might find in Slide view. Figure 1-2, on the next page, shows a sample presentation in Outline view. Because you work only with text in Outline view, you can concentrate on the words of the presentation and the flow of ideas through the slides. Outline view provides an excellent environment for organizing your thoughts and materials before you switch to a different view, where you might work on the design elements of the presentation.

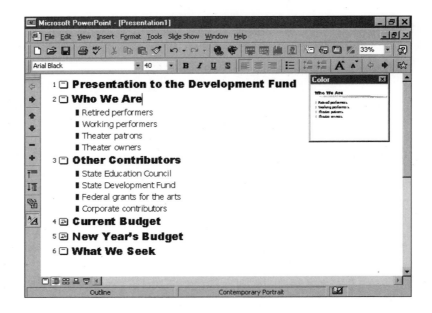

Slide Sorter View

For more information about Slide Sorter view, see Chapter 11, "Using Slide Sorter View," page 301.

In Slide Sorter view, you see the slides of the presentation laid out in neat rows and columns, as in Figure 1-3. Here you can see the results of sweeping changes to the appearance of the entire presentation, such as a change to the background design and color scheme. You cannot make changes to the content of individual slides in Slide Sorter view, but you can cut extraneous slides, duplicate slides, and shuffle the order of slides just as if you had laid out real 35-mm slides on a light table.

By using Slide Sorter view before you print a presentation or generate slides, you can check for inconsistencies among slides and gross errors such as a chart that is positioned on the wrong part of a page. You can also give your presentation a design overhaul by switching to a different template. When you change templates, virtually everything about your presentation's appearance changes too. As a result, a lively, colorful presentation for the sales force can become a stately, elegant presentation for the board of directors. Slide Sorter view is also the place to add and edit the transition effects used between slides during a slide show.

FIGURE 1-3.
Slide Sorter view.

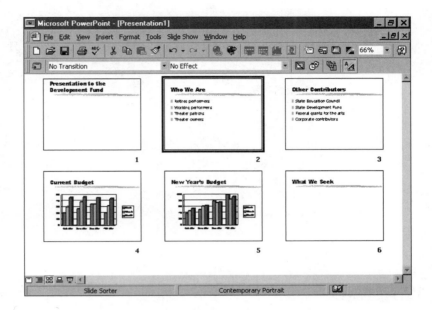

Notes Pages View

SEE ALSO
For more information about Notes Pages view, see "Adding Speaker Notes," page 322.

The fourth PowerPoint view is dedicated to creating speaker notes that the presenter can use at the podium. Notes Pages view produces a smaller version of the slide on the top part of a page and leaves the bottom part free for notes that the speaker can use during the presentation. While in Notes Pages view, you can view a reduced version of each slide and type in the accompanying text notes. Figure 1-4, on the next page, shows a slide in Notes Pages view.

FIGURE 1-4.

Notes Pages view.

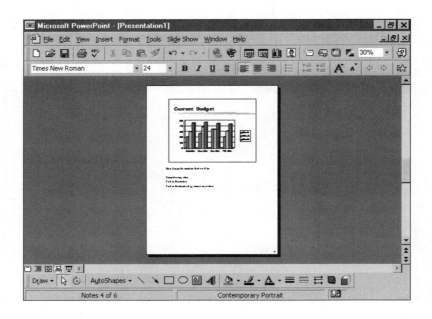

Slide Show View

For more information about Slide Show view, see Chapter 16, "Creating Slide Shows," page 387.

The fifth PowerPoint view, Slide Show view, does not display a single, static image. Instead, it shows the presentation progressing from slide to slide just like a real slide show using projected 35-mm slides. However, unlike a real slide show, which at best can only fade out of one slide before fading into the next, a PowerPoint slide show can use eye-popping special effects to make the transition from slide to slide and to introduce new elements to the current slide. As one slide dissolves off the screen, for example, the next slide can reveal itself gradually from top to bottom, and its bulleted lines of text can glide in one by one from the side. Figure 1-5 shows a chart during the slide show as a third set of columns fades in to view.

FIGURE 1-5.
Slide Show view
showing a third set
of columns in a
chart as it fades in
to view.

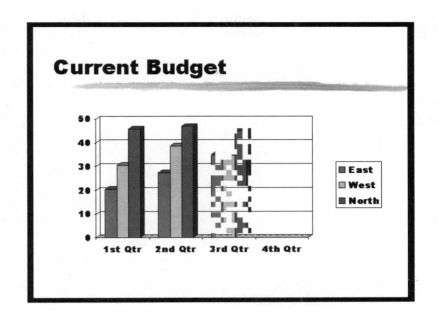

Starting PowerPoint

Before you can see how easy it is to switch from one view to another, you must get PowerPoint up and running. After PowerPoint is installed, its name is added to the Programs menu. To begin using PowerPoint, click the Start button at the end of the Taskbar, point to Programs to display a menu of the programs on your system (at this point, your screen should be similar to that shown in Figure 1-6 on the next page), and then click Microsoft PowerPoint.

⭐ TIP

How to Place a PowerPoint Shortcut on the Windows desktop.
Here's the easiest way to put a copy of the PowerPoint icon directly on the Windows desktop so that it is within easy reach. First, click the Start button and choose Find from the Start menu. In the Find dialog box, enter POWERPNT.EXE into the Named edit box. Then, choose My Computer from the Look In drop-down list. Click Find Now. When POWERPNT.EXE shows up on the list in the Find dialog box, drag it from the list to the Windows desktop.

Introducing PowerPoint

FIGURE 1-6.
Opening PowerPoint from the Start button on the Windows 95 Taskbar.

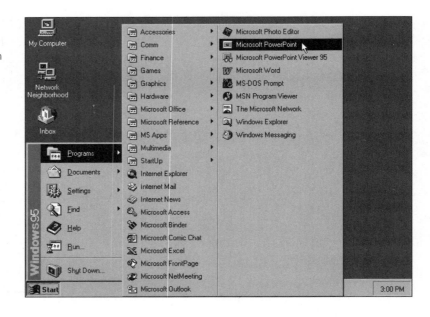

TIP

To remove the Microsoft PowerPoint icon from the Windows desktop (or to remove any program icon that you have added to the desktop), point to the icon and press the Delete key on the keyboard.

SEE ALSO

For more information about the PowerPoint dialog box and autolayouts, see Chapter 2, "The Essential Steps," page 29.

When you start PowerPoint for the first time, you will see the Office Assistant, an animated little figure who's ready and all-too-eager to help you work. For now, you can dismiss the Assistant by clicking the close button at the upper-right corner of the Assistant window. You now see the PowerPoint dialog box shown in Figure 1-7. You use this dialog box to select a method for creating a new presentation.

FIGURE 1-7.
The PowerPoint
dialog box.

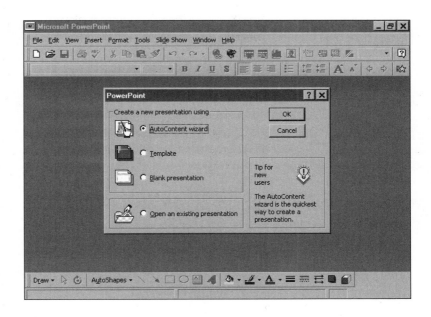

To follow along with the rest of this brief tour, select the Blank
Presentation option and then click OK, or simply double-click Blank
Presentation. As shown in Figure 1-8, the next dialog box to appear is
labeled New Slide. You use this dialog box to select a slide layout for
your presentation. PowerPoint offers 24 slide layouts, called
autolayouts, from which to choose. For now, click OK to create the
first slide with the default Title Slide autolayout, which is the appropriate slide for the opening of a presentation.

FIGURE 1-8.
The New Slide
dialog box.

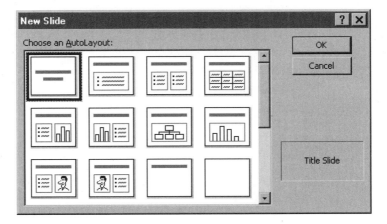

Switching Views

If you have successfully started a blank presentation and selected the Title Slide autolayout, you are now in Slide view, looking at the first slide. Getting to a different view is simply a matter of clicking one of the five buttons in the lower left corner of the presentation window, as shown in Figure 1-9.

Go ahead and click the first four buttons one by one. When you click the fifth button, the blank first slide of the presentation appears full-screen as a Slide Show. No, your system hasn't crashed. You just haven't created any slides to present in Slide Show view yet. Simply press the Esc key to return to the previous view.

FIGURE 1-9.

To switch views, click one of the view buttons near the lower left corner of the PowerPoint window.

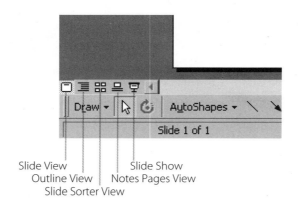

Slide View
Outline View
Slide Sorter View
Slide Show
Notes Pages View

Another way to switch between views is to use the View menu. To open the View menu, click the word *View* on the menu bar, as shown in Figure 1-10, or hold down the Alt key and then press the underlined letter in the menu name, in this case *V*.

FIGURE 1-10.

You can also change views by choosing from the options on the View menu.

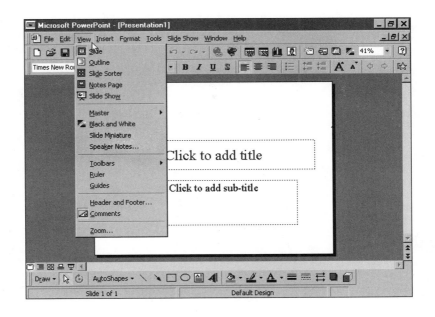

The first four entries on the View menu lead you to the first four views. The fifth entry, Slide Show, starts up an electronic presentation without any further adieu.

> **NOTE**
>
> If a command on a menu is dimmed, the command is currently unavailable. If a command is followed by an ellipsis (three dots), a dialog box appears when you choose the command. If a command is preceded by a check mark, the command is currently active and can be toggled on and off. If a command is followed by an arrowhead, choosing the command displays a submenu of additional commands. Commands that have toolbar equivalents are preceded by a picture of the toolbar button.

Controlling the PowerPoint Window

Like all windows in Microsoft Windows 95 or Microsoft Windows NT, the PowerPoint window has Minimize, Maximize, and Close buttons in its upper right corner. Clicking the Minimize button shrinks the PowerPoint window to the Taskbar, and clicking the Maximize button expands the window to fill the screen. Clicking the Close button shuts down PowerPoint and closes all open windows. Clicking the Control button in the upper left corner displays a menu with additional commands for restoring the PowerPoint window to its previous size, for moving and sizing the window, and for closing PowerPoint.

NOTE

When the PowerPoint window is maximized, the Maximize button becomes the Restore button. If you click this button, the window is restored to its previous size. To return the window to full size, click the Maximize button or choose Maximize from the Control menu.

TIP

How to Use the Mouse to Adjust the PowerPoint Window
When the PowerPoint window is not maximized, you can use the mouse to move and resize the window. For example, click and drag the window's title bar to move the window to a new location. To change the window's size, position the mouse pointer on one side of the window's frame, and when the pointer changes to a double-headed arrow, hold down the left mouse button and drag the frame in the desired direction.

Manipulating the Presentation Window

When you create a new presentation in PowerPoint or edit an existing one, the presentation window occupies most of the PowerPoint window. To change the presentation window's location or size, you can use its buttons and Control menu commands just like you use the PowerPoint window's buttons and commands.

You can have more than one presentation open at a time so that you can compare presentations or copy graphics or text from one presentation to another. To open more than one presentation, choose Open from the File menu, and when the Open dialog box appears, locate the presentation you want to open, and click the Open button. The new presentation window covers any windows that are open, but you can use the commands on the Window menu to rearrange the windows. For example, the Arrange All command places the open windows side by side, as shown in Figure 1-11.

FIGURE 1-11.

Two presentations arranged side by side using the Window menu Arrange All command.

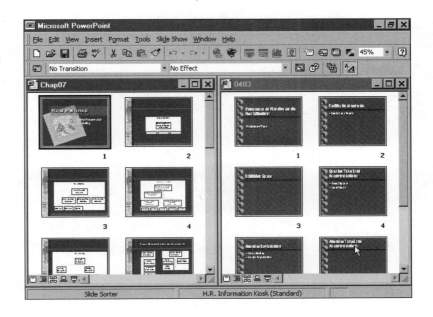

The Cascade command on the Window menu arranges open presentation windows in sequence so that you can see all their title bars. You can then click any title bar to bring that presentation window to the front. The Fit To Page command sizes the currently selected window so that it neatly fits the presentation slide.

NOTE

> After you use any of the commands on the Window menu, you can still manipulate each window individually by using the window's buttons and Control menu commands.

Using the Toolbars

Every command in PowerPoint resides on one of PowerPoint's menus. This fact isn't very comforting, however, when you're in a rush and you'd rather not have to rummage through PowerPoint's menus. Fortunately, to make life a little easier, PowerPoint features several toolbars that contain buttons for the commands you use most often. These toolbars are conveniently displayed in the PowerPoint window so that you can access a command simply by clicking the corresponding toolbar button. As shown in Figure 1-12, the default PowerPoint window displays three toolbars: the Standard, Formatting, and Drawing toolbars. In addition to these toolbars, PowerPoint provides others, which often appear automatically whenever they would be helpful as you use the program.

FIGURE 1-12.
The Standard, Formatting, and Drawing toolbars

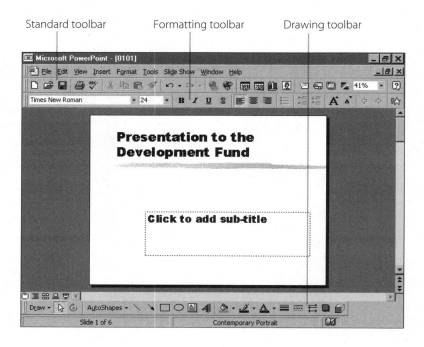

Displaying Toolbars

? SEE ALSO
For more information about customizing toolbars, see "Customizing Toolbars," page 491.

To display a toolbar that does not appear by default, choose the Toolbars command from the View menu; when the list of main toolbars appears, as shown in Figure 1-13, click the toolbars you want. Menu items like these act as toggles—you click once to turn on the option (add the check), and you click again to turn off the option (remove the check).

Try turning on an additional toolbar now by clicking WordArt on the list. The WordArt toolbar appears in the PowerPoint window. The WordArt toolbar contains buttons that you can use to add fancy text logos and text effects. To remove the WordArt toolbar, return to the Toolbars list and clear the WordArt check box by clicking it again.

FIGURE 1-13.
The Toolbars menu.

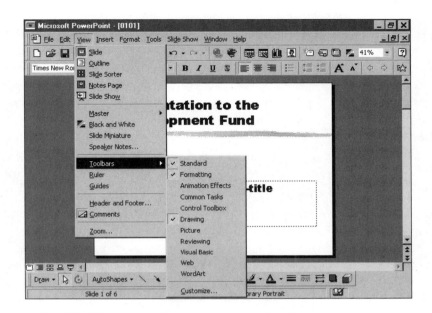

To see even more toolbar choices, click Customize at the bottom of the toolbar list. In the Customize dialog box, you see all the toolbars that are available.

 **TIP**

> **How to Get Toolbars Quickly**
> A neat, little shortcut is to click any toolbar with the right mouse button. Then you can choose the toolbars you want from the shortcut menu.

All of PowerPoint's toolbars can be customized to include only the buttons you want. You can also move buttons from one toolbar to another. And you can make the toolbar buttons large or small and display them with or without color.

Positioning Toolbars

By default, PowerPoint arranges its toolbars where they fit best on the screen, but you can change this arrangement to create a workspace that you find more comfortable. A toolbar can be located along one of the four sides of the PowerPoint window, or it can be free-floating within the window. You might want to leave the default arrangement of toolbars for now. When you become more familiar with Power-Point, you can position the toolbars to suit your needs.

To move a toolbar, first place the mouse pointer within the borders of the toolbar, but not on top of any button. Then hold down the left mouse button and drag the toolbar to a new location on the screen. When you release the mouse button, the toolbar drops into its new position, and, if necessary, the presentation window inside the PowerPoint window adjusts to make room. If you drag a toolbar to one side of the PowerPoint window, the toolbar automatically changes shape to fit the space. If you drag the toolbar toward the middle of the screen, the toolbar becomes a "floating" box. After you drop a toolbar into place, you can reshape it by dragging its borders just as you reshape a window. Figure 1-14 shows the Drawing toolbar as a box within the PowerPoint window.

FIGURE 1-14.
The floating Drawing toolbar.

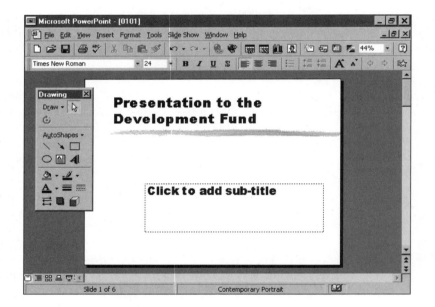

ScreenTips

PowerPoint provides a handy feature called ScreenTips to help you keep track of all those toolbar buttons and other items on the screen. To see a description of any toolbar button or of any button on the screen, simply place the mouse pointer on the button and pause. A small ScreenTip box pops up nearby, displaying the button's name; a brief description of the button appears in the status bar at the bottom of the PowerPoint window. Whenever you display a new toolbar in

PowerPoint, use ScreenTips to get acquainted with its buttons. To turn off ScreenTips, choose Toolbars from the View menu, select Customize on the Toolbars menu, and then deselect the Show ScreenTips on Toolbars option on the Options tab of the Customize dialog box.

Moving Through Slides

In Slide view, you see only one slide at a time, but the presentation may contain many slides. To move to another slide in your presentation, use any of the following methods:

- Press PgDn to move forward one slide, or press PgUp to move back one slide.

- Click the Next Slide button at the bottom of the presentation window's vertical scroll bar to move forward one slide, or click the Previous Slide button to move back one slide (see Figure 1-15 on the next page).

- Drag the scroll box up or down in the presentation window's vertical scroll bar (see Figure 1-15 on the next page) to move backward or forward through the presentation. As you drag the scroll box, the current slide number and title appear next to the scroll bar.

To practice moving through slides in a ready-made presentation, you can open one of the ready-made presentations that comes with PowerPoint. Click the Open button on the Standard toolbar or choose the Open command from the File menu. When the Open dialog box appears, select Presentation Templates from the Files Of Type drop-down list and click the Up One Level button on the toolbar. Now navigate to the Templates folder within the Microsoft Office folder (it's probably within MSOFFICE in the PROGRAM FILES folder). Then double-click the Presentations folder within the Templates folder and double-click the Generic (Standard) presentation filename. In the Generic presentation, you can try moving through the slides by using any of the methods listed above. When you finish viewing the slides, choose Close from the File menu to close the presentation window.

FIGURE 1-15.

The vertical scroll bar
and scroll box and the
Previous Slide and
Next Slide buttons in
Slide view.

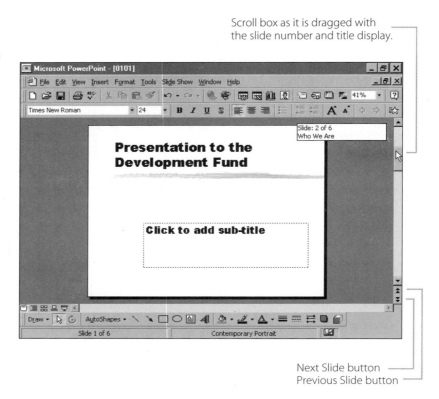

Scroll box as it is dragged with
the slide number and title display.

Next Slide button
Previous Slide button

Saving Your Work

You've heard it before, but it always bears repeating: Save your work
often. Don't wait until you've finished a presentation to save it. Save a
presentation after you create the first slide. Save it again a little while
later. The more frequently you save your work, the less you stand to
lose if you fall victim to a power failure, a coffee spill, or a rambunc-
tious child who decides to play piano on your keyboard.

To save a file, click the Save button on the Standard toolbar (that little
picture on the button is a disk, not a TV) or choose Save from the File
menu. If you have not yet named the file (if the presentation title bar
still displays the name *Presentation*), the Save dialog box appears. As
shown in Figure 1-16, you enter a filename in the File Name edit box.
The filename can be one word, a few words, or up to 255 letters and
spaces. Use something that will make sense to you later when you
want to find this presentation. The Save In box at the top of the

dialog box, indicates where PowerPoint will save the file. You can change where the file is saved by clicking the arrow at the right end of the Save In box and opening the folder you want.

FIGURE 1-16.

The File Save dialog box.

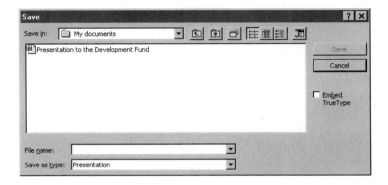

After you enter a filename and click Save, PowerPoint may display the Summary tab of the Properties dialog box for the presentation. As shown in Figure 1-17 on the next page, you can enter information in this dialog box to help you search for files later. For example, if you always enter the project name for all presentations belonging to a particular project in the Keywords edit box, you can later use these Keywords to extract a list of those presentations. (See the tip below.) You can also save a preview picture of your presentation, in case you find it easier to remember faces than names.

TIP

How to Search for a Presentation

To search for a presentation, click the Open button on the Standard toolbar or choose Open from the File menu. In the Look In box, locate the drive or folder you want to search by clicking the down arrow and making your selection. At the bottom of the Open dialog box, specify part of the filename or, if you know it, either an approximate time when the presentation was last modified, or some text that should appear within the presentation. Then click the Find Now button. If the search is successful, the filename appears in the Name list. If the search isn't successful, you can refine the search to look for information you entered in the Properties dialog box, by clicking the Advanced button, selecting a category (such as Author or Keywords) from the Property drop-down list, and entering the information in the Value edit box.

FIGURE 1-17.
You can use the
information in the
Properties dialog
box to search for
specific files.

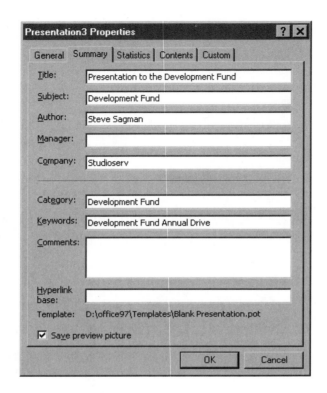

To enter information in the Summary tab of the Properties dialog box,
type text directly in the edit boxes, using the Tab key to move to the
next edit box and Shift+Tab to move to the previous edit box. When
you've filled in as many edit boxes as you want, click OK to close the
dialog box.

Getting Help

PowerPoint's online Help system is extensive and easy to use. To
access Help, press F1 while PowerPoint is displayed, or choose
Microsoft PowerPoint Help from the Help menu. The Help Topics
window shown in Figure 1-18 appears.

FIGURE 1-18.

The PowerPoint Help Topics window.

Clicking the Contents tab displays a set of book icons, and double-clicking a book icon displays its contents—either more book icons or topic icons that look like a page with a question mark. When you find the topic you want, double-click the topic icon to open it.

Clicking the Index tab in the Help Topics window displays a list of words associated with PowerPoint Help topics. Type the first few letters of the word you are looking for. As you type, the list of words advances to match the letters you type. You can also scroll through the word list until you find the word you want. Once you find the desired word, select it and click Display to see the topic.

The first time you click the Find tab, you will see the Find Setup Wizard, which walks you through the process of creating a list of all of the words in PowerPoint Help so that you can locate the information you are searching for. You can choose whether to include all of the Help files associated with PowerPoint or only some of them by clicking the Customize Search Capabilities option. After the list is created, you can use the options on the Find tab to locate specific words in Help.

As you read a Help topic, you'll see words with dotted underlines and words with solid underlines. A dotted underline indicates that when you click the word, a pop-up definition of the word is displayed. A solid underline indicates that when you click the word, the Help topic for the word is displayed. To see other related topics, click the Related Topics button at the end of a topic.

Within a Help topic, you may see a picture of a toolbar button or other object that you can click for more information. Within an instruction, you may see a shortcut button that you can click to open the dialog box you need to complete that step. Some topics may also have a small button that you can click to open another topic with more details.

Some Help topics have an Examples and Demos button at the top of their window. When you click this button, Help displays a graphical representation of the topic or gives you a step-by-step demonstration of how to carry out a corresponding task.

While in the Help system, you can click the Back button at the top of the Help window to return to the previous topic, or you can click the Help Topics button to redisplay the Help Topics window.

Clicking the Options button in the Help window displays a list of commands. Choose Annotate to read an existing note or to type a new note. When a topic has an annotation attached to it, a paper clip is displayed next to the topic title. To copy the information in the Help window, select the text you want to copy, and then choose Copy from the Options menu. You can also press Ctrl+C to copy selected text. Choose Print Topic to print the current topic. Choose Font to set the Help font to small, normal, or large size. Choose Keep Help on Top to display Help on top of the PowerPoint window while you work. Choose Use System Colors to change the colors that are used to display Help.

Keeping a Help Topic Visible

When you find a Help topic pertinent to the task you are trying to accomplish, you can keep the topic on your screen and refer to it while you work in PowerPoint. In the Help window, select the Options button, choose Keep Help On Top, and then choose On Top from the submenu. Choose Not On Top if you want Help to step back when you work in PowerPoint.

The Office Assistant

Always ready to serve, the Office Assistant is an animated character that pops up whenever it thinks it has a way to help you. If the Office Assistant is installed in your machine (it's a custom option during the setup process) you'll see it appear in its own window. Whenever the Assistant thinks it can help, a light bulb appears in its window. Click the Assistant to find out what it has to offer. You can also click the Assistant any time you need help while using PowerPoint. The Assistant will offer help options related to the work you are doing in PowerPoint at the moment, as shown in Figure 1-19.

FIGURE 1-19.

The Office Assistant.

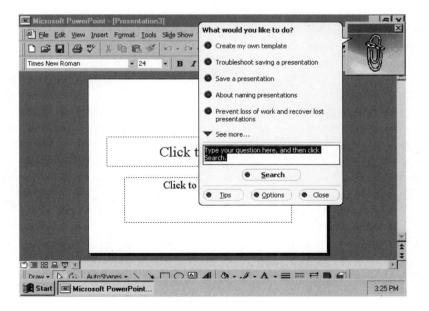

The Office Assistant button.

If the Assistant does not appear, you can click the Office Assistant button on the Standard toolbar.

Visiting Microsoft on the Web

Microsoft offers extensive online help and a number of additional resources for PowerPoint on its World Wide Web site on the Internet. If you can connect to the Internet, you can choose Microsoft on the Web from the Help menu, and then select any of the shortcuts to Microsoft Internet addresses from the Microsoft on the Web menu.

Other Ways of Getting Help

To get help about a button or a menu command, choose What's This from the Help menu or press Shift+F1. When the pointer displays a question mark, click the button or menu command you want information on. Help then displays the corresponding topic for the button or menu command you've chosen.

The Essential Steps

L ike any good software, PowerPoint offers a cornucopia of resources that were designed for a broad range of needs. Uses for the software are limited only by your time and imagination. Yet there's one well-trodden path that most users follow, taking excursions into the finer points of the program only when required. This chapter focuses on the steps that form the basic presentation-making process. Follow these footsteps, and you'll never get lost in the woods.

As you learn to use PowerPoint, you'll discover that it always guides you through the process of creating a presentation. After you start a slide, for example, PowerPoint displays a prompt that tells you to *Click here to add a title*. Simply follow PowerPoint's lead. Remember, the software was written with ease of use in mind. Whenever PowerPoint's designers could anticipate your next logical move, they instructed the software to do the same.

Although this chapter covers the nine steps involved in creating a presentation, you won't actually create one yet. Instead, you'll become familiar with the sequence of the steps, which also forms the structure of this book.

Step 1: Starting the Presentation

The presentation process gets under way as soon as you launch PowerPoint and start a new presentation. After the PowerPoint banner, the PowerPoint dialog box, shown in Figure 2-1, is displayed. The first option in the PowerPoint dialog box activates the AutoContent Wizard. This option asks you to select a presentation type from a list of predefined types and then loads a set of slides with relevant text already in place. Of course, the text is generic, such as *Details about this topic*, but it nevertheless guides you in structuring the presentation.

The second option, labeled Template, displays a list of design templates you can choose from. These templates automatically format everything in the presentation, giving the entire presentation a consistent "look." You won't use this option until you're more familiar with PowerPoint. The third option, Blank Presentation, starts a blank presentation devoid of any design or sample text. You will, however, select a slide layout to get started.

FIGURE 2-1.

The PowerPoint dialog box.

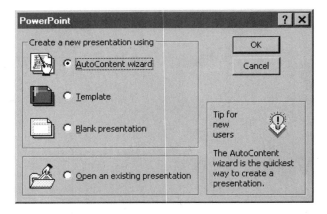

If you've already used PowerPoint to create a presentation, you can select the last option, Open An Existing Presentation. When you select this option, PowerPoint displays the Open dialog box so that you can open a presentation that has already been created and filed away.

The New
Button

If you are already working in PowerPoint, you can always click the New button on the Standard toolbar or choose New from the File menu to start a new presentation.

Step 2: Choosing the Content and Appearance

Step 2 consists of two tasks that you can perform in either order: entering the presentation content and establishing its design. You can focus on the text of the slides first and leave the design for later, or you can select a design and have it applied to each new slide as you enter the text. The simplest way to take care of both tasks is to use the AutoContent Wizard. This wizard lets you select sample content for a set of presentation slides, as shown in Figure 2-2. One caveat, though: The AutoContent Wizard also institutes a presentation design. Of course, you can always change the design at Step 6, "Tweaking the Presentation."

Another way to choose a design for a new presentation is to select Template from the PowerPoint dialog box. This option is especially helpful after you've had the chance to develop your own designs, logos and color schemes in custom templates.

FIGURE 2-2.
You can use the AutoContent Wizard to help you choose the content and design of your presentation.

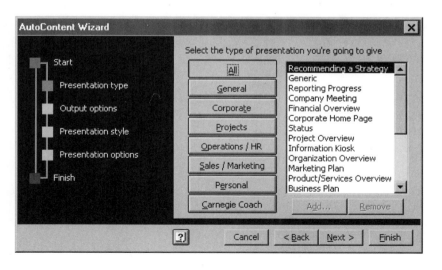

Step 3: Entering and Editing the Text

? SEE ALSO

For more information, see Chapter 4, "Working with Text in Outline View," page 53, and Chapter 5, "Working with Text in Slide View," page 89.

Even if you use the AutoContent Wizard rather than type in your own text, you still need to replace the wizard's generic text with your own. You can step through the presentation slide by slide and substitute your words for PowerPoint's, or you can work in Outline view as shown in Figure 2-3, where you can focus on the overall flow of the text as well as the text on individual slides. Outline view is the easiest place to enter and edit text, rearrange text, and copy or move text from slide to slide.

FIGURE 2-3.

Outline view lets you focus on the flow of your presentation.

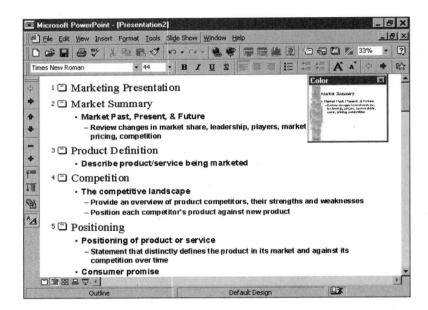

Step 4: Adding Charts, Organization Charts, and Table Slides

Not every topic is best communicated with written statements. Sometimes pictures or charts are the ticket, and sometimes tables are most effective. You can add a chart or table to a text slide, or you can create a new slide devoted to a chart or table. When you request a new slide or begin a blank presentation, PowerPoint displays the New Slide dialog box, which offers a variety of slide autolayouts, as shown in Figure 2-4. Some slide autolayouts have text only—a slide title and a block of text below, usually with bulleted lines of text—and others have charts, organization charts, and tables in addition to a title. Some even have combinations of text, graphics, pictures, and media on the same slide. You simply click the autolayout you want, and then click OK. The selected autolayout appears full-screen in Slide view, as shown in Figure 2-5.

FIGURE 2-4.
The New Slide dialog box with a chart autolayout selected.

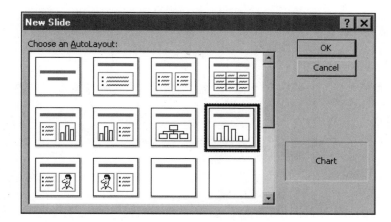

FIGURE 2-5.
After you select an autolayout, it appears full-screen in Slide view.

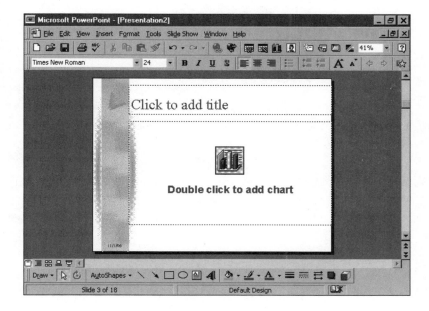

As you can see, an autolayout contains a combination of placeholders, which are dashed, rectangular boxes with text prompts. Some place-holders, such as chart placeholders, contain icons as well as text prompts. The text prompt in each placeholder tells you how to use the placeholder. For example, in Figure 2-5, on the previous page, one placeholder tells you to *Click to add title*. Another tells you to *Double click to add chart*. The autolayout shown in Figure 2-6 has three placeholders: one for a title, one for bulleted text, and one for a graph. With placeholders, you can't go wrong. When you click a text placeholder, such as *Click to add title*, PowerPoint displays an inser-tion point so that you can type text directly in the placeholder. If you double-click a chart placeholder, PowerPoint loads the special module you use to create charts.

FIGURE 2-6.

An autolayout with title, bulleted text, and chart placeholders.

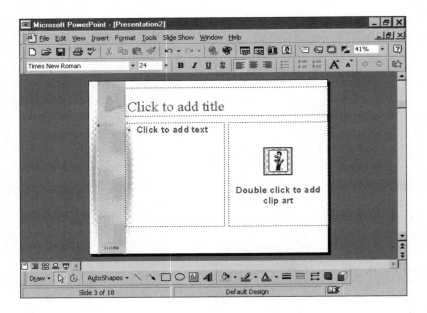

Autolayouts and placeholders are the keys to making your way through a presentation. When you select an autolayout and then click one of its placeholders, PowerPoint displays all the tools you need so that you don't have to hunt around for specific commands or toolbars.

Step 5: Adding Annotations and Graphic Embellishments

? **SEE ALSO**

For more information about adding annotations and graphics, see Chapter 12, "Working with Text Annotations and Speaker Notes," page 315, and Chapter 13, "Drawing Graphic Objects," page 325.

By step 5, you're ready to add the finishing touches to your presentation. The text and charts are complete, but you should take a moment to review each slide before continuing. On some slides, a little additional explanation might help the audience. With the Text Box tool on the Drawing toolbar, you can add free-floating blocks of text as annotations that highlight or explain a special feature. You can also use the Drawing toolbar to add graphics to accompany an image or text on a slide. The simplest case is a line that connects a text annotation to the subject it describes, such as the line connecting the label to the pie chart in the slide shown in Figure 2-7. But you can also draw more complex images with PowerPoint's drawing tools.

FIGURE 2-7.

A simple line connects a text label to the pie chart in this slide.

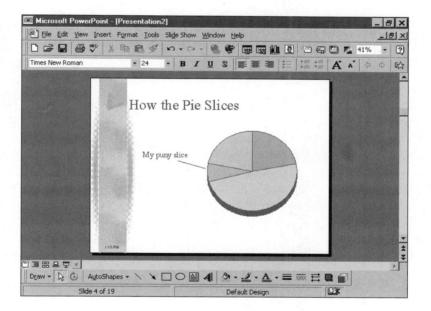

If drawing is not your thing, you can take advantage of the Clip Gallery—PowerPoint's extensive library of ready-made images—or you can use the AutoClipArt command on the Tools menu to help you select drawings. PowerPoint organizes the images by category in the Clip Gallery, as shown in Figure 2-8 on the next page.

FIGURE 2-8.

The Clip Gallery.

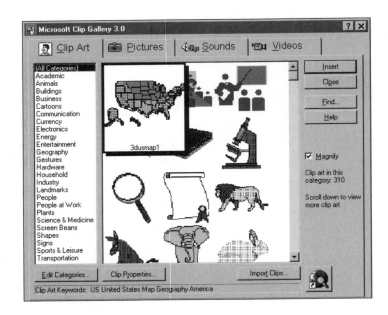

As Figure 2-9 shows, you can increase the effectiveness of a slide by adding a clip art image to the text.

FIGURE 2-9.

A clip art image on a slide.

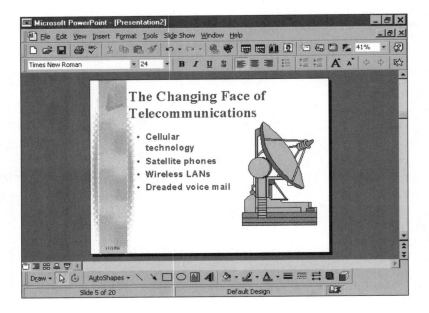

⊘ SEE ALSO

For more information about clip art, photos, sounds, and movies, see "Using the Clip Gallery," page 358.

In addition to using clip art, you can also incorporate pictures you've drawn in other software programs and display photos you've scanned with a scanner. PowerPoint can import and display both drawings and pictures from other applications.

If you plan to display the slide show onscreen, you can add sound and movie files from the Clip Gallery, too.

Step 6: Tweaking the Presentation

What would you do with all that extra time if it weren't for last-minute changes? Because your presentation is stored electronically in PowerPoint rather than drawn on paper, you can make changes as easily as you edit a document in a word processor or update numbers in a spreadsheet. You can also try out a different design template to see if your presentation would benefit from a different look.

PowerPoint's Slide Sorter view, shown in Figure 2-10, is the best place to see and make sweeping changes to your slides because you can view an entire segment of the presentation at once. While in Slide Sorter view, you can also adjust the order of the slides or delete extraneous slides.

FIGURE 2-10.

Use Slide Sorter view to make sweeping changes to the entire presentation.

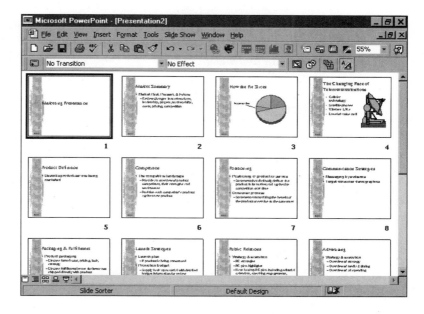

Step 7: Saving Your Work

The Save
Button

To store a completed presentation, you save it in a file by clicking the Save button on the Standard toolbar or by choosing Save from the File menu. Each PowerPoint file holds an entire presentation of slides, so you don't have to worry about lost slides the next time you display a presentation. At this point, you can also save a PowerPoint presentation as the content for a World Wide Web site by choosing Save As HTML. Of course, you shouldn't wait long to save for the first time. Remember—Save early and save often.

Step 8: Generating Printed Output, Slides, and Electronic Presentations

Even if it's just for immediate gratification, you'll probably want to print a set of slides as soon as they're complete. PowerPoint can print your slides on paper with just about any printer you install in Windows. Laser printers and color ink-jet printers, today's business standards, produce especially attractive printouts.

PowerPoint is equally adept at generating 35-mm slides. Unfortunately, slides do not pop out of a slide-making device the same way that pages emerge from a printer. You must either attach a film recorder, which records your slides onto slide film that must then be developed, or send the presentation file to a service bureau that can create and develop the slides for you.

A special form of output, the electronic presentation, is quickly overtaking even slides in popularity. An electronic presentation displays images on a computer screen or on a large screen with the aid of a computer projector. Electronic presentations can incorporate fancy fades and slick transitions between slides, and they can play sound and video, too. If you are connected to an office network or the Internet, you can deliver a slide show to others who "tune in" across the network or the Internet. Electronic presentations can also be interactive, so you can control their flow during the presentation, stepping back to a previous slide or advancing to an additional topic.

What's more, in an electronic presentation, you can "drill down" to the spreadsheet file that contains the figures for a graph so that the audience can see the original worksheet. Best of all, electronic presentations can be updated at the very last second. You'd be surprised by how many concluding slides are prepared even while a presentation is in progress.

Step 9: Collecting Accolades

The final step is the easiest. Leave your phone line clear and your door open for the flood of praise that will come your way. With a PowerPoint presentation, you'll not only enlighten an audience but entertain them as well. So say goodbye to the chalkboard, flip chart, and Orator ball.

In the next chapter, you'll get an opportunity to try the procedures you've learned about here.

PART II

The Basic Presentation

Getting Started on the Presentation

I f you are new to preparing presentations, you'll find Microsoft PowerPoint 97 ready to help you through the process step by step. If you're a presentation veteran, on the other hand, PowerPoint provides easy-to-use tools for performing familiar tasks. If you're somewhere in between, PowerPoint offers only as much assistance as you need.

PowerPoint recognizes that creating a professional presentation involves two initial tasks: drafting the content and creating a consistent design. Amazingly, PowerPoint can help you with both of these tasks. It's easy to find a presentation graphics program that comes with a selection of professionally designed templates. But it's rare to find a program that helps you work out what to say and how to say it.

In this chapter, you'll learn how to start a new presentation and determine how much assistance PowerPoint will offer as you work. In the following chapters of this section, you will also learn to work with the sample content PowerPoint provides, enter your own text, and add graphs, organization charts, and fancy visual effects.

Starting with the Presentation Content

When you already know the general content of your presentation, you can translate your thoughts into a concrete PowerPoint presentation in three ways:

- You can use the AutoContent Wizard to select a ready-made presentation, complete with sample slides, which suggest topics and presentation approaches. The rest of the job—replacing the the sample text with your own; dropping in graphs, charts, and other elements; and customizing the generic design (adding your own logo, for example)—is up to you.

- If you've drafted a presentation outline in Word, you can bring it into PowerPoint's Outline view in one step. With this option, you start your work in PowerPoint with your own content rather than a generic sample. The topics in the outline will become the slides of the presentation. Later, you can add graphs, pictures, and other elements to complete the content.

- You can start from scratch in PowerPoint, laying out the text in Outline view or entering it right onto slides, and then dropping in graphs, pictures, and annotations wherever you need them.

The first part of this chapter explains each of these options in detail.

Using the AutoContent Wizard

PowerPoint can't possibly know what you need to say, but it does know how successful communicators organize their presentations. So, in the AutoContent Wizard, PowerPoint offers a few handfuls of tried-and-true predefined outlines as starting points for your own presentation. You can select outlines to fit any of these needs:

- Corporate

- Operations/HR

- Sales and Marketing

- Personal

To set up a presentation, the AutoContent Wizard asks you to choose:

- A presentation type for the presentation (the overall theme)

- The type of output you'll need (whether the presentation will be a formal dog-and-pony show where the speaker elaborates on each slide or an unattended kiosk display, for example)

- What materials you'll need PowerPoint to generate (pages printed on paper, slides, or an onscreen electronic presentation, for example)

- A presentation title and information for the opening slide.

The Wizard then displays a general outline for the presentation in Outline view.

To activate the AutoContent Wizard, either:

- Start PowerPoint, and when the PowerPoint dialog box (shown in Figure 2-1 on page 30) appears, double-click the AutoContent Wizard option.

- Or, if PowerPoint is already on your screen, choose New from the File menu to open the New Presentation dialog box, and then click the Presentations tab. If you now see the New Presentation dialog box, double-click the AutoContent Wizard icon.

No matter how you activate the AutoContent Wizard, you see this dialog box.

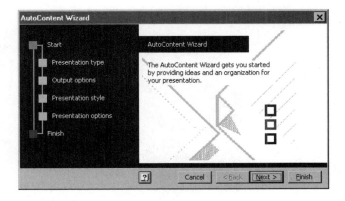

II

The Basic Presentation

The AutoContent Wizard has four screens of queries for you. Use the wizard by following these instructions:

1 The first screen introduces you to the AutoContent Wizard. Click Next or press N to move to the next screen.

2 The Presentation Type screen in the AutoContent Wizard asks you to choose a presentation type. Click one of the presentation category buttons and then choose a presentation type from the list. Finally, click Next to move on to the Output Options screen.

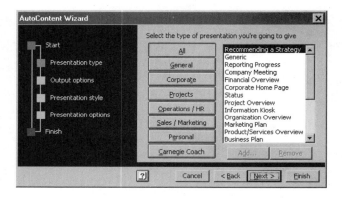

3 The Output Options screen asks you to select whether the new presentation will be given by someone (such as presentations, informal meetings, handouts) or whether it will be navigated by a self-paced viewer at a kiosk or across an internet (a corporate intranet or the Internet). Click the appropriate option in this screen and then click Next to proceed.

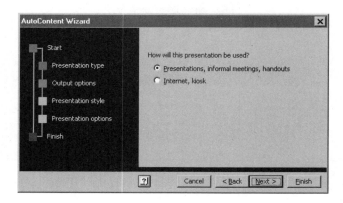

4   The Presentation Style screen asks you to choose an output type
(black and white or color overheads, a slide show displayed on
your computer, or 35-mm slides) and whether you will print
handouts. Click the options you want and click Next.

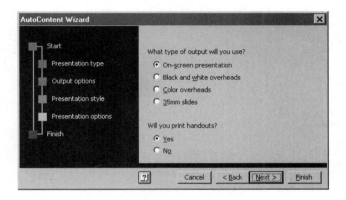

5   The final screen, Presentation Options, asks you for information
to be placed on the presentation's title page, such as a presentation title, your name, and "additional information" to be used as
the presentation subtitle. Enter or revise the text in the three edit
boxes and click Next.

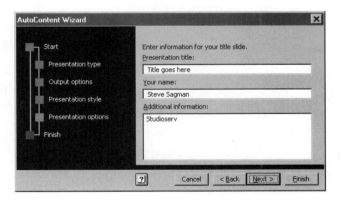

6   When the Finish AutoContent Wizard screen is displayed, click
Finish. The outline of the new presentation appears in Outline
view, as shown at the top of the next page.

The Basic Presentation

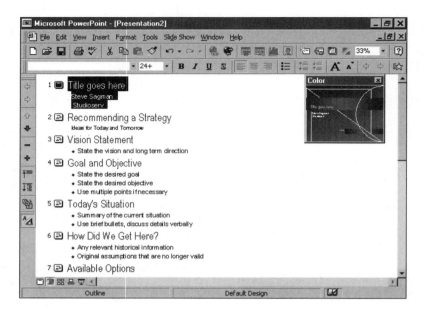

**SEE ALSO**

For more information about Outline view, see Chapter 4, "Working with Text in Outline View," page 53.

Notice that the presentation includes suggestions for the content of each slide in addition to the slide titles.

TIP

> **How to Customize the AutoContent Presentations**
> You can customize the existing presentations used by the AutoContent Wizard by modifying text on the slides or changing the template that gives the presentation its design. Simply open one of the presentations in the Presentations subfolder, and edit the text and/or change the design template. Then resave the Presentation in the same subfolder without renaming it. The next time you use the AutoContent Wizard, you'll get the same presentation types, but they'll reflect your customized changes.

Adding Custom Presentations

In addition to the standard set of presentations that come as part of the AutoContent Wizard, you can add presentations you've created. Not only does this make your own custom presentations easily available in the future, but it also helps categorize commonly used presentations because you must place each custom presentation into one of six categories in the wizard.

To add a custom presentation to the AutoContent Wizard, follow these steps:

1 Open the presentation that you want to add to the AutoContent Wizard.

2 Choose Save As from the File menu, and then, in the Save As dialog box, select Presentation Template from the Save As Type drop-down list.

3 Double-click the Presentations folder in the display of folders to open it, enter a file name for the presentation, and click Save.

4 Start the AutoContent Wizard. You can do this by choosing AutoContent Wizard or by choosing New from the File menu and then selecting AutoContent Wizard from the Presentations tab of the New Presentation dialog box.

5 Click Next to get to the Presentation Type screen.

6 In the Presentation Type screen, click any of the presentation category buttons except for the first (All) or the last (Carnegie Coach).

7 In the same screen, click the Add button below the list of presentations in the current category.

8 In the Select Presentation Template dialog box, choose the presentation template you just saved.

To delete an AutoContent presentation, click the Delete button on the Presentation Type screen of the AutoContent Wizard.

Using an Outline from Microsoft Word

SEE ALSO
For more information about using existing outlines, see "Importing Outlines," page 84.

If you've prepared an outline for your presentation in Microsoft Word, you can easily send the outline to PowerPoint by viewing the outline in Word and then, from the File menu, choosing Send To. On the Send To submenu, select Microsoft PowerPoint. The Outline immediately shows up in PowerPoint's Outline view exactly as it appeared in Word. Level 1 headings become slide titles, and lower-level headings become indented, bulleted items on the slides.

Entering the Text from Scratch

When you know what you want to say and you just want to create the slides, you can always jump right into a new presentation and start entering the text from scratch. Simply start PowerPoint and select Blank Presentation in the PowerPoint dialog box. Then select an autolayout from the New Slide dialog box. Or, if PowerPoint is already on your screen, do one of the following:

The New button

- Click the New button on the Standard toolbar, and select an autolayout in the New Slide dialog box.

- Choose New from the File menu, double-click the Blank Presentation icon on the General tab of the New Presentation dialog box, and select an autolayout from the New Slide dialog box.

- Choose New from the File menu, click the Presentation Designs tab, double-click one of the design template icons, and then select an autolayout from the New Slide dialog box. You'll learn more about design templates in the next section.

No matter which procedure you follow, PowerPoint displays the first slide of a new presentation in Slide view. You can switch to Outline view and concentrate on the text, or you can stay in Slide view and add slides one by one, entering text and graphics as you go.

Starting with the Presentation Design

If you want to see the presentation's design while working on its content, you can select a design template first. Each slide you create picks up the design of the template so that your presentation has a consistent look. You can choose from among PowerPoint's many ready-made design templates, or, if you're feeling creative, you can create your own design.

To select one of PowerPoint's ready-made design templates, follow the steps on the facing page.

1   Choose New from the File menu, and when the New Presentation dialog box appears, click the Presentation Designs tab to display template options similar to those shown here:

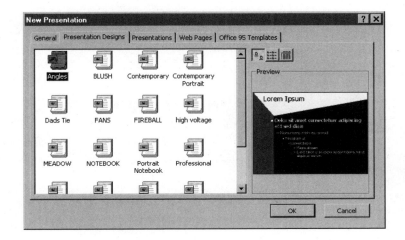

2   Click each template icon to see a sample of the template design in the Preview box on the right. (You can also use the arrow keys to move from one template to the next.) When you find the template you want, click its icon once and then click OK, or double-click its icon.

SEE ALSO

For more information about creating a template, see Chapter 9, "Making Overall Changes," page 215.

To store an existing presentation as a template to use as the design of a new presentation, follow this procedure:

1   Open the existing presentation and make any changes you want to the design.

2   Choose Save As from the File menu, and when the Save As dialog box appears, select Presentation Templates from the Save As type drop-down list.

3   Double-click the Presentation Designs folder in the folder list, type a name for the new template in the File name edit box, and click Save.

All you have to do to use the new template is double-click its icon on the Presentation Designs tab of the New Presentation dialog box.

The Basic Presentation

TIP

How to Place Your Own Templates on the General Tab
If you want your template to appear on the General tab of the New Presentation dialog box, save it in the Templates folder. If you save a template in a new *folder* in the Templates folder, the name of the new folder appears as a separate tab in the New Presentation dialog box. For example, you can create a special folder to hold your company-specific templates.

Starting a Design from Scratch

SEE ALSO
For more information about creating a template, changing the background, color scheme and fonts of your presentation, see Chapter 9, "Making Overall Changes," page 215.

If none of the templates suits your fancy or if you need to create a special presentation with a unique appearance, you can start with a blank presentation and then custom design the background, color scheme, and font choices.

To start with a blank presentation, follow these steps:

1   Choose New from the File menu.

2   On the General tab of the New Presentation dialog box, click the Blank Presentation icon and then click OK, or double-click the Blank Presentation icon.

3   In the New Slide dialog box, select an AutoLayout format for the first slide and click OK.

No matter what choices you make when starting a presentation, your next stop will probably be Outline view, where you can enter and edit the text that will form the backbone of your presentation. Chapter 4, "Working with Text in Outline View," is devoted to this next, logical step. But if you want, you can skip Outline view and head straight to Slide view, where you can work on slides one by one. In that case, Chapter 5, "Working with Text in Slide View" will give you the guidance you need.

CHAPTER 4

Working with Text in Outline View

C hapter 3 introduced the three ways of producing the text of a presentation: using the AutoContent Wizard; importing an outline created in Microsoft Word (or another application); and creating an outline from scratch in Outline view. The second and third methods are the topics of this chapter.

Starting a presentation in Outline view lets you mull over the themes and topics of the presentation, hone the flow of your arguments before you worry about how the presentation will look, and build a case that will be overwhelmingly persuasive. That, after all, is the purpose of a presentation.

Understanding Outline View

Outline view offers these advantages:

- In Outline view, you see only the presentation text—you don't see graphs, tables, or the design elements of the presentation, such as the background design. This way you can concentrate on the content of the presentation—what it says—without being distracted by its appearance.

- In Outline view, you can easily enter the list of main topics of your presentation. Entering the main topics generates all the presentation slides you need because each main topic becomes the title of a slide.

- In Outline view, you can easily rearrange the topics, thereby changing the order in which you will address issues in the presentation. You can enter supporting statements that will become bulleted items on the slides, and you can move the statements from topic to topic until you are sure a discussion point is addressed in just the right spot during the presentation.

Figure 4-1 shows the topics and supporting statements of a presentation in Outline view.

FIGURE 4-1.

A presentation outline in Outline view.

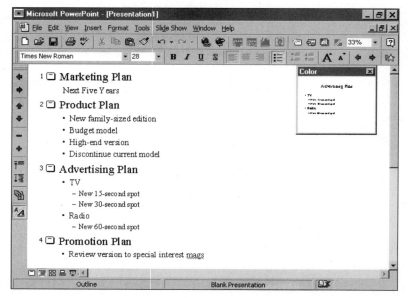

Figure 4-2 shows the resulting titles and bulleted items on slides in Slide Sorter view.

FIGURE 4-2.

The slides in Slide Sorter view.

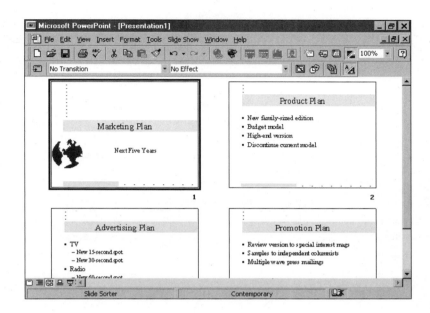

Switching to Outline View

When you start a new presentation using any option in the New Presentation dialog box other than AutoContent wizard, PowerPoint automatically opens the presentation in Slide view. If you want to concentrate on the topics you'll cover in the presentation and enter text to support each topic, you can easily switch to Outline view. After you finish with the text in Outline view, you can return to Slide view and add graphs and tables for information that is not readily communicated with words.

Assuming that you have launched PowerPoint and started a new presentation, here's how to switch to Outline view at any time: With the title slide displayed on your screen, click the Outline View button in the lower left corner of the presentation window, shown at the top of the next page, or choose Outline from the View menu.

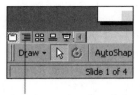

Click the Outline View button.

When you switch to Outline view to begin a new presentation, the insertion point is positioned beside blank slide number 1, as shown in Figure 4-3. When you begin typing, PowerPoint inserts your text at the insertion point. Also, when Outline view is active, a special Outlining toolbar appears on the left side of the presentation window, as shown in Figure 4-3.

FIGURE 4-3.
Starting a new presentation in Outline view.

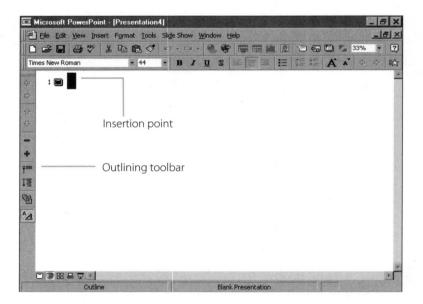

Insertion point

Outlining toolbar

Entering the Main Topics

When you reach Outline view, you'll enter a title for the presentation and a list of the topics you plan to discuss. The title and topics will become your preliminary slide titles. Don't worry about entering the topics in exact order. You can always rearrange them later.

To enter the topics for your presentation, follow these steps:

1 Type the presentation title and Press Enter.

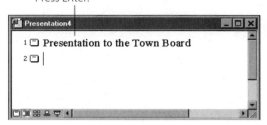

2 Type the first topic, and press Enter. If you don't yet have a topic precisely pinned down, type a two- or three-word place-holder. You can always edit it later.

3 Type the next topic, and press Enter.

4 Type the topic for each successive slide, pressing Enter after each one except the last.

Figure 4-4 shows a completed list of topics for a presentation about the construction of a new store.

FIGURE 4-4.
A list of topics for the slides of a new presentation.

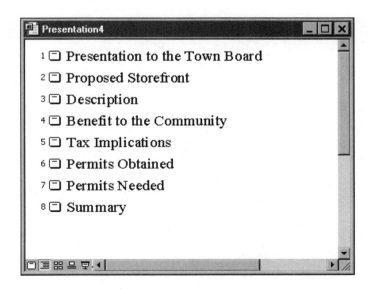

The Basic Presentation

⭐ **TIP**

Use Fewer Words for a More Powerful Presentation

On each slide, use the fewest words possible to communicate your message. The fewer words used, the more impact the text has, and the larger and more readable it can be. Try to write newspaper-like headlines, not whole sentences. Write *Profits up 26%* rather than *Our profits increased by 26%*.

Next, examine your list of topics to determine the best way to communicate to your audience. Some topics are best conveyed with a few bulleted items added below the topics. Other topics involve numeric data. Later, you can switch to Slide view and add graphs or tables to these slides to bring the numbers to life. You can also add organization charts and drawings.

⭐ **TIP**

How to See More Text on the Screen

If your presentation outline has many topics, you may want to use the Zoom Control box on the Standard toolbar or the Zoom command on the View menu to reduce the magnification of the text so that more of it fits on the screen. For more information about zooming, see the sidebar titled "Zooming In and Out," page 69.

The Outline View-Slide View Connection

Each main topic entered in a presentation in Outline view becomes a title on a slide in Slide view. Similarly, each supporting statement entered under a main topic in Outline view becomes a bulleted item on a slide in Slide view. This connection between Outline view and Slide view is a two-way street. If you edit a title or bulleted item in Slide view, the changes you make show up in Outline view as well.

Adding Bulleted Items

After entering a list of topics, you're ready to enter the supporting statements for those topics.

To add bulleted items under a topic, follow these steps:

1 Move the insertion point to the end of the topic that requires bulleted items.

2 Press Enter to create a new line. PowerPoint adds a slide icon and renumbers the existing topics.

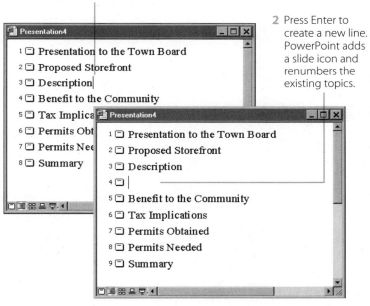

The Demote button

3 Click the Demote button on the Outlining toolbar or press the Tab key to move the insertion point one level to the right. PowerPoint removes the slide icon, readjusts the numbers, and inserts a bullet, as shown on the next page.

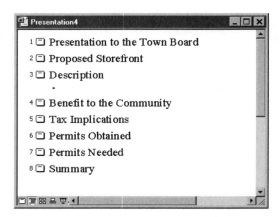

4   Type the first bulleted item. If you type more text than will fit on one line, the text wraps to the next line.

5   Press Enter to start another bulleted item.

6   Repeat steps 4 and 5 until you've added all the bulleted items you need.

Figure 4-5 shows the completed set of bulleted items for the third slide of the store-construction presentation.

FIGURE 4-5.
A complete set of bulleted items.

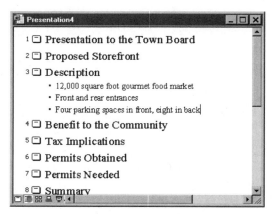

 NOTE

Text indented under the presentation title on slide 1 is not given a bullet; it becomes a subtitle on slide 1.

If you add bulleted items below a topic of your outline and then you want to add a new topic below, press Enter at the end of the last bulleted item, and then click the Promote button on the Outlining toolbar or press Shift+Tab to move the insertion point one level to the left. Then type the new topic. For example, Figure 4-6 shows the store-construction presentation with a new topic added after the bulleted items for slide number 3.

The Promote
button

FIGURE 4-6.

Press Enter and click
the Promote button
after typing a
bulleted item to
add another slide.

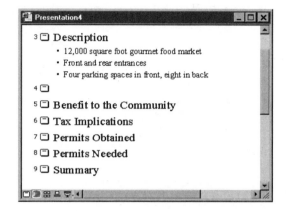

You can have five levels of items on a slide, as shown in Figure 4-7 on the next page. Each level is indented from the preceding level and has its own default bullet style. To demote a bulleted item by one level, thereby indenting it farther to the right, click the Demote button on the Outlining toolbar or press Tab before typing the bulleted item. To promote a bulleted item by one level, click the Promote button on the Outlining toolbar or press Shift+Tab. With five indent levels, you can have points under the main topics, subpoints under the points, and so on. But don't get carried away. Remember, when it comes to presentations, less is more.

Promoting or Demoting an Existing Bulleted Item
To demote or promote an existing bulleted item, place the insertion point anywhere in the item, and click the Demote or Promote button or press Tab or Shift+Tab.

FIGURE 4-7

The five levels of
bulleted items.

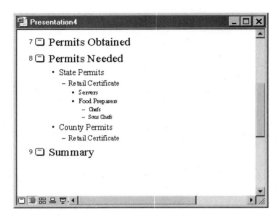

> **Another Approach to Creating Outlines**
>
> Typing all the topics and then adding bulleted items is one approach to creating the outline. It lets you reorganize the list of main topics before adding any detail to the presentation. (For information about reorganizing the outline, see "Reorganizing Text in Outline View," page 75.) Another approach is to enter a topic and then press Tab to enter its supporting bulleted items. Then, after the last bulleted item, press Shift+Tab and type the next topic. When you finish the last topic, you can still reorganize the presentation before switching to Slide view, where the topics become slide titles and where you can add graphs, tables, and other elements.

Creating a Summary Slide

New in this version of PowerPoint is the ability to quickly and easily create a summary slide from a series of slides. A summary slide shows the slide titles of other slides as bulleted text items. You can place a summary slide at the end of a series of slides, or place it before the series, so it will act as an agenda for the upcoming presentation.

To create a summary slide, follow the steps on the next page.

1 Select the slides to summarize.

The summary slide appears in front of the selected slides.

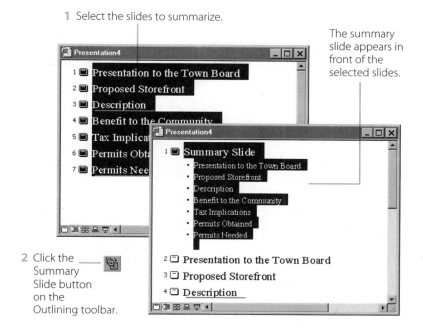

2 Click the Summary Slide button on the Outlining toolbar.

Editing Text in Outline View

After you've entered topics and bulleted items, you can revise the text to reword entries or make corrections. To edit text in Outline view, you must first move the insertion point to the spot that needs editing. The simplest way is to click where you want the insertion point to be in the text. For example, clicking to the left of the B in Board positions the insertion point as shown in Figure 4-8.

FIGURE 4-8.
An insertion point appears where you click.

Click to place an insertion point in the text.

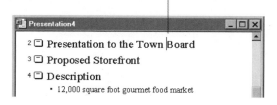

You can also move the insertion point with the keyboard by using one of the keys or key combinations listed in Table 4.1.

TABLE 4.1. Keyboard Shortcuts for Moving the Insertion Point.

Keys	Moves the Insertion Point
Left, Right, Up, or Down	One character left/right or one line up/down
Ctrl+Left arrow key	To the beginning of the previous word
Ctrl+Right arrow key	To the beginning of the next word
Ctrl+Up arrow key	To the beginning of the current topic (or to the beginning of the previous topic if the insertion point is already at the top of a topic)
Ctrl+Down arrow key	To the beginning of the next topic
Home	To the beginning of the current line
End	To the end of the current line
Ctrl+Home	To the top of the outline
Ctrl+End	To the bottom of the outline

After correctly positioning the insertion point, simply start typing to insert text. You can press the Backspace key to delete the character to the left of the insertion point or press the Delete key to delete the character to the right of the insertion point. You can also press Ctrl+Backspace to delete the word to the left or press Ctrl+Delete to delete the word to the right.

 NOTE

Unlike Microsoft Word, PowerPoint is *always* in Insert mode. Anything you type is inserted at the insertion point. You cannot press the Insert key to switch to Overtype mode.

Selecting Text for Editing

In PowerPoint, the easiest way to make more drastic editing changes is to select the text you want to modify so that your changes affect the entire selection rather than single characters.

To select a block of text with the mouse, click to the left of the first character in the block, hold down the left mouse button, and then drag across the text past the last character in the block. PowerPoint highlights the text as the mouse pointer passes across it, as shown in Figure 4-9. To select more than one line, drag down to the next line. Note that if you select a single word in one topic and then drag down to the next line, the entire first topic is selected.

FIGURE 4-9.
Selected text.

Drag across a word to select it.

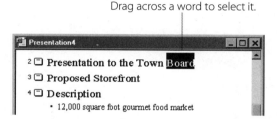

TIP

Shortcuts for Selecting Text with the Mouse
You can select a single word and its trailing space by double-clicking the word. You can select a series of words by double-clicking the first word, holding down the mouse button on the second click, and dragging across the remaining words. To select all of the text that follows a bullet, click the bullet once; to select a topic and all of its bulleted items, click the slide icon to the left of the topic text. You can select the entire presentation by choosing Select All from the Edit menu or by pressing Ctrl+A.

A special editing option called Automatic Word Selection makes it easy to select multiple words with the mouse. When you drag across any part of a word and continue to drag to the next word, PowerPoint selects both the first and second words. If you want to select an entire sentence, all you have to do is click anywhere in the first word and then drag to anywhere within the last word. PowerPoint then highlights the first and last words and all of the words in between. This option is on by default. To disable Automatic Word Selection, choose the Options command from the Tools menu, deselect the Automatic Word Selection option on the Edit tab, and click OK.

If you have trouble dragging across the text without also selecting part of the line above or below, you're not alone. You may want to use

II

The Basic Presentation

this technique instead: Click anywhere in the first word you want to select, hold down the Shift key, and then click anywhere in the last word of the block you want to select. PowerPoint highlights the first word, the last word, and all of the text in between. This technique selects the characters between the clicks if the Automatic Word Selection option is turned off.

 TIP

Using the Keyboard to Select Text

You can select text with the keyboard by moving the insertion point to the beginning of the text you want to select, holding down the Shift key, and then using the keys and key combinations listed earlier in Table 4-1 to move the insertion point to the end of the desired text block.

To practice selecting and editing text, try the following: Start a new presentation, and use the AutoContent Wizard to load the presentation called Selling Your Idea. When the presentation appears, click an insertion point in the *Goal and Objective* topic. Press the End key to move the insertion point to the end of the line, and then type an *s* to change the title of the slide to Objectives. Next, click the bullet in front of *State the desired objective* to select the entire line, and then type *To make you happy* to replace the selected text.

Later in this chapter, you'll make further changes to the outline, so you might want to save the presentation now by choosing Save As from the File menu and entering a filename.

Moving and Copying Text

Want to take the easiest and most direct approach to moving or copying selected text to another position within the outline? Then drag-and-drop editing is for you.

To move text using drag and drop, follow these steps:

1 Select the text you want to move or copy.

2 Point to the selected text. The I-beam
pointer becomes an arrow.

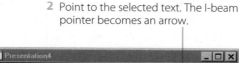

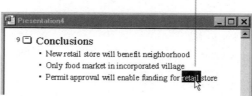

3 Hold down the mouse button, drag the pointer to the destination
for the selected text, and release the mouse button. The text
appears in its new location, as shown here:

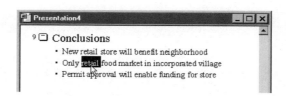

To copy text using drag and drop, follow the same procedure, but
hold down the Ctrl key while dragging the pointer. With drag and
drop, you can drag text clear to another slide.

In addition to using the drag-and-drop techniques, you can move or
copy selected text using the following methods:

The Cut
button

The Paste
button

The Copy
button

- To *move* selected text, first click the Cut button on the Standard
  toolbar, choose Cut from the Edit menu, or press Ctrl+X. Then
  move the insertion point to the destination for the text (even if
  it's on another slide), and click the Paste button on the Standard
  toolbar, choose Paste from the Edit menu, or press Ctrl+V.

- To *copy* selected text, start by clicking the Copy button on the
  Standard toolbar, choosing Copy from the Edit menu, or pressing
  Ctrl+C. Then move the insertion point to the destination for the
  text, and click the Paste button, choose Paste from the Edit
  menu, or press Ctrl+V.

II

The Basic Presentation

The Cut, Copy, and Paste commands are available on the text shortcut menu as well as on the Edit menu. To use a shortcut menu, select text with the right mouse button or point to an object or a selection and click the right mouse button. A menu pops up with options that are relevant to the object or text.

For example, to use the shortcut menu to move or copy a text selection, follow these steps:

1 Hold down the right mouse button and select the text you want to move or copy.

2 From the shortcut menu, choose Cut or Copy.

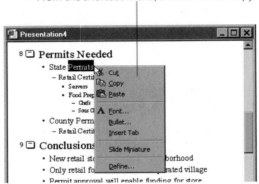

3 Move the insertion point to the destination for the text.

4 Click the right mouse button to open the shortcut menu again, and then choose Paste.

Deleting Text

To delete selected text, simply press the Delete key or the Backspace key. You can also delete selected text by clicking the Cut button on the Standard toolbar, choosing Cut or Clear from the Edit menu, or by pressing Ctrl+X.

Zooming In and Out

While working in Outline view, you can use the Zoom Control box on the Standard toolbar, shown below, to change the magnification level, or zoom percentage, of your view of the outline. When you use a higher zoom percentage, the text appears larger. Use a smaller zoom percentage to fit more text on the screen.

Zoom Control box.

To change the zoom percentage, click the current percentage number in the Zoom Control box on the Standard toolbar, type a new zoom percentage, and press Enter. To select a preset magnification level, click the arrow to the right of the Zoom Control box, and then select one of the zoom percentages from the drop-down list.

You can also change the zoom percentage by first choosing Zoom from the View menu to display this Zoom dialog box:

Then select one of the Zoom To percentages or edit the number in the Percent edit box. You can also click the arrows to the right of the Percent edit box to adjust the percentage up or down by one. Click OK to implement the new zoom percentage.

By default, Outline view uses a smaller zoom percentage than Slide view so that you can see more of your outline on the screen at one time. If you make Outline view's zoom percentage the same as Slide view's, the text size is identical in both views.

The Basic Presentation

Undoing Editing

The Undo
button

Retrieving something you've deleted is as simple as clicking the Undo button on the Standard toolbar, choosing Undo from the Edit menu, or pressing Ctrl+Z.

By repeatedly clicking the Undo button, you can undo up to your last 20 actions in PowerPoint. (If you want to increase—up to 150—or decrease this number, choose Options from the Tools menu, and change the Maximum Number Of Undos setting on the Edit tab of the Options dialog box.)

The Redo
button

When you use the Undo button or command to reverse an action, the Redo button on the Standard toolbar and the Redo command on the Edit menu become available. You can then quickly redo the last change you made in a presentation by clicking the Redo button or choosing the Redo command. For example, after applying bold format and then clicking the Undo button to remove the bold formatting, you can click the Redo button to reapply the bold formatting.

Repeating Actions

You can repeat many of the actions you take in PowerPoint—editing, formatting, or checking spelling, for example—by choosing the Repeat command from the Edit menu. The name of the command changes, depending on your last action—for example, Repeat Typing or Repeat Bold. If you cannot repeat your last action, the Repeat command changes to Can't Repeat.

Finding and Replacing Text

While editing an outline, you can search for a word or a string of characters and replace it with another. For example, you can use the Find command to find a former client's name in a presentation, and then use the Replace command to replace that name with a new client's name throughout the presentation.

To search for specific text, follow these steps:

1   Choose Find from the Edit menu or press Ctrl+F. PowerPoint displays the Find dialog box shown on the facing page.

2   Enter the text you want to find in the Find What edit box.

3   Then click Find Next or press Enter.

To have PowerPoint find only those words or strings of characters that match the capitalization entered in the Find What edit box, select the Match Case option. (Then PowerPoint will not find *Man* when you enter *man*.) To have PowerPoint find the text you've entered only when it is a whole word rather than part of a word, select the Find Whole Words Only option. (Then PowerPoint will not find *constitutional* when you enter *constitution*.)

To replace text, follow these steps:

1   Choose Replace from the Edit menu or press Ctrl+H. (Or, if the Find dialog box is open, you can click the Replace button.) PowerPoint displays the Replace dialog box shown here:

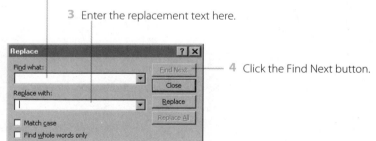

2 Enter the text to replace here.

3 Enter the replacement text here.

4 Click the Find Next button.

5   After PowerPoint locates the Find What text, click the Replace button to substitute the Replace With text for the selected text.

To replace every occurrence of the Find What text throughout the presentation, click the Replace All button instead of the Find Next button and the Replace button. You may want to use the Match Case option and the Find Whole Words Only option to be sure you do not replace text that does not exactly match the Find What text.

PowerPoint keeps a log of the text you have searched for or used as a replacement. To perform the same search or replace again, open the Find dialog box or the Replace dialog box, click the down arrow next to the Find What edit box or Replace With edit box, and then select a previous entry from the drop-down list.

Checking the Spelling of Presentation Text

Before your presentation goes public, take a moment to use PowerPoint's very capable spelling checker. Nothing looms larger than a silly little typo when it is projected full-screen.

To spell-check a presentation, follow these steps:

The Spelling
button

1 Click the Spelling button on the Standard toolbar, choose Spelling from the Tools menu, or press F7. PowerPoint checks each word against two dictionaries: the main dictionary and a supplemental dictionary called CUSTOM.DIC, which is empty until you add words to it. When PowerPoint finds a word it considers misspelled, it displays the dialog box shown here:

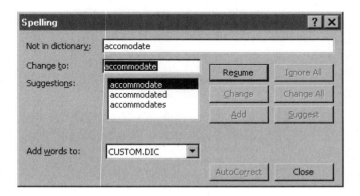

The questionable word is displayed in the Not In Dictionary edit box. The first and most strongly suggested replacement is highlighted in the Suggestions list and appears in the Change To edit box.

2 Indicate what you want PowerPoint to do next:

- If you know that the word is spelled correctly—if the word is a company name, for example—click the Ignore button.

- If the word is spelled correctly and occurs frequently in this presentation, you may want to click Ignore All instead of Ignore.

- If the word is spelled correctly and occurs frequently in other presentations, you can click Add to add the word to a custom dictionary. In future spelling checks, the word will not be flagged as a misspelling.

- If the word is misspelled and you want to change it to the word in the Change To edit box, click Change.

- If the word is misspelled and you want to make the same change throughout the entire presentation, click Change All instead.

Using Custom Dictionaries

When you click the Add button to add a word to a custom dictionary, the word is added to the dictionary file listed in the Add Words To box in the Spelling dialog box. The default custom dictionary is CUSTOM.DIC, the same custom dictionary file used by Microsoft Word and other Microsoft Office applications. If you have created custom dictionaries in another Microsoft Office application, you can select one of those dictionaries from the Add Words To drop-down list. If you enter words in a custom dictionary while working in another Microsoft Office application, those words won't be flagged as incorrect in PowerPoint either.

When PowerPoint completes the spelling check of the presentation, it informs you with an on-screen message. Click OK to remove the message and return to your outline.

WARNING

PowerPoint cannot check the spelling of text in graphs, organization charts, and tables. It also cannot check the spelling of text in objects created in other applications that are embedded in PowerPoint.

The Basic Presentation

Using AutoCorrect

If you frequently transpose the same letters in the same words while typing, you can use the AutoCorrect feature to recognize and then correct your mistakes. For example, if you type *captial* instead of *capital*, AutoCorrect can change the incorrect spelling to the correct one. In addition, you can use AutoCorrect to change two consecutive capital letters to one, to correct the accidental use of the Caps Lock key, and to capitalize the names of the days of the week. Best of all, PowerPoint's AutoCorrect feature already contains a large list of commonly misspelled words (such as *teh*), which are corrected when you press the Spacebar or type punctuation.

To add a word to the AutoCorrect list, follow these steps:

1   Choose AutoCorrect from the Tools menu. The AutoCorrect dialog box appears as shown below:

2   Be sure the Replace Text As You Type option is selected.

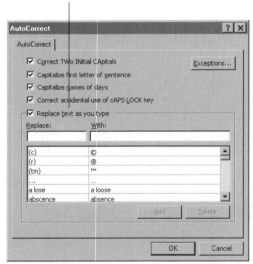

3   Enter the misspelled word in the Replace edit box, enter the correctly spelled word in the With edit box, and then click OK.

The next time you type the word incorrectly, PowerPoint will correct the misspelling as soon as you press the Spacebar or type punctuation. If you want to add more than one word to the list in the AutoCorrect dialog box, click the Add button after you complete the Replace and With edit boxes for each entry. If you want to delete a word in the AutoCorrect list, select the word and then click Delete.

If the presentation you are creating is strictly text, as most presentations are, and you do not need to reorganize the text, your basic presentation is now complete. You can skip ahead to Chapter 9 and beyond. But if you want to work on your text in Slide view, or add graphs, organization charts, or tables to your presentation, take a close look at the next four chapters.

Reorganizing Text in Outline View

The power of Outline view becomes obvious as soon as you need to reorganize the text of a presentation. You can change the order of the topics covered in the presentation, change the order of bulleted items under individual topics, and even move bulleted items from one topic to another. You can also delete topics, duplicate topics, and insert new topics.

Selecting Topics and Bulleted Items

Before you can reorganize a presentation, you must select the element you want to work with. You can select an entire topic (the topic text and its bulleted items), several topics, or one or more bulleted items within a topic.

To select an entire topic, you can use any of the following methods:

- Click the slide number or click the space to its left.

- Click the slide icon to the left of the topic.

- Triple-click the topic text.

- Click the topic text, and press Ctrl+Shift+Down arrow key.

II

The Basic Presentation

Whichever method you use, the result is similar to that shown in Figure 4-10.

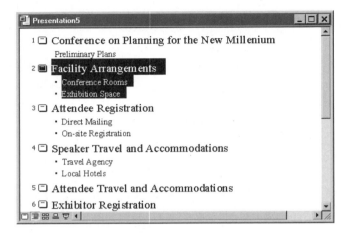

To select multiple slides, you can use one of these methods:

- Hold down the Shift key while clicking each slide's icon.

- If the slides are consecutive, point to the left of the title on the first slide, hold down the mouse button, and drag downward in the space to the left of the slides you want to select.

To select a bulleted item, as shown in Figure 4-11, do one of the following:

- Click in the space to the left of the text but to the right of the vertical line that separates the slide number and the slide icon. This method selects the bulleted item and any items indented below it.

- Triple-click a word in the bulleted item to select the entire bulleted item. Any items indented below it are also selected.

- Drag through the text of the bulleted item with the mouse.

- Click the first word of the bulleted item, hold down the Shift key, and then click the last word.

- Position the insertion point at the beginning of the bulleted item, hold down the Shift key, and press the End key to move the insertion point to the end of the bulleted item.

FIGURE 4-11.

A selected
bulleted item.

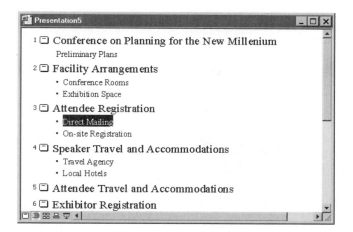

Reordering Topics and Bulleted Items

After you select a topic or a bulleted item, you can move it up or down in the outline to solidify the logic of your presentation. For example, you can move a touchy topic to the front of a presentation to get it over with early. Then move some good news to the end so that your audience can leave on a high.

To move an entire topic, follow these steps:

1 Point to the slide icon for the selected topic.

2 Hold down the mouse button, and drag up or down. When you drag, the pointer becomes a double-headed arrow, and a horizontal line indicates where the topic will drop when you release the mouse button.

3 Release the mouse button. The topic and its bulleted items move to the new position.

For example, Figure 4-12, on the next page, shows the result after the *Attendee Registration* topic was moved down in the New Millennium Conference presentation.

II

The Basic Presentation

FIGURE 4-12.

Dragging a selected topic's slide icon moves the topic within the presentation.

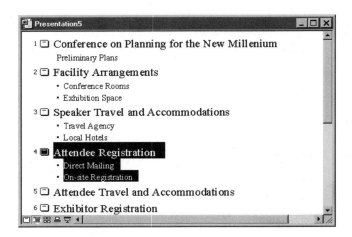

You can also move the selected topic up or down by clicking the Move Up or Move Down button on the Outlining toolbar. In fact, if you've selected multiple topics, you must use the Move Up or Move Down button to move them.

You can change the order of entire topics just as easily in Slide Sorter view. But what makes Outline view special is that you can reorder bulleted items under a topic and move them from topic to topic, as well as reorder entire topics. To move a bulleted item up or down, follow these steps:

1 Select the bulleted item.

2 Click the Move Up button or the Move Down button until the bulleted item is positioned where you want it. Alternatively, point to the left of the bulleted item, hold down the mouse button, and drag up or down in the outline. Release the mouse button when the bulleted item is in the correct position.

Using either the mouse or the button technique, you can move the selected bulleted item all the way to another topic if you want. Working this way in Outline view saves you from having to cut and paste text from one slide to another in Slide view.

TIP

> **How to Use the Keyboard to Organize an Outline**
> If you want to use the keyboard to organize an outline, you can press Alt+Shift+Up arrow to move selected text up and Alt+Shift+Down arrow to move selected text down. (These are the same key combinations used to reorganize outlines in Microsoft Word.)

Now try reorganizing the outline you've started. Load the presentation you created earlier in this chapter, and click the slide icon for slide 2. All the text related to the *Objectives* topic is now selected. Point to the slide icon, hold down the mouse button, and drag down to just below the last text item on slide 3. As you drag, a horizontal line shows where the text will drop. Release the mouse button. *Objectives* becomes slide 3, and *Customer Requirements* becomes slide 2.

Now try moving a bulleted text item from one topic to another. Click the bullet at the beginning of *This section may require multiple slides*, on slide 4. Drag the bullet up and drop it under *Customer Requirements* on slide 2. Be sure to save the presentation again because you'll have the opportunity to make further changes later in this chapter.

Promoting and Demoting Topics and Bulleted Items

Earlier in the chapter, you learned that *promoting* text moves it one level to the left and *demoting* text moves it one level to the right. If you need to split a topic into two slides, you can promote one of the bulleted items to the main topic level to start a new slide. When an existing topic should be a supporting statement for the previous topic, you can demote it to a bulleted item.

To promote a bulleted item, select it and then take one of the following actions:

The Promote button

- Click the Promote button.

- Click just to the left of the item, hold down the mouse button, and drag to the left.

- Press Shift+Tab or Alt+Shift+Left arrow.

Figure 4-13 shows the result after the second bulleted item under *Facility Arrangements* in the New Millennium Conference presentation is promoted to a topic. As you can see, a new slide number and slide icon appear to the left of the promoted text, which becomes the title of a new slide in Slide view.

FIGURE 4-13.

Promoting a bulleted item creates a new topic on a new slide.

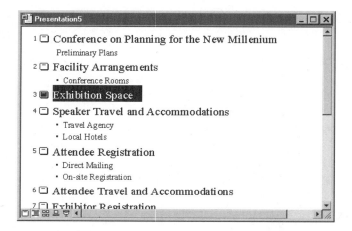

To demote a topic or a bulleted item, select it and take one of the following actions:

The Demote button

- Click the Demote button.

- Click to the left of the selected text, hold down the mouse button, and drag to the right.

- Press Tab or Alt+Shift+Right arrow.

All of the promotion and demotion techniques discussed so far promote or demote not only the selected text but also bulleted items below the selected text. What if you want to promote or demote a line but leave any subpoints at their current levels? You can click once anywhere in a topic or bulleted item, and then press the Tab key to demote the line, or press Shift+Tab to promote the line without affecting any subordinate text.

Be aware when you are organizing topics and bulleted items that you can fit only a certain amount of text on any one slide. For example, in the presentation on the left in Figure 4-14, the list of bulleted items under the topic *What I Love About New York* is far too long. To get all these points across, move the insertion point to the end of *The action*, and press Enter to start a new bulleted item. Then type *What I Love to Do in New York* as a new bulleted item. Finally, drag the bullet in front of the new bulleted item one level to the left so that the bulleted item becomes a new main topic. The outline then looks as shown on the right in Figure 4-14.

FIGURE 4-14.

A long list of bulleted items (left) divided between two slides for greater impact (right).

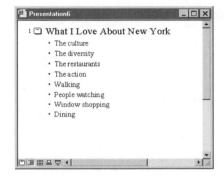

Hiding and Revealing Detail

Sometimes you need to step back to see the big picture while working on a presentation outline. If the entire outline is displayed, the volume of detail can muddle the big themes. By *collapsing* bulleted items, you can temporarily hide them from view and show only the larger topics. To redisplay the bulleted items, you *expand* them. You can collapse and expand outlines using the Collapse button and the Expand button on the Outlining toolbar.

To collapse bulleted items under a topic, follow these steps:

1 Click anywhere in the topic or click the slide icon that is to the left of the topic.

The Collapse button

2 Click the Collapse button or press Alt+Shift+Minus. PowerPoint draws a gray line under the topic to indicate the presence of collapsed bulleted items, as shown on the next page.

The Basic Presentation

 TIP

Why to Collapse Bulleted Items

When you collapse bulleted items under a topic, they remain an intrinsic part of the topic. If you move that topic, the collapsed bulleted items also move. In fact, you may find it easier to reorganize a presentation with many bulleted items if you collapse them under their topics and then reorder the topics.

To expand the collapsed bulleted items, follow these steps:

1 Click anywhere in the topic.

2 Click the Expand button or press Alt+Shift+Plus.

The Expand button

To quickly collapse all bulleted items under their topics, click the Collapse All button or press Alt+Shift+1. Then to expand all of the items again, click the Expand All button or press Alt+Shift+A.

The Collapse All button

Try hiding detail in this chapter's sample presentation. With the presentation displayed on your screen in Outline view, click the Collapse All button on the Outlining toolbar to show only the main topics. Drag topic 2, *Customer Requirements*, to just after topic 3, *Objectives*. Then click the Expand button on the Outlining toolbar to see that the collapsed bulleted items have come along for the ride. Finally, click the Expand All button on the Outlining toolbar to redisplay all the presentation text.

The Expand All button

You may want to save the sample presentation you've made for posterity, but you'll be making no further changes to it in this chapter.

Formatting Text in Outline View

Slide view is usually the best place to format the text of a presentation because you can see how the text fits with the background design. However, while entering and editing the presentation in Outline view, you can format any words or characters that are sure to need it. For example, you can italicize a special term or change a character in a formula name to superscript.

SEE ALSO
For more information about selecting text, see "Selecting Text for Editing," page 64.

To format text in Outline view, you must first select it. Then you can use the character formatting buttons on the Formatting toolbar or the character formatting commands on either the Format menu or the shortcut menu. For example, choosing the Font command from the Format menu or the shortcut menu displays the Font dialog box shown in Figure 4-15. The character formatting buttons and commands work the same way in both Outline view and Slide view.

FIGURE 4-15.
The Font dialog box.

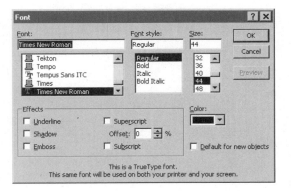

SEE ALSO
For more information about formatting text, see "Formatting Text in Slide View," page 99.

Whether you apply character formatting in Outline view or in Slide view, you can display the outline in Outline view without character formatting. Just click the Show Formatting button on the Outlining toolbar or press the slash key above the numeric keypad on your keyboard. The Font Face box and the Font Size box on the Formatting toolbar still show accurate information about the selected text, but the entire outline is displayed in a standard font and size (Arial, 28 points). To redisplay the character formatting in Outline view, click the Show Formatting button again or press the slash key again.

Importing Outlines

If you have already created a perfectly good outline in another application, it would be tedious to have to recreate it in PowerPoint. And you don't have to. You can import the outline as a starting point for your presentation.

Importing an Outline from Microsoft Word

You can generate a presentation outline in Microsoft Word and then easily export the outline to PowerPoint. Developing the outline in Word lets you take advantage of Word's sophisticated text capabilities. For example, you can use the thesaurus to replace ordinary outline words with vibrant, vigorous, pulsating, dynamic, energetic words.

Because PowerPoint imports Word outlines so easily, anyone can generate an entire text presentation in Word and hand the file over to you. You can then import the outline, give the presentation a distinctive look, and generate slides in no time.

To import a Word outline:

1   Open the outline in Word.

2   From Word's File menu, choose Send To.

3   From the Send To submenu, choose Microsoft PowerPoint. Word opens PowerPoint if necessary, opens a new presentation in Outline view, and exports the outline to PowerPoint.

For example, Figure 4-16, on the facing page, shows an outline in Word. Figure 4-17, also on the facing page, shows the same outline after it has been imported into PowerPoint.

⭐ **TIP**

If the Word outline contains a lot of detail, the PowerPoint slides you get may be too crowded for your liking. To automatically distribute the bulleted text points of a slide onto multiple slides you can use Expand Slide, described in the Expand Slide Tip, page 306.

FIGURE 4-16.

An outline in Microsoft Word.

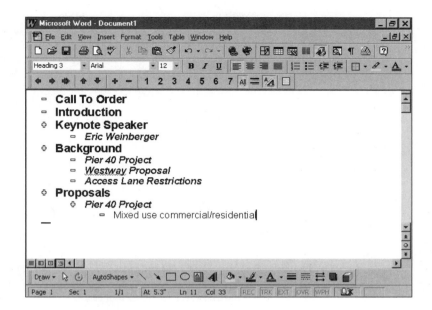

FIGURE 4-17.

The Word outline in PowerPoint.

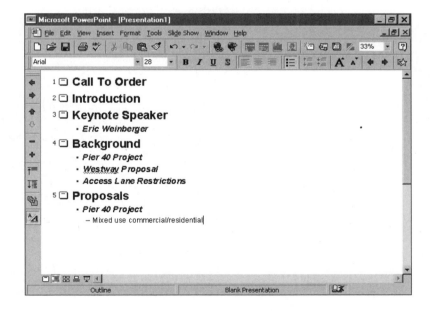

The Best Way to Copy a Word Outline to PowerPoint
A super-slick method you can use to create a new PowerPoint presentation from a Word outline is to drag and drop the Word outline file from Windows Explorer to the PowerPoint window. A new presentation opens in PowerPoint with the Word outline in place.

Imported Word outlines can have up to nine indent levels. However, when you import an outline into PowerPoint, levels beyond level five are all converted to fifth-level entries.

Importing an Outline from Another Application

You can import an outline from most word processing programs as well as from other presentation applications that can export their presentation outlines. If the application can generate an RTF (Rich Text Format) file, you should use that format when saving the outline to disk. When you import the file, PowerPoint uses the styles in the file to determine the outline structure. For example, a Heading 1 style becomes a slide title, a Heading 2 style becomes an indented bulleted item, and so on. If the file contains no styles, PowerPoint uses the paragraph indents to determine the outline structure.

If the application cannot generate an RTF file, you should generate a plain ASCII text file. PowerPoint then picks up the outline structure from the tabs at the beginning of paragraphs. A paragraph preceded by no tabs becomes a slide title, a paragraph preceded by one tab becomes an indented bulleted item, and so on.

To import an outline file, follow these steps:

1 Click the Open button on the Standard toolbar or choose Open from the File menu.

2 In the File Open dialog box, select All Outlines from the Files Of Type drop-down list.

3   Navigate through the folders list, select the file you want to import, and then click Open. PowerPoint opens the file and displays it as a PowerPoint outline.

Inserting an Outline in an Existing Presentation

As a starting point for a presentation, in addition to importing an outline created in an application such as Word you can also insert an outline file created with another application into an existing PowerPoint presentation.

To supplement a PowerPoint outline with an imported outline, follow these steps:

1   In Outline view, click the topic after which you want the imported outline to appear.

2   Choose Slides From Outline from the Insert menu. PowerPoint displays this dialog box:

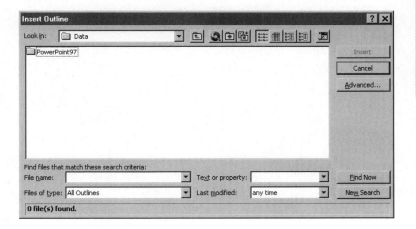

3   In the Insert Outline dialog box, navigate through the folders and filenames, select the outline file you want to insert, and then click Insert. PowerPoint inserts the imported outline in the current outline, assigning numbers, slide icons, and indent levels

to create a seamless presentation. If you import an outline with more than five levels, PowerPoint converts all levels beyond five to fifth-level entries.

> You can also import an outline in Slide view. First move to the slide after which you want the outline to appear, and then follow steps 2 and 3 on the previous page. PowerPoint imports the outline into the presentation as slides.

After you import an outline from another application as a new presentation or insert an imported outline in an existing PowerPoint presentation, you can manipulate it just like an outline created from scratch in Outline view.

In this chapter, you learned how to develop and modify a presentation outline in Outline view—the best place for concentrating on the text and the flow of ideas. In the next chapter, you'll learn how to create the text for a presentation in Slide view, where you can see the design of each slide, but you cannot easily see the progression of the presentation from one slide to the next.

Working with Text in Slide View

Creating and organizing a presentation in Outline view is still the best way to focus exclusively on the text of your presentation, but you may prefer to devote your creative energy to crafting a single slide at a time in Slide view. Slide view may also be the best place to start when your job is not to conceive a presentation but to produce slides for someone else from handwritten notes and napkin sketches. Figure 5-1 on the next page shows a completed slide as it appears in Slide view.

In this chapter, you'll learn how to create text slides in Slide view. By the time you finish, you'll be just as far along as if you'd entered the presentation text in Outline view and then switched to Slide view. The task still remaining is to drop in the graphs, tables, and drawings you want to include in the presentation. You'll learn how to do this in the next several chapters.

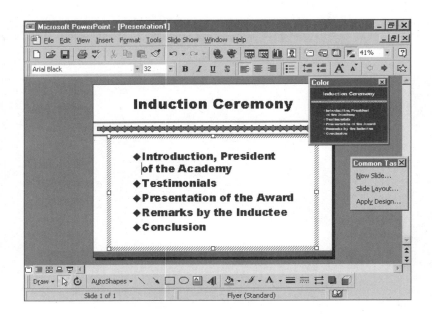

Creating a New Presentation in Slide View

If you do not use the AutoContent Wizard to start a new presentation (which leaves you in Outline view), you are dropped off in Slide view with the New Slide dialog box displayed on the screen. The Title Slide autolayout in the New Slide dialog box is selected so you can simply click OK or press Enter to move to Slide view with a blank title slide displayed. If PowerPoint is correct in assuming that you plan to create a complete presentation, you should fill out this title slide.

> If you're using PowerPoint to create a single slide, you may want to use a slide layout other than the Title Slide layout. To work with a graph chart layout or organization chart layout, for example, click Slide Layout on the Common Tasks toolbar and select a different slide layout in the Slide Layout dialog box. (For more information about selecting a slide layout, see "Adding a New Slide," page 94.)

If you need to switch to Slide view from another view, click the Slide View button in the lower left corner of the presentation window or choose Slide from the View menu.

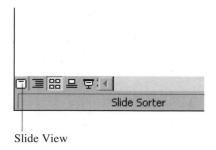

Slide View

Creating the Title Slide

As shown in Figure 5-2, the Title Slide layout displays two text *placeholders*—dashed boxes that show the location for an object on a slide. All placeholders tell you to click to add text, a chart, or another presentation element. In this case, you're prompted for a title and a sub-title for the new presentation.

FIGURE 5-2.
The Title Slide layout that appears when you create a new presentation.

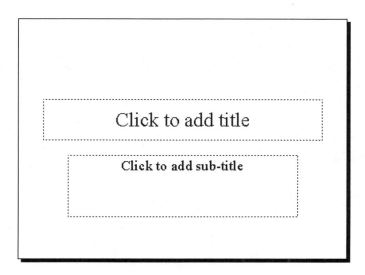

The Basic Presentation

II

To enter a presentation title in the Title Slide layout, follow these steps:

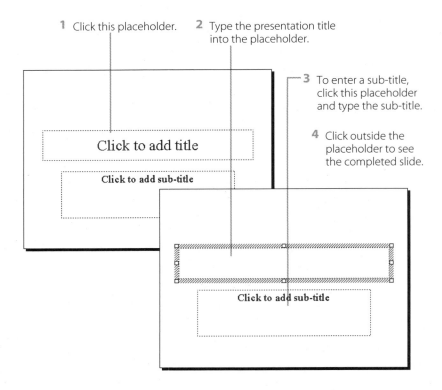

Figure 5-3 on the next page shows a completed slide we happened to have laying around.

Figure 5-3 on the next page

 TIP

When you add a new slide, you can start typing without clicking the *Click to add title* placeholder. The first text you type is automatically entered in the placeholder.

FIGURE 5-3.
A completed
title slide.

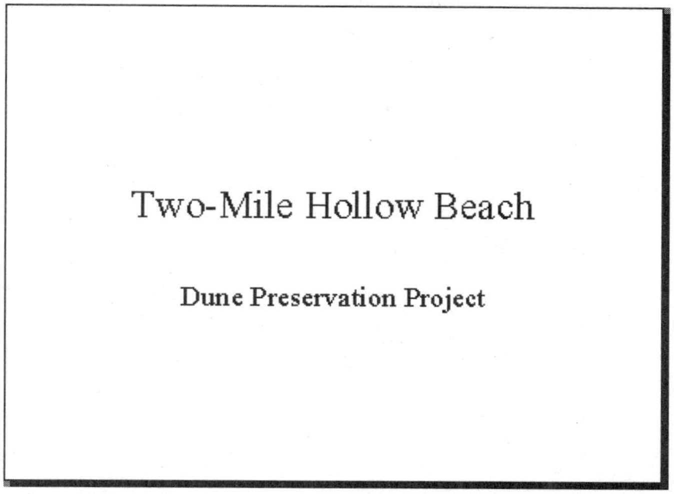

Two-Mile Hollow Beach

Dune Preservation Project

 NOTE

The formatting of the text (its font, size, color, and so on) is determined by the formatting of the text on the title master and slide master. To change the appearance of the text on any single slide, you can apply your own formatting, which overrides the title master's and slide master's formatting. (For more information, see "Formatting Text in Slide View," page 99.) To change the appearance of the text on all the slides of a presentation, you might want to change the formatting of the title master or slide master, instead. (For more information, see "Editing the Title Master or Slide Master," page 227.)

If you want to try creating the sample title slide shown in Figure 5-4 on the next page, start a new presentation by choosing New from the File menu. In the New Presentation dialog box, click the Presentation Designs tab, and then double-click the Contemporary Portrait template. When the New Slide dialog box appears, select the Title Slide autolayout, and click OK. Then click the *Click to add title* placeholder, and type *Person to Person*. Click the *Click to add sub-title* placeholder or press Ctrl+Enter, and type *Our New Care-Giving Partnership*. Finally, click anywhere outside the subtitle frame to see the completed title slide.

II

The Basic Presentation

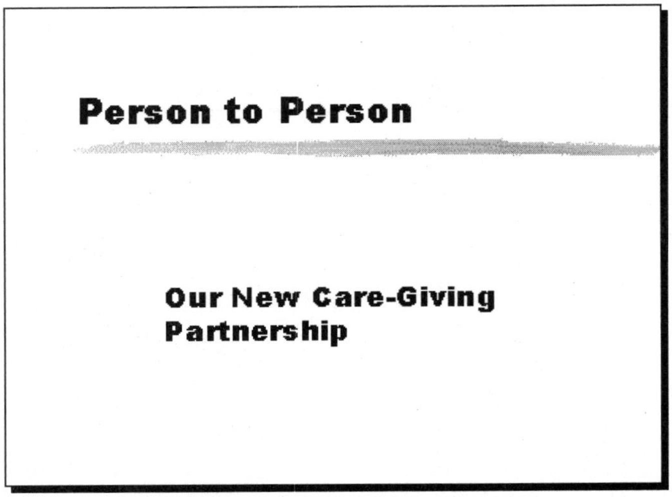

FIGURE 5-4.

A sample title slide.

TIP

How to Work Quickly with the Keyboard

After typing text in a placeholder, you can press Ctrl+Enter to move to the next placeholder. If the current slide has no more placeholders, PowerPoint creates a new slide and puts the insertion point in the *Click to add title* placeholder on that slide.

Adding a New Slide

After completing the title slide, you are ready to add the next slide. Before you add a slide, however, you must select an autolayout from the New Slide dialog box. Like the Title Slide autolayout, PowerPoint's other autolayouts contain placeholders. For example, the Bulleted List autolayout has a *Click to add title* placeholder and a *Click to add text* placeholder; the Chart autolayout has a *Click to add title* placeholder and a *Double click to add chart* placeholder; and so on. PowerPoint offers 24 autolayouts that should meet nearly all of your presentation needs.

To add a new slide to your presentation, follow these steps:

1 Click the New Slide button on the Standard toolbar or click New Slide on the Common Tasks toolbar. The New Slide dialog box appears, as shown here:

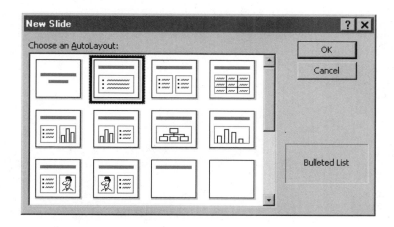

You can scroll through the display of autolayouts using the scroll bar. To see the name of an autolayout, click the autolayout once.

TIP

The Common Tasks toolbar has three text options—New Slide, Slide Layout, and Apply Design. These same options appear as buttons on the Standard toolbar. If you do not see a Common Tasks toolbar, choose Toolbars from the View menu and click Common Tasks on the Toolbars submenu.

2 When you've decided which autolayout you want, either double-click it or click it once and then click OK. A new slide with the selected autolayout appears on the screen.

The rest of this chapter focuses on entering text in text slides. When you finish one slide, you can repeat the previous steps to create the next one. If you need to look at a slide you've already completed, you can move back to the slide by pressing the PgUp key. Press the PgDn key to move forward through your slides. You can also move from one slide to another by dragging the scroll box in the vertical scroll bar up or down.

II

The Basic Presentation

Entering Text in a Bulleted List AutoLayout

If you add a new slide with a layout that has bulleted text, such as the Bulleted List autolayout or the 2 Column Text autolayout, a *Click to add title* placeholder appears on the new slide along with one or more *Click to add text* placeholders.

To complete a slide with bulleted items, follow these steps:

1 Type a slide title. (You don't have to click the *Click to add title* placeholder first.)

2 Click this placeholder or press Ctrl+Enter.

3 Type the first bulleted item, press Enter, type the next item, and so forth.

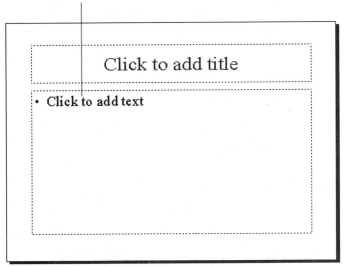

4 After typing the last bulleted item, click outside the placeholder frame to see the completed slide.

NOTE

If you want text without bullets (for a paragraph that is a quote, for example), never fear. You can turn off the bullets at any time. For more information about turning off bullets, see "Adding and Removing Bullets," page 108.

New Slide
button

As an example, try adding the bulleted slide shown in Figure 5-5 to the slide you created earlier using the Contemporary Portrait template. Click the New Slide button on the Standard toolbar, and then double-click the Bulleted List autolayout—the second layout in the first row. Type *Activities* in the title placeholder. Then click the *Click to add text* placeholder or press Ctrl+Enter, type *Home visits*, and press Enter. Type *Hospital bedside visits,* and press Enter. Finally, type *County Community Center work*, and click outside the placeholder frame.

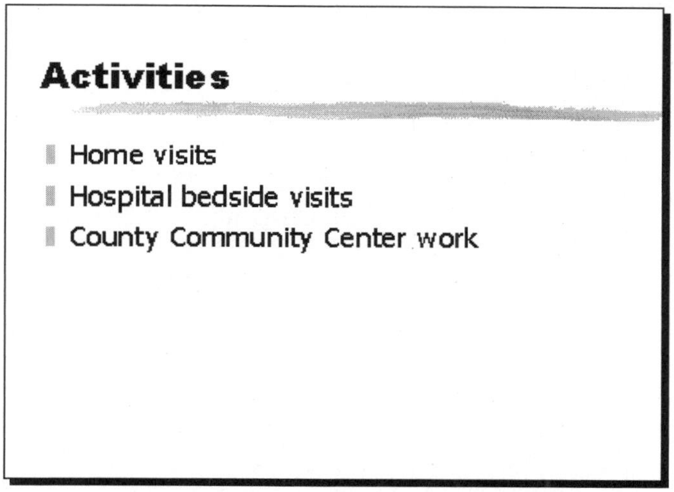

FIGURE 5-5.
A sample slide with bulleted items.

Activities

▌ Home visits
▌ Hospital bedside visits
▌ County Community Center work

As in Outline view, you can create up to five levels of bulleted items in Slide view using the same buttons and keystrokes that you use in Outline view. The Demote and Promote buttons are available on the Formatting toolbar, and you can also press Tab at the beginning of a line to demote an item or Shift+Tab to promote it.

Editing Text in Slide View

While creating presentation text in Slide view, you can use all the text editing techniques available in Outline view. In fact, everything you type flows through to the presentation outline; you see the presentation as an outline if you switch to Outline view.

To edit text directly on a slide in Slide view, first position the insertion point in the spot you want to edit. The keyboard methods for moving the insertion point in Slide view are nearly the same as those used in

II

The Basic Presentation

SEE ALSO

For more information about moving text in Outline view, see "Moving and Copying Text," page 66.

SEE ALSO

For information about editing text, see "Editing Text in Outline View," page 63.

Outline view. The notable exceptions: Pressing Ctrl+Up arrow or Ctrl+Down arrow moves the insertion point to the previous or next paragraph, respectively, rather than to the previous or next topic; and pressing Ctrl+Home or Ctrl+End moves the insertion point to the beginning or end of the current *text object* (all the text in a single placeholder) rather than to the beginning or end of the entire outline. If no placeholder is active, Ctrl+Home takes you to slide 1, Ctrl+End takes you to the last slide.

After clicking an insertion point or positioning the insertion point with the keyboard, you can type to insert text, press the Backspace key to delete characters to the left of the insertion point, or press Delete to delete characters to the right of the insertion point. As in Outline view, you can make larger edits most efficiently by first selecting the text you want to edit.

Selecting text with the mouse is the same as it is in Outline view: Position the insertion point at the beginning of the text, hold down the left mouse button, and drag to the end of the text. (Automatic Word Selection is active in Slide view, so when you drag across any part of a word, the entire word is selected.) Selecting text with the keyboard is also the same: Move the insertion point to the beginning of the text, hold down the Shift key, and then use the appropriate keys to move the insertion point to the end of the text.

To select an entire text object, click the border of the object. The border changes from a fine diagonal strip to a fine pattern of dots as shown on the right side of Figure 5-6.

FIGURE 5-6.

A selected bulleted item (left) and a selected text object (right).

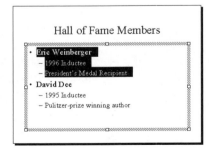
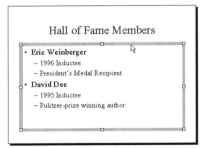

After you select text on a slide, you can delete, move, or copy it using the same buttons, commands, and key combinations you use in

Outline view. You can also use drag-and-drop editing to move text within one placeholder or to move text between placeholders. Reorganizing Text in Slide View

Reorganizing bulleted items is not as easy in Slide view as it is in Outline view, but it's not that difficult, either. Because the Outlining toolbar, with its Move Up and Move Down buttons, is not present, you must select bulleted items and then press Alt+Shift+Up arrow or Alt+Shift+Down arrow to move them.

Formatting Text in Slide View

? SEE ALSO
For more information about changing the slide master, see "Editing the Title Master or Slide Master," page 227.

The appearance of the text on all text slides is determined by the slide master for that particular presentation. By editing the slide master, you can change the formatting of text throughout the presentation. You can also override the slide master's control of the text on any individual slide by applying your own formatting. This section discusses formatting that you apply to individual slides.

Many of PowerPoint's text formatting options are available as buttons on the Formatting toolbar or as key combinations. Others are available only as menu commands. You'll soon get a feel for the quickest way to apply specific types of formatting.

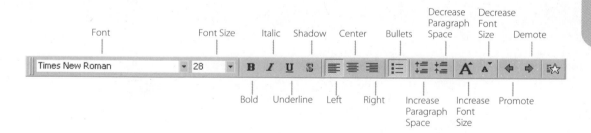

Selecting Text for Formatting

You can apply two types of formatting to the text on your slides: character formatting that affects individual characters, and a broader type of formatting that affects an entire text object. Selecting text for character formatting is just like selecting text for editing. You drag across characters to select them, and then make your formatting changes.

You can also drag to select entire text objects, but you might want to use a special technique to select all the text in the object containing the insertion point. Either press Ctrl+A to highlight all the text within the object, as shown on the left side of Figure 5-7, or press F2 to select the text object itself, as shown on the right side of Figure 5-7. When you press F2 to select a text object, the object is surrounded by handles. Press F2 again to select the text within the object. After you select a text object, you can press Tab to select the next text object on the slide either before or after you make formatting changes. (You can select the previous text object by pressing Shift+Tab.)

FIGURE 5-7.

Selected text within a text object (left) and a selected text object (right).

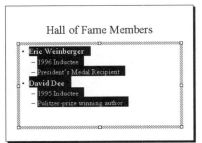

TIP

Instead of pressing F2 to select the object, you can click the gray border that surrounds the text object.

Changing the Font, Font Style, Size, Color, and Font Effects

You can emphasize individual characters, words, or phrases by changing their font, font style, size, or color. You can even apply special font effects, such as shadows or embossing, to selected text. All of these options are available in the Font dialog box.

To make formatting changes using the Font dialog box:

1 Select the text you want to format. You can select an individual character; you can place the insertion point in a word to format the entire word; or you can select several words or sentences.

2 Choose Font from the Format menu, or point to the selection, click the right mouse button and choose Font from the shortcut menu to display the Font dialog box shown below:

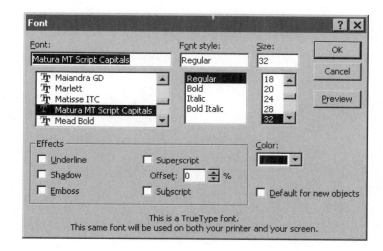

3 Select a Font, Font Style, and Size from the lists in the Font dialog box. The Font list includes the fonts installed on your Windows system. The sizes are measured in points (with 72 points comprising 1 inch).

4 Select any combination of Effects options by clicking the appropriate check boxes. If you turn on Superscript or Subscript, you can change the percentage by which the text is set above or below the line by increasing or decreasing the Offset.

5 To change the color of the selected text, first click the down arrow next to the Color box. Then click one of the eight colors available for the current color scheme, or click More Colors to select from the full palette of available colors.

6 Click the Preview button if you want to see the changes you've made. (If necessary, drag the title bar of the Font dialog box to move the box out of the way.)

7 Click OK to implement the changes.

TIP

Try formatting some text on the bulleted slide you created earlier in this chapter. Select *County Community Center work*, click the right mouse button, and choose Font from the shortcut menu to display the Font dialog box. Then select Bold Italic as the Font Style option, and click OK.

The choices you make for the selected text in the Font dialog box are cumulative. You might make certain changes during one pass, such as changing the font and font style, and then come back later and make more changes, such as changing the color. When you select already formatted text and return to the Font dialog box, all the changes you've made to the formatting up to that point are reflected in the dialog box's settings.

After you select the text you want to format, you can also change the font and font size by using the Font and Font Size drop-down lists on the Formatting toolbar. The Increase Font Size or Decrease Font Size button increases or decreases the font size by specific increments. The increments become larger as the font size increases. The largest theoretical font size is 4000 points, but you will probably run out of paper long before you can print a character that large.

You can apply the bold or italic font styles by clicking the Bold button or the Italic button on the Formatting toolbar, and you can apply the underline or shadow effects by clicking the Underline button or the Text Shadow button. Clicking the Font Color button on the Drawing toolbar pops up a palette of the eight colors available with the current color scheme. Most text formatting options are available as keyboard shortcuts, too. Rather than using menus or the Formatting toolbar, you can select the text and then use one of the keyboard shortcuts listed in Table 5-1 on the facing page.

TABLE 5-1. Keyboard shortcuts for formatting text.

Text Formatting	Keyboard Shortcut
Change font	Ctrl+Shift+F
Change font size	Ctrl+Shift+P
Increase font size	Ctrl+Shift+>
Decrease font size	Ctrl+Shift+<
Bold	Ctrl+B or Ctrl+Shift+B
Underline	Ctrl+U or Ctrl+Shift+U
Italic	Ctrl+I or Ctrl+Shift+I
Subscript	Ctrl+=
Superscript	Ctrl+Shift+=
Plain text	Ctrl+Shift+Z
Restore default formatting	Ctrl+Spacebar

TIP

You can replace all instances of a certain font with another font—for example, replacing Times New Roman with Arial—by using the Replace Fonts command on the Format menu. In the Replace box, select the font you want to replace and then in the With box, select the font you want to use instead. Click the Replace button, and all of the instances of the Replace font are immediately changed to the With font.

Changing the Indents, Alignment, and Spacing

You can perform certain types of text formatting only on entire text objects, not individual characters or words. These formatting types include changing the left and first-line indents of paragraphs, changing the alignment of paragraphs, and changing the spacing between and within paragraphs.

Remember, a text object includes all the text in a single placeholder. For example, a bulleted list slide has only two text objects, the title and the bulleted list, even though the bulleted list probably consists of more than one paragraph.

Changing the Left Indent and First-Line Indent

Increasing the left indent of a bulleted list text object pushes all the text to the right, increasing the space between the bullets and the text for each bullet. To change the indents of a text object, you must click anywhere in the text object and then drag the corresponding markers in the top ruler.

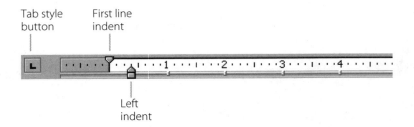

If the ruler is not visible, you can display it in one of the following ways:

■ Choose Ruler from the View menu.

■ Point to the slide background, click the right mouse button, and choose Ruler from the shortcut menu.

 **NOTE**

> If a text object has bulleted items at two or more levels, the ruler contains a pair of markers (a left indent marker and a first-line indent marker) for each level.

To increase the space to the right of the bullets, follow these steps:

1 Click any of the text in the object.

2 Drag the left indent marker to the right.

 TIP

> Be sure to drag the lower, triangular marker that points upward. Dragging the rectangular marker located below the left indent marker moves the first-line indent marker and the left indent marker at the same time.

Dragging the first-line indent marker (the upper, triangular marker that points downward) to the left or the right changes the starting position of the first line of the paragraph. Because a bullet starts the first line of a bulleted list paragraph, dragging the first-line indent marker to the right moves the bullet to the right. Figure 5-8 below, and Figure 5-9 on the next page, show the indent settings on several rulers and the corresponding indents of the text below. If a text object contains paragraphs that have no bullets, dragging the first-line indent marker to the left creates a hanging indent, as shown in Figure 5-10 on the next page.

FIGURE 5-8.

Notice how the ruler settings correspond to the text on these two slides.

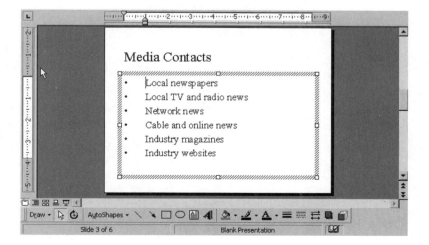
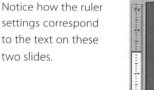
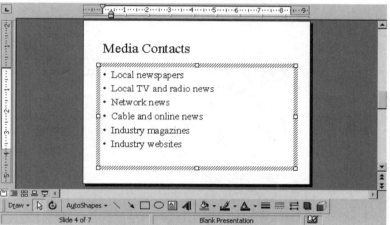

FIGURE 5-9.
Notice how the ruler settings correspond to the text on this slide.

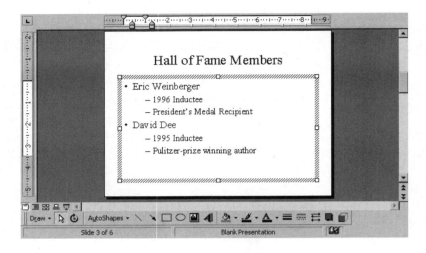

FIGURE 5-10.
Paragraphs with hanging indents.

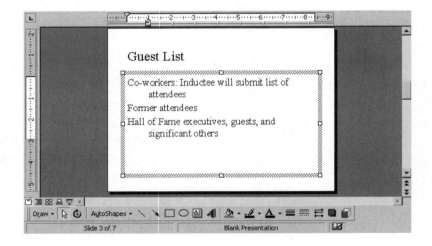

Changing Paragraph Alignment

The *alignment* of a text object determines the horizontal placement of its lines. The alignment options are shown in table 5-2 on the facing page.

TABLE 5-2.   Alignment options.

Button	Option	Keystroke	Effect
≣	Left	Ctrl+L	Text within a text object is flush with the left edge of the object.
≣	Center	Ctrl+E	Text within a text object is centered horizontally within the object.
≣	Right	Ctrl+R	Text within a text object is flush with the right edge of the object.
None	Justify	Ctrl+J	Extra spaces are added between words to make the text flush with both the left and right edges of the object.

The alignment options for the paragraphs of a text object can also be found in the Alignment submenu. To get to this submenu, follow these steps:

1 Select the text object.

2 Choose Alignment from the Format menu, or click the right mouse button and choose Alignment from the shortcut menu.

3 Select the alignment option that works best from the Alignment submenu.

To left-align, center, or right-align text, you can click the Left Alignment, Center Alignment or Right Alignment buttons on the Formatting toolbar. You can also use one of the keyboard shortcuts listed in Table 5-2 to align text in various ways.

Changing Line and Paragraph Spacing

The *line spacing* value determines the amount of vertical space between lines within a paragraph, and the *paragraph spacing* value determines the amount of space between paragraphs within a text object. You may want to add extra space between paragraphs to separate them or add extra space between the lines of a paragraph to make the paragraph easier to read, for a design effect, or to make the text fill more vertical space on the page.

II

The Basic Presentation

To change the line spacing in a text object, follow these steps:

1 Select the text object.

2 Choose Line Spacing from the Format menu. The dialog box, shown beklow, appears:

3 Enter a number or click the arrow buttons to change the spacing.

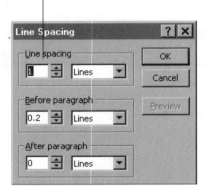

The Increase Paragraph Spacing button

The Decrease Paragraph Spacing button

The other two options in the Line Spacing dialog box allow you to add extra space before or after each paragraph. By using the Before Paragraph and After Paragraph options, you can spread out the paragraphs vertically. You can also use the Increase Paragraph Spacing or Decrease Paragraph Spacing button on the Formatting toolbar to adjust the spacing.

Adding and Removing Bullets

The Bullets button

Each bullet that appears at the beginning of a text line emphasizes the statement that follows. In addition, bullets are only appropriate when a slide contains a series of statements of equal value. As a result, there may be times when you don't need bulleted text, such as when a slide contains a single phrase. Fortunately, you can easily add and remove bullets in PowerPoint by using the Bullets button on the Formatting toolbar to toggle a bullet on or off..

To remove the bullet from a line of text:

1 Click anywhere in the line.

2 Click the Bullets button on the Formatting toolbar.

For example, in Figure 5-11, the bullet has been removed from the second of two text statements. To remove the bullets from all the text in a placeholder, first select the text by pressing Ctrl+A, or select the placeholder object by pressing F2 or by clicking the object's gray border, and then click the Bullets button. The Bullets button is a toggle, so if you select the text and click the Bullets button again, PowerPoint restores the bullets.

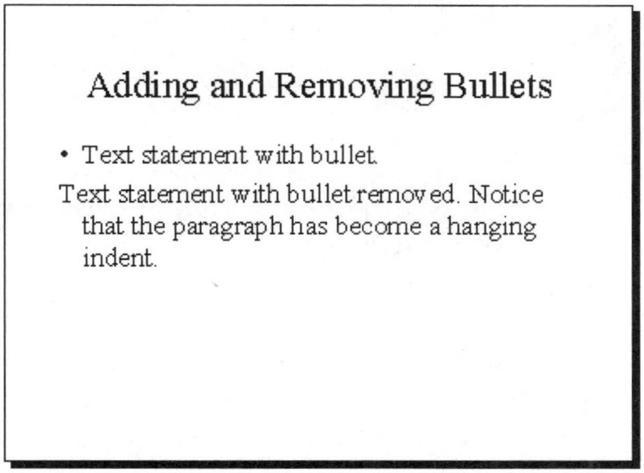

FIGURE 5-11.
The bullet has been removed from the second text statement.

Adding and Removing Bullets

- Text statement with bullet.

Text statement with bullet removed. Notice that the paragraph has become a hanging indent.

Another way to add or remove bullets is to select the text to the right of the bullets, and choose Bullet from the Format menu or the short-cut menu. Then, when the Bullet dialog box appears, select or deselect the Use a Bullet option to turn the bullets on or off.

When you remove the bullet from a bulleted paragraph that contains more than one line of text, you'll notice that the first line of text shifts to the left. The paragraph's hanging indent is still present, as you can see in the second text statement in Figure 5-11. To remove the hanging indent in a nonbulleted paragraph, follow the steps on the next page.

II

The Basic Presentation

1 Check that the ruler is visible. (If it is not, choose Ruler from the View menu or the shortcut menu.)

2 Drag the left indent marker to the left so that it aligns with the first-line indent marker, as shown below. Be careful to drag the triangular part of the left indent marker, not the rectangular part, which moves both the first-line and left indent markers simultaneously.

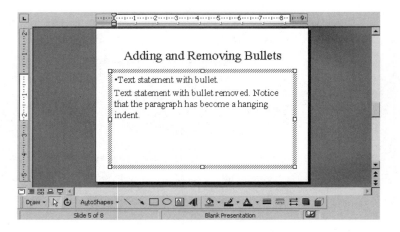

Notice that the text in the second bulleted item is now properly left aligned, but the top bulleted item has been affected, too. That's because changing indents affects all the paragraphs in a text object when the entire text object is selected.

Changing the Bullet Shape, Color, and Size

The default bullets that precede the text on your slides are only one of the almost limitless options for bullet shape, color, and size. You can use any character from any TrueType font on your system, and you can change the color and size of the bullets on any slide.

To select a special bullet character, follow the steps on the facing page.

1 Select the text following the bullet or bullets you want to change.

2 Choose Bullet from the Format menu, or point to the selection, press the right mouse button and choose Bullet from the shortcut menu. The Bullet dialog box appears.

3 Select a font from this list.

4 Click any of the characters displayed. The character will be magnified temporarily so that you can see it better.

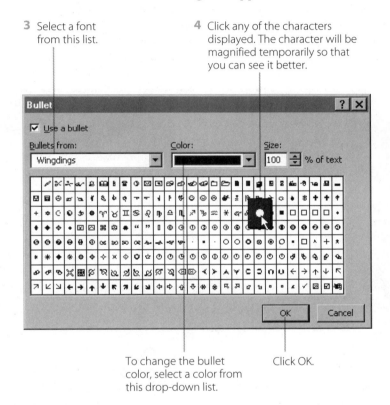

To change the bullet color, select a color from this drop-down list.

Click OK.

To change the bullet size, type a new size in the Size edit box, or click the up or down arrows at the right end of the edit box to increase or decrease the size of the bullet as a percentage of the text size.

Figure 5-12, on the next page, shows a bulleted list slide with bullets that are far more interesting than the defaults.

The Basic Presentation

FIGURE 5-12.

Interesting characters used as bullets.

Media Contacts

☎ Local newspapers
☎ Local TV and radio news
☎ Network news
☎ Cable and online news
☎ Industry magazines
☎ Industry websites

Creating Numbered Lists

PowerPoint cannot automatically number paragraphs in a text object. You must first turn off the bullets, and then type a number at the beginning of each paragraph. After the number, press the Tab key. Then align the text of the numbered paragraph by changing the first tab marker on the ruler. For more information about tabs, see the following section.

Setting and Removing Tab Stops

Creating tables in PowerPoint is so easy that you'll probably want to use a table whenever you need to place text in columns on a slide. But you can also place tab stops in a text object to space text horizontally across a slide. As described in Table 5-3, PowerPoint provides four different types of tab stops. All of these are available on the ruler.

TABLE 5-3.   Powerpoint's tab stops.

Tab Button	Tab Stop	Description
L	Left-aligned tab stop	Aligns the left edge of text with the tab stop
⊥	Centered tab stop	Aligns the center of text with the tab stop
⌐	Right-aligned tab stop	Aligns the right edge of text with the tab stop
⊥	Decimal tab stop	Aligns the decimal points of numbers with the tab stop

To switch from one tab type to the next, click the Tab Alignment button at the left end of the ruler until the tab type you want appears on the face of the button. Figure 5-13 shows the location of the Tab Alignment button and the appearance of text entered at a set of tab stops.

To enter tab stops, follow these steps:

1 Click anywhere in the text within a text object. (All of the text in the object will be formatted with the same tab stops.)

FIGURE 5-13.

The Tab Alignment button and text entered at various tab stops. (The ruler shows the current tab stops.)

2 Click the Tab Alignment button until the type of type you want appears.

3 On the ruler, click the position for the tab stop.

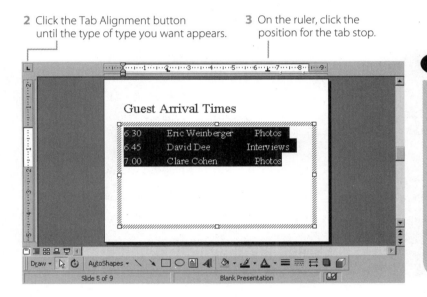

4 Continue clicking different positions in the ruler to add tab stops of the same type, or select a different tab type and then click the ruler.

 NOTE

To remove a tab stop you have set, point to the tab stop, hold down the left mouse button, and drag the tab stop down and off the ruler.

Changing the Case of Text

To change the capitalization of text on a slide, select the text you want to modify, and then, from the Format menu, choose Change

Case. Figure 5-14 shows the Change Case dialog box, which offers case options for text. You might want to try each option to see its effect. Simply select an option, and then click OK. You can also cycle between uppercase, lowercase, and title case for the selected text by pressing Shift+F3.

FIGURE 5-14.

The Change Case
dialog box.

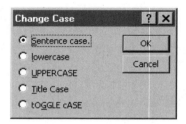

Transferring Text Styles

After you format one selection of text, you can transfer the same formatting, called the *text style,* to another selection of text. By transferring a text style, you save time because you don't have to reopen menus, reselect options, and so on.

To transfer the formatting of one text selection to another text selection, follow the step on the facing page.

1 Select the text whose formatting you want to transfer, as shown below.

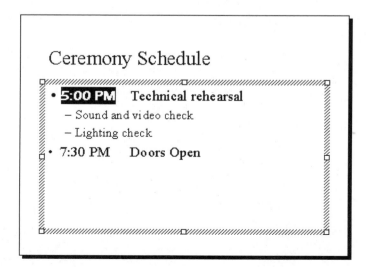

The Format
Painter button

2 On the Standard toolbar, click the Format Painter button.

3 Click and drag across the text that you want to transfer the formatting to.

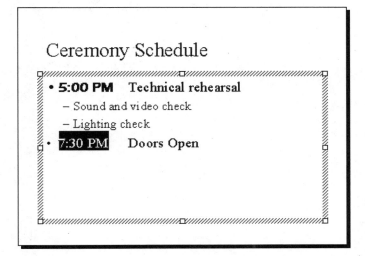

As shown below, the formatting of the original text selection is transferred to the other text selection when you release the mouse button.

TIP

> **How to Transfer a Format to Several Other Items**
> To transfer the formatting of an object to multiple objects, select the object and *double-click* the Format Painter. The format of the object will be transferred to each new object you select until you click the Format Painter button once more to turn off format painting.

Moving and Resizing Text Objects

The text you enter in a placeholder appears at the position of the placeholder text. But after you enter all the text you need, you may want to move the text object or change its size, perhaps to make room on the slide for a chart or graphic.

To move or resize a text object you have been editing, you must select the entire object with one of these procedures:

■ Choose Object from the Edit menu.

■ Press F2.

■ Click the gray border that surrounds the object.

In each case, the border changes from fine diagonal stripes to fine dots, as shown in Figure 5-15.

FIGURE 5-15.
Border and handles of a selected object.

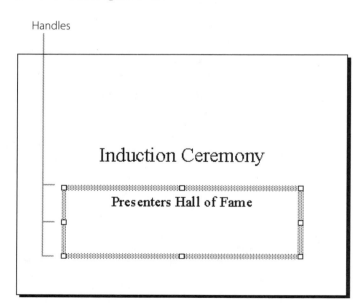

After you select the text object, to move the object, position the mouse pointer on the object's border away from a handle, hold down the left mouse button, and drag the object to a new position; or press the arrow keys to move the object incrementally. To resize the object, drag one of the object's handles.

NOTE

By holding down the Shift key and dragging one of the object's corner handles, you can change the object's scale. That is, both the object's width and height are resized proportionally. By holding down the Ctrl key and dragging one of the object's corner handles, you can resize the object while leaving it centered at its current position.

Turning Word Wrap On or Off

When you resize an object, the text inside wraps to fit the new size, as shown in Figure 5-16. Words in a paragraph that can no longer fit on a line within the object move to the following line. Words in a paragraph that can fit on the previous line after the object is resized move to the previous line.

FIGURE 5-16.
Word wrapping allows words of text to wrap to the next line to fit the boundaries of a text object.

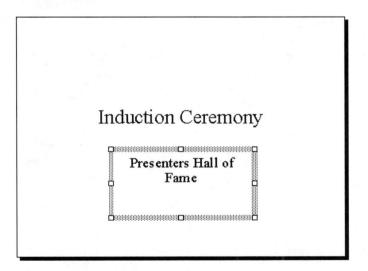

You can turn word wrap off by first selecting the text object or any of the text within the object, and then choosing AutoShape from the

Format menu. Click the Text Box tab on the Format AutoShape dialog box, as shown in Figure 5-17.

The Word Wrap Text in AutoShape option controls word wrapping. Click the option's check box to turn word wrapping on or off.

When word wrapping is turned off, any text you add to a paragraph continues across the slide, beyond the borders of the text object, and even beyond the edge of the slide if necessary.

FIGURE 5-17.

The Text Box tab of the Format AutoShape dialog box.

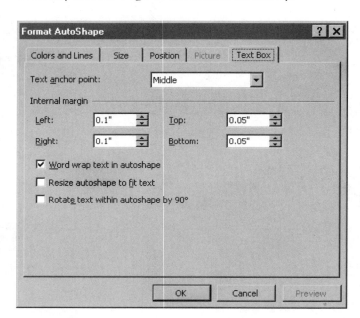

Changing the Text Box Margins

The four Internal Margin settings on the Text Box tab, shown above, let you adjust the interior margins of the text object. Increasing the margins adds space between the text and the borders of the object. Increasing the margins is helpful when you add an actual graphic box to the borders of a text object, as you'll learn in the section titled "Special Text Object Formatting." As shown in Figure 5-18, larger margins pad the interior of the box so that the text does not appear to be so cramped

FIGURE 5-18.

The text object on the bottom has larger internal margins.

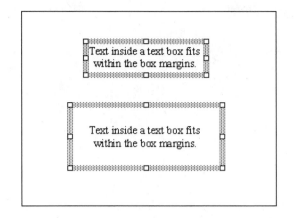

Fitting Text Objects to the Text

Sometimes, the text you enter in a placeholder does not completely fill the placeholder. For example, the bottom border of the text object shown on the left in Figure 5-19 is some distance from the text. To automatically shrink the text object to fit the text you've entered, select the text, and then select the Resize AutoShape To Fit Text option in the Format AutoShape dialog box. The text object immediately shrinks to fit the text inside, as shown on the right in Figure 5-19. If you enter additional text, the text object will grow vertically to accommodate the new text.

FIGURE 5-19.

The size of the text object on the left is not automatically adjusted to fit the text. The text object on the right shrank vertically to accommodate the ezxisting text.

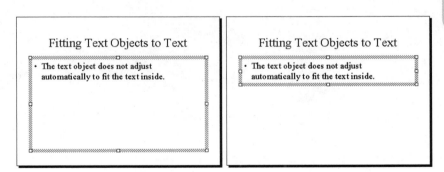

When the Resize AutoShape To Fit Text option is turned on, you can stretch the sides of a text object horizontally, but the bottom border always snaps to fit the last line of the text. When Resize AutoShape To

Fit Text is turned off, newly typed text overruns the bottom border of the text object, and you have to resize the object manually.

Decreasing the margins while the Resize AutoShape To Fit Text option is turned on brings the borders of the text object closer to the text.

Rotating Text

Clicking Rotate Text Within AutoShape By 90° rotates the text clockwise within a text box.

To rotate a text object, select the object, or any of the text within the text object, choose AutoShape from the Format menu, and then change the Rotation setting on the Size tab of the Format AutoShape dialog box. You can also rotate text to any angle by selecting the text object and clicking the Free Rotate button on the Drawing toolbar. Drag one of the green handles to rotate the object. Figure 5-20 shows the result.

FIGURE 5-20.

Rotating text.

Drag a handle to rotate the text.

Special Text Object Formatting

A text object can have its own special formatting. You can surround it with a line, add a shadow to it, fill it with color, rotate it, resize it, and scale it. In fact, you can use any of the commands that you use to change the appearance of other drawing objects. You will learn about formatting drawing objects in Chapter 13, "Drawing Graphic Objects."

Two special commands you may find helpful are Scale and Position. After selecting a text object, you can change its size by selecting options on the Size tab of the Format AutoShapes dialog box. The Height and Width settings allow you to resize an object by percentage. You can reduce a text object to 90 percent of its former size, for example, to make room for a graphic. Clicking the Lock Aspect Ratio check box insures that the object will change size without changing shape. The Horizontal and Vertical settings on the Position tab of the Format AutoShapes dialog box allow you to place a text object at a precise point. You can pin an object to the same spot in a sequence of slides, for example.

FIGURE 5-21.
The Size tab of the Format AutoShape dialog box.

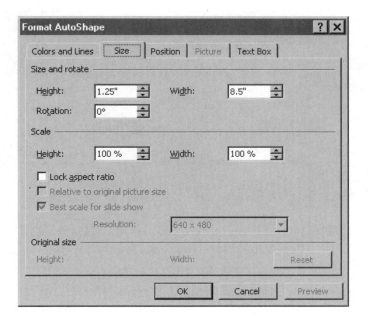

Microsoft WordArt

When your presentation title needs a little pizzazz, you can use Microsoft WordArt to create spirited titles with one or more eye-catching special effects. WordArt can create shadowed, stretched, rotated, and skewed text of any size, and text that has been contoured to fit a number of predefined shapes.

To add WordArt text to a title slide, or to any slide, click the Insert WordArt button on the Drawing toolbar. (Before you click the WordArt button, you can delete the *Click to add title* placeholder on the title slide so that it doesn't get in your way.) When WordArt's visual menu of styles appears on the screen, choose a style, click OK, and then type the desired text in the Text box on the Edit WordArt Text dialog box and choose any special format settings you want. Click OK to place the WordArt on the slide.

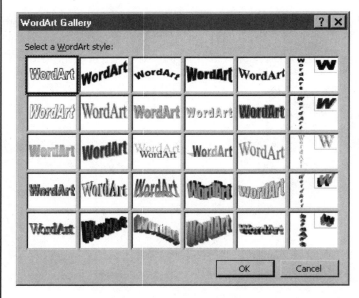

The WordArt toolbar will appear so you can change WordArt options or make still more formatting choices such as rotating the WordArt object or making the height of all characters within the WordArt object the same.

To edit WordArt, double-click any WordArt text.

If the presentation you are creating is strictly text, as most presentations are, then you have now done everything required to create the presentation, and you can skip ahead to Chapter 9. But if you want to add graphs, organization charts, and tables to your presentation, go on to the next three chapters.

CHAPTER 6

Adding Chart Slides

You can reel off numbers until you're blue in the face, but nothing gets your message across like a chart. Microsoft Graph, included with Microsoft Power-Point, offers 18 different chart types with all the pizzazz you could want, and it makes the process of creating charts simple and automatic. In this chapter, you'll learn how to use Graph to add the charts to slides. You'll also learn how to enter and edit the data that supports your charts, and you'll discover ways to incorporate data and charts from sources outside of PowerPoint into your chart slides.

A chart can communicate any information that can be quantified, so don't hesitate to pull out and use a chart whenever your message is numeric—even if your numbers aren't precise.

Because a chart is a visual representation of data, it can have a much greater impact than words alone. For example, the statement *We outproduced any of our competitors by 2 to 1* is impressive, but not as impressive as this chart:

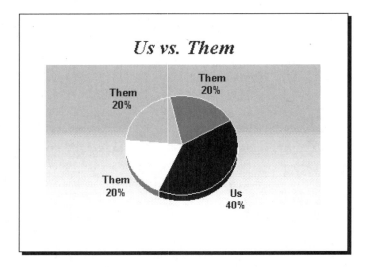

Graphs are your best bet for illuminating trends, deviations, and other measurements that don't require a great deal of explanation. If an explanation is needed, you can simply add text to the chart or include a text slide. By the time you finish this chapter, you'll probably think of new ways that you can use charts to enhance your PowerPoint presentations.

What Is Microsoft Graph?

Microsoft Graph is a program shared by all the Microsoft Office products that creates charts for use in Windows-based applications such as Microsoft Word, Microsoft Excel, and, of course, PowerPoint. If you're already familiar with graphing in Excel, you'll find it easy to jump to graphing in PowerPoint because both programs use the same Graph application. If you're not familiar with graphing in Excel, don't worry. At every step of the way, Graph guides you through the process of converting raw numbers into professional, colorful, and illuminating charts.

When you create or modify a chart, Graph's menus and Standard toolbar replace PowerPoint's menus and toolbars, as shown in Figure 6-1, so only the commands and controls you need are on the screen.

FIGURE 6-1.

Graph's menus and Standard toolbar take over the screen when you create a chart.

Graph's menu   Graph's Standard toolbar   Graph's Formatting toolbar

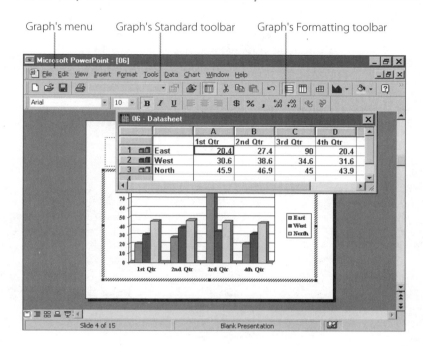

The chart you are creating in Graph appears on the current slide. When you are entering or editing chart data, a datasheet containing the numbers overlays the chart. Any change to the numbers in the datasheet is reflected immediately in the chart.

Understanding Chart Basics

You can create a special chart slide devoted to an entire chart, or you can add a chart to an existing slide to enhance a text message. Then you can select from an array of 18 basic chart types to ensure that the chart presents your data effectively.

Creating a Chart Slide

To create a chart slide in an existing presentation, follow these steps:

1 In Slide view, display the slide that the new slide should follow, and click the New Slide button on the Standard toolbar, or choose New Slide from the Insert menu or Common Tasks toolbar to display the New Slide dialog box shown below:

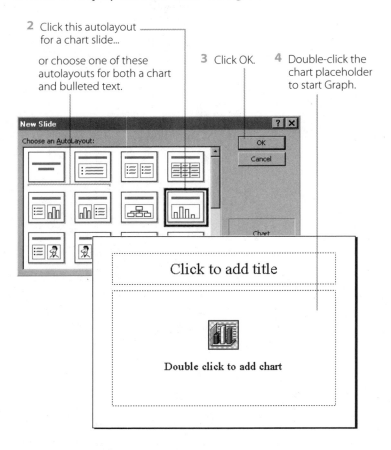

2 Click this autolayout for a chart slide...

or choose one of these autolayouts for both a chart and bulleted text.

3 Click OK.

4 Double-click the chart placeholder to start Graph.

A sample chart appears within the placeholder, and the datasheet window containing the sample data for the chart overlays the chart as shown in Figure 6-1 on page 125.

Adding a Chart to an Existing Slide

To add a chart to an existing slide, click the Insert Chart button on PowerPoint's Standard toolbar or choose Chart from the Insert menu. Either way, Microsoft Graph loads and displays a sample chart and datasheet. Don't worry about the positioning or size of the chart at this point. After you enter your data, you can move and size the chart as needed.

Selecting a Chart Type

After you create a chart slide or add a chart to an existing slide, you can select a chart type from PowerPoint's 18 basic chart types. Selecting a chart type before you begin entering data is a good first step because you are compelled from the start to consider the message your data conveys. It also modifies the appearance of the datasheet window to show how the data will be represented. You'll see bars in the datasheet window if you select a bar chart, or pie slices if you select a pie chart. Of course, because PowerPoint always lets you change your mind at any time, you can begin with one chart type and change to other types later.

Keep in mind that PowerPoint can produce variants, called *sub-types*, of most of the 18 basic chart types. You can also go beyond these sub-types and modify any chart to a virtually unlimited degree. You can even mix chart types within the same chart, showing some data with lines and some with bars, for example.

TIP

Keeping the Chart Type Palette Handy

You can "tear off" the palette of chart types and drop it on an unused part of the screen for easy access later. Simply click the arrow next to the Chart Type button to drop down the palette. Next, position the mouse pointer on the palette's title bar, hold down the left mouse button, and drag the palette away from Graph's Standard toolbar. You can close the Charts palette by clicking the Close button at the right end of the Chart Type title bar.

II

The Basic Presentation

To select a chart type for a chart, follow these steps:

1 Double-click the chart, if necessary, to activate Microsoft Graph.

2 Click the down arrow to the right of the Chart Type button on the Standard toolbar.

3 Click the chart type you want.

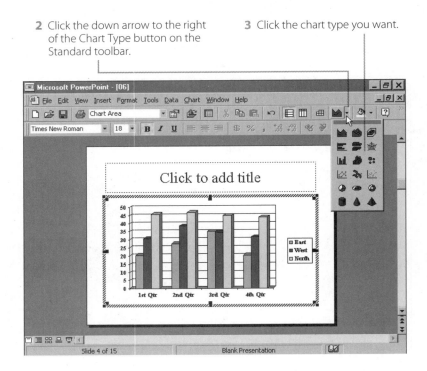

You can also use the Chart Type command on the Chart menu or shortcut menu to select a chart type. When you choose this command, Graph displays the Chart Type dialog box shown in Figure 6-2 on the facing page. Note that samples of the various chart types appear in large, easy-to-see panes.

To further refine your selection choose a chart sub-type from the right side of the `dialog box. For example, Figure 6-3 shows the Chart Type dialog box that appears when you select the pie chart type. You can select a sub-type and then preview your data plotted using the

FIGURE 6-2.

The Chart Type dialog box.

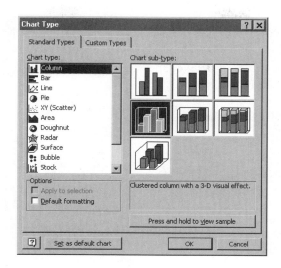

subtype by clicking the Press And Hold To View A Sample button in the dialog box. Either click OK to implement the selected chart subtype, or click another Sub-type option and click OK. If you want to use a particular chart type and sub-type frequently in the presentation, select them and click the Set As Default Chart button on the Chart Type dialog box. The next Chart slide you create will display the chart type you've chosen.

FIGURE 6-3.

You can use the Chart Type dialog box to select a chart sub-type.

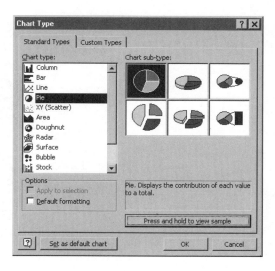

The following sections discuss PowerPoint's 14 basic chart types and explain how each chart type presents information. Figure 6-4 provides an example of each chart type.

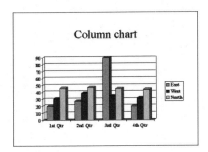

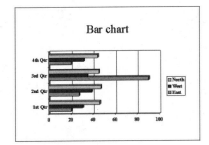

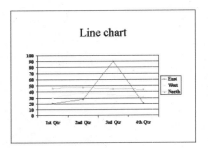

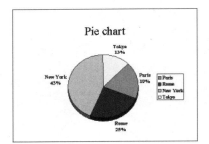

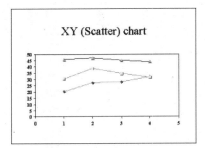

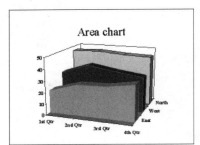

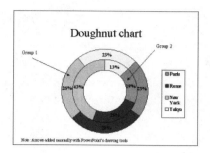

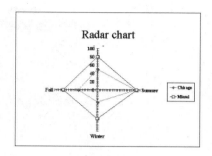

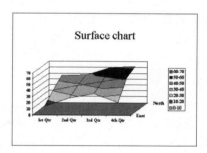

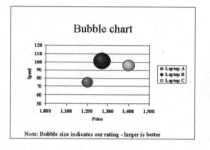

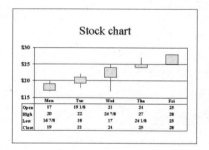

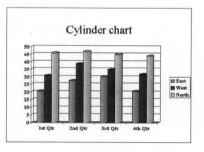

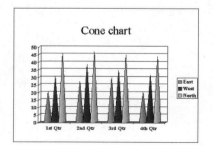

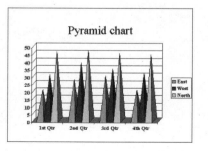

Bar Charts

Bar charts compare measurements at intervals. They emphasize measurements at discrete times rather than the changes over time. Their bars run horizontally. The stacked bar sub-type shows the contributions of each measurement to a whole. The 100% stacked bar sub-type shows the percentage contribution of each measurement to the whole without identifying specific numeric contributions.

Column Charts

Column charts are much like bar charts except their bars run vertically rather than horizontally. Like bar charts, they compare measurements at intervals and provide snapshot views of data taken at specific moments rather than a depiction of the change of data over time. Column charts also have stacked and 100% stacked sub-types.

Line Charts

Line charts show changes in data or trends over time. You can show the same data using bars or columns, but lines emphasize change rather than comparisons at intervals.

Pie Charts

Pie charts show the breakdown of a total. You can separate slices of the pie to emphasize certain values. The values depicted by slices are contained in a single series on the Graph datasheet.

XY (Scatter) Charts

XY (scatter) charts show the degree of correspondence between two series of numbers. Generally used for scientific data, XY charts also let you depict two sets of numbers as one set of XY coordinates.

Area Charts

Area charts show the amount of change in a set of values during an interval of time. Line charts are similar, but they emphasize the *rate* of change rather than the *amount* of change.

Doughnut Charts

Like pie charts, doughnut charts show breakdowns of totals, but they let you depict several series of data in successive rings around a doughnut hole.

Radar Charts

Radar charts compare change in values of a several series. Each value is plotted on axes that radiate from the center of the chart. Series of values are connected by a line that runs from axis to axis and circles the center of the chart.

Surface Charts

Surface charts depict the best and worst combinations of numbers. Colors or patterns designate areas with the same value. The three Surface sub-types show: a wire-frame-only view of the surface chart, and a 2-D view of the surface chart from above, with and without the wire frame.

Bubble Charts

A bubble chart is like an XY (Scatter) chart with the addition of different sized bubbles at the data points to indicate the value of a third number.

Stock Charts

Stock charts (also called high-low-close charts) show the (hopefully) rising values of stocks or other financial instruments. They can also depict scientific data, such as daily variations in temperature, air pressure, or humidity. Stock charts can also depict volume of sales. The typical stock chart depicts five variables: date, high, low, close, and volume.

Cylinder, Cone, and Pyramid Charts

Cylinder, cone, and pyramid charts are just like 3-D column or 3-D bar charts, except they use more interesting and dramatic shapes to display values.

Entering the Data

The generic entries in the datasheet window (1st Qtr, 2nd Qtr, etc.) when you start a new chart provides an example of how text and numbers should be arranged in a datasheet. The chart peeking out from behind the datasheet window displays the text and numbers in the datasheet graphically, and it is updated immediately as you enter and edit data in the datasheet. Figure 6-5 shows the datasheet.

FIGURE 6-5.

The datasheet.

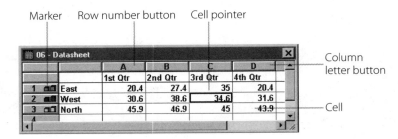

The datasheet is made up of *cells,* which are the rectangular spaces at the intersections of the rows and columns. In Figure 6-5, text labels appear in the leftmost and topmost cells of the datasheet. The actual numbers to be graphed occupy the cells below and to the right of the labels. Each cell in this section has an *address* that consists of a column letter and row number. For example, the address of the cell at the intersection of column A and row 1 is *A1.*

To create a proper chart, PowerPoint must know whether the *series* (the sets of related numbers) are entered in rows or columns. By default, PowerPoint assumes that the series are arranged in rows. PowerPoint places small pictures of the *markers* that will be used in the chart (the bars, columns, lines, or other graphic shapes) on either the row number or column letter buttons in the datasheet. If the markers are on the row number buttons, the data is organized in the chart by row. If the markers are on the column letter buttons, the data is organized by column. If you place your series in columns instead of rows, you can choose Series In Columns from the Data menu.

Entering the Labels

Your first step in entering the data for a chart is to replace the text labels in the first row and first column of cells. To replace a label, use the mouse or the arrow keys to move the *cell pointer*—the highlight surrounding a single cell—to the cell containing the label, and then type over the existing entry. You can also double-click or press F2 to place an insertion point in a selected cell and then edit its contents. You can use the same text editing techniques that you use elsewhere in PowerPoint to edit the contents of a cell in the datasheet.

Because PowerPoint's default setting arranges chart data by row, each label entered in the leftmost cell of a row appears in the graph's legend. The labels entered in the topmost cells of columns often have time or date designations, such as a specific year or month, but they can be any other text that distinguishes the individual data points in a series of numbers. Remember, if you want the column labels to appear in the graph's legend rather than in the row labels, choose Series In Columns from the Data menu.

To try your hand at entering labels, start by creating a new chart:

1 Click New Slide on the Standard toolbar.

2 In the New Slide dialog box, select an autolayout that includes a chart placeholder.

3 In Slide view, double-click the *Double click to add chart* place-holder to start Microsoft Graph.

Stick with the default chart type when the chart and datasheet appear, and then follow these steps, using the suggested labels or your own:

1 Select the first cell in row 1 (the cell containing the label *East*).

2 Type *Regular mail* and press Enter. Don't worry that the label is too long to fit in the cell. The length of the label won't affect the resulting chart, and you can widen the entire column to accommodate the label at any time (see the sidebar titled "Changing the Widths of Columns" on the next page).

3 Now replace *West* with *Overnight* and press Enter.

4 Replace *North* with *Courier*, and then select the first cell in column A, and replace *1st Qtr* with *Package*.

5 Press Tab to move to the cell to the right, replace *2nd Qtr* in column B with *Box*, and press Tab again.

6 Replace *3rd Qtr* in column C with *Letter*. Leave the text in Column D as is—you'll plot only three columns of data in the chart. Here's how the datasheet should look now:

06 - Datasheet		A	B	C	D	
		Package	Box	Letter	4th Qtr	
1	Regular m	20.4	27.4	90	20.4	
2	Overnight	30.6	38.6	34.6	31.6	
3	Courier	45.9	46.9	45	43.9	
4						

Changing the Widths of Columns

When the label you enter in a cell exceeds the width of the cell, you won't be able to see the entire label. To widen the entire column, place the mouse pointer between the current column letter button and the column letter button to the right (the pointer changes to a double arrow). Then hold down the left mouse button, and drag to the right. In the datasheet shown below, the first column is being widened to accommodate the longest label.

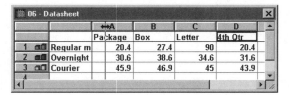

To change the width of more than one column, click the column letter button for the first column, hold down the mouse button, and drag across the other column letter buttons. Then, when you widen the first column using the technique described above, the other selected columns are also widened.

In addition, you can double-click between two column letter buttons to automatically adjust the width of the first column to accommodate the column's longest entry. Select several columns and double-click between any two to automatically fit them all to their longest entry.

Entering the Numbers

After you enter the labels to create a framework for the data, you must replace the sample numbers with your own. You can select any single cell, type over the cell's contents, and then move to the next cell. However, the best way to quickly enter all the numbers is to select the range of cells that will contain the numbers, and then begin typing columns of replacement numbers. To select a range of cells, place the mouse pointer on the first cell, hold down the mouse button, and then drag across to the cell at the opposite corner of the range. You can also move the cell pointer to the first cell, hold down the Shift key, and then use the arrow keys to move to the cell at the opposite corner.

When you type a number and press Enter, the cell pointer moves to the cell below. When you type a number in the last cell of a selected range of cells and press Enter, the cell pointer returns to the first cell in the range.

To enter the data for the chart you've created, follow these steps. (Again, you can use the suggested data or supply your own.)

1 Place the mouse pointer on cell A1, which is located at the intersection of column A and row 1.

2 Hold down the left mouse button, and drag the pointer to cell C3.

3 Release the mouse button. The rectangular range of cells from A1 to C3 is selected, as shown here:

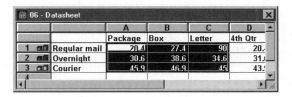

4 Type the numbers shown below, pressing Enter after each number. Be sure to enter the numbers by column, *not* by row.

8.60	10.75	.32
17.90	22.00	9.95
48.00	56.00	17.50

The datasheet now looks like this:

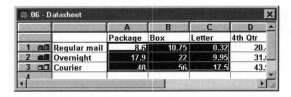

To use the quick data-entry technique, you must enter the numbers in columns, even if you're charting the data by rows.

TIP

How to Control the Cell Pointer
You can control whether the cell pointer moves to the next cell or remains on the selected cell when you press Enter by first choosing Options from Graph's Tools menu. Then click the check box next to the Move Selection After Enter option to deselect it, and click OK.

Formatting the Labels and Numbers

You can use Graph's Formatting toolbar (shown in Figure 6-6) to select a different font and numeric format for a datasheet. The changes you make to the font are displayed only in the datasheet, whereas the changes you make to the numeric formatting appear in both the datasheet and the chart.

NOTE

If Graph's Formatting toolbar is not present, choose Toolbars from Graph's View menu, select the Formatting option, and click OK.

FIGURE 6-6.

The Formatting toolbar of Graph.

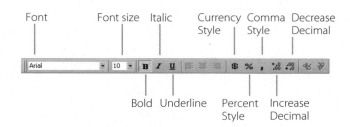

Font   Font size Italic   Currency Comma Decrease
                                 Style   Style Decimal

Bold Underline   Percent Increase
                  Style   Decimal

From Graph's Formatting toolbar, shown above in Figure 6-6, you can select a font, a point size, and character formatting attributes such as bold, italic, and underline for the text and numbers in your datasheet. You cannot change the alignment while working in the datasheet because the paragraph alignment buttons are inactive, but you should keep in mind that text is always left-aligned in the datasheet and numbers are always right-aligned.

In addition to Graph's Formatting toolbar, you can use the Font command on Graph's Format menu or shortcut menu to change the formatting of the data in the datasheet. When you choose the Font command, the Font dialog box is displayed so that you can make your formatting selections.

To change the numeric formatting of the numbers in a datasheet, you must first select the numbers, and then either use the number formatting buttons on Graph's Formatting toolbar or choose the Number command from Graph's Format menu or shortcut menu. You can select one set of numbers and format them as decimal and then select another set and format them as percentages, for example.

Five number formatting buttons are located at the right end of Graph's Formatting toolbar. You use the first three buttons to apply a general format to your numbers, and the last two buttons to increase or decrease the number of decimal places. For additional number formatting options, choose Number from Graph's Format menu or shortcut menu. Then in the Format Number dialog box, shown in Figure 6-7 on the next page, select a formatting category from the list at the left, and make any other formatting choices before clicking OK to implement your changes.

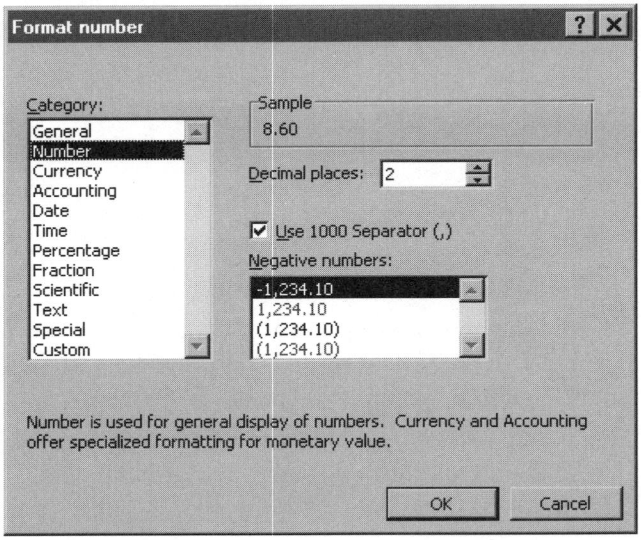

FIGURE 6-7. The Format Number dialog box.

To format the numbers in your sample chart, follow these steps:

1. Select the rectangular range of numbers from cell A1 to cell C3.

The Currency Style button

2. Click the Currency Style button on Graph's Formatting toolbar. The numbers should look like this:

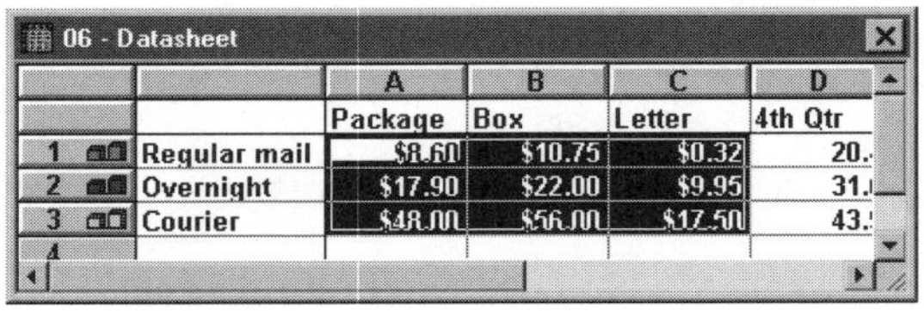
06 - Datasheet

		A	B	C	D
		Package	Box	Letter	4th Qtr
1	Regular mail	$8.60	$10.75	$0.32	20.
2	Overnight	$17.90	$22.00	$9.95	31.
3	Courier	$48.00	$56.00	$17.50	43.
4					

SEE ALSO
For more information about formatting charts, see Chapter 10, "Formatting Charts," page 243.

To remove formatting from the data in your datasheet, select the data, choose Clear from Graph's Edit menu, and choose Formats from the Clear submenu. Choosing Contents from the Clear submenu removes the data from selected cells without deleting the cells. (You can also remove the data from selected cells by choosing Clear from Graph's shortcut menu.)

Viewing the Chart

As you revise the data in the datasheet, the chart adjusts to reflect the changes. To see the chart clearly, close the datasheet window by clicking the View Datasheet button on Graph's Standard toolbar or by clicking the Close button at the right end of the datasheet's title bar. Figure 6-8 shows the chart created from the sample datasheet. If you close the datasheet window, you can always reopen it by clicking the View Datasheet button again or by choosing the Datasheet command from Graph's View menu.

The View Datasheet button

> **NOTE**
>
> Before closing the sample datasheet window, we double-clicked the column letter button at the top of column D to exclude the data in column D from the chart. For more information about excluding data, see "Excluding Data," page 145.

The numbers along the vertical axis of the chart in Figure 6-8 are formatted with the currency style you specified earlier in the datasheet window. Other aspects of the graph's appearance are controlled by the template that formats the current presentation and by the chart type you selected. The template gives the chart its color scheme and font selections. The chart type gives the chart its overall design and special option settings. If necessary, you can now start revising the content of the chart and adjusting the appearance of the chart.

FIGURE 6-8.

Sample chart with vertical axis numbers formatted with the currency style.

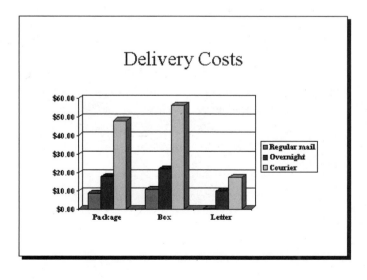

The Basic Presentation

Editing the Data

PowerPoint offers a variety of ways to edit the data displayed by the chart, including moving, copying, inserting, and deleting. Before you can put any of these techniques to work, however, you must activate the datasheet by clicking the View Datasheet button on Graph's Standard toolbar or by choosing the Datasheet command from Graph's View menu.

 TIP

> **How to Change the Numbers by Dragging the Bar, Pie Slice, or Line**
> If you are using a 2-D chart, you can click a bar, column, pie slice, or line two times (not double-click) and drag the handle that appears to change the number represented by the marker.

Moving and Copying Data

You might want to move the data in your datasheet to make room for new data. Or you might want to rearrange the data so that the chart becomes more meaningful. For example, by ordering the data in your datasheet from largest to smallest or vice versa, you can enhance the impression the chart makes. You can move or copy data in the datasheet window by selecting it and then using the Cut, Copy, and Paste buttons on Graph's Standard toolbar; the Cut, Copy, and Paste commands on Graph's Edit menu or shortcut menu; or the shortcut key combinations. You can also use the drag-and-drop method to drag the data to a new location.

To move data with drag and drop, select a rectangular region of cells in your datasheet, place the pointer on the border of the selected cells (the pointer changes to an arrow), hold down the mouse button, and then drag the cells to a new location. Release the mouse button when the cells are in the correct position in the datasheet.

By holding down the Ctrl key as you drag, you can copy the selected cells and then drop the copy in a new location on the datasheet. A small plus sign appears next to the pointer when you hold down the Ctrl key.

Now try using drag and drop to rearrange the data in your chart:

1 Select the three columns of data you've entered by dragging across the column letter buttons A, B and C.

2 Place the pointer on the border of the selected range, hold down the mouse button and drag the data to columns E, F and G.

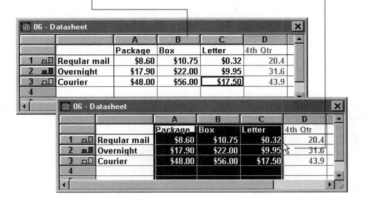

3 Release the mouse button to drop the data into place. (Be careful not to overwrite the contents of column D.)

4 Click the Column G button to select the contents of column G.

5 Drag the border of column G to the left until it's over column A, and then release the mouse button.

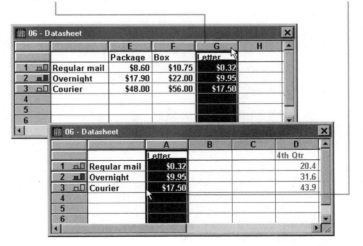

5 Finally, select columns E and F, and drag them to columns B and C. Now the data is arranged sequentially from least expensive to most expensive.

06 - Datasheet		A	B	C	D	
		Letter	Package	Box	4th Qtr	
1	Regular mail	$0.32	$8.60	$10.75	20.4	
2	Overnight	$9.95	$17.90	$22.00	31.6	
3	Courier	$17.50	$48.00	$56.00	43.9	
4						
5						
6						

NOTE

Graph displays a warning if you inadvertently try to drop data on a cell that already contains data. To continue the drag-and-drop operation, just click OK in the message box.

Inserting and Deleting Data

To insert a row or column of cells in the datasheet, click a row number or column letter button, and then choose Cells from Graph's Insert menu. To remove a row or column from the datasheet, click the row number or column letter button for the row or column you want to delete, and then choose Delete from Graph's Edit menu or shortcut menu. To add or remove more than one row or column at a time, drag across the row number or column letter buttons for as many rows or columns as you want to add or remove before you choose the Cells command or the Delete command. For example, to add three columns, drag across three column letter buttons, and then choose Cells from Graph's Insert menu.

When you select only some of the cells in a row or column and then choose Cells from Graph's Insert menu or shortcut menu, the Insert dialog box appears, shown in Figure 6-9. Here you can specify whether you want to push aside (shift) the other cells in the row or column or insert an entire row or column. If you want to push the cells aside, select Shift Cells Right or Shift Cells Down. If you want to insert an entire row or column, select Entire Row or Entire Column. Then click OK.

FIGURE 6-9.

The Insert dialog box.

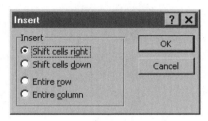

Excluding Data

You can temporarily exclude data from a chart without deleting the data from the datasheet. Excluding data can be helpful when you want to use the same set of data to create several charts. In one chart, you can compare only certain sets of data, and then, in another chart, you can compare different sets of data from the same data pool.

To exclude a row or column of data, double-click the corresponding row number or column letter button. The selected data in the row or column is dimmed, and the chart adjusts immediately. To include the selected data once again, double-click the same row number or column letter button.

You can also exclude multiple adjacent rows or columns of data by first selecting one or more cells in the rows or columns you want to exclude. Then choose the Exclude Row/Col command from Graph's Data menu. When the Exclude Row/Col dialog box appears, as shown in Figure 6-10, select the appropriate option and click OK.

FIGURE 6-10.

The Exclude Row/ Col dialog box.

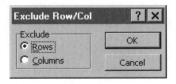

To return excluded data to a chart, select the excluded row or column, and choose the Include Row/Col command from the Data menu.

Data Arrangements for Special Chart Types

For each chart type, Graph expects you to follow certain rules when it comes to arranging the data in the datasheet. Otherwise, the chart may deliver a message that is different from the one you intended.

Pie Charts and Doughnut Charts

A pie chart can plot only one series, with each number in the series represented by a pie slice. To plot more than one series, you must use a doughnut chart, which plots multiple series in two dimensions as concentric rings in the chart. To show multiple breakdowns in three dimensions, you might want to consider using the stacked or 100% stacked subtype of a bar or column chart. Each bar or column can show the breakdown of a different series.

If you've entered more than one series in the datasheet for a pie chart, the chart plots the first series only. To plot a different series, exclude the earlier series. For example, to plot the third series in a datasheet, exclude the first and second series. Figure 6-11 shows a pie chart that plots the data in row 1 of the datasheet. Notice that rows 2 and 3 have been excluded and that a pie chart marker appears on the row 1 button.

FIGURE 6-11.

This pie chart plots the numbers in the first series, row 1, in the datasheet.

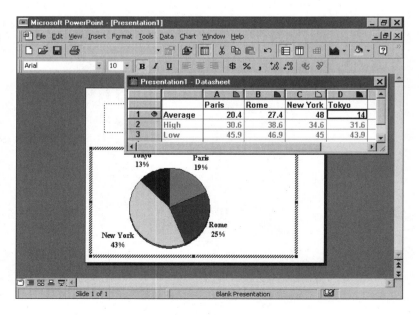

Area, Bar, Column, Line, Surface, Cylinder, Cone, and Pyramid Charts

Charts with areas, bars, columns, lines, or a surface as their markers all require the same arrangement of data in the datasheet. You enter each series of numbers in a row or a column, and then allow Graph to create the chart. By default, Graph interprets each row of numbers as a series. If you want Graph to interpret each column of numbers as a series, you must choose the Series In Columns command from Graph's Data menu.

FIGURE 6-12.

A chart plotted by row.

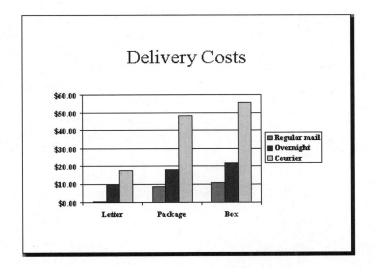

FIGURE 6-13.

The same chart plotted by column.

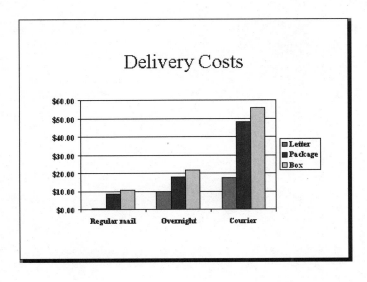

Choosing Series In Columns after you've entered numbers in rows can give you an equally legitimate view of the data, whether you create a bar chart or column chart. In fact, you may want to try both options to see which makes your case more clearly. For example, Figure 6-12, on the previous page, shows a chart plotted by row. Figure 6-13, also on the previous page, shows the same chart plotted by column. The chart in Figure 6-11 emphasizes the comparison of delivery methods, whereas the one in Figure 6-12 emphasizes the comparison of package types.

XY (Scatter) and Bubble Charts

To create an xy (scatter) chart, enter the X values in one column and the Y values in adjacent columns. To create a Bubble chart, enter the X values, Y values, and Bubble sizes in adjacent columns. Figure 6-14 shows an xy (scatter) chart and its data. Figure 6-15 shows a bubble chart and its data.

FIGURE 6-14.
An xy (scatter) chart and its data.

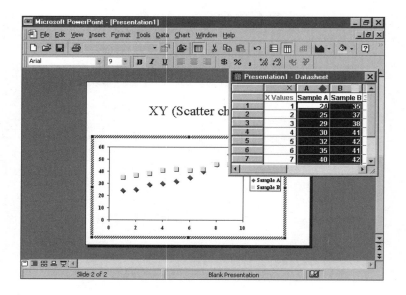

FIGURE 6-15.
A bubble chart and
its data.

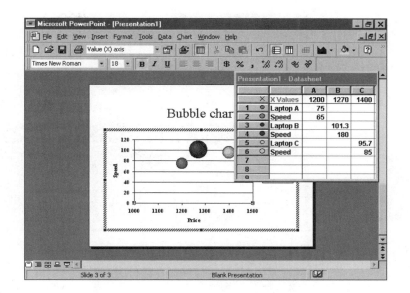

Radar Charts

The numbers in a series are represented as data markers on different radial axes of a radar chart. All the data markers in the same series are connected by a line that forms a ring around the chart.

When you enter series in rows, each column is represented by a different radial axis. (The labels at the top of the columns identify the axes.) Figure 6-16 shows a radar chart and its datasheet.

FIGURE 6-16.
A radar chart and
its datasheet.

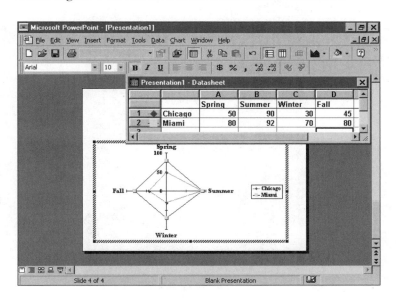

Stock Charts

To create a stock chart, you must enter all the high numbers in one series, all the low numbers in another series, and so forth. The order in which you enter the numbers is important. If the chart depicts data series in rows, follow one of these patterns:

Row	High-Low-Close Chart	Open-High-Low-Close Chart
1	High Value	Opening value
2	Low value	High value
3	Closing value	Low value
4		Closing value

Figure 6-17 shows an open-high-low-close chart and the datasheet that underlies it.

To add volume numbers to a chart, enter the volume values as the first series and choose Stock as the chart type and choose Volume-Open-High-Low-Close as the sub-type. Volume values will be plotted as a secondary value axis at the right side of the chart. You can format this axis separately from the primary value axis.

FIGURE 6-17.

An Open-high-low-close chart and its datasheet.

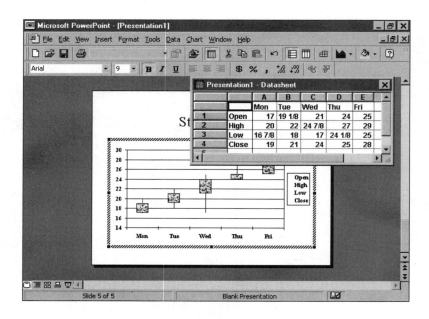

Using Data from Microsoft Excel

If you've already typed the numbers for a chart in a Microsoft Excel worksheet, the last thing you want to do is retype the numbers in PowerPoint. Fortunately, there's an easy way to transfer your Excel data to PowerPoint. In fact, you can set up a link between the original numbers in Excel and the copies in PowerPoint. Then, if you change the numbers in Excel, the numbers in PowerPoint are updated automatically. You can also import an existing Excel chart into PowerPoint by dragging it from an Excel window directly onto a PowerPoint slide.

Importing Excel Data into Graph

To perform a simple transfer of data from an Excel worksheet to Graph, you can use the Import File command on Graph's Edit menu. You can then specify the Excel file and the range that contains the data you want to import.

Use the Import File command when you want to copy data from an Excel worksheet. To establish a link between the Excel data and the PowerPoint chart, however, you must use a different procedure, as described in the next section.

To import data from an Excel worksheet like the one shown here, follow the steps below.

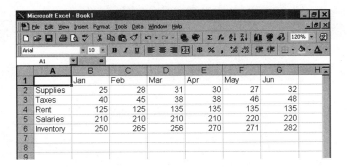

1   Switch to the Graph datasheet by clicking the View Datasheet button on Graph's Standard toolbar or by choosing Datasheet from Graph's View menu.

2 In the datasheet, click the cell located in the upper left corner of the area into which you want to import the data.

3 From Graph's Edit menu, choose the Import File command. The Import File dialog box appears, as shown here:

4 Use the Look In drop-down list and File Name list to navigate to the Excel file containing the data.

5 Double-click the file name.

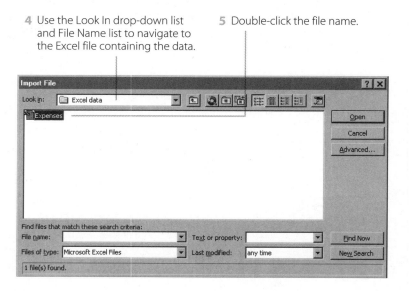

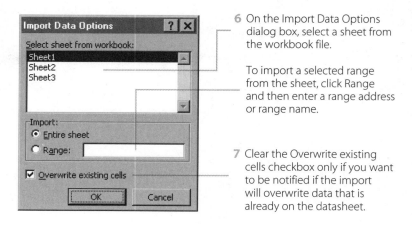

6 On the Import Data Options dialog box, select a sheet from the workbook file.

To import a selected range from the sheet, click Range and then enter a range address or range name.

7 Clear the Overwrite existing cells checkbox only if you want to be notified if the import will overwrite data that is already on the datasheet.

8 Click OK to import the data.

9 If the destination cells in the datasheet already contain data, and Graph displays a message warning you that the data will be overwritten, click OK to proceed, or click Cancel to cancel the import operation. If you click Cancel, you can then select a different destination in the datasheet and begin the procedure again. When the data is successfully imported, it appears in the Graph datasheet like this:

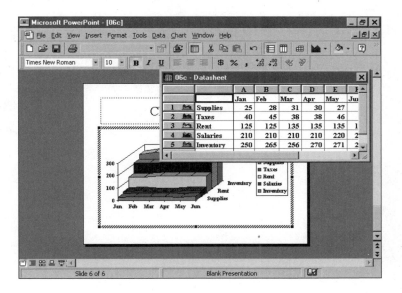

TIP

You can use the Import Data command to consolidate data from several Excel worksheets into a single Graph datasheet. After you import data from the first worksheet, select another location in the datasheet, import data from the second worksheet, and so on.

Creating a Link Between Excel and Graph

Establishing a link between the data in an Excel worksheet and the data in a Graph datasheet allows you to update the numbers in Excel and then see the changes automatically reflected in PowerPoint.

To create a link, you use a special feature of Windows called OLE. Windows takes care of all the behind-the-scenes complexity. Simply by copying the data to the Windows Clipboard in Excel and then

The Basic Presentation

using the Paste Link command in Graph's Edit menu to paste the data from the Clipboard to the datasheet, you automatically establish a link.

To create a link, follow these steps:

1   In Excel, select the range of data you want to link to PowerPoint, as shown here:

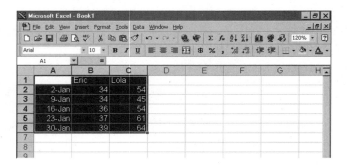

2   Choose the Copy command from Excel's Edit menu to copy the data to the Windows Clipboard.

3   Switch to the datasheet window in PowerPoint, and then select the cell in the upper left corner of the area into which you want to paste the data.

4   From Graph's Edit menu, choose the Paste Link command. If Graph displays a message box cautioning you about overwriting existing data, click OK to continue or click Cancel and try again in another location. The data appears in the Graph datasheet.

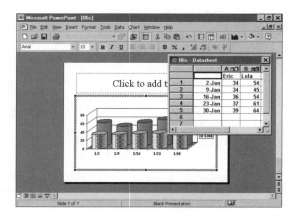

Updating the Link

After you create a link between Excel and PowerPoint, the link will be updated automatically unless you change it to a manual update link. Just for interest's sake, you can arrange the Excel and PowerPoint windows side by side to see the link in action; when you change a number in Excel, you can immediately see the number updated in PowerPoint.

To change the characteristics of the link, choose the Links command from the Graph Edit menu. The Links dialog box appears, as shown in Figure 6-18. To change the link so that it updates only when you click the Update Now button, select the Manual option at the bottom of the Link dialog box. Other options in this dialog box allow you to open the original data in Excel for editing; select a different data source—perhaps a different range in the Excel worksheet; or break the link between Excel and PowerPoint. If you break the link, the data remains in the Graph datasheet, but it is no longer updated when you make changes in the Excel worksheet.

FIGURE 6-18.

The Link dialog box.

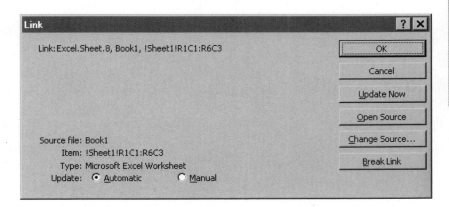

Using Text and Data from Data Files

When the data you need for a chart is stored in an ASCII text file (a text file without formatting), you can import the file into Graph using the Import File command. The columns of data in the file should be separated by tabs, semicolons, commas, or spaces.

To import an ASCII text file, follow these steps:

1   In the Graph datasheet, click the cell in the upper left corner of the destination area for the data.

2   Choose the Import File command from Graph's Edit menu, and when the Import File dialog box appears, select Text Files (*.prn, *.txt, *.csv) in the List Files of Type drop-down list.

3   Use the Directories and File Name lists to navigate to the file you want to import, and then double-click the filename. The Text Import Wizard opens, as shown below:

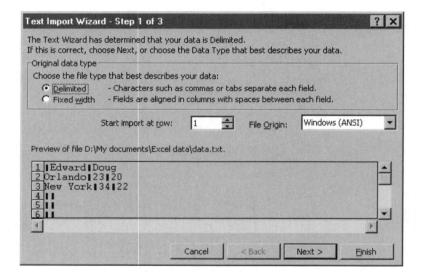

If the columns of data are separated by tabs, semicolons, or commas, the file is *delimited*, and by default the Delimited option is selected as the file type. If the columns of data are separated by spaces, the Fixed Width option is selected. A preview at the bottom of the first Text Import Wizard dialog box shows the data to be imported.

4   Click the Next button to move on to step 2, shown on the facing page.

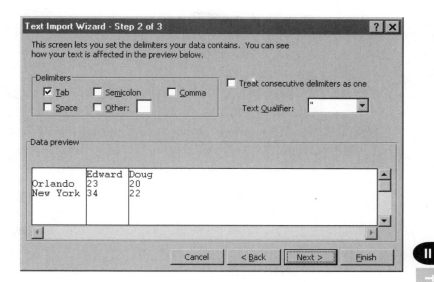

5 If the Text Import Wizard has not properly identified the delimiter used in the file (tabs or commas, for example), select the correct delimiter in the Step 2 dialog box. Vertical lines should properly separate the columns of data in the Data Preview box.

6 Click the Next button to get to step 3, shown below:

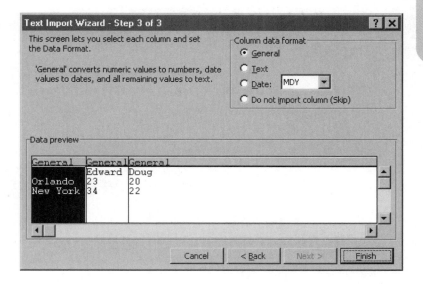

7　Select each column of data in the Data Preview box by clicking anywhere in the column. Then check the Column Data Format section that appears in the upper right corner of the Step 3 dialog box. If the Text Import Wizard has selected the incorrect data format, select the correct format now.

8　Click the Finish button to complete the import procedure. The data appears in the Graph datasheet, and you can then format the resulting chart to suit your needs.

That completes your introduction to creating charts and chart slides. In Chapter 10, "Formatting Graphs," you'll learn how to create custom charts that you can tailor to meet the most demanding requirements. For now, you might want to spend some time reviewing PowerPoint's graphing features before moving on to the next chapter, where you'll learn how to add organization chart slides to your presentations.

Adding Organization Chart Slides

An organization chart, or *org chart*, shows the hierarchy of an organization using a series of boxes and connecting lines. A classic hierarchy is the military's chain of command—officers and enlisted men and women. But an org chart can also depict the structure of a company, a division within a company or a government department, or even groups of organizations that are affiliated in a "top-down" arrangement. It might even be used to represent information other than an organization of people, such as types of books by different authors or categories of events at a sporting competition.

This chapter introduces you to PowerPoint's built-in organization chart tool. You'll learn how to create an org chart slide from scratch, how to add an org chart to an existing slide, and how to incorporate an existing org chart in a presentation. In addition, you'll learn how to create and modify the org chart's structure and how to format its text, boxes, and connecting lines.

Understanding Org Chart Basics

The procedure you use to add an organization chart to your presentation depends on where you want the chart to appear. If you want the org chart to be on a new slide that is dedicated to the chart, you can create a new slide and then select a layout that includes an org chart placeholder. If you want the chart to be on an existing slide or if you want to use an existing org chart, you can add an org chart object to a slide.

Creating an Org Chart Slide

PowerPoint's autolayouts make it easy to create an org chart slide for a presentation. When you start a new slide and select the Organization Chart autolayout, PowerPoint creates a new slide with an org chart placeholder.

Here are the specific steps for creating an org chart slide:

1 In Slide view, display the slide that you want the org chart slide to *follow*.

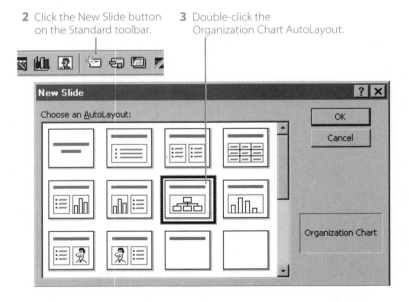

2 Click the New Slide button on the Standard toolbar.

3 Double-click the Organization Chart AutoLayout.

4 Double-click the org chart placeholder
to start a new org chart

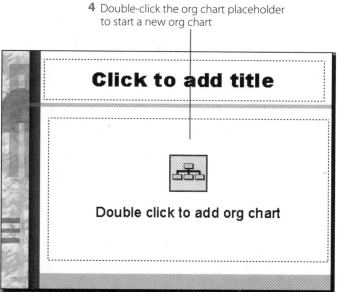

The Microsoft Organization Chart window opens.

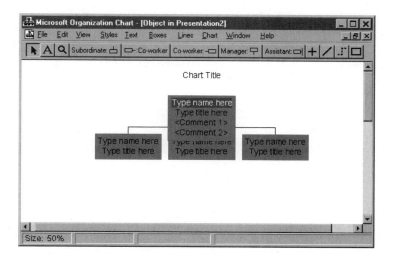

As you can see, the org chart contains a number of placeholders to simplify the task of entering information in the chart. And Microsoft Organization Chart comes equipped with a menu bar and a toolbar so that you can edit and format the org chart.

Adding an Organization Chart to an Existing Slide

To include both an org chart and another object, such as a group of bulleted text items or a graph on a slide, you can add an org chart to an existing slide. The bulleted text items can help explain the org chart, and a graph can depict a numeric achievement that resulted from a change in the organization's structure.

To add an org chart to an existing slide, display the slide in Slide view, choose Picture from the Insert menu, and then choose Organization Chart on the pop-out menu.

 TIP

> If you'll be creating org charts frequently, you can add an Insert Organization chart button to the Standard toolbar using the procedure described in "Customizing Toolbars," page 491.

Here's another method for adding a new org chart to an existing slide:

1   In Slide view, display the slide that will contain the org chart.

2   Choose Object from the Insert menu to display the Insert Object dialog box, shown below:

3 Make sure that Create New is selected.

4 Double-click MS Organization Chart 2.0.

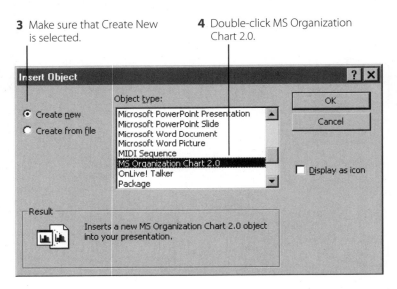

Microsoft Organization Chart opens in a window so that you can create the org chart.

Using an Existing Org Chart

If you've already created and saved an org chart, you can pull it into a presentation by inserting the chart as an object. If you follow the procedure below, you can double-click the chart to edit it from within PowerPoint:

1   In Slide view, display the slide you want to add the org chart to.

2   Choose Object from the Insert menu.

3 Click Create from file.   **4** Enter the org chart's file name or click the Browse button to search for the org chart.

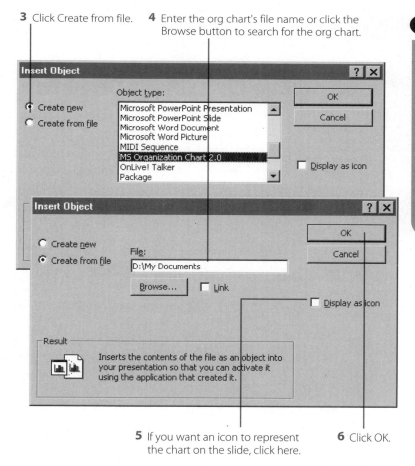

5 If you want an icon to represent the chart on the slide, click here.   **6** Click OK.

If you choose to place an icon for the chart on a slide, you can then "drill down" to the organization chart by double-clicking the icon. The org chart opens so you can modify it right in front of your audience.

> If you want to establish a link between the original org chart file and the picture of the org chart that will be displayed in PowerPoint, select the Link option in the Insert Object dialog box. Linking allows the chart in the presentation to reflect any subsequent changes that are made in the original org chart file. But be careful: If you select Link and then move the presentation to another computer, the chart will not come along for the ride. That's because the data for the chart is stored in the external org chart file rather than in PowerPoint. To store the data for the org chart in PowerPoint, you must leave the Link option unselected in the Insert Object dialog box.

Creating the Org Chart Structure

When the Microsoft Organization Chart window opens, the beginning of a hierarchy (one manager and three subordinates) is displayed in four boxes. (If you see only one box in the Organization Chart window, you can choose Options from the Organization Chart Edit menu, select the Use Standard 4-Box Template For New Charts option, and click OK. Then close the Organization Chart window, and click No when the program asks whether to update the presentation. You can then create a new org chart with four boxes.)

Before you begin entering text in the org chart's boxes, you may want to give the chart a title. Select the text *Chart Title* at the top of the chart, and type a new title, such as *Our Division*. You can press Enter at the end of the title line to add a line for a subtitle. In fact, you can create a series of subtitles, but then you'll have little room left for the chart!

> **Depicting Complicated Organizations**
> You may want to diagram each division of a complicated organizational structure in a separate chart to avoid overcrowding. You can create a preliminary organization chart that depicts the broad picture (the branches of the organization without any of the "leaves"), and then show each division in detail in a separate chart.

Filling in the Boxes

To start entering names in the org chart's boxes, follow these steps:

1   Click to select the first box.

2   Type a name into the first box and press Enter. You can also press Tab or the Down arrow key.

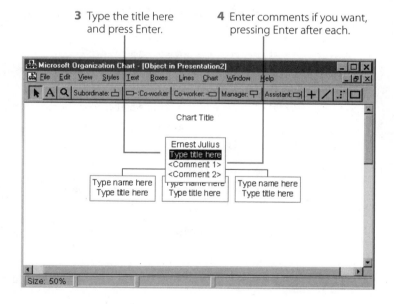

3 Type the title here and press Enter.

4 Enter comments if you want, pressing Enter after each.

5   Press Ctrl+Down arrow key to move to the first subordinate box.

6   Enter a name, title, and comments into this box.

7   To move to the box to the right, press Ctrl+Right arrow key. You can also press Ctrl+Left arrow key to move to the box to the left, or press Ctrl+Up arrow key to move to the top box.

Editing the Text

After you enter text in an org chart box, you can edit the text by clicking the box once to select it and then clicking an insertion point in the text you want to edit. You can use all the same text selection and editing techniques you use elsewhere in PowerPoint.

After you enter text in a box, you can press Esc to complete the entry but leave the box selected. Then you can immediately edit the text if necessary.

SEE ALSO
For more information about text editing techniques, see "Editing Text in Outline View," page 63.

You can also edit the text in an org chart by clicking the Enter Text button on the Organization Chart toolbar and then clicking any of the text in the chart. As you'll learn later, the Enter Text button is useful for typing text directly on the chart background as well.

Adding and Deleting Boxes

Chances are, your organization has more than three members, so you need to know how to add more boxes to the org chart. Fortunately, adding boxes is easy. On the Organization Chart toolbar, click the button for the type of box you want to add, and then click the box that you want to connect the new box to. To add more than one box at a time, click the appropriate toolbar button the desired number of times, and then click an existing box.

The boxes you can add to an org chart are shown on the facing page in Table 7-1, along with their corresponding buttons and a description of each button's function.

To add a subordinate to one of the three subordinates already in the chart, follow these steps:

The Subordinate button.

1 Click the Subordinate button on the Organization Chart toolbar.

2 Click one of the three boxes in the second row of the chart. A new box appears, ready for you to type in a name, title, and comments.

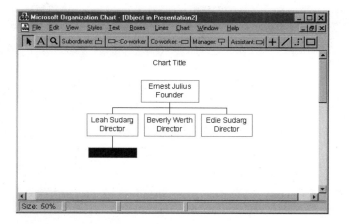

TABLE 7-1. The org chart boxes and toolbar buttons.

Button	Name	Function
Subordinate:	Subordinate	Adds a box at the level below the selected box
Co-worker	Left Co-worker	Adds a box to the left of the selected box at the same level.
Co-worker:	Right Co-worker	Adds a box to the right of the selected box at the same level.
Manager:	Manager	Adds a box at the level of the selected box and moves the selected box down one level. The selected box is attached to the new box as a subordinate.
Assistant:	Assistant	Adds a box below the selected box. The new box is attached to the line of command but is not a part of it (a staff position).

Deleting an org chart box is as easy as adding one. Simply select the box you want to delete, and then press the Delete key or choose Clear from the Organization Chart Edit menu. To delete two or more boxes, first select the boxes by clicking one box, then hold down the Shift key, and click the other boxes. After you select multiple boxes, press Delete to delete all of them.

TIP

> **Quickly Deleting Adjacent Boxes**
> If the org chart boxes you want to delete are adjacent to one another, you can click the Select button on the toolbar and drag a selection box around the boxes. Then you can press Delete to delete the selected boxes.

A Sample Org Chart

To try your hand at creating an org chart with an assortment of boxes, follow this example: Imagine that you need to diagram the structure of a nonprofit organization and its regional affiliates. If you've been following along by creating an actual chart, choose Exit And Return To *<Presentation>* from the Organization Chart File menu, and then click No when you are asked if you want to update the chart. When you return to PowerPoint, start a new org chart by double-clicking the org chart placeholder, and then follow these steps:

1 After the Organization Chart window opens, select the text *Chart Title* at the top of the new chart, and type *League of Lefties*.

2 Click the topmost box once, type *Renee A. Gauche* as the name, press Enter, and type *National Director* as the title.

3 For the first comment, type *Wash., D.C.* You won't enter a second comment, so press Ctrl+Down arrow key to move to the first subordinate box.

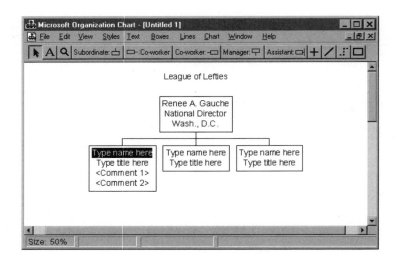

4   In the first subordinate box, type *Greta Links,* press Enter, and
    type *Director* as the title and *California* as the first comment.
    Then press Ctrl+Right arrow key to move to the second subordi-
    nate box.

5   In the second subordinate box, type *Leanora Izquierda,* press
    Enter, and type *Director* as the title and *New York* as the first
    comment.

6   The League of Lefties does not have a third individual at the
    Director level, so click the third subordinate box, and press
    Delete. The chart now looks like this:

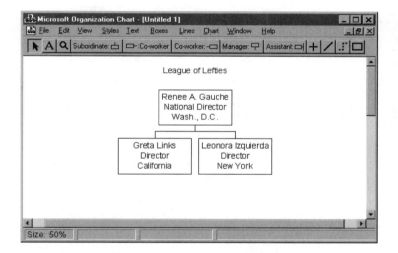

7   Greta Links has two subordinates, so click the Subordinate
    button on the toolbar twice, and then click Greta's box. Two
    subordinates appear.

8   Leanora Izquierda has three subordinates, so click the Subordi-
    nate button three times, and then click Leanora's box.

9   Renee A. Gauche has an assistant, so click the Assistant button,
    and then click Renee's box. Next, type *Sylvia Southpaw* as the
    name, type *Assistant* as the title, and then click anywhere
    outside the org chart.

10 Enter the names of the subordinates under both Greta and
    Leanora. Click the first subordinate box under Greta, type

Tiffany, press Ctrl+Right arrow key, and type *Bijou.* Type *Sal, Howie,* and *Clarice* as the subordinates under Leonora.

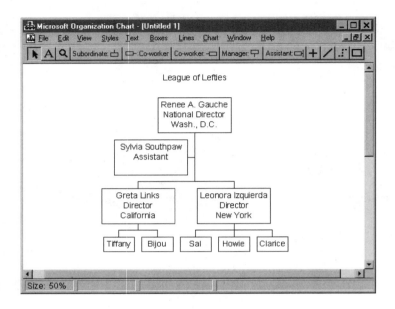

Later in this chapter, you'll modify the structure and change the formatting of the org chart you've just created. For now, return with the chart to PowerPoint by first choosing Update *<Presentation>* from the Organization Chart File menu and then choosing Exit And Return To *<Presentation>* from the same menu. In a moment, the chart appears on the current PowerPoint slide. Save the PowerPoint presentation with a name of your choosing so that you can retrieve it later.

Moving Boxes

The ease with which you can modify the structure of an org chart suits today's dynamic organizations. But fortunately or unfortunately, depending on your place in the organization, restructuring an actual org chart in PowerPoint is far easier than restructuring an actual organization.

Restructuring an organization in real life often results in moving people from one manager to another. The counterpart in PowerPoint is dragging a box from one place in the org chart to another. You can drag boxes to other positions at the same level in the chart, or move them up or down within the organization's structure.

To move a box in an org chart, follow these steps:

1 Open the org chart in the Organization Chart window.

2 Place the mouse pointer on the frame of the box you want to move.

3 Hold down the left mouse button and drag the box's frame.

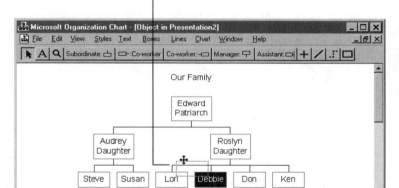

4 When the frame is in position, release the mouse button.

When you drag a box's frame near the left or right inside edge of another box and release the mouse button, the moved box appears to the left or right of the other box, at the same level. When you drag the frame near the bottom inside edge of another box, the moved box appears below the other box, as a subordinate.

When you drag the frame onto another box, an indicator appears inside the frame. The indicator is a left arrow when the moved box will appear at the left side of the existing box, as shown in Figure 7-1 on the next page. The indicator is a right arrow when the moved box

The Basic Presentation

will appear at the right side of the existing box. The indicator is a subordinate box icon when the moved box will appear below the existing box, as a subordinate.

FIGURE 7-1.

The left arrow indicates that the moved box will appear to the left of the existing box.

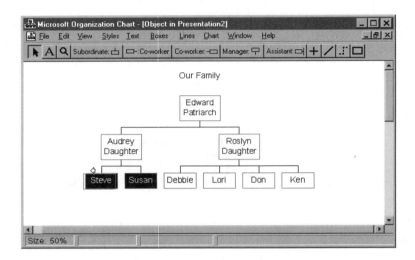

Try moving a box in the org chart you created earlier by first opening the presentation file (if necessary), double-clicking the org chart to open the Organzation Chart window, and then placing the mouse pointer on Sal's box. Next, hold down the left mouse button, and drag Sal's box onto Greta's box without releasing the mouse button. Then move Sal's box toward the bottom of Greta's box, and when the subordinate indicator appears, release the mouse button to drop Sal's box into place. (Sal now appears to the right of Bijou.) Next move Sal between Tiffany and Bijou by clicking anywhere outside the chart to deselect Sal's box and then dragging Sal's box onto Bijou's box. Notice the
left arrow inside Bijou's box when you drag it onto Bijou's box. The arrow indicates that Sal's box will drop to the left of Bijou's box, just as you want. Release the mouse button to see the results shown in Figure 7-2.

Finally, return to the presentation by choosing Update *<Presentation>* from the Organzation Chart File menu and then choosing Exit And Return To *<Presentation>* from the same menu. To save the presentation file with the changes in PowerPoint, click the Save button on the Standard toolbar, choose Save from the File menu, or press Ctrl+S.

FIGURE 7-2.
The revised org chart.

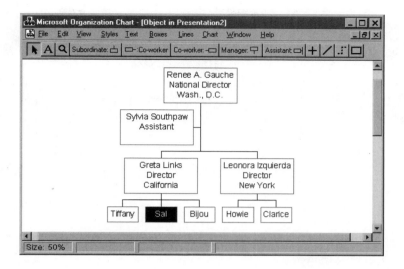

II

The Basic Presentation

Changing the Style of Groups and Branches

The subordinates under a manager are called a *group*. By default, PowerPoint displays a group in boxes that are side by side. But, from the Styles menu, you can choose several other ways to display a group. For example, the members of a group can be shown as a vertical list, or they can be depicted as leaves that emanate from a central branch.

Before you can change the style of an org chart group, you must select the group. So your first step is to double-click any member of the group, or click a member and then press Ctrl+G (*G* for *Group*) to select the entire group. You can also select a group by selecting one member of the group and choosing Select and then Group from the Organzation Chart Edit menu. Figure 7-3 on the next page shows the members of a group after they have been selected. Note that the group members all report to the same manager.

After you select a group, open the Styles menu, and click one of the six group style buttons at the top of the menu. For a group at the lowest level of a chart, a useful style is that shown on the second button in the second row of styles. Arranging a group in this style can reduce the horizontal space needed by a chart whose organizational structure is wide rather than deep.

Just as you can change the style of an org chart group, you can also change the style of an org chart *branch*. A branch consists of a manager and all the manager's subordinates. To select a branch, select the manager at the top of the branch, and then press Ctrl+B (*B* for *Branch*), or choose Select and then Branch from the Organzation Chart Edit menu. After you select a branch, you can choose one of the styles from the Styles menu.

FIGURE 7-3.

The members of a selected group.

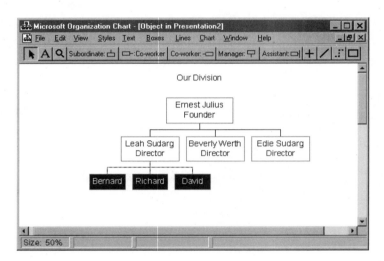

How to Select a Chart Group or Branch
You can also select an org chart group or branch by clicking the Select button on the toolbar and dragging a selection box around the group or branch.

Two special styles at the bottom of the Styles menu let you change the rank of members of a group. The first style, Assistant, changes selected members of a group to assistants. For example, Figure 7-4 displays two org charts on a slide. The left chart shows three subordinates under a manager. The right chart shows the result after two of the subordinates are converted to assistants with the Assistant style.

The second style at the bottom of the Styles menu is the Co-manager style. You can use this style to indicate two or more members of the organization who report to the same manager and share power. After you select the members you want to make comanagers, click the Co-manager style on the Styles menu. Figure 7-5 shows two subordinates who have become comanagers.

FIGURE 7-4.
Subordinates converted to assistants with the Assistant style.

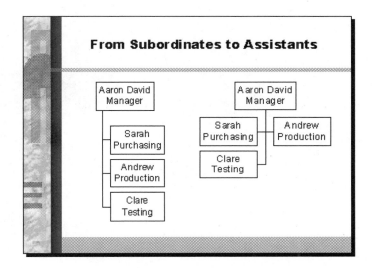

FIGURE 7-5.
Subordinates converted to comanagers with the Co-manager style.

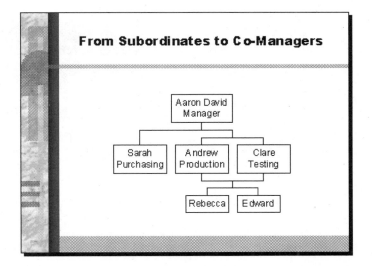

Try changing the style of the groups in the org chart you created earlier, by first opening the presentation file, if necessary, and then double-clicking the org chart to open the Organization Chart window. Next, click one of the subordinates under Greta, and press Ctrl+G to select the entire group of subordinates who report to Greta. Open the Styles menu, and click the second style in the second row. The three side-by-side boxes of the group change to a small ladder that lists the three subordinates. You can try other styles or choose the same style for Leanora's group of subordinates. Figure 7-6 shows Greta's group with its new style.

FIGURE 7-6.

The new style applied to the group of subordinates who report to Greta Links.

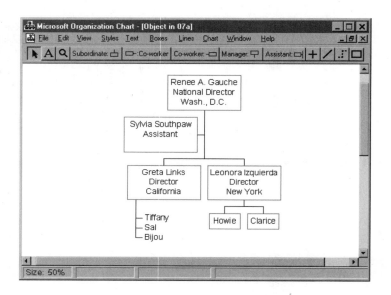

Formatting the Org Chart

An organization chart inherits the design characteristics of the template that you attached to the current presentation. For example, the template determines the font of the text and the color of the boxes in the org chart. But, as you'll learn in this section, after you complete an organizational structure, you can still make changes to the appearance of the chart. For instance, you can emphasize the titles of the organization members with a special color or change the box borders.

Zooming In and Out

Before you start formatting an org chart, you should get acquainted with the Organization Chart zoom feature. That way, you can see exactly what you're doing when you make changes to a chart.

The Zoom
button

To zoom in on an org chart, click the Zoom button on the toolbar, and then click the area of the org chart you want to zoom in on. To zoom out, click the Zoom button again (the Button now displays a miniature org chart instead of a magnifying glass), and then click the org chart. You can also use the following commands to change the zoom percentage of the chart: Choose Size To Window from the View menu or press F9 to fit the entire chart within the Organzation Chart window; choose 50% Of Actual or press F10 to reduce the chart to 50 percent of its actual size, which, in turn, is approximately 50 percent of its printed size; and choose 200% Of Actual or press F12 to enlarge the chart so that you can focus on some of the chart detail.

Formatting the Text

The procedures for formatting the text in an org chart are similar to the procedures for formatting text elsewhere in PowerPoint. Rather than use commands on the Format menu, however, you use commands on the Organization Chart Text menu. These commands allow you to change the font, color, and alignment of the text in organization chart boxes.

Of course, before you can use the commands on the Text menu, you must select the text you want to format. To select all the text in a box, click the box. To select all the text in several boxes, hold down the Shift key as you click each box. You can also select specific boxes by using the Select commands on the Organization Chart Edit menu. Table 7-2 on the next page describes each of the Select commands.

TIP

> ### Selecting Adjacent Boxes
> You can also select several adjacent boxes by clicking the Select button on the toolbar and dragging a selection box around the boxes.

To format specific text in a box, such as the title only, click the box, and then click an insertion point in the text that you want to format. Next, use any of the standard text selection techniques to select the text in the box. For example, drag across the text with the mouse, double-click a word, or hold down the Shift key as you press the Left or Right arrow key. By selecting only certain text within a box, you

II

The Basic Presentation

can change the appearance of as little or as much text as you want. You can even format a single character with a special font or color.

Unfortunately, PowerPoint offers no easy method to select all names or all titles in an org chart. You must move from box to box, selecting the name or the title, if you want to apply special formatting to only those elements.

TABLE 7-2. The Select commands.

Command	Function
All	Selects all boxes in the org chart.
All Assistants	Selects all assistants.
All Co-Managers	Selects all members who have been made comanagers with the Co-manager style.
All Managers	Selects only members who have subordinates.
All Non-Managers	Selects only members who do not have subordinates.
Group	Selects the other members of a group. You must have one group member selected first.
Branch	Selects the other members of a branch. You must have one branch member selected first.
Lowest Level	Selects only the boxes at the lowest level of the org chart.
Connecting Lines	Selects only the connecting lines between boxes.
Background Objects	Selects only the boxes and lines drawn with the drawing tools.

Formatting the Boxes

By selecting an org chart box and then using the commands on the Boxes menu, you can change the box's color, add a shadow, and modify the box's borders. Before you can make any of these changes, however, you must select the box or boxes you want to format using the techniques described in the previous section. Then simply choose the desired commands from the Boxes menu. For example, to format a box with the color red and an extra-thick border, first click the box to select it, choose the Color command from the Boxes menu, click the red color option in the Color dialog box, and then click OK. Next choose the Border Style command from the Boxes menu, and click the second border option in the second column of the Border Style submenu.

The Color command allows you to apply any of the colors in the current color palette to the interior of the selected box or boxes. (After you finish creating the org chart, you'll see it on the slide, against the slide background, and you'll be able to determine whether the box interior color clashes with the slide background color.)

The Shadow command allows you to apply a shadow that extends in one or more directions behind the selected box or boxes. Shadows give boxes a three-dimensional look. Figure 7-7 shows shadows added to the boxes in the sample org chart.

FIGURE 7-7.
The sample org chart with shadows added.

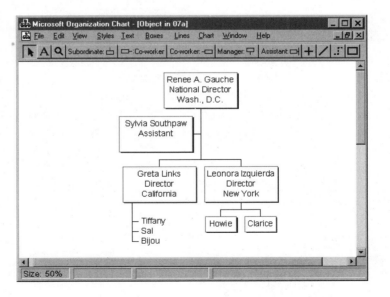

To change the style, color, and line style of a selected box's border, use the three Border commands on the Boxes menu. Figure 7-8 shows the sample org chart formatted with double borders.

FIGURE 7-8.

The sample org chart formatted with double borders.

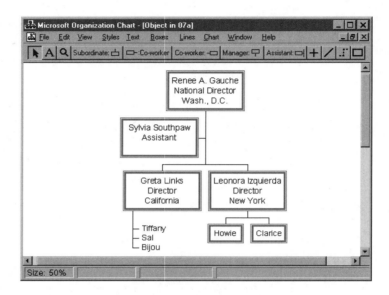

Formatting the Lines

You can change the thickness, style, and color of the lines that connect org chart boxes just as easily as you change the formatting of the boxes. Before you can change the formatting of a line, you must select the line by clicking it. The line then changes to a dashed light gray to show that it is selected. You can select multiple lines by holding down the Shift key as you click each line, or you can select all the lines by choosing Select and then Connecting Lines from the Edit menu.

> **Selecting Multiple Lines**
> You can also select multiple lines by clicking the Select button on the toolbar and dragging a selection box around the lines.

After you select the line or lines you want to format, choose the Thickness, Style, or Color command from the Lines menu. Each command offers a set of options that are fairly self-explanatory. Figure 7-9 shows the the sample org chart formatted with thicker connecting lines. Figure 7-10 shows the chart's connecting lines with the dotted line style.

FIGURE 7-9.

The sample org chart formatted with shadowed boxes and thicker connecting lines.

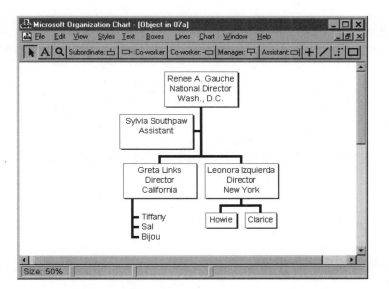

FIGURE 7-10.

The sample org chart formatted with shadowed boxes and dotted connecting lines.

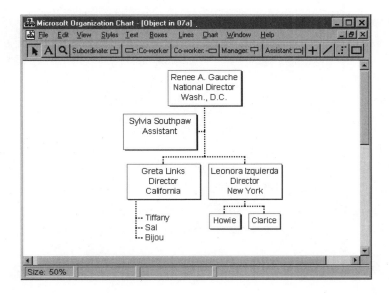

The Basic Presentation

Drawing Boxes and Lines with the Drawing Tools

Sometimes the built-in box arrangements (subordinates under managers, assistants below managers, and co-managers sharing power) simply cannot describe the complicated, spaghetti-like reporting structures in an organization. Fortunately, you can add new boxes and lines easily with the Microsoft Organization Chart module's drawing tools, shown below.

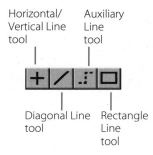

> **NOTE**

If you don't see four drawing tools to the right of the Assistant button on the toolbar, choose Show Draw Tools from the View menu or press Ctrl+D.

To draw a horizontal or vertical line or a diagonal line on the chart, click the Horizontal/Vertical Line or Diagonal Line tool, place the cross-hair pointer at the starting point for the line, hold down the left mouse button, and then drag to draw the line. After you add a line, you can select the line by clicking it with the mouse. You can then delete the line with the Delete key, format the line with the commands on the Lines menu, or change the line's length by dragging the handle at either end. You can also move a selected line by dragging it with the mouse.

To connect two boxes with a line, click the Auxiliary Line tool, place the pointer at the edge of the first box, and then drag to the edge of the second box, as shown in Figure 7-11. As you drag, you'll see the connecting line appear. If the connecting line has three segments (like the one in Figure 7-11), you can drag the middle segment to change the size or shape of the line. You may have to move the middle segment if the connecting line overlaps an existing line or box.

FIGURE 7-11.
A new connecting line has been added to the sample org chart.

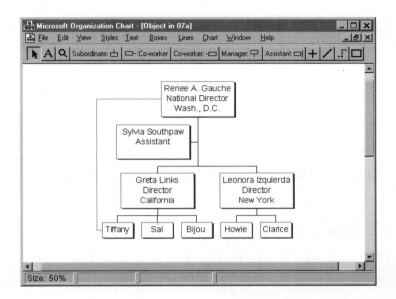

To draw a new box, as shown in Figure 7-12 on the next page, click the Rectangle tool, place the cross-hair pointer where you want the box to appear, and then drag to create the new box. To adjust the size or shape of the new box, drag one of the handles at the sides or corners of the box. To move the box, place the mouse pointer on the border of the box, between two handles, and drag in the desired direction.

You cannot use the Auxiliary Line tool to connect new boxes with existing chart boxes or with other new boxes. To connect new boxes, you must draw lines with the Horizontal/Vertical Line tool or the Diagonal Line tool.

II

The Basic Presentation

FIGURE 7-12.
A new box has been added to the sample org chart.

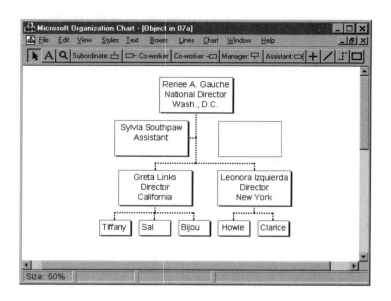

> **NOTE**
>
> To save an org chart in a separate file, choose Save Copy As from the File menu of the Organization Chart module. The chart will be saved as an OPX file that can be opened in Microsoft Organization Chart and used in other PowerPoint presentations.

Returning to PowerPoint

When the org chart is complete, choose Update *<Presentation>* from the Organization Chart File menu, and choose Exit And Return To *<Presentation>* from the same menu. If you exit without choosing Update *<Presentation>* first, PowerPoint displays a dialog box asking whether you want to update the chart. Click Yes to proceed.

The new org chart appears on the current PowerPoint slide. You can move the entire chart or drag a corner handle to resize the chart, but the chart always remains the same shape. To edit the chart, double-click it. The Organization Chart window reopens with the chart inside.

In this chapter, you've learned to place organization charts on slides. In the next chapter, you'll continue the survey of special object types by learning about table slides.

Adding Table Slides

When you want to display text paragraphs side by side—to lay out the pros and cons of an issue, for example—you can use the row-and-column format of a table. PowerPoint's table slides are quick to make and easy to modify, especially when compared to the alternative, which is to align text in columns with tab stops.

Table slides often hold text only, but they can hold numbers just as easily. When you don't need the power of a graph to illustrate a result, a table can do quite nicely. Tables are also useful as a backup to a graph, when the audience needs to see the raw data.

This chapter focuses on how to create a slide devoted entirely to a table and how to add a table to an existing slide. Because PowerPoint uses the table-making feature from Microsoft Word, not everyone can create a table in PowerPoint. If you do not have Word, you must create a table in another application (such as Microsoft Excel) and import it into PowerPoint as an object—a complex process.

By borrowing Word's table-making capabilities, PowerPoint gives you all of Word's advanced text handling and formatting capabilities as you create tables. For example, you can use Word's thesaurus to find a synonym. In fact, you gain access to all of Word's menus and tools without ever having to leave PowerPoint.

Understanding Table Basics

When you need to include a table in a presentation, you can create a new slide with the Table autolayout or you can add the table to an existing slide that already contains other objects, such as a group of bulleted text items.

Creating a Table Slide

Creating a table slide for a presentation is easy. Just follow these five steps:

1   In Slide view, display the slide that you want the table slide to follow.

2   Click the New Slide button on the Standard toolbar.

3   In the New Slide dialog box, double-click the Table autolayout:

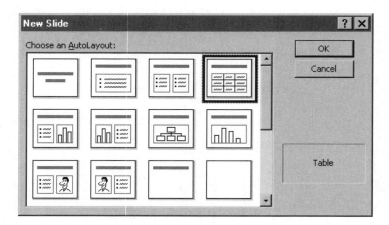

As you can see in the figure on the facing page, the new slide contains two placeholders: one for the slide title and one for the table.

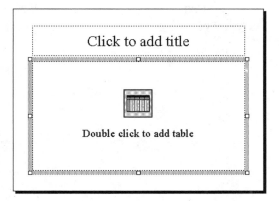

4 Double-click the table placeholder to display the Insert Word Table dialog shown below:

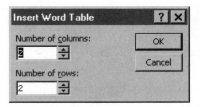

5 In the Insert Word Table dialog box, enter the number of columns and the number of rows you want to include in the table by typing new numbers in the Number Of Columns and Number Of Rows edit boxes, or by clicking the up or down arrows next to the edit boxes. Then click OK to create the table.

Using a Microsoft Excel Table

If the data for a table comes from Microsoft Excel, you might want to reserve a slide to display the Excel spreadsheet as a backup slide. (If someone asks for clarification of the table's data, you can produce the original Excel table.) When you embed an Excel table in a PowerPoint slide, the table appears just as it does in Excel, plus you gain all the advantages of Excel's data calculation powers from within PowerPoint. For example, Excel tables (actually small worksheets embedded in PowerPoint slides) can include formulas that carry out complicated calculations, and the formula results are updated automatically when any of the numbers change. For information about embedding an Excel table, see "Using PowerPoint with Microsoft Excel," page 448.

Adding a Table to an Existing Slide

You can use either of two methods to add a table to an existing slide. Here are the steps for the first method:

1 Click the Insert Microsoft Word Table button on the Standard toolbar to display a 4 x 5 grid of empty cells as shown.

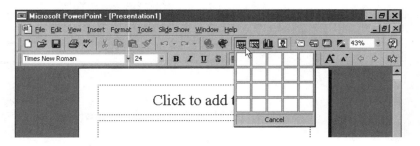

2 Position the mouse pointer on the cell in the upper left corner of the grid, hold down the left mouse button, and drag across the number of columns and down the number of rows you want in the table. For example, the result of the grid selected below would be a table with five rows and three columns.

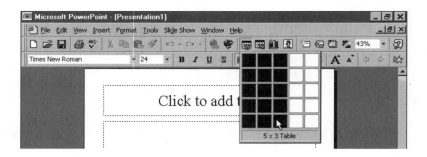

 **TIP**

In the example above, you could also have clicked the cell at column 3, row 5 without doing any dragging.

3 Release the mouse button to add the table to the current slide.

The second method you can use to add a table to an existing slide involves the following steps:

1 Choose the Picture command from the Insert menu.

2 Choose Microsoft Word Table from the Picture pop-out menu.

3 When the Insert Word Table dialog box appears, enter the number of columns and rows you want in the table, and click OK.

 TIP

> If you've already created a table in Word, you can drag and drop the table onto a PowerPoint slide, as you'll learn in "Using PowerPoint with Microsoft Word," page 436.

Entering Text in a Table

When you create a new table slide, an empty table appears within a gray frame on the slide. Vertical and horizontal rulers adjoin the table, and dotted lines called *gridlines* mark the boundaries of the columns and rows of cells in the table. Figure 8-1 shows a slide with a brand-new table.

FIGURE 8-1.
A slide with a new table.

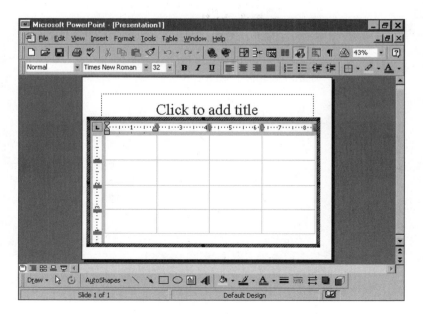

The Basic Presentation

When the new table appears on the current slide, the menus and toolbars from Word replace the PowerPoint menus and toolbars. In fact, if it weren't for *PowerPoint* in the title bar, you might think you had switched to Word entirely. PowerPoint's chameleon-like ability to transform itself lets you use all of Word's menus and tools without leaving PowerPoint.

After you finish the table, you must click outside the gray table frame. Only the section of the table within the gray frame is placed on the slide, and PowerPoint's menus and toolbars reappear.

WARNING

If you move a table's gray frame before you add the table to a slide, you may not see the entire table on the slide.

If you have created a table in Word before, you know exactly what to do after you specify the dimensions of the table. The close partnership among all the Microsoft Office 97 applications makes it easy to move from one application to another. But if you haven't used Word's table features, don't worry. This chapter leads you through everything you need to know.

The first thing you should consider is the structure of the table. For example, you'll probably want to use the cells at the tops of columns or beginnings of rows for table headings. Then, after you enter the table headings, you can enter data in the remaining cells. As you'll learn later in the chapter, it's not necessary to know exactly how many columns and rows you need from the start because you can easily add columns and rows at any time.

When you start a table, the insertion point flashes in the first cell in the upper left corner of the table. As always, you type to enter text at the location of the insertion point. To move the insertion point to another cell, press the Tab key or click the destination cell. Press Shift+Tab to move back one cell.

As you type, the text wraps within the current width of the cell. In other words, when you've typed all the way across a cell, the next word you type moves to a second line within the cell, as shown in Figure 8-2. In fact, as shown in Figure 8-3, the entire table row grows vertically rather than horizontally to accommodate its longest text entry. Later in this chapter, you'll learn how to change the height of rows, as well as the width of columns, manually.

FIGURE 8-2.

The text in four cells of this table has wrapped to the second line.

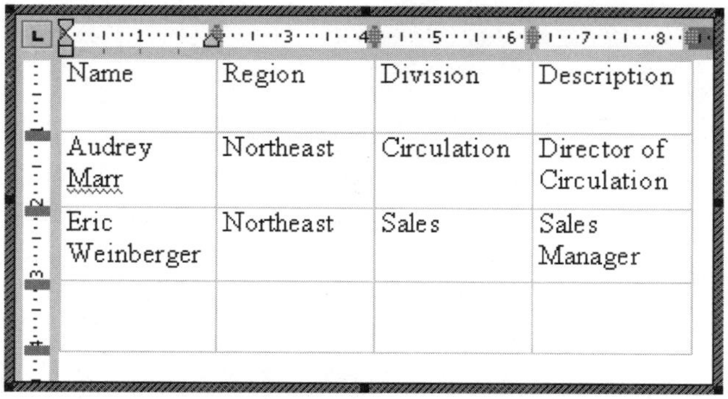

FIGURE 8-3.

A table row grows vertically to accommodate its longest text entry.

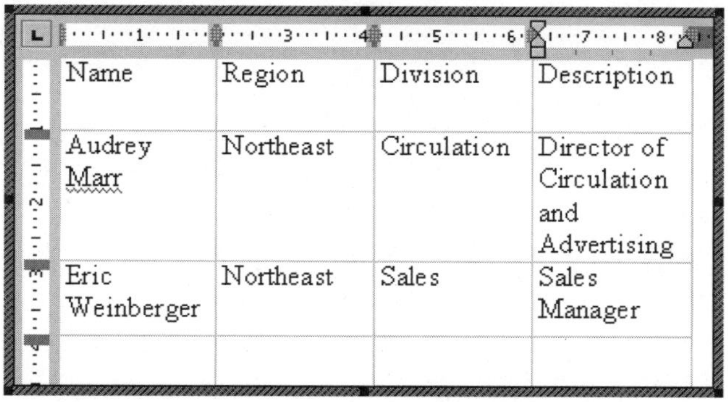

TIP

Although a cell can accommodate lengthy text entries, try to use short text entries to avoid overwhelming the screen with words. Type a word or two rather than a sentence. Keep in mind that in tables, as in charts, less is more.

You can use a variety of keys and key combinations to move around in a table. For example, to move quickly to the end of a row, press Alt+End. To move to the first cell in a column, press Alt+PgUp. Table 8-1, on the next page, summarizes the keystrokes you can use to move around in a PowerPoint table.

TABLE 8-1. The navigation keys for a PowerPoint table.

To Move...	Press...
To the next cell	Tab
To the previous cell	Shift+Tab
To the first cell in a row	Alt+Home
To the last cell in a row	Alt+End
To the first cell in a column	Alt+PgUp
To the last cell in a column	Alt+PgDown

When you press Tab to move to a cell that contains text, the text is high-lighted. You can then replace the highlighted text by simply typing new text. (Remember, any selected text is instantly replaced when you type.)

As you enter text in a cell, you can end a paragraph and start a new paragraph by pressing Enter. When you get to the end of the last cell in the last row, you can add a new row at the bottom of the table by pressing Tab.

A Sample Table

You can try your hand at creating a sample table. Imagine that you need to compare two vendors who want to supply coffee for your office kitchen. You can start by creating a new presentation, or you can use an existing presentation. Then follow the steps below.

1 Click the New Slide button on the Standard toolbar to start a new slide. When the New Slide dialog box appears, double-click the Table autolayout.

2 On the new slide, double-click the table placeholder to start the table. When the Insert Word Table dialog box appears, enter *3* in the Number of Rows edit box, and then click OK to create the empty 3 x 2 table.

3 With the insertion point in the first cell of the table, type *The Coffee Pot,* press Tab to move to the next cell, and type *Roast and Brew.* Now you can begin typing the benefits provided by each service in the cells below.

4 Press Tab to move to the second cell in the first column, and type *Freshly ground beans each week*. Then press Tab to move to the second cell in the second column, and type *Free donuts on Fridays*.

5 Press Tab again to move to the third cell in the first column, and type *Daily 7 AM service*. Then press Tab one more time, and type *Jelly donuts, too*. Your table should now look something like the table shown below:

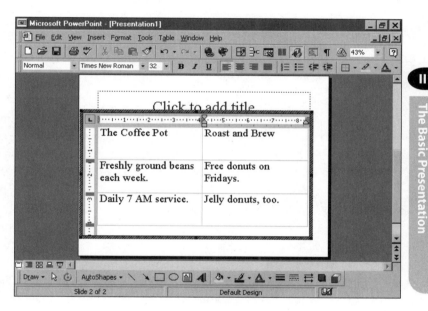

6 Click anywhere outside the gray frame surrounding the table to place the table on the current slide.

As you can see, this table could use a little formatting. The text is too large, the rows are too tall, and the column headings are not distinguished in any way. Later in this chapter, you'll learn how to make these improvements, and others as well. But first, you need to learn how to make basic modifications to the structure of the table, such as inserting a new column if a third vendor makes a bid.

Modifying the Table

After you've created a table, you can modify its structure by adding, deleting, moving, and copying cells, columns, and rows. You can also change the widths of columns, the heights of rows, and merge and split cells to accommodate the contents of your table. All these changes are easy to accomplish. If you've already clicked outside the gray frame to place a table on a slide, you must double-click the table to reactivate it for modifications.

Selecting Cells, Columns, and Rows

If you want to modify something in PowerPoint, you must select it first. This section discusses the various ways you can select cells, columns, and rows in a table.

Clicking the middle of a cell places an insertion point inside the cell, so the usual approach of clicking something to select it doesn't apply to tables. Instead, you must carefully position the mouse pointer near the left inside edge of the cell you want to select, and when the pointer changes to a right arrow, click the cell. To select adjacent cells in the same column, click anywhere in the first cell, and drag down the column. To select adjacent cells in the same row, click anywhere in the first cell, and drag across the row. Word's Automatic Text Selection feature ensures that everything in the cells is also selected. In addition, you can click one cell, hold down the Shift key, and then click another cell to select both cells and any cells in between. Figure 8-4 shows a table with all the cells in one row selected.

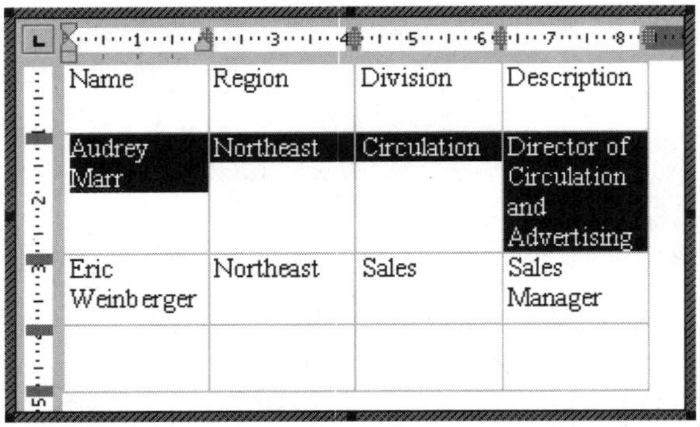

Name	Region	Division	Description
Audrey Marr	Northeast	Circulation	Director of Circulation and Advertising
Eric Weinberger	Northeast	Sales	Sales Manager

FIGURE 8-4.
All the cells in the second row have been selected.

A shortcut for selecting a column of cells is to first position the mouse pointer on the top border of the column. Then, when the pointer changes to a down arrow, click the left mouse button to select the entire column, as shown in Figure 8-5.

FIGURE 8-5.

The third column in this table has been selected. (Note the down arrow at the top of the column.)

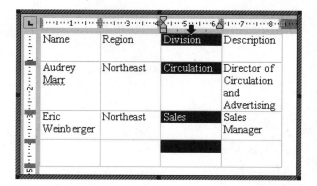

Just to make things a bit complicated, there's a difference between selecting all the cells in a row and selecting a row. You select all the cells in a row when you want to modify the contents of all the cells. You select a row when you want to add a new row or delete the current row. To select a row, you must also select the end-of-row marker that sits just to the right of the last cell in the row, as shown in Figure 8-6.

FIGURE 8-6.

The second row in this table has been selected.

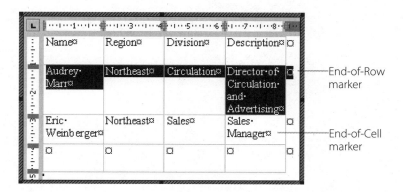

End-of-Row marker

End-of-Cell marker

¶

The Show/Hide ¶ button.

If you don't see any end-of-row markers in your table, click the Show/Hide ¶ button on the Standard toolbar. (You may also need to drag the right side of the table's gray frame a little to the right.) When the end-of-row markers appear, you'll also see end-of-cell markers that mark the end of the contents of each cell.

 TIP

> If you have trouble selecting rows and columns with the mouse, you can use Table menu commands instead. First use the arrow keys and the Tab key to move the insertion point to a cell in the row or column you want to select, and then choose Select Row or Select Column from the Table menu. After you place the insertion point in a cell at one end of a range of cells that you want to select, you can also hold down the Shift key, and press the arrow keys to select adjacent cells.

Adding and Deleting Cells, Columns, and Rows

Depending on whether you've selected a cell, column, or row, the command on the Table menu becomes Insert Cells, Insert Columns, or Insert Rows. When you insert new cells, the Insert Cells dialog box appears, as shown in Figure 8-7. You can then specify where the currently selected cell (or cells) should be moved in order to accommodate the new cell (or cells).

FIGURE 8-7.
The Insert Cells dialog box.

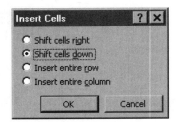

When you insert a new column, the column appears to the left of the selected column. When you insert a new row, the row appears above the selected row.

 NOTE

> If you want to add a new row to the end of a table, click the last cell in the table, and then press Tab.

Like the Insert command, the Delete command on the Table menu becomes Delete Cells, Delete Columns, or Delete Rows depending on whether you've selected a cell, column, or row. When you delete a cell, the Delete Cells dialog box appears. The options in this dialog box are similar to those in the Insert Cells dialog box. When you delete a column or row, the contents of the cells in the column or row are also deleted.

TIP

> You can also use the Insert Cells and Delete Cells dialog boxes to insert and delete entire columns or rows. In addition, the Insert and Delete commands are available on the shortcut menu that appears when you select a cell, column, or row and click the right mouse button while pointing to the cell.

Moving and Copying Cells

After you select the contents of a cell, you can move or copy the contents to another cell using the drag-and-drop techniques. As an alternative, you can use the Cut, Copy, and Paste buttons on the Standard toolbar or the commands on the Edit menu. The Cut, Copy, and Paste commands are also available on the shortcut menu that appears when you select the contents of a cell and then click the right mouse button.

When you select only the contents of a cell without selecting the end-of-cell marker and then you move or copy the contents to a different cell, the contents of the destination cell are not overwritten. When you select both the contents of a cell and the end-of-cell marker, the contents of the destination cell are overwritten.

To move or copy a cell's contents using drag and drop, follow these steps:

1 Select the information you want to move or copy. If you want the contents of the cell to replace the contents of the destination cell, you should also select the end-of-cell marker. The figure on the left shows the contents of a cell selected without the end-of-cell marker selected. At the top of the next page, the figure on the right shows what it looks like when both the contents of a cell and the end-of-cell marker are both selected.

The Basic Presentation

2 Position the mouse pointer over the selected information, hold down the left mouse button, and drag the information to the destination point in another cell. To copy rather than move the contents of a cell, hold down the Ctrl key as you drag the contents. The left figure below shows the result when only the contents are selected. The right figure shows the result when the end-of-cell marker is dragged to another cell, too—the moved or copied contents replace the contents in the destination cell.

Moving and Copying Columns and Rows

To move a column or row in a table, select the column or row and drag it between two other columns or rows. To copy a column or row in a table, simply hold down the Ctrl key as you drag the column or row. You can also move or copy multiple columns or rows by selecting all the columns or rows that you want to move before you drag.

When you select a row (or rows) to move or copy, you must be sure to select the end-of-row marker as well; otherwise, the contents of the moved or copied row will overwrite the contents of the destination row. In addition, when you move or copy a row (or rows), you must drag the row to the beginning of the first cell in the destination row. If you don't, the contents of the moved or copied row will be added to the destination row, overwriting its contents. Figure 8-8 shows a second set of rows created by copying the first set.

FIGURE 8-8.
The second set of
rows was copied from
the first set.

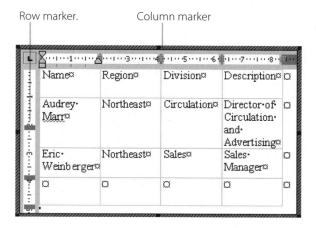

Changing Column Width and Row Height

To decrease or increase the width of a column in a table, drag the
dotted column border at the right side of the column to the left or
right, respectively. You can also drag the column markers on the
table's horizontal ruler, shown in Figure 8-9, to the left or right to
change the width of a column. When you reduce the width of a
column so that some of the text no longer fits within the width of the
column's cells, the extra text in each cell wraps to a second line.

FIGURE 8-9.
The column and row
markers on the table
rulers.

Row marker.   Column marker

To decrease or increase the heights of rows in a table, drag the
corresponding row markers on the table's vertical ruler up or down,
respectively. As shown in Figure 8-9, the row marker for a row aligns
with the bottom of the row. Changing the heights of rows is especially
important because the default row height is determined by the number of rows in the table and the amount of space allotted for the

table. Thus, the fewer the rows, the taller they must be. You may prefer shorter row heights that better fit the text height.

To change column widths and row heights in a table, you can also use the Cell Height And Width command on the Table menu.

To change the column width of one or more columns using the Cell Height And Width command, follow these steps:

1 Select as many columns as you want to modify.

2 Choose Cell Height And Width from the Table menu.

3 On the Column tab of the Cell Height And Width dialog box, enter a new width in the Width Of Column edit box by typing directly in the edit box or by using the up and down arrows on the right side of the edit box. Then click OK.

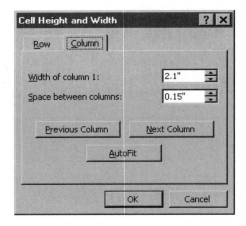

You can also use the Space Between Columns option on the Column tab to add a little breathing room to a crowded table. Or click the AutoFit button to set the width of each selected column to fit the longest text entry in the column. If you want to change the width of individual columns, click the Previous Column or Next Column button until the number of the column you want to change is displayed in the Width Of Column option. Then enter a new width in the Width Of Column edit box and click OK.

To change the row height of onr or more rows using the Cell Height And Width command, follow these steps:

1   Select as many rows as you want to modify.

2   Choose Cell Height And Width from the Table menu or from the shortcut menu.

3   On the Row tab of the Cell Height And Width dialog box, click the arrow on the right side of the Height Of Rows edit box to display a drop-down list of options.

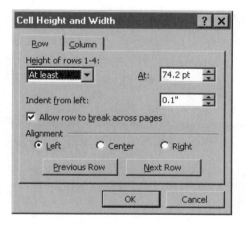

- Select the Auto option to set the row height to the height of the tallest cell in the row.

- Select the At Least option to set a minimum row height. When you select At Least, the row becomes taller if the contents of the cells are taller than the row height.

- Select Exactly to set an exact row height. Any text that does not fit in the cells at the exact row height is cut off. Note that when you select the At Least or Exactly options, you can enter a point size in the At edit box to specify a particular row height.

You can also use the Indent From Left setting on the Row tab to indent the row from the left side of the table. In addition, you can select Left, Center, or Right to specify the Alignment of the row. The Allow Row To Break Across Pages option lets you determine whether

The Basic Presentation

the contents of the row are split at an automatic page break or whether the entire row is moved to the following page. To format the previous or next row, click the Previous Row or Next Row button.

Dragging the column and row markers to change column widths and row heights is usually the easiest way to go, but you may want to select the entire table by clicking any cell and choosing Select Table from the Table menu. Then use the Cell Height And Width dialog box to set all the columns or rows to a uniform width or height, respectively.

Merging and Splitting Cells

To create one cell that spans two or more cells, you can merge adjacent cells. As shown in Figure 8-10, merging cells allows you to enter a column heading in one large cell that occupies the same width as several smaller cells below.

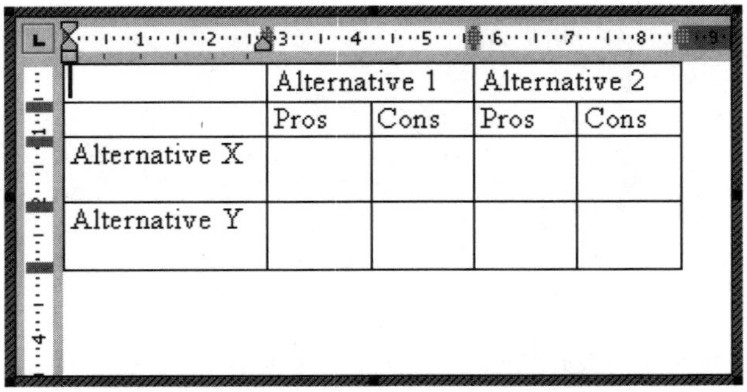

	Alternative 1		Alternative 2	
	Pros	Cons	Pros	Cons
Alternative X				
Alternative Y				

FIGURE 8-10.
The cells in row 1 of columns 2 and 3 and columns 4 and 5 have been merged to accommodate the column headings.

To merge two or more cells, simply select the cells, and then choose Merge Cells from the Table menu. Even when two or more cells have been merged, they retain their separate identities so that you can always select the merged cell and choose Split Cells from the Table menu to return to the original grouping of individual cells.

Formatting the Table

After you enter the contents of the table and make any necessary structural changes, you can turn your attention to the overall appearance of the table. By default, PowerPoint uses the current presentation template to format elements of the table such as text font and color. You can change the formatting of table text by using the same methods that you use to change the formatting of text elsewhere in PowerPoint. Simply select the text, and then use the buttons on the Formatting toolbar or the commands on the Format and shortcut menus.

In addition to the text, however, there are other elements that you should consider when you format a table, such as borders and shading. These elements are discussed in the next section.

Adding Borders and Shading with Table AutoFormats

The dotted gridlines that depict the boundaries of table cells on the screen do not appear when you view the completed table on the slide, so you must add borders to make the gridlines visible. You can also add shading to certain cells to give them a little emphasis.

PowerPoint provides both a Tables And Borders toolbar and a Borders And Shading command on the Format menu, but the easiest way to add borders and shading is to use one of the table autoformats. Each table autoformat offers its own combination of cell borders, cell shading, fonts, and color selections. In addition, while applying a table autoformat, you can automatically size the table so that its columns and rows fit the contents of the cells perfectly.

To apply a table autoformat, follow these steps:

1   Click anywhere in the table.

2   From the Table menu or the shortcut menu, choose Table AutoFormat. Be careful not to choose the AutoFormat command from the Format menu by mistake.

3 In the Table AutoFormat dialog box, select a format from the Formats list, and view the result in the Preview box.

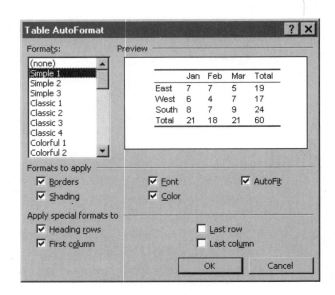

As you click each option, the sample table in the Preview box changes to reflect your selections.

4 To format specific elements in your table, select any or all of the options in the Formats To Apply section.

Option	Effect
Borders	Applies the cell borders shown in the preview.
Shading	Applies the shading shown in the preview.
Font	Applies the fonts shown in the preview. Leave Font unselected to use a font that matches your presentation font.
Color	Applies the colors shown in the preview. Leave Color unselected to use shades of gray.
AutoFit	Automatically sizes columns and rows to fit the largest entry.

5 To add special formatting to other table elements, select any or all of the options in the Apply Special Formats To section. Again, as you select options, the sample table in the Preview box changes to reflect your selections. Depending on the options you select, the special formatting may be shading, a bold font, a wider column, or special cell borders.

Option	Effect
Heading Rows	Applies a special format to the heading rows of the table.
First Column	Applies a special format to the first column of the table.
Last Row	Applies a special format to the last row of the table.
Last Column	Applies a special format to the last column of the table.

6 Click OK to implement the table autoformat you have selected. The table below is formatted using the Simple 3 table autoformat.

Circulation and Sales Staff

Name	Region	Division	Description
Audrey Marr	Northeast	Circulation	Director of Circulation and Advertising
Eric Weinberger	Northeast	Sales	Sales Manager

TIP

To undo a table autoformat, choose Undo Auto Format from the Edit menu or press Ctrl+Z. You can also choose Table AutoFormat from the Table menu, and then select [none] in the Formats list.

The Basic Presentation

Adding Custom Borders and Shading

Rather than use a table autoformat to apply a preset combination of borders and shading, you can add borders and shading to table cells by using the Borders And Shading command on the Format menu or the Tables And Borders toolbar, which offers everything you get with the Borders And Shading command, plus additional options.

The Tables and Borders button

The Draw Table button

The Eraser button

The Shading Color button

To use the Tables And Borders toolbar, click the Tables And Borders button, which appears on the Standard toolbar when you are working on a table. On the Tables And Borders toolbar, you can choose a line style, line weight, and border color and then click the Draw Table button and either draw new lines or draw over existing lines to change their appearance. Use the Eraser button to remove existing table lines. You can also select individual cells or groups of cells and apply borders and shading from the pull-down palettes on the Borders And Shading toolbar. For example, to choose a shade of gray to fill the cells of a column, you select the cells, click the down arrow next to the Shading Color button on the Tables And Borders toolbar, place the mouse pointer on a gray shade and pause to see the shade's name. Figure 8-11 shows a 20% gray shade applied to one column.

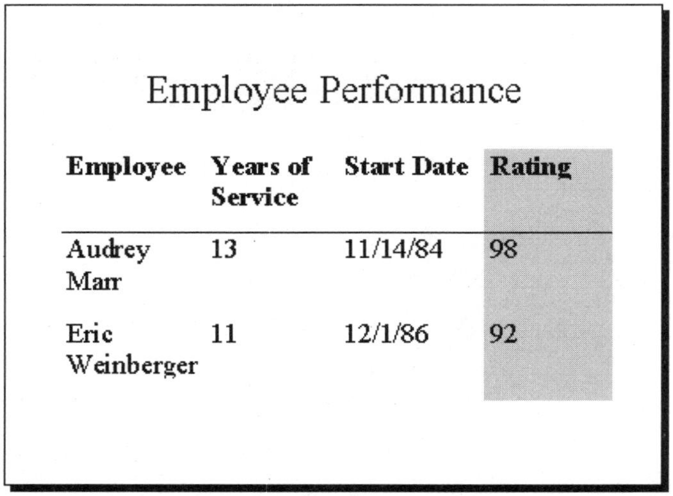

FIGURE 8-11.

The rightmost column has been formatted with the Gray-20% shade.

Employee Performance

Employee	Years of Service	Start Date	Rating
Audrey Marr	13	11/14/84	98
Eric Weinberger	11	12/1/86	92

When you use the Borders And Shading command rather than the Tables And Borders toolbar, you can select a color for the borders as well as a pattern Style and Color for the shading. Simply select the cells you want to format, and then choose Borders And Shading from the Format menu. Next, click the Borders tab of the Borders And Shading dialog box to set the borders of the selected cells, or click the Shading tab to set the shading of the selected cells. Figure 8-12 shows the Borders tab (top) and the Shading tab (bottom).

FIGURE 8-12.

The Borders and Shading tabs of the Borders And Shading dialog box.

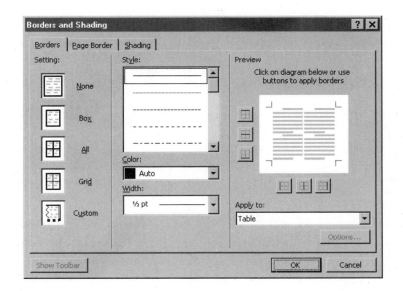

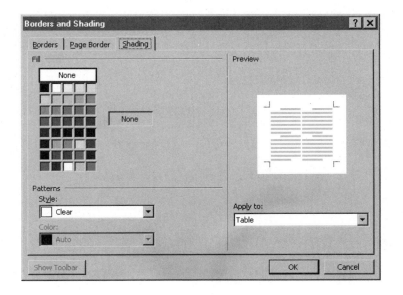

On the Borders tab, you can select a line style, color, and width and then click specific borders on the Preview diagram. Rather than click specific borders, you can also choose a setting from the left side of the Borders And Shading dialog box to select a combination of borders. Choosing Box will add a border to the outside of the selected cells, Grid will add a border around each individual cell in the selection, and All adds borders everywhere. To remove a specific border, simply click the border in the Preview section.

When you click the Shading tab of the Cell Borders And Shading dialog box, you can select a Fill color and a pattern Style and Color. The selections you make are then displayed in the Preview box. The Fill can be a solid color, a shade of a certain percentage, or a pattern. To see just the background color, select None.

After you select a border, shading, or both, click OK to apply the border and shading to the selected cells.

Distributing Columns and Rows Evenly

Distribute Rows
Evenly button

Distribute Columns
Evenly button

A new feature on the Tables And Borders toolbar lets you distribute columns or rows evenly. In other words, you can quickly and easily make them all the same width within a certain space. To distribute a number of columns or rows, position the rightmost edge of the rightmost column or the bottom edge of the bottom row, select the columns or rows to distribute and then click the Distribute Rows Evenly or Distribute Columns Evenly button.

 TIP

You can also select and distribute evenly certain cells in a column or row.

Working with the Table Data

When the table you need to create is complex, you might be better off dragging in and dropping a table you've created in Excel. But PowerPoint can now perform some Excel-like tasks, such as summing a column of numbers or sorting a table's rows.

Sorting and Summing Data in Tables

New to this version of PowerPoint is the ability to sort and sum the information in a table. To sort a table, select a cell in the column or row upon which you want to sort the table and then, select Sort from the Tables menu. The Sort command allows you to sort informationa in the table by one or more columns or rows.

To sum a column or row, click in a blank cell at the bottom of a column or at the end of a row, and then click the AutoSum button on the Tables And Borders toolbar.

Performing Advanced Calculations

In addition to sorting and summing data, PowerPoint also inherits from the newest version of Word the ability to calculate formulas in tables just as a spreadsheet can. To perform a calculation, click in an empty cell below or to the right of the numbers you want to work with. Then from the Table menu, choose Formula. In the Formula dialog box, you may see a proposed formula, such as =SUM(ABOVE). To enter a different formula, erase the proposed formula, type an equal sign (=), click the Paste function list box, and choose a function from the list. This pastes a function into the Formula area on the Formula dialog box. To complete the formula, you must enter the cell references, the cells upon which the function will operate, between the parentheses. Just like in Excel, table cell references are a combination of a column letter and row number. The first cell at the upper left corner of the table is A1, for example. A range of cells is referenced the same way it is referenced in Excel: first cell, colon, last cell. To obtain the maximum value of cells in column B, the formula might be =MAX(B1:B5). To reference specific cells, list them separated by commas. Table 8-2, on the next page, lists the available functions you can use in tables, and their results.

The Basic Presentation

⭐ **TIP**

To calculate all the cells in a row or column, enter just the column letter or row number as the beginning and ending cell references. For example, to total the cells in column B, you'd enter =SUM(B:B).

Table 8-2. The Formula Functions and Their Results

Function	Result
ABS(x)	The positive value of a number or formula, regardless of its actual positive or negative value.
AND(x,y)	The value 1 if the logical expressions x and y are both true, or the value 0 (zero) if either expression is false.
AVERAGE( )	The average of a list of values.
COUNT( )	The number of items in a list.
DEFINED(x)	The value 1 (true) if the expression x is valid, or the value 0 (false) if the expression cannot be computed.
FALSE	0 (zero).
IF(x,y,z)	The result y if the conditional expression x is true, or the result z if the conditional expression is false. Note that y and z (usually 1 and 0 (zero)) can be either any numeric value or the words "True" and "False."
INT(x)	The numbers to the left of the decimal place in the value or formula x.
MIN( )	The smallest value in a list.
MAX( )	The largest value in a list.
MOD(x,y)	The remainder that results from dividing the value x by the value y a whole number of times.
NOT(x)	The value 0 (zero) (false) if the logical expression x is true, or the value 1 (true) if the expression is false.
OR(x,y)	The value 1 (true) if either or both logical expressions x and y are true, or the value 0 (zero) (false) if both expressions are false.
PRODUCT( )	The result of multiplying a list of values. For example, the function { = PRODUCT (1,3,7,9) } returns the value 189.
ROUND(x,y)	The value of x rounded to the specified number of decimal places y; x can be either a number or the result of a formula.
SIGN(x)	The value 1 if x is a positive value, or the value −1 if x is a negative value.
SUM( )	The sum of a list of values or formulas.
TRUE	1.

Finally, to choose a number format for the result of a calculation, click the Number format drop-down list in the Formula dialog box and select a number format. Click OK to insert the formula into the cell. To update the formula, click the formula and then press the F9 key.

NOTE

Formulas in cells reside within fields. To revise the formula in a cell, right-click the cell and choose Toggle Field Codes from the shortcut menu. Now you can edit the formula. Choose Toggle Field Codes again to switch back to the formula's result.

Now that you've learned how to create table slides and add them to a presentation, you know how to work with all the basic presentation building blocks. In Part 3, you'll learn how to make overall changes to the presentation and how to add enhancements to strengthen its powers of communication.

II

The Basic Presentation

PART III

Modifying the Presentation

CHAPTER 9

Making Overall Changes

As you've seen, PowerPoint offers a sophisticated system for creating an entire presentation's worth of slides that share a common design. This chapter focuses on the central controls behind the presentation design process: the template, the color scheme, and the title master and slide master. You can use these controls to make overall changes to your presentation, such as redesigning the background or applying a different combination of colors to all the slides. The following list describes the elements that are managed by each of the three controls:

- The template contains a color scheme, a title master and slide master, and a set of autolayouts that control where objects are positioned on slides.

- The color scheme contains a background color and seven other colors that are applied to particular elements in the presentation.

- The title master and slide master contain a background design and default text formatting for the slide titles and main text items. The background design can contain graphic objects or can be shaded, patterned, or textured. The default text formatting is applied to the slide titles and the bulleted text items.

What is so powerful—and potentially confusing—about these controls is the way they overlap. When you alter the title master or slide master, for example, you can change the current color scheme, which can change the background color. To make things even more interesting, you can also change the background color directly, without changing the color scheme. To help you understand how these controls interact, this chapter first looks at the big picture. It begins with a discussion of the controls that have the broadest influence on a presentation and then goes on to cover the controls that affect a single aspect of a slide.

Applying a Different Template

The easiest—and most sweeping—step you can take when you want to change the appearance of a presentation is to apply a different template. Changing the template makes a wholesale change to just about every aspect of the presentation's appearance. Figure 9-1, on the facing page, shows a basic presentation, both before (top) and after (bottom) the Contemporary Portrait template is applied.

The template is the most powerful and far-reaching of the central controls. Among other things, changing the template:

- Changes the color scheme that controls the colors used in the presentation
- Changes the title master and slide master, which in turn changes the background design and default text formatting

The templates that come with PowerPoint were created by professional artists so they produce polished, attractive presentations. Therefore, you may not need to make further changes to the appearance of the presentation after you apply a template.

FIGURE 9-1.

A basic presentation slide before (top) and after (bottom) the Contemporary Portrait template is applied.

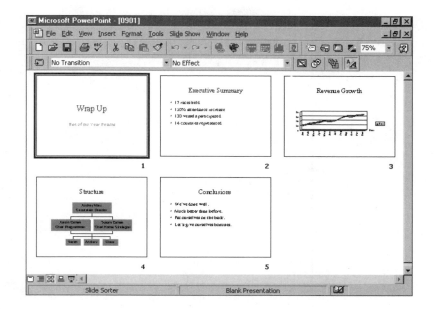

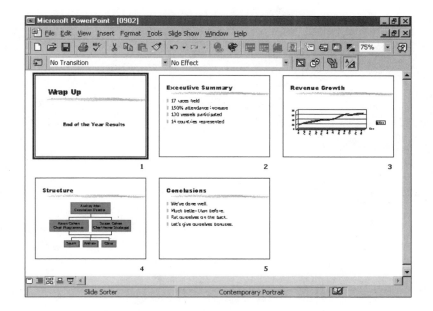

Other Ways to Change the Design

By changing the template, you can give your presentation an entirely new look: All the slides in the presentation get the same new background and new color scheme, and even a new selection of text fonts. But you can control each of these design aspects individually without having to apply a new template. You can even make design changes on selected slides, leaving the other slides to conform to the template's design. Some of the overall changes you can make without changing the template are:

- Decorating the background with a company logo or project name

- Adding special text to the background that spells out the presentation's subject

- Modifying the presentation colors to match a client's corporate color palette

- Changing the font and text formatting used in slide titles to give the presentation a more playful or more serious character

If someone else has created a unique new presentation design, he or she may have saved it in a template that you can use. When you apply the custom template to your presentation, you get the same special presentation design. Often, the chief PowerPoint user in an organization will create a template you can use to conform to the company look. In fact, the design guru may have changed the characteristics of the default template so that each new presentation you create gets the standard, approved presentation design automatically.

TIP

How to Check the Name of the Current Template
To find out which template is applied to the current presentation, check the status bar at the bottom of the PowerPoint window. The template name appears just to the right of the slide number.

Selecting an Existing Template

When you create a new presentation using the AutoContent Wizard, a template is attached to the presentation. To select a template by name as you start a new presentation, click the Presentation Designs tab of the New Presentation dialog box, and then select a template.

To change the template for an existing presentation, follow these three steps:

1   Click the Apply Design button on the Standard toolbar.

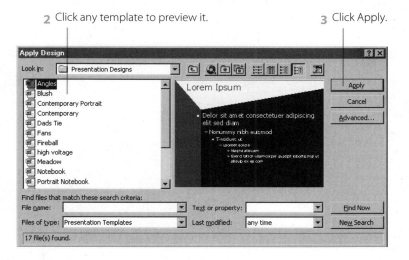

2 Click any template to preview it.   **3** Click Apply.

The new template reformats every slide in the presentation.

If you've never changed a template before, you can get some practice by creating a simple presentation. (You can use the AutoContent Wizard to quickly generate a multipage dummy presentation.) You can then click Apply Design and select a template name from the Apply Design dialog box. Notice the different effects that are created when you apply different templates.

TIP

How to Search for a Template
You can search for a particular template by entering text into any of the four text boxes at the bottom of the Apply Design dialog box and clicking the Find Now button. Clicking the Advanced button leads to a more detailed search.

III

Modifying the Presentation

Creating a New Template

To create a custom look for future presentations, you can create your own template based on the changes you've made to a presentation's color scheme and its title and slide masters. (Later in this chapter, you'll learn how to change the color scheme and the title and slide masters.) It's not a bad idea to model your template on an existing one. When you apply the template, the color scheme, background items, and text formatting will be the same as those you've used in the presentation.

To create a template, follow these steps:

1   Open or create a presentation that you want to use as the basis for a template.

2   Make any changes to the presentation that you want to save in the new template.

 NOTE

All the existing text, clip art, and links will be saved in the template unless you remove them now.

3   From the File menu, choose Save As.

4   Locate the folder in which you want to save the template.

5   In the Save As type box, select Presentation Templates.

6   In the File name edit box, type a name for the template, and then click Save.

Changing the Color Scheme

Every template you apply contains a color scheme that provides the various parts of a presentation with a coordinated set of eight default colors. The most distinctive part of the presentation is the background, so the first color in the color scheme is the background color. The other seven colors tastefully match the background color and are applied to text, charts, and other objects that appear against the background. Whenever you choose a command that allows you to change the color of an object, such as the Font command, you can display the default color scheme by clicking the arrow at the right end of the Color box. Figure 9-2 shows the default color scheme displayed in the Font dialog box.

FIGURE 9-2.

The default color scheme in the Font dialog box.

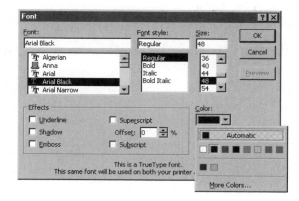

Changing the colors of the color scheme without making additional changes to the presentation can be enough to dramatically transform the look. When you modify the color scheme, you can apply the revised scheme to the entire presentation (by clicking the Apply To All button) or to the current slide only (by clicking the Apply button). If you apply the color scheme to all the slides in a presentation, the new colors are applied to every object in the presentation as well. The only exceptions are objects to which you have assigned specific colors. For example, if you have selected a special color for certain words in a slide title, that color remains even when you change the overall color scheme.

SEE ALSO

For more information about transferring color schemes, see "Copying Color Schemes Among Slides," page 311.

As always, you can save a modified color scheme for future use. After you've carefully matched your organization's standard colors, for example, you can save the color scheme in a template and distribute the template to coworkers. That way, every presentation delivered by a representative of your organization can have the uniform look you desire. In addition, if you've modified the color scheme for one presentation, you can copy the color scheme directly to another.

PowerPoint also allows you to use a different color scheme for speaker's notes and handouts by revising the color schemes of their masters. The revised color schemes of the notes and handouts have no effect on the overall color scheme applied to the presentation.

III

Modifying the Presentation

NOTE

You cannot save a color scheme in its own file. A color scheme is always part of a template, so you must save the template with a new name in order to save the revised color scheme.

Selecting a Standard Color Scheme

The easiest way to change the color scheme of a presentation is to select one of PowerPoint's standard color schemes, which were created by professional artists.

TIP

If you create a custom color scheme you should click the Add As Standard Scheme button on the Custom tab of the Color Scheme dialog box to add your custom scheme to the list. That way, you can always return to use the custom color scheme by simply selecting it on the Standard tab.

To select a predefined color scheme, follow these steps:

1   Open the presentation whose color scheme you want to modify.

2   Choose Slide Color Scheme from the Format menu.

3 Click a different color scheme.

4 Click Apply to All to apply to every slide or Apply to apply to the current slide.

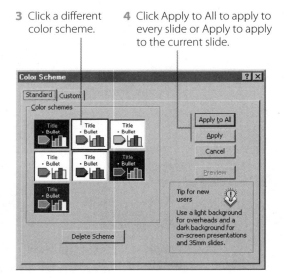

You may need to drag the Color Scheme dialog box to one side to preview the presentation.

> If you previously applied a color to a specific element in your presentation, that element will not be affected by the new color scheme.

Creating a Custom Color Scheme

Occasionally, the standard color schemes won't quite work for your presentation. You might want to vary the brightness or the shade of one or more colors, or you might want to select a different set of colors entirely. If this is the case, you can create a custom color scheme. You'll probably want to first select a template for your presentation that has a color scheme similar to the one you want to create.

To create a custom color scheme, follow these steps:

1 Click the Open button or choose Open from the File menu, and open an existing presentation.

2 Choose Slide Color Scheme from the Format menu or the shortcut menu to display the Color Scheme dialog box, and then click the Custom tab, shown below. (See Table 9-1 on the next page for more information about the eight scheme colors listed in the Color Scheme dialog box.)

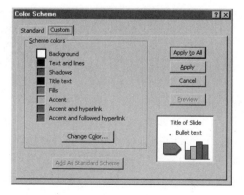

TABLE 9-1.   The eight color boxes in the Color Scheme dialog box.

Color Box	Description
Background	The color applied to the background of the slides. The background color can be shaded in a template from light to dark or dark to light, and, on selected slides, it can be superseded by a different background color that you select.
Text And Lines	The color applied to bulleted text and to text blocks typed onto the slides with the Text Tool. Also used for lines and arrows drawn with the Line Tool and as the outline color for autoshapes and objects drawn with the other drawing tools.
Shadows	The color applied to shadows created with the Shadow command.
Title Text	The color applied to slide titles and subtitles.
Fills	The color used to fill autoshapes and objects drawn with any drawing tool. Also the color used to fill the first series in a graph.
Accent	The color used as a second color in graphs, org charts, and other added elements.
Accent And Hyperlink	The color used as a third color in graphs, org charts, and other added elements. Also used for hyperlinks (jumps to other slides, presentations, or Internet addresses on pages).
Accent And Followed Hyperlink	The color used as a fourth color in graphs, org charts, and other added elements. Also used for hyperlinks that have already been used on pages.

3   To change one of the eight scheme colors, double-click the corresponding box, or click the box once and then click Change Color. For example, to change the fill color, double-click the Fills box to open the Fill Color dialog box, then click the Standard tab, as shown at the top of the facing page. The Fill Color dialog displays dozens of colors and several shades of gray from which you can select a new color. (Note that the current color's pane is highlighted.)

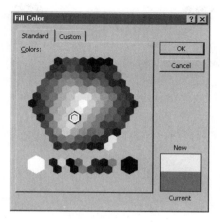

4 Select a color by clicking its pane, and then click OK. If you
don't see the color you want, click the Custom tab shown here:

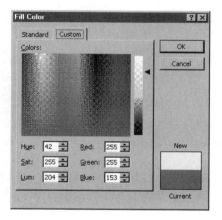

You can use the two controls in the upper part of the Custom
tab to select a color. The large box has a cross hair that identifies
the general color (the hue) and the intensity of the hue (the
saturation level) when you drag it across the box. The vertical
strip to the right of the box has a triangular marker that indicates
how much black or white is mixed with the color (the luminance of the color) when you drag it up or down the strip. Two
color boxes in the lower right corner show the new color and
the currently selected color. The remaining boxes contain

numeric values for the hue, saturation, and luminance (HSL) and for the red, green, and blue (RGB) of the color. You can use the HSL and RGB numbers to specify an exact color. For example, you can record the numbers of a color you like in one color scheme and then enter the numbers in another color scheme to reproduce the same color. (You can enter either the three HSL numbers or the three RGB numbers—you don't need both sets.)

5 On the Custom tab, drag the cross hair in the large box to the general color you want, and then drag the marker on the vertical strip to brighten or darken the color. Check the New Color box in the lower right corner of the tab to see the new color, or click Preview to see how the new color will appear in the presentation. (You may need to drag the Color Scheme dialog box to one side to preview the presentation.)

6 When you're satisfied with the new color, click OK to return to the Color Scheme dialog box.

7 Follow steps 3 through 6 to change any of the other Scheme Colors. Then click Apply To All to apply the color scheme to the entire presentation, or click Apply to apply the scheme to the current slide only.

After you create a custom color scheme, you may want to add it to the presentation as a standard scheme. That way, if you change one or more slides to another color scheme, you can always return the slides to the custom color scheme you created.

To add a custom color scheme as a standard scheme, follow these steps:

1 Choose Slide Color Scheme from the Format menu or the shortcut menu to display the Color Scheme dialog box, and then click the Custom tab. The custom color scheme appears on the tab.

2 Click Add As Standard Scheme. PowerPoint copies the custom color scheme to the Standard tab.

PowerPoint's Color System

Although PowerPoint provides a broad palette of colors from which to choose, it does not follow the commonly used color matching systems for selecting and specifying colors, such as the Pantone system or the Trumatch system. To match a color, such as the dominant color in your company's logo, you must go through the trial-and-error process of selecting a color, sending it to your color output device, examining the output, and then adjusting the color in PowerPoint. The process can be time-consuming because most output devices produce colors that are lighter or darker than they appear on your screen. In addition, the number of colors you see on the screen and the precision with which they are displayed depend on the color capabilities of your hardware. Even the brightness control on your monitor affects how a color looks. When you do find the correct color, you might want to make note of its HSL or RGB number so that you can reproduce it later.

Editing the Title Master or Slide Master

In addition to the color scheme, the title master and the slide master are the other elements you can modify in a presentation. Changes you make to the Title Master affect only the slides that you add with the Title autolayout; changes you make to the Slide Master affect all the other slides in a presentation. Both masters contain:

- A background color that can be shaded

- A scheme of fonts and text formatting for the slide titles and bulleted text

- An optional group of graphic objects placed on the background and arranged to form a design

The Title Master and Slide Master give the presentation an overall look by providing the background and the design of the text, as well as saving you the tedium of having to format each slide individually. This section discusses how to open the Title Master and Slide Master and how to customize their background color and shading, title and text, and background design.

III

Modifying the Presentation

Opening the Title Master or Slide Master

Before you can actually edit the Title Master or Slide Master, you must display it on your screen.

To display the Title Master shown in Figure 9-3, first make sure that a title slide is displayed. (To determine whether the slide you are in is a title slide, click the Slide Layout button on the Standard toolbar to see which layout is selected. Click cancel to return to your slide.) Then hold down the Shift key, and click the Slide View button at the bottom left of your screen. You can also choose Master and then Title Master from the View menu.

FIGURE 9-3.

The Title Master.

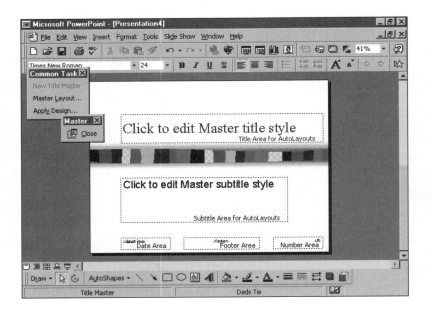

To display the Slide Master shown in Figure 9-4 on the next page, first make sure that a slide other than the title slide is displayed. (If you're unsure, click the Slide Layout button and check which layout is selected, and then click Cancel.) Then, you can use one of these two methods:

- Choose Master and then Slide Master from the View menu.

- Hold down the Shift key and click the Slide View button.

FIGURE 9-4.

The Slide Master.

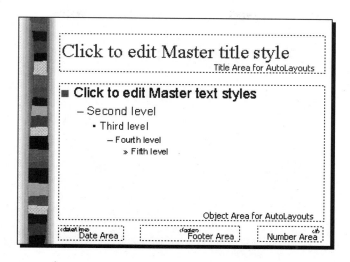

As you can see, the Title Master or the Slide Master temporarily takes over the screen. A new Master toolbar also appears containing two buttons—a Slide Miniature icon button to display a small version of the slide, and a Close text button to close the master and toolbar..

Altering the Custom Background

Although the color scheme supplies a background color for a presentation, you can modify the background color when you change the slide background for the master. Modifying the background color on a master is just like modifying the background color in the color scheme. In fact, when you return to the Color Scheme dialog box, you'll see the background color you applied in the master.

In addition to the color, you can also make other changes to the master's background. For instance, you can set a shading for the background color and then lighten or darken the shading.

To make changes to the master's background, choose the Background command from the Format menu or the shortcut menu. (Remember, the master must be displayed on your screen before you choose the command.) The Background dialog box appears, as shown in Figure 9-5 on the next page. You use the controls in the drop-down list of the Background dialog box to change the appearance of the background, including its shading, pattern, and texture. If you'd like, you can even insert a picture for a "watermark" effect. The current background appears in the drop-down list. To return to a background color that complements the color scheme, select Automatic or one of the eight colors that appear in the drop-down list.

FIGURE 9-5.

The Background dialog box.

Click here to apply the settings to both the title master and the slide master.

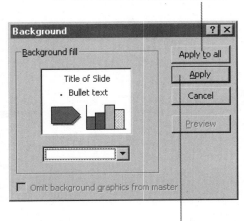

Click here to apply the settings to the current master only.

 TIP

You can click the Preview button in the Background dialog box to preview the new background. After you click Preview, you may need to drag the dialog box aside to see the background. If you're not satisfied with the background shading, the Background dialog box is still on the screen, so you can select a different setting.

Applying Shading

You can shade the background of a Title Master or Slide Master using one color, two colors, or a preset color scheme. Shading can make the presentation look like it has been lighted from one side. To apply shading to the background, first select Fill Effects from the drop-down list in the Background dialog box.

To select a different background color altogether, first select the One Color, Two Color, or Preset option on the Gradient tab of the Fill

Effects dialog box. Then use the drop-down lists to select a color or preset color scheme. You can also select More Colors to specify a different color using the techniques described earlier for selecting a standard or custom color scheme. If you are using just one color, try using the scroll bar under the Color drop-down list to vary the intensity of the shading.

Now you are ready to select a Shading Styles option and one of its variants—just click the options you want. For example, to create a background shade that runs vertically from dark to light, click Vertical as the shading style and then click the variant that shows a transition from dark to light. Other variants allow you to shade the background from light to dark, from light to dark to light, or from dark to light to dark. You get the idea.

Applying a Pattern

Rather than shade the background, you can apply a pattern made up of two colors. PowerPoint offers more than 35 patterns and many colors to choose from. To apply a pattern to the background, first select Fill Effects from the drop-down list in the Background dialog box, then select the Pattern tab.

The patterns shown are composed of the foreground and background colors displayed in the Foreground and Background boxes. You can select a different pattern and different foreground and background colors to create the combination you want.

Applying a Texture

Yet another way to change the background of the title master or slide master involves applying a texture. Applying a texture can change the overall "feel" of your presentation. You can choose from several textures, including medium wood, white marble, cork, and paper. To apply a texture to the background, first select Fill Effects from the drop-down list in the Background dialog box, and then click a texture on the Texture tab of the Fill Effects dialog box. Figure 9-6, shown on the following page, shows a slide that has been formatted with a textured background.

III

Modifying the Presentation

FIGURE 9-6.
A slide formatted with the Water droplets texture.

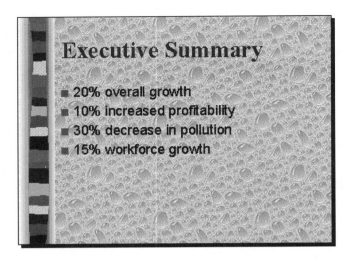

? SEE ALSO

For more information about inserting pictures, see Chapter 14,"Adding Multimedia," page 357.

Inserting a Picture

If you prefer, you can insert a picture into the background of either master. Select Fill Effects from the drop-down list in the Background dialog box and then click the Picture tab in the Fill Effects dialog box. Click the Select Picture button to choose a background picture. PowerPoint will scale the picture to fit the entire background area of the slide. Bright, bold pictures work well on title slides, such as the one in Figure 9-7. Because text will be displayed over the picture on other slides, you may want to choose something simple rather than complex. A muted version of the title slide picture often works well.

FIGURE 9-7.
A bright, bold picture works well on title slides. A muted version works well on the rest of the slides.

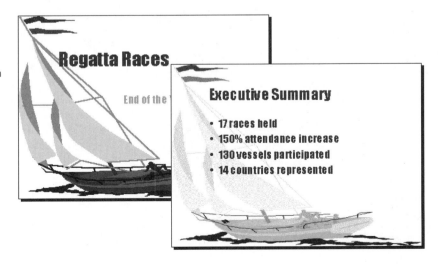

Formatting the Title Master or Slide Master

With the background set, you can turn your attention to the appearance of the text in the presentation.

Figure 9-8 shows the title master of the High Voltage template. As you can see, the title master displays text in five areas indicated by dashed boxes: The Title, Subtitle, Date, Footer, and Number areas contain sample text for you to format. When you change the formatting of the sample text on the title master, only the formatting on the title slide changes. To change the formatting on the remaining slides, you must change the formatting of the text of the slide master.

FIGURE 9-8.

The title master of the High Voltage template.

Click to edit Master title style

Click to edit Master subtitle style

As shown in Figure 9-9 on the next page, the slide master looks similar to the title master, but it contains an object area for autolayouts instead of a subtitle area. The object area for autolayouts holds sample text at each of the five bulleted text levels. When you change the formatting of the sample text on the slide master, the formatting of the text on every slide—except for the title slide—changes accordingly.

III

Modifying the Presentation

FIGURE 9-9.

The slide master of the High Voltage template.

The initial colors of the text in the title, subtitle, and object areas are determined by the colors of the color scheme. For example, the Title Text color of the color scheme sets the title area text color, and the Text And Lines color of the color scheme sets the object area and subtitle area text color. But changing the color of the sample text on the master overrides the color scheme. Even when you change the actual color scheme, the text colors on the Title Master or Slide Master are applied rather than the color scheme's text colors.

To change the appearance of the slide titles or subtitles, format the text in the title or subtitle area by selecting the text and then using buttons on the Formatting toolbar or commands on the Format or shortcut menus. To change the font and color of the title, for example, click the title to select it, click the right mouse button to display the shortcut menu, choose the Font command, and then select options in the Font dialog box. To change all instances of a particular font to another font, choose the Replace Fonts command from the Tools menu.

If you want to make uniform changes to all the bulleted text in a presentation, click the object area of the slide master to select all the bulleted text, and then use the text formatting commands.

To change the formatting of the bulleted text at only one of the indent levels, select the text at that level, and then make a formatting change. For example, to change the font used by bulleted text lines at the second level, select the text *Second Level,* as shown in Figure 9-10, and then use the text formatting commands. Similarly, to change the bullet used at the second level, select the second level text, choose Bullet from the Format menu, and then select a different bullet shape, color, and size from the Bullet dialog box.

FIGURE 9-10.
To change the formatting of the bulleted text at the second level, select the level, and then use the text formatting commands.

TIP

Although you can apply different formatting to the text at each level, you probably shouldn't deviate too much from the formatting of the first level. Otherwise, you might end up with a jumble of formatting. You might consider using the same font for each level, but make them distinctive by varying the size.

Creating a New Background or Modifying the Existing Background

You can create your own background design or modify an existing one by using PowerPoint's drawing tools to place graphic objects on the background of the title master or slide master. Professional artists can do wonders with simple drawing tools, creating entire scenes like those found in the templates that come with PowerPoint. If your

III

Modifying the Presentation

artistic skills are not strong, you might prefer to add a few simple geometric shapes to the background. A line or two, or a row of small shapes that you create with the AutoShape tool, can look quite nice.

Rather than compose a background design of your own, you can make minor modifications to the background objects in one of the templates. Simply by moving some of the existing objects, duplicating objects, or changing the objects' positions, you can create a new background design with a unique look. Figure 9-11 shows a slide with a floral graphic added to the Meadow template.

FIGURE 9-11.

A custom background design.

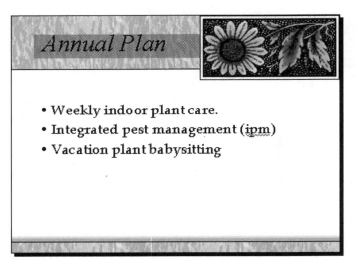

NOTE

Any graphic objects that are already a part of the title master or slide master have been grouped into a single object. You must select the group of objects and then use the Ungroup command on the Draw menu before you can work with the individual objects. You'll learn more about grouping and ungrouping objects in "Grouping Objects," page 348.

SEE ALSO

For more information about using PowerPoint's drawing tools, see Chapter 13, "Drawing Graphic Objects," page 325.

Text annotations, clip art, and scanned pictures saved as bitmapped files are other elements you can add to the background of the Title Master or Slide Master so that they appear on every slide. When you read about adding text annotations, clip art, and pictures to slides in Chapters 12 and 14, bear in mind that these elements can be added to the Title Master or Slide Master background as well.

Adding a Header or Footer

PowerPoint makes it easy to add three special text elements to the background of every slide: the date, the time, and the slide number. You can display these elements when you display the presentation in a slide show or print the presentation as slides, handouts, or notes pages. To add a header or footer to your presentation, choose Header And Footer from the View menu, and then click the Slide tab. The Header and Footer dialog box appears, as shown in Figure 9-12.

FIGURE 9-12.

The Header And Footer dialog box for a slide with the date, slide number, and some text in the footer.

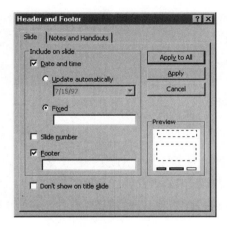

To add the date or time, select the Date and Time check box, and then select the Update Automatically option (to automatically update the date and time each time you display or print your presentation) or the Fixed option (to enter a fixed date). The format of the date and time is determined by the format you select in the corresponding drop-down list or the format you type in the edit box. The Preview window shows the placement of the options you select.

To add the slide number, select the Slide Number check box. You can also add some additional text to every slide by selecting the Footer check box and typing the text in the corresponding edit box. If you don't want the date, time, slide number, or footer text to appear on the title slide, be sure to select the Don't Show on Title Slide check box.

When you are satisfied with your choices, click Apply To All to apply the header or footer to the entire presentation, or click Apply to apply the header or footer to the current slide only.

III

Modifying the Presentation

If you want to add a header or footer to your notes or handouts, click the Notes And Handouts tab of the Header And Footer dialog box, and select the options you want. Then click Apply To All to apply the header or footer to the entire presentation.

You can position the date, time, slide number, and footer text anywhere on the slides. To reposition one of these elements, first open the Title Master or Slide Master and select the frame that contains the element you want to move. Then drag it to a new location.

You may want to use the date and time to keep track of versions while the presentation is in the draft stage, and then remove them when you're ready to display or print the final presentation. To remove the date and time, simply choose Header And Footer from the View menu, click the Slide tab, and deselect the Date And Time check box.

Inserting the Slide Number, Date, or Time on Selected Slides

If you want to add the date, time, or slide number on a selected slide, first move to the slide and then select the Text Box button on the Drawing toolbar. With the Text Box tool, draw a text box outside the title, subtitle, and object areas of the title master or slide master. Then choose the Date And Time command or the Slide Number command from the Insert menu. If you choose Date And Time, select a format in the Date And Time dialog box, figure 9-13.

FIGURE 9-13.
The Date And Time dialog box.

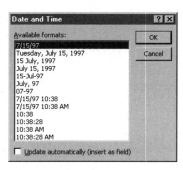

You can start slide numbering at a number other than 1 by choosing Page Setup from the File menu and then altering the number in the Number Slides from edit box. Changing the starting slide number is helpful when the presentation you're creating is a continuation of an earlier presentation.

Checking Your Presentation's Style

After you've made all the changes to your presentation, you may want to use PowerPoint's handy Style Checker to ensure consistency across all your slides. With the Style Checker, you can do a final check on the spelling in your presentation, make sure your slides are easy to read, and verify that the case of bulleted text and titles and their end punctuation are the same throughout.

To open the Style Checker, shown in Figure 9-14, choose Style Checker from the Tools menu.

FIGURE 9-14.
The Style Checker checks each slide for inconsistencies.

To start checking your presentation for inconsistencies, select the options you want to check, and then click Start. PowerPoint displays a dialog box for each error in the presentation, similar to the one shown in Figure 9-15.

FIGURE 9-15.
The Style Checker dialog box.

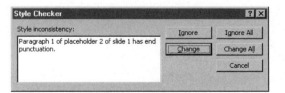

More often than not, the Style Checker's default settings for visual clarity, case, and end punctuation will work for most presentations. There are times, however, when you may want to change the settings.

III

Modifying the Presentation

For example, you may need to comply with an in-house style guide that determines how many bulleted items you can have on a slide or that dictates a period at the end of each bulleted item.

To change the Style Checker settings, open the Style Checker dialog box, and click Options. Then click the Case And End Punctuation tab of the Style Checker Options dialog box, as shown in Figure 9-16.

In the Case group, select from the drop-down lists how you want the titles and body text of your slides to appear. You can select sentence case, title case, uppercase, or lowercase. If you created a presentation with the Caps Lock key accidentally turned on, you can even ask the Style Checker to toggle the case in your presentation, changing uppercase to lower, and lowercase to upper. If you want the Style Checker to ignore case when reviewing your slides, remember to deselect the Slide Title Style and Body Text Style options.

FIGURE 9-16

The Case and End Punctuation tab of the Style Checker Options dialog box.

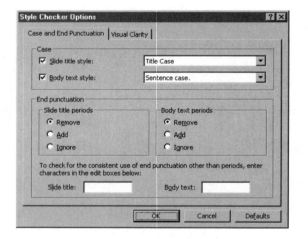

The End Punctuation group of the Case And End Punctuation tab lets you standardize the end punctuation for the titles and body text of your slides. You can ask the Style Checker to remove all end punctuation, add end punctuation, or ignore how your slides are punctuated. The default end punctuation is a period. If you want the Style Checker to use something else, such as a semicolon or a comma, enter the punctuation in the Slide Title and Body Text edit boxes.

With PowerPoint's flexible formatting, it's easy to apply several different fonts and font sizes to text in your presentation. If more than one person works on a presentation and each person has a different formatting style, the Style Checker can check the presentation for visual clarity. The Visual Clarity tab of the Style Checker Options dialog box, shown in Figure 9-17, lets you tell the Style Checker how you want the presentation to look, ensuring that it can be easily read.

The Fonts group of the Visual Clarity tab lets you set the maximum number of fonts within a presentation. You can also set the size of the font used for title text and for body text. The Legibility group defines the maximum number of bullets per slide and the maximum number of lines per title and per bullet. The Style Checker can also check to make sure that your text doesn't overrun the edges of the slide. If you don't want the Style Checker to check a particular option, simply deselect it.

FIGURE 9-17

The Visual Clarity tab of the Style Checker Options dialog box.

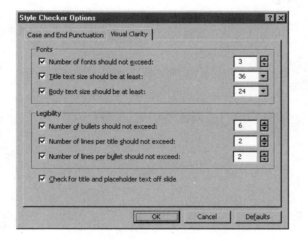

Once you've selected or modified all the options, click OK to return to the Style Checker dialog box. Then click Start, and the Style Checker is off and running!

The changes you have learned about in this chapter are broad in scope and affect an entire presentation. They allow you to govern the overall appearance of a presentation and to customize its look. In the next two chapters, you'll learn to make further modifications to a presentation by formatting graphs you've added and using Slide Sorter View to rearrange the presentation's slides.

III

Modifying the Presentation

Formatting Charts

When all you need is a standard-issue chart to get your message across, the basic steps of entering data and selecting a chart type or autoformat—covered in Chapter 6—are as far as you need to go. Microsoft Graph 97, the graphing module used by Microsoft PowerPoint, creates a professional-quality chart that vividly portrays your data and harmonizes with the design of your presentation.

But in many cases, the basic chart that PowerPoint produces is not sufficient. You want the chart to *communicate*—to accentuate a trend, de-emphasize an outcome, or call attention to a result. At times like these, creating the basic chart is only the first step. Formatting the chart to make it truly expressive is an equally important part of the process.

In this chapter, you'll learn how to emphasize patterns or trends in your charts in a variety of ways, including getting down to the nitty gritty of changing the appearance of the markers that represent numbers, and changing the structure and design of the chart axes. You'll also learn how to format the titles, legend, gridlines, and other parts of the chart to communicate your data more effectively.

Activating a Chart for Formatting

After you create a basic chart by following the steps in Chapter 6, the chart appears on a slide with the default formatting prescribed by its particular chart type. For example, a new pie chart has the default formatting for pie charts.

To activate the chart so that you can modify any aspect of its formatting, use one of these methods:

- Double-click the chart.

- Select the chart and press Enter. (Remember, you can cycle through the objects on a slide by pressing Tab.)

- Select the chart, choose Chart Object from the Edit menu, and then choose Edit from the submenu.

When you activate a chart, Graph's menus and Standard toolbar replace PowerPoint's menus and toolbars. The chart appears on a slide within a frame surrounded by handles, as shown in Figure 10-1. You haven't left PowerPoint, but you can now use any of Graph's Standard toolbar buttons to make changes to the entire chart. You learned about these buttons in Chapter 6, but they are shown in Figure 10-2, on the facing page, for review.

FIGURE 10-1.

An active chart on a slide.

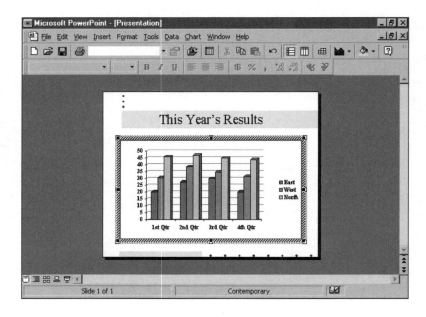

FIGURE 10-2.
The Formatting
toolbar.

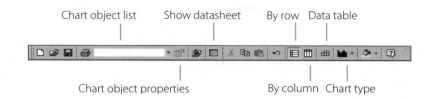

Chart object list   Show datasheet   By row   Data table

Chart object properties   By column   Chart type

Although it adds an unnecessary window to your screen, you can open Microsoft Graph so that its menus and its toolbar appear within a separate Graph window that overlays PowerPoint. (This is how Graph worked in previous versions of PowerPoint.) First select the chart, and choose Chart Object and then Open from the Edit menu. When you finish editing in Graph, choose Update from Graph's File menu, and then choose Exit And Return To *<Presentation>* from the File menu.

After you finish formatting the chart, click outside the gray frame to exit Graph and to redisplay PowerPoint's menus and toolbars.

TIP

To use the Zoom command on Graph's View menu, you must first select the chart in the PowerPoint window. Next, choose Chart Object and then choose Open from PowerPoint's Edit menu. Graph is loaded, and the Zoom command on Graph's View menu becomes available. You can also quickly zoom in on a chart in the PowerPoint window by using PowerPoint's Zoom Control box or Zoom command.

Selecting a Chart Object for Formatting

In addition to changing the entire chart, you can change individual components, called *chart objects*. To understand which chart objects you can change, you need to know a little about the anatomy of a chart. Figure 10-3, on the next page, shows a typical chart and its chart objects. Don't worry if you can't remember the names of all the chart objects right now. You'll have plenty of opportunity to become familiar with them as you read the sections of this chapter, which cover each chart object in depth.

III

Modifying the Presentation

To check the name of a chart object, place the mouse pointer on the object without clicking. The name appears in a ScreenTip.

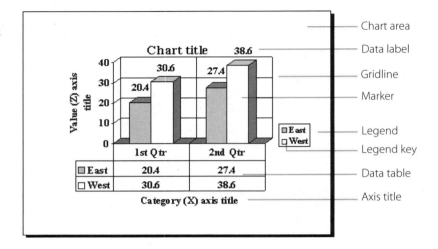

To change a chart object, double-click the object after you've activated the chart. A dialog box opens with formatting options for the selected object. You can double-click each object in the chart in succession, and make formatting changes in a series of dialog boxes. You can double-click and format the bars in a bar chart, for example, and then double-click and format the legend.

To use the keyboard to select a chart object, first press the Up or Down arrow key to move from one group of chart objects to the next. Then, to select an individual chart object from the group, such as one of the columns of a column series or one of the legend entries of the legend, press the Right or Left arrow key. After you select an object in this way, you can choose the first command on the Format menu (or press Ctrl+1) to display a dialog box with formatting options for the selected object. The name of the menu command changes depending on which chart object is selected. If you select an axis, for example, the command is Selected Axis. If you select a legend, the command is Selected Legend, and so on.

A third method for indicating which chart object you want to format is to point to the object and then click the right mouse button to open the shortcut menu. Select the Format command at the top of the shortcut menu to open a dialog box with formatting options for the corresponding object. Like the first command on the Format menu, the name of the Format command on the shortcut menu changes to reflect the chart object you've selected, such as Format Legend or Format Data Series.

⭐ **TIP**

How to Save a Chart Type for Future Use

When you have formatted as many chart objects as necessary to create a chart with the look you want, you can save the combination of formatted chart objects as a custom chart type. Then you can select the custom chart type to quickly apply its settings to all the chart objects in any new chart. For more information about saving a formatted chart as custom chart type, see "Saving Chart Formatting as a Custom Chart Type," page 297.

Basic Chart Formatting

Each chart object has its own special formatting options. This section, which covers basic formatting options for charts, assumes that you have already activated the chart and are ready to select a chart object for formatting.

Changing the Color of a Data Series

In a chart, a data series is represented by one or more markers: an area, a group of bars or columns, a line, the slices of a pie, the rings of a doughnut chart, the lines of a radar chart, or the groups of points in an XY (scatter) chart. The color of a data series is the color displayed by the markers of that series. These markers can also contain a pattern of another color or an image, such as a texture or picture.

The easiest way to change the color of a data series is to click the series and then use the Fill Color button on Graph's Standard toolbar. To select a different color, click the down arrow to the right of the Fill Color button, and then click a color in the palette of colors, as shown in the graphic on the next page.

III

Modifying the Presentation

Color palette

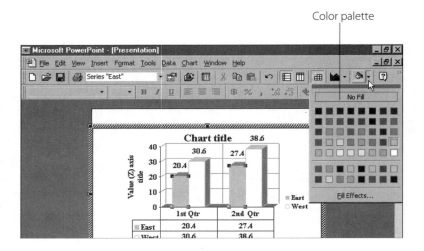

To select a pattern, texture, or picture, click the down arrow to the right of the Fill Color button on the Standard toolbar, and then click Fill Effects. Click one of the four tabs in the Fill Effects dialog box (Gradient, Texture, Pattern, or Picture), and then choose the settings you want.

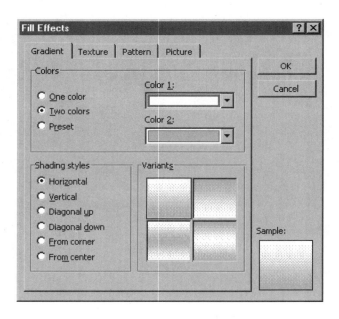

To select a color or pattern for the markers of a data series as well as a color for the border of the markers, you must use the Format Data Series dialog box instead. Follow these steps:

1 Double-click any of the markers in a data series to open the Format Data Series dialog box shown below.

The Format Data Series dialog box contains at least two tabs. The Patterns tab gives you options that change the patterns and colors of the series. The Data Labels tab lets you add numbers that show the numeric values of the data points. Other tabs that might appear in the dialog box provide advanced formatting options for types of charts that are covered later in this chapter.

2 Modify the border with these controls, or choose Automatic for a default border.

3 Modify the marker appearance with these controls.

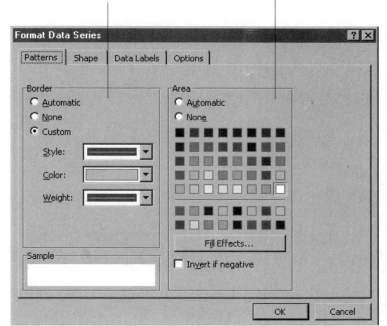

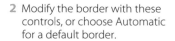

III

Modifying the Presentation

> **NOTE**
>
> If the series is represented by a line, the options in the Border section control the appearance of the line.

If, for example, you want to surround an area marker in an area chart with a white line and fill the area marker with dark blue, first double-click the marker. Then, in the Format Data Series dialog box, select white as the Color option in the Border section and dark blue as the color in the Area section, and click OK.

TIP

> When you change the color of a data series, be sure you select a color that properly contrasts with the background of the chart and with the colors of the other data series.

Adding and Formatting Titles

After you enter your data, the basic chart that PowerPoint draws displays no text other than the labels that mark increments along the axes and the text in the legend. Figure 10-4 shows a chart at this earliest stage. You may want to enter a title for each of the chart axes to identify what they measure. You may also want to add a title above the chart to describe the particular chart's purpose, especially if you've used the slide title to describe the slide in general rather than the specific chart.

FIGURE 10-4.
A basic chart without titles.

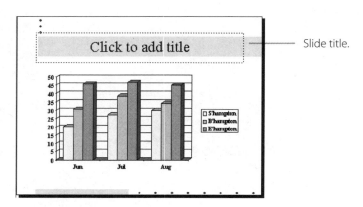

Click to add title

Slide title.

To remove a title, display the chart in Graph, select the title, and press delete, or click the right mouse button, and choose Clear from the shortcut menu. To replace a title, click the title, and then type the replacement text. To edit a title, click the title once, and then click an insertion point in the text. Edit the text as you would edit any text in PowerPoint. Press Esc or click elsewhere on the chart to complete the editing process.

Adding the Titles

To add titles for the chart and its axes, follow these steps:

1   With the chart activated, choose Chart Options from the Chart menu or the shortcut menu. Graph displays the Chart Options dialog box, shown below:

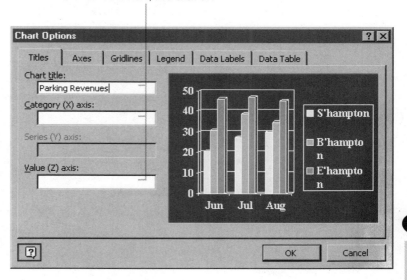

2 Enter titles here, and click OK.

After you add a title, you can reposition it on the chart by following the sequence of steps below:

1   Click the title. Graph displays the title's text box surrounded by handles, as shown on the next page.

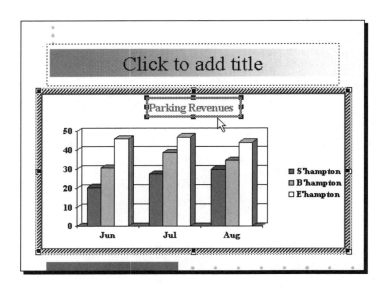

2 Place the pointer on the outline of the text box or on one of the handles, and drag to move the box.

Dragging the handles does not stretch the box, as you might expect. Instead, the entire box moves.

Formatting the Titles

The default formatting of the chart determines the formatting of the titles. However, you can select and format each title separately—making the chart title larger and the axis titles smaller, for example. You can format both the text of the title and the rectangle that contains the text. You must select and format each title separately.

To format both a title and its box, double-click the title or click the title border once and click the Format Chart Title button on the Standard toolbar. A Format dialog box appears, as shown in Figure 10-5. (If the title is already selected, be sure to double-click the title border, or you will end up selecting title text.)

FIGURE 10-5.
The Format Chart Title
dialog box appears
when you double-
click the chart title.

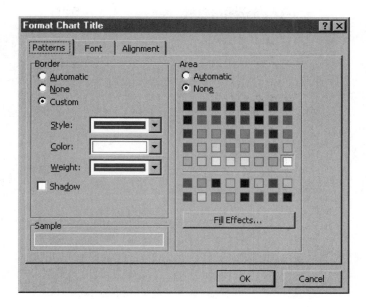

Alternatively, you can click the title and display the Format dialog box by choosing the first command from the Format menu (which is either Selected Chart Title or Selected Axis Title), by pressing Ctrl+1, or by clicking the right mouse button and choosing the Format command from the shortcut menu.

To format only part of a title, click the title and then select only the text you want to format. (The Format dialog box consists of only the Font tab when you select part of the title.) You can also format the text of a title by selecting the text and then using the text formatting buttons on the Formatting toolbar.

To format the title's text box rather than its text, you use the options on the Patterns tab in the Format dialog box. The Border settings control the appearance of the border of the text box. The Area settings control the color and pattern of the interior of the text box. A sample in the lower left corner shows the results of the Border and Area settings. You can select the appropriate None option if you want the text box to have no border or a clear interior. To restore the defaults for the Border or Area settings, select the Automatic option.

III

Modifying the Presentation

⊕ TIP

When you select an Area color for the text box, be careful to select a color that properly contrasts with both the plot area of the chart and the text of the title. You may have to change the text color to contrast with the text box color, as described below.

To add a border, select a Style, Color, and Weight option from the drop-down lists under Custom in the Border section. To add a shadow, click the Shadow check box. The color of the shadow is determined by the Shadow color of the color scheme.

To change the appearance of the title's text, select the title and then click the Font tab of the Format dialog box. Figure 10-6 shows the Font tab options. Use the Font, Font Style, Size, Underline, and Color options to change the look of the text. Leaving the Color option set to Automatic applies the Text Color specified by the Text And Lines color in the color scheme for the active template. Leaving Auto Scale checked automatically resizes the text to fit changes you make to the chart's size.

FIGURE 10-6.
The Font tab of the Format Chart Title dialog box.

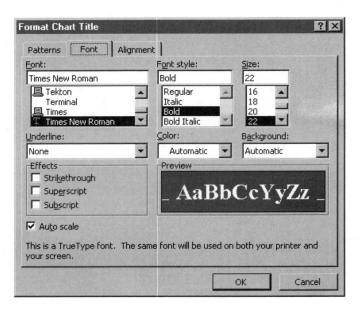

The Background option on the Font tab is a fine-tuning control. Leave it set to Automatic to let Graph select a background that contrasts properly with the foreground text color. If the text and text box are the same color, the Automatic setting fills the area behind the letters of the text with a contrasting color to ensure that the text is readable. You can select Transparent to make the area behind the letters transparent so that the text box color shows through, or you can select Opaque to make this area a solid color. When you select Opaque, any pattern is removed from the area behind the text.

The Effects options on the Font tab let you turn on Strikethrough (a horizontal line through the text), Superscript, or Subscript. Figure 10-7 shows an axis title with a subscript character.

To change the alignment of the text in the text box, click the Alignment tab of the Format dialog box. (Figure 10-8 on the next page shows the Alignment tab options in the Format Axis Title dialog box.) You can then position the text within the text box by selecting options in the Text Alignment section. For example, selecting Left for Horizontal and Center for Vertical aligns the text against the center-left interior edge of the text box.

FIGURE 10-7.

An axis title with a subscript character.

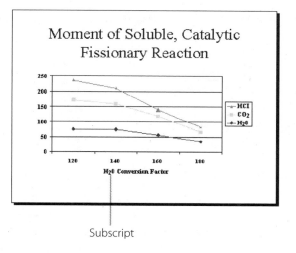

Subscript

The Orientation option is especially useful for rotating the title next to the vertical of the chart, as shown in Figure 10-9 on the next page. (In a 3-D chart, the value axis is called the Z axis.)

FIGURE 10-8.

The Alignment tab of the Format Axis Title dialog box.

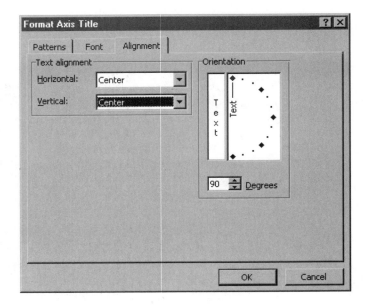

FIGURE 10-9

The value (Z) axis title, *Thousands*, rotated 90 degrees.

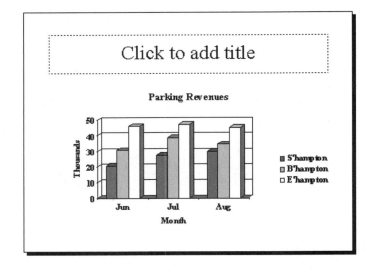

Formatting All the Chart Text

By double-clicking the chart area, you can display the Format Chart Area dialog box. You can then use the Font tab of this dialog box to make changes to all the text in the chart. This is an efficient way to change the font for all the chart text, for example.

Adding and Formatting a Legend

The Legend Button

If the chart you've created does not already have a legend, you can add one by clicking the Legend button on Graph's Standard toolbar or by choosing Legend from the Insert menu. The plot area of the chart shrinks, moving in from the right to allow space for the legend. If you change your mind, you can quickly remove the legend by clicking the Legend button again or by selecting the legend and pressing the Delete key.

Repositioning the Legend

If you want the legend to appear above, below, or to the left of the chart instead of to the right, you can select a preset legend location by choosing a menu command, or you can drag the legend into position. The advantage of using the menu command is that Graph adjusts the plot area to make room for the legend and adjusts the shape of the legend to fit its new location. The advantage of dragging the legend is that you can place it anywhere you want—even within the chart, if you can find a position that won't obscure the chart's data. Placing the legend within the chart allows you to recover the space formerly occupied by the legend. You can then stretch the plot area of the chart to make the chart larger and easier to read.

To reposition a legend using a menu command, follow these steps:

1   Select the legend, and then choose Selected Legend from the Format menu, or click the Format Legend button on the Standard toolbar.

III

Modifying the Presentation

2 Click the Placement tab.   3 Click one of these options and click OK.

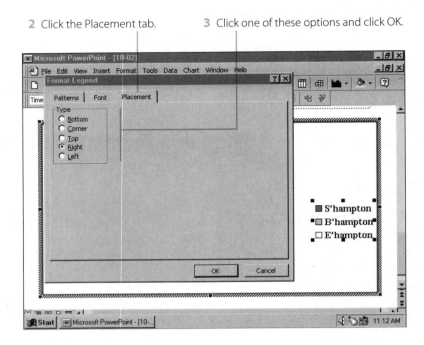

When you drag a legend above, below, or to the left of the chart, the plot area of the chart does not adjust to make space. Also, the legend does not automatically change shape to fit its new location. You must size the legend and chart by selecting them and dragging the handles of the plot area and the legend. You can reshape a legend by dragging one of its corner handles. As the boundaries of the legend move, dotted boxes in the legend show the new arrangement of the legend entries. For example, when you stretch the legend horizontally, the boxes indicate that the legend entries will be arranged side by side, as shown in Figure 10-10.

TIP

How to Emphasize Positive Change

When you move a legend from the right or left of the chart to the top or bottom, you can widen the chart to reclaim the legend's space. But when you widen an area, bar, column, or line chart, you decrease the impression of change over time. The lines of a line chart, for example, do not appear to climb or fall as rapidly. You can use this fact to your advantage. To emphasize positive change, place the legend on the left or right side of the chart; to de-emphasize negative change, place the legend above or below the chart.

FIGURE 10-10.
Stretching a vertical legend horizontally.

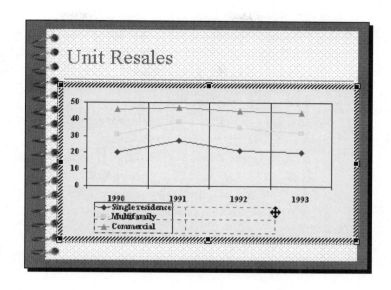

Formatting the Legend Entries

SEE ALSO

For more information about using the Patterns and Font tabs, see "Formatting the Titles," page 252.

You can format the legend box, the text within the legend, and even an individual legend text entry or legend key (the small box within the legend that shows the identifying color or pattern). To format the legend box and all the text within it, double-click the legend to display the Format Legend dialog box. To format a legend entry or legend key, double-click the legend entry or legend key to display the corresponding dialog box.

NOTE

> When you change the color or pattern of a legend key, the color or pattern of the corresponding data series changes, too.

In the Format Legend dialog box, you use the options on the Patterns tab to format the legend box and legend key, and you use the options on the Font tab to format the legend text. Both tabs work the same way with legends as they do with chart titles.

Formatting the Axes and Tick Marks

The axes of an area, bar, column, line, XY (scatter), bubble, or radar chart are the scales against which the values of the markers in the chart are measured. Pie and doughnut charts do not have axes. By scaling the axes (changing the minimum or maximum values), you

III

Modifying the Presentation

can emphasize or de-emphasize the chart's data. By adding, removing, and formatting tick marks and tick mark labels, you can make the chart easier to interpret—or harder, if that's your goal.

Showing or Hiding the Axes

By default, axes are displayed on the basic chart that Graph creates, but you can turn off one or both axes if you need to display only the markers of the chart. For example, you may not need to give your audience a scale against which to measure the actual values in the chart. Or you may prefer to omit the axes and instead display data point labels, which specify the exact value of each data point.

To turn off an axis, follow these steps:

1   Choose Chart Options from the Chart menu.

2   Click the Axes tab in the Chart Options dialog box.

3   Select check boxes on the Axes tab to turn on X and Y axes. Deselect checkboxes to turn them off.

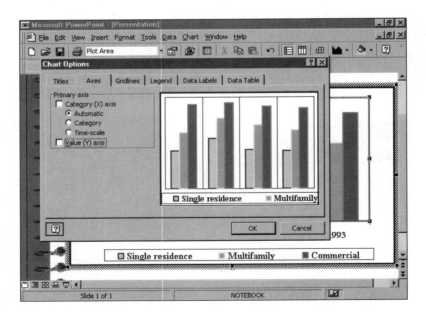

For example, deselecting the Value (Y) Axis option and adding data point labels (you'll learn how later in this chapter) produces the chart shown on the facing page.

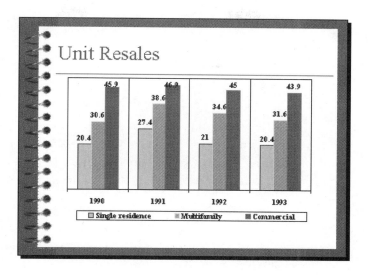

To remove an axis, you can select the axis, and then press the Delete key or choose Clear from the shortcut menu.

Formatting the Axes

To change the color or line style of an axis, start by double-clicking the axis. Alternatively, select the axis and then choose Selected Axis on the Standard toolbar. When the Format Axis dialog box appears, click the Patterns tab, shown in Figure 10-11.

FIGURE 10-11.

The Patterns tab of the Format Axis dialog box.

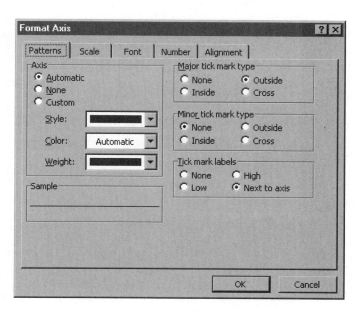

TIP

An Easier Way to Select an Axis
If you have trouble double-clicking the axis, you can double-click any of the labels along the axis to open the Format Axis dialog box.

You can select a line style, line color, and line weight from the three drop-down lists under Custom in the Axis section. The Sample box shows the result of your changes. Click OK to return to the chart, or click a different tab to make other changes to the axis.

Scaling the Axes

Graph automatically determines appropriate axis scaling for the numbers you entered in the datasheet. The maximum value of the value axis is set to the next major interval above the largest value in the data. However, you might want to change the automatic settings to achieve specific effects. To accentuate change in a line chart, for example, you can reduce the maximum value and increase the minimum value.

To change the scale of an axis, double-click the axis. In the Format Axis dialog box, click the Scale tab. Figure 10-12 shows the Scale tab for a value (Y) axis. Figure 10-13 shows the Scale tab for a category (X) axis. If the chart is an XY (scatter) type, it has two value axes.

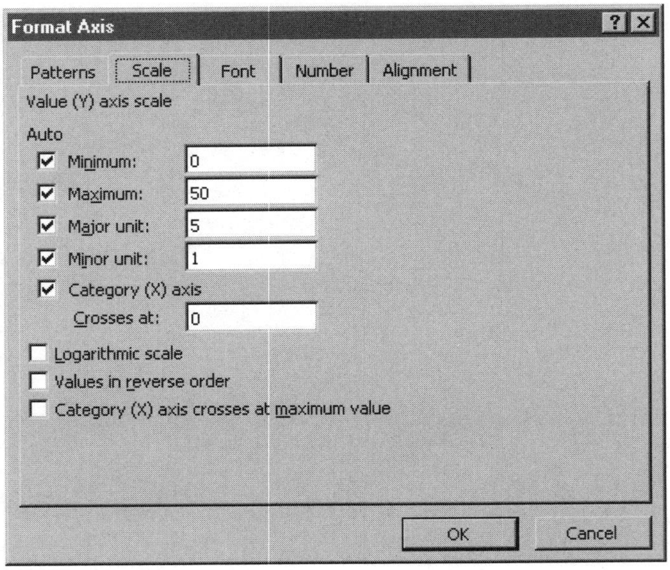

FIGURE 10-12.
The Scale tab options in the Format Axis dialog box when a value (Y) axis is selected.

Format Axis [?] [X]

| Patterns | Scale | Font | Number | Alignment |

Value (Y) axis scale

Auto
☑ Mi_n_imum: 0
☑ Ma_x_imum: 50
☑ Ma_j_or unit: 5
☑ Mi_n_or unit: 1
☑ Category (X) axis
_C_rosses at: 0

☐ _L_ogarithmic scale
☐ Values in _r_everse order
☐ Category (X) axis crosses at _m_aximum value

OK   Cancel

If you've selected a value axis, the Scale tab shows the current settings for the Minimum, Maximum, Major Unit, Minor Unit, and Category (X) Axis Crosses at options, which are described in Table 10-1. The Auto check box to the left of each option is checked to show that Graph has automatically supplied a standard setting. When you change a setting, Graph clears the Auto check box.

FIGURE 10-13.

The Scale tab options in the Format Axis dialog box when a category (X) axis is selected.

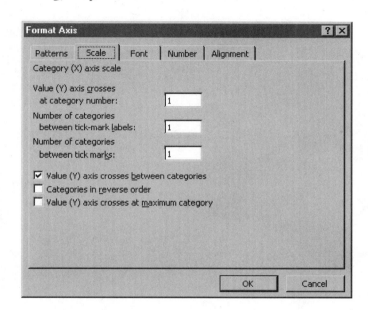

TABLE 10-1.   The Value (Y) Axis Scale options.

Option	Description
Minimum	The minimum value along the axis.
Maximum	The maximum value along the axis.
Major Unit	The distance between tick marks.
Minor Unit	The distance between the minor units that appear between the major units along the axis.
Category (X) Axis Crosses At	The point on the value axis at which the category axis intersects. This setting might be less than 0 if your data includes negative values.

The minimum value of a bar or column chart must always be 0. Anything other than 0 hides the full lengths of the bars or columns. If you can't see the full bars or columns, you can't gauge their relative lengths, and the chart is truly misleading.

The other three options on the Scale tab for a value axis serve special purposes. To use a logarithmic scale along the value axis (appropriate when your data has vast variations), click the Logarithmic Scale option. Then each successive interval along the axis is 10 times the previous interval. To invert an entire chart, click the Values in Reverse Order option. Figure 10-14 shows an inverted chart.

FIGURE 10-14.

An inverted chart created by selecting the Values in Reverse Order option on the Scale tab of the Format Axis dialog box.

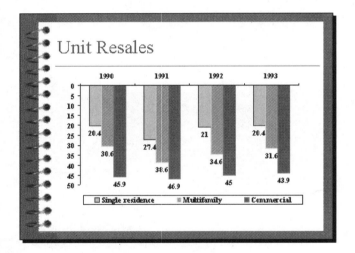

To invert a chart without inverting the value axis, click the Category (X) Axis Crosses At Maximum Value option. You can use such a chart to show the amount of progress still needed to reach a goal by setting the Maximum option to the value of the goal and entering the progress so far on the datasheet. Figure 10-15 shows such a chart.

FIGURE 10-15.
An inverted chart
created by selecting
the Category (X)
Axis Crosses at
Maximum Value
option on the Scale
tab of the Format
Axis dialog box.

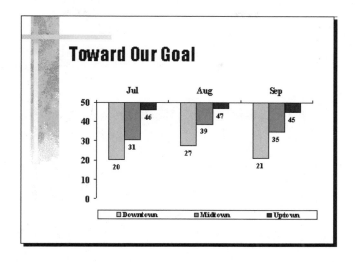

If you've selected a category axis, the Scale tab shows the three edit
boxes described in Table 10-2.

Table 10-2.   The Category (X) Axis Scale options.

Option	Description
Value (Y) Axis Crosses At Category Number	Moves the value axis to the right along the category axis to the category number in the edit box.
Number Of Categories Between Tick-Mark Labels	Determines the number of labels along the category axis. Enter 2, for example, to show every other label.
Number Of Categories Between Tick Marks	Determines the number of tick marks along the category axis. Enter 2, for example, to show every other tick mark.

The Scale tab also has three checkbox options. Deselecting the Value
(Y) Axis Crosses Between Categories option draws the value axis in
the middle of a category rather than between categories. Selecting the
Categories In Reverse Order option reverses the order of the categories along the category axis. For example, if the categories are chrono-

logical, they appear in reverse chronological order. Selecting the Value (Y) Axis Crosses At Maximum Category option moves the value axis to the right side of the chart (or to the left side if the categories are reversed).

Formatting the Tick Marks Along the Axes

Major and minor tick marks are the tiny notches that appear along the value axis of a chart to indicate the major and minor units specified on the Scale tab of the Format Axis dialog box. Tick marks also appear between categories on the category axis.

An axis can have major and minor tick marks inside, outside, or crossing the line of the axis. These tick marks automatically have the same color and pattern as the axis to which they are attached. You can change the position of the tick marks by changing the Tick Mark Type options on the Patterns tab of the Format Axis dialog box, shown in Figure 10-16. Figure 10-17, on the facing page, shows a chart with major tick marks that appear outside the value axis and minor tick marks that appear inside the axis.

FIGURE 10-16.
The Patterns tab of the Format Axis dialog box.

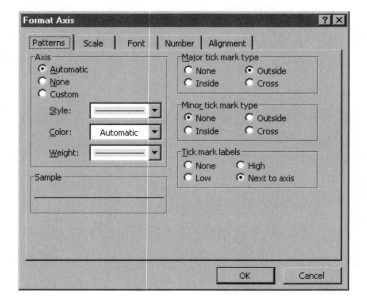

III

Modifying the Presentation

FIGURE 10-17.
An axis with major tick marks outside and minor tick marks inside.

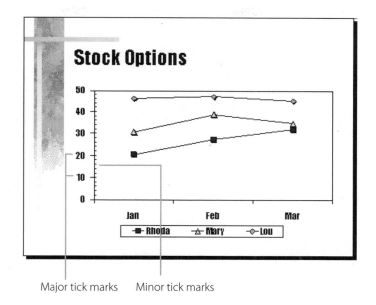

Major tick marks   Minor tick marks

Formatting the Labels Along the Axes

Tick mark labels appear at the major tick marks of the value axis and between tick marks on the category axis. You control the formatting of these labels by using options on the Patterns, Font, Number, and Alignment tabs of the Format Axis dialog box.

To change the location of the tick mark labels, use the Tick Mark Labels options on the Patterns tab of the Format Axis dialog box, shown in Figure 10-16. The default setting, Next To Axis, places the labels near their own axis. To place them near the maximum or minimum values of the other axis, select High or Low, respectively. For example, selecting High moves the tick mark labels to the opposite side of the chart, adjacent to the maximum value on the other axis, as shown in Figure 10-18 on the next page.

To remove tick mark labels, click None, but unless you want to show only relative values in a chart, be sure to use data point labels to specify the absolute values.

FIGURE 10-18.
A chart for which the
Tick Mark Labels
option is set to High.

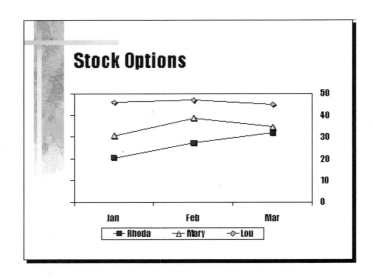

NOTE

The Font tab options for formatting the text of tick mark labels work just like the Font tab options for formatting titles. For more information about the Font tab options, see "Formatting the Titles," page 252.

The options on the Number tab, shown in Figure 10-19 on the facing page, let you modify the formatting of the numbers along a numeric axis. If the Linked To Source option is selected, these numbers have the same formatting as the numbers in the datasheet. To change the formatting, select a category from the Category list, and then select any other appropriate options. The Sample number in the dialog box reflects the selected formatting.

The options on the Alignment tab let you change the orientation of the tick mark labels. The Automatic setting (horizontal) usually works best for the value tick mark labels, but you may want to select a vertical orientation for the category tick mark labels if the labels are long. Figure 10-20 shows a chart with –90 degree tick mark labels along the category axis.

FIGURE 10-19.
The Number tab of
the Format Axis
dialog box.

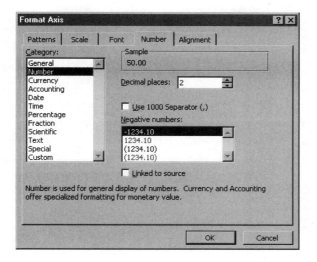

FIGURE 10-20.
A chart with −90
degree tick mark
labels along the
category axis.

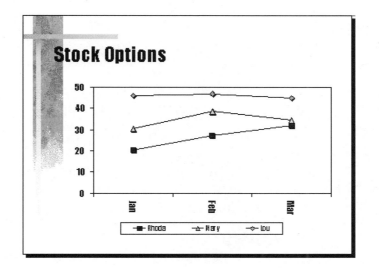

> **NOTE**
>
> Be aware that setting the tick mark label orientation to vertical leaves less
> vertical space for the chart, so the chart becomes shorter without a corre-
> sponding change in its width. Changing a chart only vertically or only
> horizontally increases or decreases the impression of change in the chart.

Showing or Hiding Gridlines

Gridlines extend from major unit tick marks and help you gauge the heights of areas and lines, the lengths of bars and columns, and the position of data points. The easiest way to turn gridlines on or off is to click the Axis Gridlines buttons on Graph's Standard toolbar. Click once to turn on gridlines, and click again to turn them off. You can also choose Chart Options from the Chart menu and then change options on the Gridlines tab of the Chart Options dialog box.

Formatting the Gridlines

After you turn on gridlines, you can format them by double-clicking any gridline to display the Format Gridlines dialog box. Then use the options on the Patterns tab to set the style, color, and weight of the gridlines. You can click Automatic to return to the default settings.

 NOTE

The options on the Scale tab in the Format Gridlines dialog box allow you to set the scaling of the axis from which the gridlines emanate.

Modifying the Chart Background

A chart has two background areas you can format: the plot area immediately behind the markers, axes, and axis tick mark labels; and the chart area within the heavy border surrounding the chart, including the area occupied by the legend and the chart title. To identify each area of the chart, point to the area and view the ScreenTip.

Formatting the Plot Area

To format the plot area, first double-click within the chart but away from the axes or markers. If the chart is three-dimensional, you must double-click just outside the chart, but away from the axes or axis labels. You can also click once to select the plot area and, when you see a border appear around the plot area, choose Selected Plot Area from the Format menu. The Format Plot Area dialog box contains only the Patterns tab. Use the options in the Border and Area sections to change the look of the plot area. Figure 10-21 shows the plot area of a chart filled with a texture.

FIGURE 10-21.

The plot area of a chart filled with a texture.

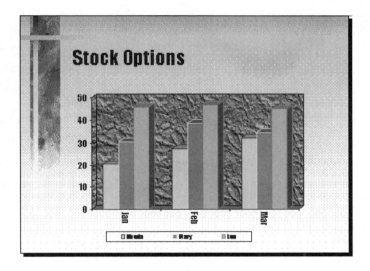

Formatting the Chart Area

To format the chart area, double-click within the heavy border of the chart but outside the plot area, or click once to select the chart area and then choose Selected Chart Area from the Format menu. The Format Chart Area dialog box appears, as shown in Figure 10-22 on the next page.

Use the options in the Border and Area sections of the Patterns tab to change the look of the border and the interior of the chart area. You can select a border style, color, and weight, and you can fill the chart area with a background color and pattern. Use the Font tab options to change the look of all the text in the chart. Figure 10-23, also on the next page, shows a line chart with contrasting formatting in the plot and chart areas.

III

Modifying the Presentation

FIGURE 10-22.
The Format Chart Area dialog box.

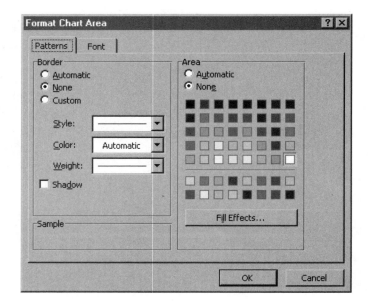

FIGURE 10-23.
A line chart with contrasting chart and plot area formatting.

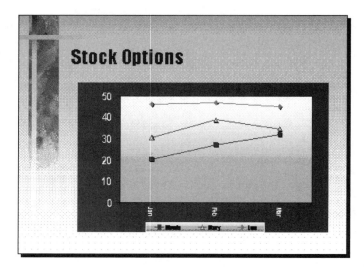

NOTE

The Replace Fonts command on the Tools menu, which changes the fonts used throughout a presentation, does not affect the fonts used by chart text. After changing the presentation font, you can quickly change a chart's font to match by using the options on the Font tab of the Format Chart Area dialog box. You won't have to select and format each chart text object individually.

Adding and Formatting Data Labels

The markers of a data series provide only an approximate representation of the numbers in the datasheet. To show the actual numbers, you must provide a table of numbers or place the numbers directly on the markers as data labels.

To add data labels to a data series, start by double-clicking the series. When the Format Data Series dialog box appears, click the Data Labels tab, which is shown in Figure 10-24.

FIGURE 10-24.

The Data Labels tab of the Format Data Series dialog box.

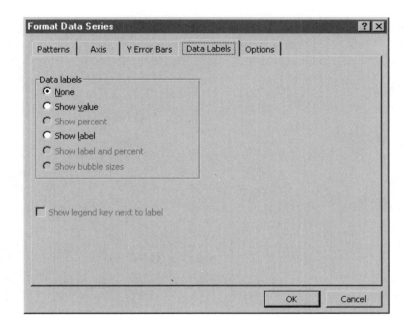

To add data labels to all the markers in the chart, you can select the chart and then choose Chart Options from the Chart menu. The Data Labels tab of the Chart Options dialog box shows the same options as the Data Labels tab of the Format Data Series dialog box.

When you have displayed the dialog box, click Show Value to display the numeric value of each data point in the series. Click Show Percent if the chart is a stacked bar, stacked column, pie, or doughnut chart and you want to show the percentages represented by the segments or slices. Click Show Label to display the category assigned to the data point. (In an area chart, clicking Show Label displays the series names.) Click Show Label And Percent to display both the category or series names and the percentages. Click Show Bubble Sizes to display the size of the bubbles in a bubble chart. If an Automatic Text check box appears on the Data Labels tab, the data labels of the datasheet are being used. Click this check box to synchronize the data labels with those on the datasheet. If the Show Legend Key Next To Label check box is available, you can check it to place the legend key, which displays the color of the series, next to the data label.

TIP

How to Add a Data Label to a Single Marker
You can add a data label to a single marker—an outstanding result, for example—by clicking the marker to select it and then double-clicking the marker to open the Format Data Point dialog box, which contains the same Data Labels and Patterns tabs as the Format Data Series dialog box.

To format the data labels on a chart, double-click any data label in a series. The Format Data Labels dialog box appears. The options on the four tabs of the dialog box (Patterns, Font, Number, and Alignment) work just as they do when you format any other text in a chart. For example, you can use the Patterns options to create a filled box around each data label and the Number options to change the number of decimal places shown in the data labels.

To format a single data label, select the data labels for the series, and click the data label you want. Then double-click the border of the same data label, and use the options in the Format Data Labels dialog box as usual. You can also select a single data label, click an insertion point in it, and then edit or add text. For example, you might want to add text to a data label, as shown in Figure 10-25.

TIP

An Alternative to Crowding Charts
Don't try to crowd too many data labels on a chart. You might prefer to add a table to the slide or to the following slide showing the numbers.

FIGURE 10-25.
Text added to a
data label.

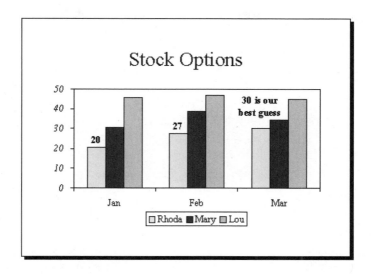

Moving and Resizing Chart Objects

You've already seen that you can move a chart's title or legend by
dragging its border. You can also drag the border of the entire chart to
move it on the slide, and drag the plot area to move or resize the area
of the chart bounded by the axes and axis labels. (Enlarging the plot
area of a chart can make interpreting the markers easier, but changing
the shape of the plot area alters the impression of change in the
chart.) You can even drag each data label to reposition it relative to its
data point or marker.

To move or resize a chart object, click the object and then drag the
object's border. To drag a data label, for example, first click the data
label to select it, and then drag the border surrounding the data label.

After you finish formatting the chart, click outside the chart's border to
redisplay PowerPoint's menus and toolbars. Later, if you want to make
additional changes to the chart, you can reopen Graph by simply
double-clicking the chart.

III

Modifying the Presentation

3-D Chart Formatting

PowerPoint's 3-D chart types are almost always worthy replacements for their 2-D equivalents. They add a touch of depth and, if you want, perspective. All the techniques that format 2-D charts apply to 3-D charts, but 3-D charts also add special formatting possibilities, which are discussed in this section.

Adjusting the 3-D View

PowerPoint offers 3-D versions of area, bar, column, line, and pie charts as sub-types when you choose a new chart type. You can slant, rotate, and change the height of 3-D charts by changing their 3-D view. For all types other than 3-D bar and 3-D pie charts, you can also increase the illusion of depth by adding perspective.

To change both the elevation (the forward slant) and the rotation of a 3-D chart, you don't even have to use a dialog box. You can simply drag the corners of the chart by following these steps:

1   Click the walls or the floor of the chart. A handle, labeled as a "corner" in the ScreenTip, appears at every corner of an imaginary 3-D box that encloses the chart. (If you see handles only at the corners of the back wall, try clicking the corner again or clicking a different corner.)

2   Place the mouse pointer on one of the corner handles, hold down the mouse button, and drag the mouse slightly. The outlines of the imaginary box appear. If you hold down the Ctrl key as you drag, you see outlines of the markers, too, as shown:

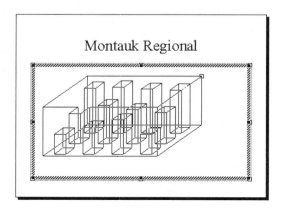

3 Still holding down the mouse button, drag the corner up or down to change the elevation, or drag the corner left or right to rotate the chart.

4 Release the mouse button to redraw the chart.

You can use the options in the 3-D View dialog box to accomplish the same task. Select the chart and then choose 3-D View from the Format menu to open the dialog box shown in Figure 10-26. As you can see, additional options in the dialog box let you change the height of 3-D charts and add perspective to those charts that are able to show perspective.

FIGURE 10-26.
The 3-D View dialog box.

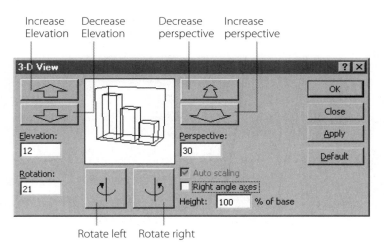

Increase Elevation · Decrease Elevation · Decrease perspective · Increase perspective

Rotate left · Rotate right

In the 3-D View dialog box, a model of the 3-D chart shows the current option settings. By viewing the model as you change the options, you can determine how the actual chart will look when you click OK.

To change the elevation of the chart, enter a number in the Elevation edit box or click the Increase Elevation or Decrease Elevation button to the left of the model. Each click changes the elevation by 5 degrees. To change the rotation, enter a number in the Rotation edit box or click the Rotate Left or Rotate Right button below the model. Each click changes the rotation by 10 degrees.

To change the height of the chart, which you can only do when Right Angle Axes is turned on (so the chart has no perspective), deselect

III

Modifying the Presentation

the Auto Scaling option, and then edit the number in the Height edit box. (You cannot change the height of 3-D pie charts.) The height of the chart is specified as a percentage of the length of the base. To let PowerPoint select a height that is appropriate for the chart, turn on Auto Scaling by clicking the option again.

To add perspective, deselect the Right Angle Axes option. (The Right Angle Axes option cannot be deselected for 3-D bar charts or 3-D pie charts because these charts cannot have perspective.) Then edit the number in the Perspective edit box or click the Decrease Perspective or Increase Perspective button to the right of the model. Each click changes the perspective by 5 units. (Valid perspective numbers are 0 to 100.) The default perspective setting of 30 is just enough to give the chart a true sense of depth without the kind of distortion shown in Figure 10-27.

After you change the options in the 3-D View dialog box, click Apply to apply the new settings without removing the dialog box, or click OK to return to the chart. If you click Apply, you can drag the dialog box aside to see the revised chart. You can also click Default to return the chart to its default 3-D view settings.

FIGURE 10-27.

A rotated, 3-D column chart distorted by a Perspective setting of 55.

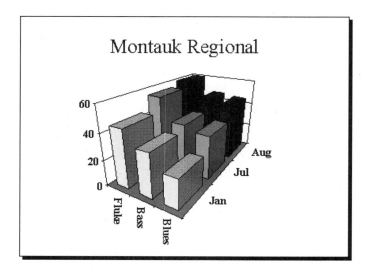

To change the depth of a 3-D chart, select a series in the chart and then choose Selected Data Series from the Format menu. In the Format Data Series dialog box, click the Options tab. Figure 10-28

shows the Options tab of the dialog box that appears when a 3-D column series is selected. Then change the Chart Depth option and click OK. (The minimum and maximum chart depths are 20 and 2000, respectively.)

FIGURE 10-28.
The Options tab of the Format Data Series dialog box.

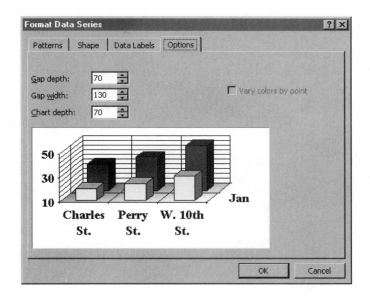

Formatting 3-D Chart Objects

3-D charts have unique chart objects that 2-D charts do not have. Figure 10-29 identifies the chart objects that are unique to 3-D charts.

FIGURE 10-29.
The unique chart objects of a 3-D column chart.

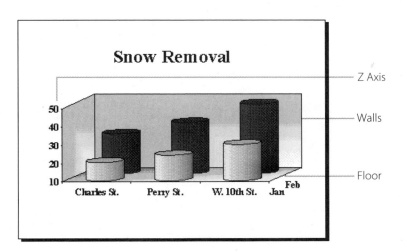

III

Modifying the Presentation

Formatting the Axes

When the series in 3-D charts appear behind one another at various depths in the chart, a third axis—the series axis—extends along the floor of the chart from front to back. The category axis remains the X axis, but the value axis rises from the floor. The chart shown in Figure 10-29 on the previous page shows all three axes.

Formatting the value axis of a 3-D chart is just like formatting the value axis of a 2-D chart. You double-click the value axis to display the Format Axis dialog box. The options on the Patterns, Font, Number, and Alignment tabs of this dialog box are the same as those for 2-D charts. However, the Scale tab has a new option, Floor (XY Plane) Crosses At, which lets you change the position of the floor within a 3-D area, bar, column, line, or surface chart. ·

When you change the vertical position of the floor, markers in 3-D area and column charts extend either above the floor or below the floor, but they do not cross the floor to reach their proper length along the value axis. Figure 10-30 shows a chart with the floor set at 35. Such a chart can show an excess above or deficiency below a budget or target value. In 3-D bar charts, the floor runs vertically, so markers extend to the left or right of the floor. In 3-D line and 3-D surface charts, the floor appears as a transparent panel within the chart and has no effect on the display of the lines or surface; values extend above or below the floor.

FIGURE 10-30.

A chart in which the floor (XY plane) crosses at 35.

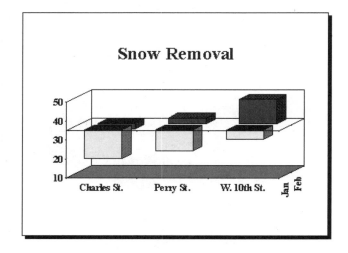

You can click the Floor (XY Plane) Crosses At Minimum Value option to place the floor at the minimum value of the value axis.

Formatting the Walls and Floor

All 3-D chart types, except 3-D pie charts, have walls and a floor. The walls are behind and to the side of the markers, and the markers rest on the floor.

By double-clicking the walls of a 3-D chart, you can open the Format Walls dialog box, shown in Figure 10-31, which displays only Patterns options. Use the options in the Border and Area sections to change the border and surface color, pattern, or texture of the walls. Figure 10-32, on the next page, shows a 3-D chart with textured walls. The floor must be formatted separately. Double-click the floor to open the Format Floor dialog box, which contains the same options as the Format Walls dialog box.

FIGURE 10-31.
The Format Walls dialog box.

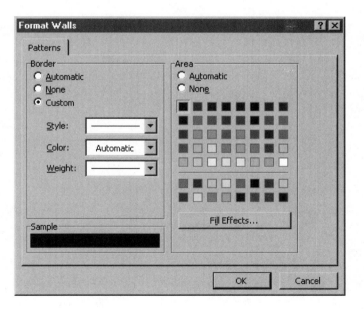

FIGURE 10-32.
Textured walls in a
3-D chart.

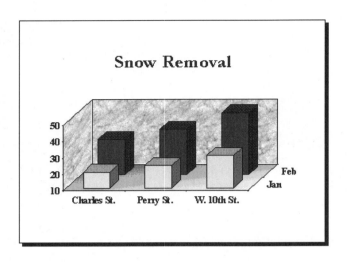

Formatting the Gridlines

When a chart has three axes, you can add major and minor gridlines
to all three axes. When you choose Chart Options from the Chart
menu, the options on the Gridlines tab of this dialog box (shown in
Figure 10-33) let you turn on major and minor gridlines for the
category, series, and value axes.

 NOTE

When 3-D charts contain markers that look three-dimensional but are not at
planes of different depths, you can display 2-D walls and gridlines by clicking
the 2-D Walls And Gridlines option at the bottom of the Gridlines dialog box.

FIGURE 10-33.
The Gridlines options
for a 3-D chart.

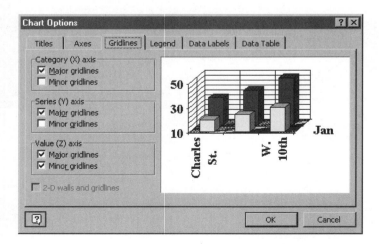

Formatting Area, Bar, Column, and Line Charts

In Chapter 6, while creating basic charts, you learned about selecting a chart type and sub-type. Each sub-type has a unique style and arrangement of markers that convey a different message. Changing the sub-type is the quickest way to dramatically change the look of a chart.

To change the sub-type of a chart, select the chart, choose Chart Type from the Chart menu, and then select one of the sub-types from the dialog box that appears.

NOTE

If you select the 2-D stacked bar or 2-D stacked column sub-type, you can click Series Lines on the Options tab of the Format Data Series dialog box to connect the series in the columns with lines.

Creating Combination Charts

PowerPoint allows you to mix 2-D chart types, selecting the best chart type for each series or group of series in the chart. You might use a line for one series and columns for another to compare the fluctuating change of a series (for example, sales volume) in response to incremental adjustments in another series (for example, price). Figure 10-34 on the next page shows such a chart.

CAUTION

You can't mix chart types in a 3-D chart.

To change the chart type of one or more series, select the series, and choose Chart Type from the Chart menu. Then select a different 2-D chart type from the palette of chart types. Be sure to choose Apply To Selection in the Chart Type dialog box. To return all series to one type, select the Chart Area and then select a chart type.

III

Modifying the Presentation

FIGURE 10-34.
A chart that compares price (shown as a line) and volume (shown as columns).

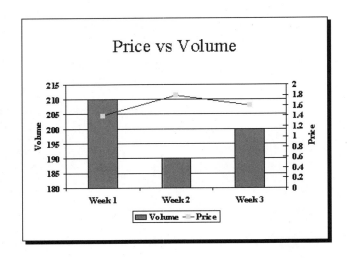

When a chart has two or more series with different chart types, you can add a secondary category or value axis against which you can plot one or more of the chart type groups. A secondary axis appears on the opposite side of the chart and is scaled according to the series assigned to it. As a result, the same chart can show two chart types that have very different ranges of values. For example, you might plot the price of a product over time against the primary axis, which ranges from $1.40 to $1.80, and plot the units sold against the secondary axis, which ranges from 190 to 210.

To add a secondary axis, choose Chart Options from the Chart menu. On the Axes tab of the Chart Options dialog box, you can choose Secondary Axis options: a Category (X) Axis and a Value (Y) Axis. Select one or both options to add one or two axes to the chart.

To assign a series to a secondary axis, double-click the series and then choose either Primary Axis or Secondary Axis on the Axes tab of the Chart Options dialog box, shown in Figure 10-35.

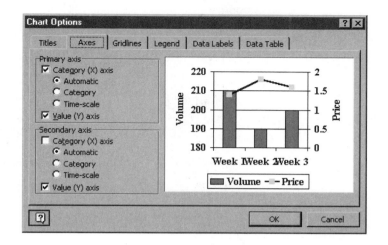

Adjusting the Spacing of Areas, Bars, Columns, and Lines

With the Gap Depth and Gap Width settings on the Options tab of the Format Data Series dialog box, you can modify the spacing between 2-D and 3-D areas, bars, and columns, and between 3-D lines. Figure 10-36 shows these options for a 3-D bar chart. For 2-D bar and column charts, you can also use the Overlap option, which won't work in 3-D charts.

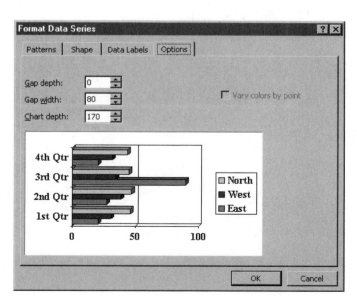

III

Modifying the Presentation

The bars or columns of a default chart are arranged in clusters along the category axis. To change the spacing between clusters, change the Gap Width setting, which can range from 0 to 500 percent of the width of a single bar or column. A setting of 0 percent creates a step chart or histogram. The default setting of 150 percent leaves 1.5 times the width of a bar or column between each cluster. As you increase the gap width, the width of the bars or columns decreases.

To separate the areas, bars, columns, or lines along the Y axis of a 3-D chart, change the Gap Depth setting on the Options tab. The gap depth, like the gap width, is calculated as a percentage of the depth of a single marker.

To change the spacing of 2-D bars or columns within a cluster, rather than between clusters, change the Overlap setting. At 0 percent, the bars or columns are side by side without overlapping. At 100 percent, they overlap completely. Figure 10-37 shows a column chart with a 50-percent overlap and a 100-percent gap width.

TIP

How to Separate Markers within a Cluster
To separate the bars or columns within a cluster, you can enter a negative overlap percentage. An overlap setting of -50 percent, for example, separates the columns within a cluster by half the width of a single column.

FIGURE 10-37.
A column chart with a 50-percent overlap and a 100-percent gap width.

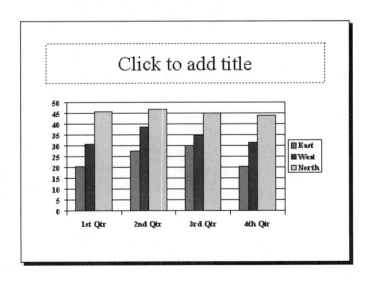

Adding Drop Lines to Area and Line Charts

Drop lines are vertical lines that help identify the data points of 2-D and 3-D area and line charts. They run from the data points of the areas or lines to the category axis of the chart. Figure 10-38 shows a 3-D line chart with drop lines.

FIGURE 10-38.

A 3-D line chart with drop lines.

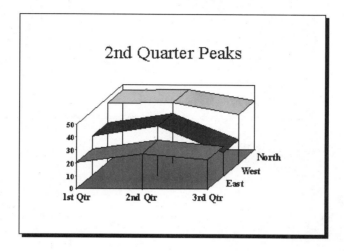

To turn on drop lines, double-click the data series, and click the Drop Lines option on the Options tab of the Format Data Series dialog box.

Adding High-Low Lines to Line Charts

High-low lines can be added to individual lines or to all lines in a 2-D line chart to depict the range over which a measurement varies, such as the high and low temperature of the day or the high and low test scores of different groups of people. Figure 10-39, on the next page, shows high-low lines added to all the data series in a temperature fluctuation chart.

To create a chart that shows discrete ranges of measurements instead of connected series, you can set the Line option on the Patterns tab of the Format Data Series dialog box to None. First, double-click any series. Then click High-Low lines on the Options tab of the Format Data Series dialog box. Figure 10-40, also on the next page, shows the temperature fluctuations chart with this setting.

III

Modifying the Presentation

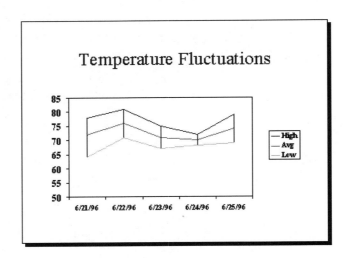

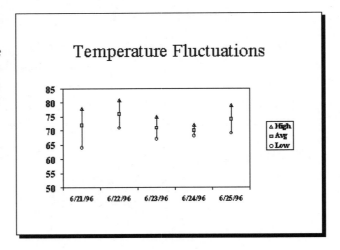

To change the style, color, and weight of drop lines and high-low lines, first double-click a line. Then change the Line options on the Patterns tab of the dialog box that appears.

Showing and
Predicting Trends with Trendlines

When working with area, bar, column, line, and XY (scatter) charts, you can add an automatic regression line that depicts the general trend of the numbers in a data series and allows you to predict approximate future data points based on the existing data. The regression line, called a *trendline*, overlays the series markers.

The default trendline is a linear regression that depicts a "best fit" straight line passing nearest to all the data points. You can select one of five other regression types, each based on a different mathematical regression formula. You can also format the trendline to set the intercept; change the number of forecast periods; or display the trendline name, the R-squared value, or the regression equation on the chart. (If terms like "intercept" and "R-squared value" puzzle you, you might want to stick with a simple linear regression trendline and leave the higher math to the statisticians.) Figure 10-41 shows standard linear regression lines in a chart.

FIGURE 10-41.
Linear regression lines on a column chart.

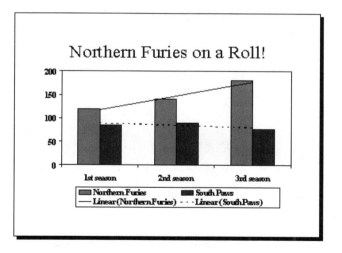

To add a trendline to a chart, choose Add Trendline from the Chart menu. On the Type tab, shown in Figure 10-42 on the next page, select a Trend/Regression Type, highlight the series the trend line will be based upon, and click OK.

FIGURE 10-42.
The Type tab of
the Add Trendline
dialog box.

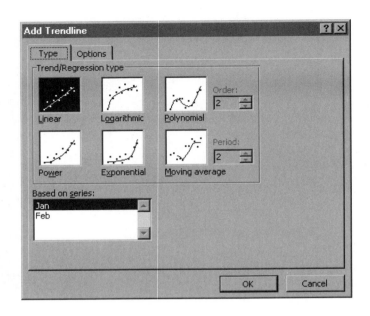

To delete a trendline quickly, select the line and then press the Delete key or choose Clear from the shortcut menu.

To format a trendline, double-click it. On the Options tab of the Format Trendline dialog box you can enter a custom trendline name that will replace the default name in the legend. The options in the Forecast section allow you to extend the trendline beyond the actual data by adding a number of forecast periods forward and backward. If regressions are the stuff of your daily life, you will want to vary the intercept by entering values in the Set Intercept edit box and display the math behind the trendline by clicking the Display Equation On Chart and Display R-Squared Value On Chart options.

To change the line style, color, and weight of the regression line, use the options on the Patterns tab of the Format Trendline dialog box.

Allowing for Error with Error Bars

Error bars in a chart allow you to depict the minor deviations that you expect in your data. You can enter this "margin of error" as a fixed number, a percentage, the number of standard deviations from the mean of plotted values, or the standard error. You can also add a custom plus and minus error value. 2-D area, bar, column, and line charts have Y error bars that apply to the Y axis only. XY (scatter) charts can have both X error bars and Y error bars. Figure 10-43 above shows a column chart with Y error bars.

FIGURE 10-43.

A column chart with Y error bars.

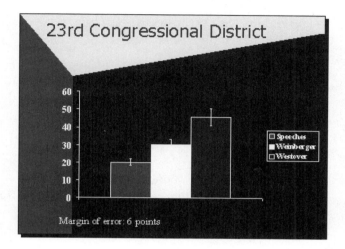

To add error bars that extend from each data point in a series, double-click each series in turn and then the Y Error Bars tab in the Format Data Series dialog box, shown in Figure 10-44.

FIGURE 10-44.

The Y Error Bars tab of the Format Data Series dialog box.

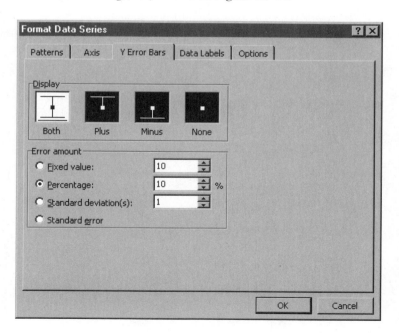

On the Y Error Bars tab of the Format Data Series dialog box, select a display type by clicking the Both, Plus, Minus, or None option in the Display section, and select an error type and amount in the Error Amount section. If the chart is an XY chart, the Format Data Series dialog box has two Error Bars tabs, one to set the X error bars and another to set the Y error bars.

To format the error bars, double-click one of the error bars, and click the Patterns tab of the Format Error Bars dialog box. You can then select the style, color, and weight of the bars, plus select one of two marker styles: a T or a straight line extending from the data point.

Varying the Colors of a Single Series Chart

When a chart displays only one series, you can have each marker in the series display a different color rather than the same color. Double-click the series, and in the Format Data Series dialog box, select Vary Colors By Point on the Options tab. The Vary Colors By Point option is not available for 2-D area, 3-D area, or 3-D surface charts.

 NOTE

A related option, Vary Colors By Slice, applies a different color to each slice in a pie or ring in a doughnut chart. This option is turned on by default.

Formatting Pie and Doughnut Charts

Pie and doughnut charts offer special formatting options that are unique to their chart types. You can select and format the entire pie or doughnut group, or you can select and format a pie slice, a doughnut ring, or a segment of a doughnut ring.

Separating Slices

To call attention to certain pie slices, you can separate them from the rest of the pie by dragging them away from the center one by one. You can also separate segments of the outermost doughnut ring by dragging them.

Labeling Slices

The easiest way to label the slices of a pie is to select Chart Options from the Chart menu, and then choose a Data Label type. (To label a single slice, select that slice before choosing Data Labels.) Selecting Show Value places the value of each slice next to the slice. Selecting Show Percent shows the calculated percentage of each slice. Selecting Show Label shows the name of the slice. (You may prefer to show slice names rather than a legend so that the viewer can see what each slice represents without having to match the legend key to the slice colors.) Selecting Show Label And Percent shows both the name and percentage next to each slice, as shown in Figure 10-45.

FIGURE 10-45.

A pie with data labels created by turning on the Show Label And Percent option in the Chart Options dialog box.

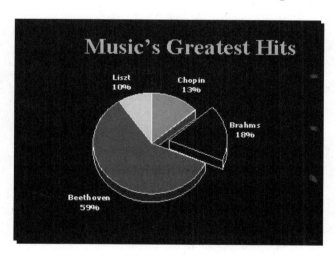

⭐ **TIP**

What You Can't Do with Pie Slice Labels

You can drag the values, percentages, or labels onto their corresponding pie slices. But if you have turned on the Show Label And Percent option, you cannot drag the percentages onto the slices and leave the labels off to the side unless you convert the pie to graphic objects. For more information, see "Converting a Chart to Graphic Objects," page 298.

III

Modifying the Presentation

Varying Colors by Slice

By default, the Vary Colors By Slice option on the Options tab of the Format Data Series dialog box is turned on. When you turn off Vary Colors By Slice, all slices get the same color, and the legend is no longer helpful unless the slices are filled with different patterns.

Changing the Angle of the First Slice

On the Options tab of the Format Data Series dialog box or the Format Doughnut Group dialog box, you can set the Angle Of First Slice option to rotate the entire pie or doughnut. Slices or segments start in the location specified by the Angle Of First Slice option and are plotted clockwise within the pie. The default setting is 0 degrees. To rotate the pie 90 degrees to the right, for example, you would change the Angle Of First Slice setting to 90 degrees.

> **NOTE**
>
> You can also rotate a 3-D pie chart by changing the Rotation setting in the Format 3-D View dialog box. For more information about rotating a 3-D chart, see "Adjusting the 3-D View," page 276.

Changing the Hole Size of a Doughnut Chart

Reducing the hole size of a doughnut chart enlarges the segments so that they are easier to see. The default hole size, specified as a percentage of the width of the chart, is 50 percent. To change the hole size, simply modify the Doughnut Hole Size percentage setting on the Options tab of the Format Data Series dialog box.

Formatting Radar and 3-D Surface Charts

The size of the ring of each data series in a radar chart shows the aggregate of the values in the series. Where the ring bulges from the center, the series shows the greatest measurements. For example, Figure 10-46 shows a radar chart in which each ring represents the yearly sales, by month, of a store in a three-store chain. As you can see, the sales of all three stores swelled during the months before

Christmas. The store with the largest ring, Fifth Ave., had the greatest overall sales.

FIGURE 10-46.
A radar chart showing the monthly sales of three stores.

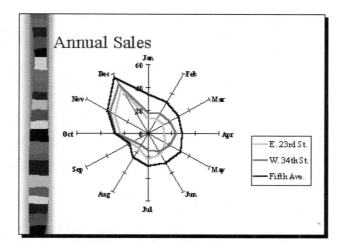

In a radar chart, value (Y) axes extend from the center of the chart, evenly spaced, in different directions. Each data point in the series has its own value axis. Double-clicking any axis and changing a setting in the Format Axis dialog box formats all the axes. Tick mark labels appear only on the axis that rises vertically from the center of the chart.

To format a radar chart, double-click a series in the chart and then change the settings in the Format Data Series dialog box. To label the axes of the radar chart, click the Category Labels option on the Options tab. To display markers at each data point, choose Chart Type from the Chart menu, and select the second radar chart sub-type. To display each series as a filled ring, select the third sub-type.

Formatting Surface Chart Intervals

In a surface chart, each height interval along the vertical (Z) axis—the 3-D axis—has its own color, as shown in the chart's legend. The color of a 3-D surface chart region indicates the height interval along the Z axis that the region has reached. If you want to change the colors of the Z axis intervals, you must double-click the legend keys and then change the Color or Fill Effects options in the Area section of the Patterns tab in the Format Legend dialog box.

III

Modifying the Presentation

Creating Picture Charts

By filling the markers of a chart with pictures, you can create a picture chart. The pictures can identify the series and communicate more information at a glance, as shown in Figure 10-47.

To turn a regular chart into a picture chart, activate the chart and then double-click one of the series of markers you want to replace with pictures. On the Patterns tab of the Format Data Series dialog box, click the Fill Effects button. In the Fill Effects dialog box, click the Picture tab. Click Select Picture to choose a picture file. The Format options on the same tab let you stretch the image to fill the markers or stack the pictures instead, using as many copies of the picture at its original size as necessary to fill the marker. You can also tell PowerPoint to stack the pictures at a size you specify.

FIGURE 10-47.

A picture chart.

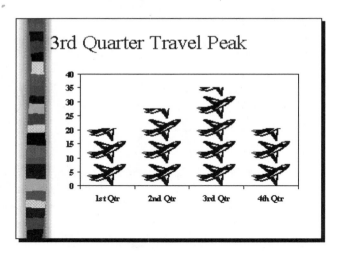

When you fill the markers of a line, XY, or radar chart with pictures, the pictures always appear at their original size. They cannot be stretched, stacked, or scaled.

Saving Chart Formatting as a Custom Chart Type

After creating a special combination of chart formatting that you like, you can save the combination as a custom chart type that you can then apply to other charts. To create a new custom chart type, follow these eight steps:

1 Activate a completed chart, and then choose Chart Type from the Chart menu. The Chart Type dialog box appears.

2 Click the Custom Types tab.

3 Click the User-Defined option in the Select From section.

4 Click the Add button. The Add Custom Chart Type dialog box appears, as shown here:

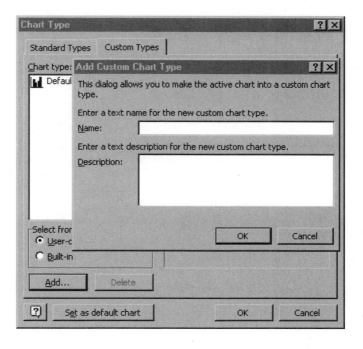

5 In the Name edit box, enter a name. (You can include spaces.)

6 Type a description in the Description edit box, if desired.

7 Click OK; the selected chart appears in the Sample dialog box.

8 Click OK to close the dialog box and return to the chart.

To delete a custom chart type, follow the procedure above, but instead of step 4, select the custom chart type to delete and click the Delete button.

Converting a Chart to Graphic Objects

PowerPoint offers a wealth of choices that allow you to change the appearance of a chart. But for the ultimate in flexibility, you can convert the chart to a collection of graphic objects, each of which can be modified individually. You can convert the columns of a column chart to a collection of rectangles, for example, and then revise them with PowerPoint's comprehensive drawing and editing commands.

When you convert a chart to a set of graphic objects, it loses its identification as a chart object that represents an underlying set of data. You can no longer use Graph's commands and controls, and the datasheet is no longer available. The result of the conversion is a picture of what was once a chart. And the conversion process is a one-way street; you cannot convert the collection of graphic objects back to a chart.

? SEE ALSO
For more information about editing graphic objects, see "Editing Objects," page 339.

Before you convert a chart to a set of graphic objects, you might want to copy the chart to another presentation slide. Then you can convert the copy of the chart to graphic objects, knowing that you can always return to the original, unchanged chart. You can even hide the slide containing the original chart so that you can access it even though it does not appear when you display the presentation.

To convert a chart to a collection of graphic objects, follow these four steps:

1 Click the chart once to select it without activating it.

2 Choose the Ungroup command from the Draw list on PowerPoint's Drawing toolbar. PowerPoint warns you that proceeding will permanently discard any embedded data, and asks whether you want to convert the chart to drawing objects.

3 Click Yes to convert the chart. After a moment, the chart reappears as a collection of graphic objects, each of which is selected.

4 Click outside the chart to deselect the objects.

Now you can select the objects one by one and make any necessary modifications.

In this chapter, you learned how to modify the appearance of the charts in your presentation. In the next chapter, you'll learn how to use Slide Sorter view to make broad changes to the entire presentation's design.

III

Modifying the Presentation

CHAPTER 11

Using Slide Sorter View

By displaying the slides of a presentation as miniatures arranged neatly on the screen, Slide Sorter
view, the third of PowerPoint's views, gives you a
working view of the presentation as a whole. But Slide
Sorter view allows you to do more than just view the
presentation. You can also do real work on the presentation
before switching to another view.

Some of the tasks you can accomplish in Slide Sorter view are:

- Checking the presentation start-to-finish for flaws and design consistency

- Rearranging slides

- Changing the template, color scheme, and background of all slides or only selected slides

- Duplicating slides

- Moving and copying slides between two presentations

- Setting up and previewing the transition and build effects that will appear in Slide Show view

All of these tasks except the last one are covered in this chapter. Creating slide shows while in Slide Sorter view is the subject of Chapter 16, "Creating Slide Shows."

Switching to Slide Sorter View

Switching to Slide Sorter view is as easy as clicking the Slide Sorter View button in the lower left corner of the presentation window. You can also choose Slide Sorter from the View menu.

When you switch to Slide Sorter view, the current presentation is displayed as a set of miniature slides, and the Slide Sorter toolbar appears below the Standard toolbar, replacing the Formatting toolbar. Figure 11-1 shows a presentation in Slide Sorter view.

To leave Slide Sorter and look at a single slide in Slide view, double-click on a slide. You can also use the arrow keys to move the highlighted border to a slide, and then press Enter.

FIGURE 11-1.

A presentation in Slide Sorter view.

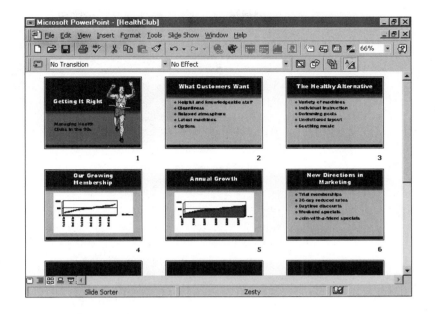

Zooming In and Out

Zooming in allows you to inspect slides more closely to check for errors. Zooming out allows you to view more of the presentation as a whole so that you can check its design consistency. To zoom in and out on the slide miniatures in Slide Sorter view, choose the Zoom command from the View menu. When the Zoom dialog box appears, select one of the preset zoom percentages or enter a new percentage in the Percent edit box.

Changing the Presentation in Slide Sorter View

In Slide Sorter view, as in most other views, you can change the appearance of the presentation by rearranging slides, adding and deleting slides, duplicating existing slides, applying a different template, and moving and copying slides between presentations. You cannot change the content of individual slides, however. Creating and editing individual slides is a task that you must perform in Slide view or Outline view.

III

Modifying the Presentation

TIP

Speeding Your Work in Slide Sorter View
By clicking the Show Formatting button on the Slide Sorter toolbar, you can temporarily display only the slide titles. Then, as you work with the slides, you don't have to wait for them to redraw. To redisplay the slide contents, click the Show Formatting button again.

Rearranging Slides

The most common use of Slide Sorter view is to move slides to new positions in the presentation, the same way you'd sort 35-mm slides on a light table before placing them in a slide projector. The simplest way to reposition a slide is to use the good old drag-and-drop technique. However, you can also move a slide by using the Cut and Paste commands or toolbar buttons.

To rearrange the order of slides using drag and drop, follow these steps:

1 Position the mouse pointer on the slide you want to move.

2 Hold down the left mouse button and drag the vertical marker to a position between two other slides.

3 Release the mouse button to drop the slide into place.

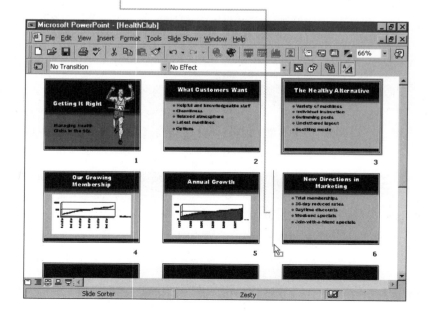

Here are the steps for moving a slide using Cut and Paste:

1   Click the slide you want to move.

2   Click the Cut button on the Standard toolbar or choose Cut from the Edit or shortcut menus.

3   Click an insertion point to indicate the slide's new position (a vertical line appears), and click the Paste button or choose Paste from the Edit or shortcut menus.

 TIP

> **How to Copy a Slide in Slide Sorter View**
> To copy a slide rather than move it, hold down the Ctrl key as you drag the slide, or click the Copy button instead of the Cut button on the Standard toolbar (or choose Copy from the Edit or shortcut menus), and choose Paste. The slide appears both at the destination and at the original location.

Rearranging a group of slides is just as easy as rearranging a single slide. After you select the group, you can use the same techniques described above for moving a single slide.

To select a group of slides, hold down the Shift key and click each slide. Each selected slide is surrounded by a highlighted border. You can use this method to select nonadjacent slides—that is, slides located in different parts of the presentation. When a group of nonadjacent slides is moved to a new location, the slides appear in the same relative order, one after the other in the new location. A slide from the first part of the presentation appears first, followed by a slide from the next part of the presentation, and so on.

To select a group of adjacent slides, you can draw a selection box across the group, like this:

1   Position the mouse pointer just outside the first slide you want to select.

III

Modifying the Presentation

2 Hold down the left mouse button, and drag the selection box across the slides you want to select.

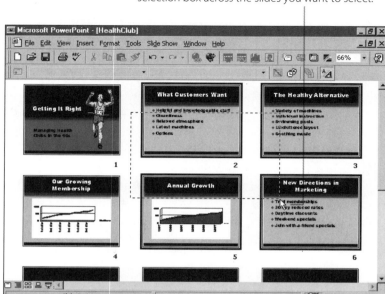

You don't need to enclose entire slides to select them. As long as any part of a slide is within the selection box, the slide will be selected.

After you select the slides, place the pointer on any slide and drag the group to its new location in the presentation. As with single slides, you can also use the Cut and Paste commands.

Adding and Deleting Slides

In addition to rearranging slides, you can also add and delete slides. Slide Sorter view is a good place to make these changes because you can quickly see their effect on the entire presentation.

Expand Slide, a new command in PowerPoint 97, can break a complex bullet slide into multiple slides by distributing the slide's bulleted points onto a series of successive slides it creates and inserts into the presentation. Select the complex slide and choose Expand Slide from the Tools menu.

To add a slide, follow these steps:

1 In the presentation, click the slide that you want the new slide to follow.

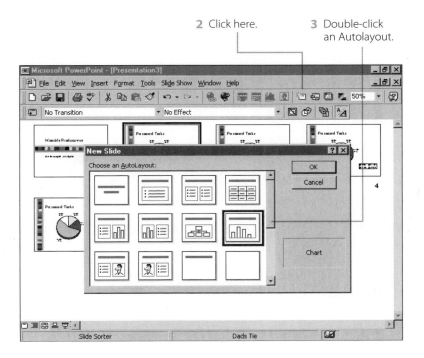

2 Click here.

3 Double-click an Autolayout.

Deleting a slide is even easier than adding one. Just click the slide you want to delete, and press Delete on the keyboard. You can also delete a group of slides by using one of the methods described earlier for selecting a group, and then pressing Delete.

Duplicating Slides

Another handy use for Slide Sorter view is to duplicate slides that have some feature you want to reproduce. Let's say you need to create the same pie graph for each salon in a chain of six beauty salons. You can create the first graph on a slide, switch to Slide Sorter view, and duplicate the slide five times. Then you can switch back to Slide view and edit the data in each of the duplicate slides. The design of the first graph and special formatting you've applied are carried over to the other slides, as in Figure 11-2 on the next page.

III

Modifying the Presentation

If you often need to use the same graph design, you can save the formatting of the graph as an autoformat that you can apply to a new graph. For more information about autoformats, see "Saving Chart Formatting as a Custom Chart Type," page 297.

To duplicate a slide in Slide Sorter view, follow these steps:

1 Click the slide.

2 Choose Duplicate from the Edit menu or press Ctrl+D. The duplicate appears to the right of the original slide.

FIGURE 11-2.
Duplicating a slide lets you carry special formatting throughout a presentation.

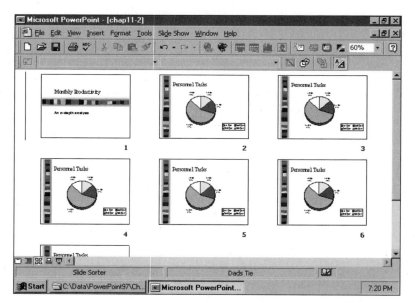

Moving and Copying Slides Between Presentations

Just as you can move and copy slides within a presentation, you can also move and copy slides between presentations. Moving and copying slides between presentations lets you transfer an existing slide to a new presentation rather than recreate its content.

Before you can actually move or copy slides between two presentations, you must arrange the presentations side by side in Slide Sorter view. Follow the steps below.

1   Open two presentations.

2   Switch to Slide Sorter view in each presentation.

3   Choose Arrange All from the Window menu to arrange the two presentations side by side, as shown below:

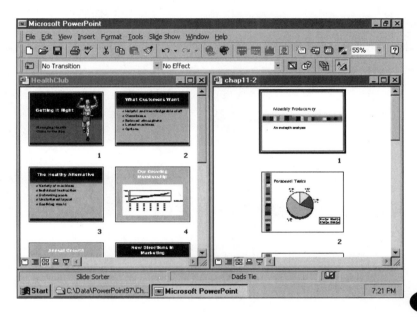

NOTE

You may want to use the same zoom percentage for both presentations. You can select a presentation by clicking it, and then change its zoom percentage independently. For more information about changing the zoom percentage, see "Zooming In and Out," page 303.

After the presentations are arranged side by side, you can move a slide from one presentation to another by clicking a slide in one presentation and dragging it to the other presentation. The moved slide takes on the design of the destination presentation's template.

III

Modifying the Presentation

To copy a slide rather than move it, hold down the Ctrl key as you drag the slide to the destination presentation.

You can also transfer slides between presentations by first selecting a slide in one presentation and using the Cut or Copy button on the Standard toolbar or by choosing the Cut or Copy command on the Edit or shortcut menus. Then you can click an insertion point in the other presentation, and click the Paste button on the Standard toolbar or choose the Paste command from the Edit or shortcut menus. Again, the slide takes on the template design of the destination presentation.

> **NOTE**

You can move or copy a group of slides between presentations by selecting the group before you use the drag-and-drop technique, the toolbar buttons, or the menu commands. To select a group of slides, hold down the Shift key as you click each slide, or drag a selection box around the group. For more information about selecting a group of slides, see "Rearranging Slides," page 304.

Changing the Design in Slide Sorter View

In Chapter 9, you learned about changing the template, color scheme, and background of a slide. Slide Sorter view is an ideal place to make these changes because you can easily see how the entire presentation is affected.

Changing the Template and Color Scheme of the Presentation

SEE ALSO
For more information about changing a presentation's template and color scheme, see Chapter 9,"Making Overall Changes," page 215.

In Slide Sorter view, you use the same techniques to change the template and color scheme of the presentation that you use in Slide view. For example, to change the presentation template, you choose the Apply Design command from the Format menu, and then select a different template in the Apply Design dialog box. As mentioned earlier, when you change the template and color scheme in Slide Sorter view, you can see the effect of the redesign on all the slides.

Changing the Color Scheme of Selected Slides

⊘ SEE ALSO

For more information about changing the color scheme, see "Changing the Color Scheme," page 220.

In Slide Sorter view, you can select specific slides and change their color scheme. For example, you can select all the slides that cover a general topic, and modify their color scheme. You can even give each segment of the presentation a different color scheme to differentiate it from the other segments.

To modify the color scheme for specific slides, first select the slides using one of the techniques described earlier. Then choose Slide Color Scheme from the Format menu, and make changes to the color scheme. Only the slides that you selected will display the revised color scheme.

Copying Color Schemes Among Slides

After you change the color scheme for selected slides, you can copy the color scheme to other slides in the presentation. Copying the color scheme can be a real time-saver because you don't have to go through the process of choosing commands and selecting options. You simply select a slide that has already been formatted with the color scheme you want and copy the scheme to one or more other slides.

To copy a color scheme from one slide to another, first select the slide with the color scheme you want to copy, and then click the Format Painter button on the Standard toolbar. Next, click the slide to which you want to copy the color scheme, or drag the mouse across the slides you want to be changed. It's that simple!

Changing the Background

You can change the background color of selected slides just as easily as you can change their color scheme. The Background command on the Format menu works as it does in Slide view: you can change only the background color, or you can apply a gradient, texture, or picture to the background without affecting the other presentation colors.

III

Modifying the Presentation

⑦ SEE ALSO

For more information about changing the background scheme of a presentation, see "Altering the Custom Background," page 229.

When you select slides in Slide Sorter view and then choose the Background command, you can also click the Omit Background Graphics From Master option to turn the background design on or off on the selected slides. You might want to select slides and turn off their background graphics when you need a simple background on which to draw diagrams or create complicated foreground images. Figure 11-3 shows a presentation with two slides that have had their display of background graphics turned off.

FIGURE 11-3.
The background graphics have been turned off on two slides in this presentation.

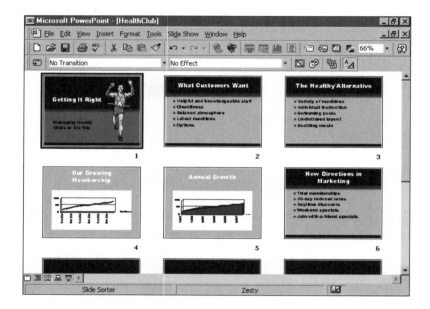

In this chapter, you've learned how useful Slide Sorter view can be when you want to rearrange slides and change a presentation's design. In Part IV, you'll learn how to refine individual slides of the presentation by adding text annotations, drawings, clip art, and bitmapped images.

PART IV

Adding Annotations and Graphics

CHAPTER 12

Working with Text Annotations and Speaker Notes

During the presentation, you'll want to direct your abundant energy and persuasive charm toward delivering your grand vision rather than detailing the minor technicalities in your graphs. Fortunately, you can leave the wherefores and the gotchas to helpful little notes that appear in text boxes alongside the other text and graphic objects on the slides. Figure 12-1, on the next page, shows a typical, useful text annotation.

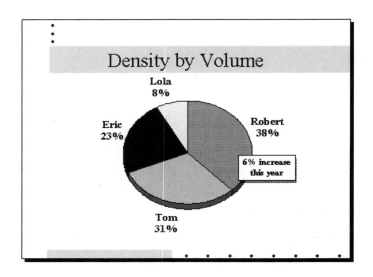

In this chapter, you'll learn how to add text annotations as well as how to add speaker notes to slides in Notes Pages view. While text annotations are designed to be seen by the audience, speaker notes are seen only by the individual delivering the presentation. On the top half of a speaker's note page, the presenter sees a reduced version of the current slide. On the bottom half of the page, the presenter sees typed notes about the slide—points to make while the slide is on the screen and supporting information to bring up, if necessary.

Text annotations and speaker notes are only two of the special additions you'll learn about in this part of the book. In Chapter 13, you'll learn how to add graphic objects that you can form into logos and diagrams, and in Chapter 14, you'll learn how to add clip art and pictures to enhance your slides.

Adding a Text Annotation

The Text Box
Button

The main difference between entering text in a text placeholder and adding text as a text annotation is in how you get started. To enter the main body text of a slide, such as bulleted text lines, you can simply click a *Click to add text* placeholder and begin typing. To create a text annotation, you must use the Text Box button on the Drawing toolbar, and then type in an annotation.

SEE ALSO

For more information about hiding slides, see "Hiding Slides", page 398.

To comment on the contents of a slide, you can add as many text boxes as you see fit, and you can move and copy them just like any other objects. But you might want to limit your use of text boxes to one every few slides to avoid cluttering the presentation or giving the impression that the exceptions to the rule are the rule. Rather than use text boxes, you can group comments, restrictions, exemptions, exclusions, and other technicalities on a subsequent slide, so they won't break the flow of your presentation. The subsequent slide can even be hidden so that you can display it only if necessary during a slide show.

To add a text box and enter a text annotation, follow these steps:

1   In Slide view, display the slide to which you want to add a text box.

2   Click the Text Box button on the Drawing toolbar.

3   Position the mouse pointer where you want the text box to appear, hold down the left mouse button, and drag out a rectangle. If you plan to type a short one- or two-word label, you can simply click the slide to add a small text box. The text box shown below was created by dragging:

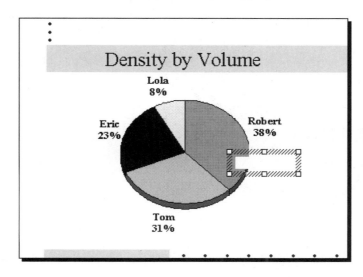

IV

Modifying the Presentation

4 Type the text of the annotation. As shown below, the box grows vertically, if necessary, to accommodate the text you enter.

NOTE

> If you simply click and then type a long note, the text box extends horizontally and eventually goes off the slide. To reformat the text in the text box, you need to turn on word wrap for the text box.

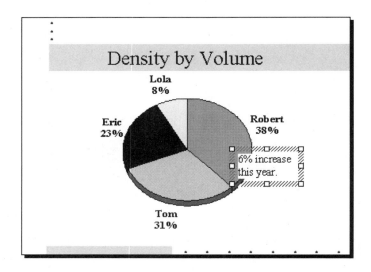

5 Click elsewhere on the slide to complete the text annotation or click the Text Box button again to add another text box.

Formatting a Text Annotation

SEE ALSO

For more information about formatting text, see Chapter 5, "Working with Text in Slide View," page 89.

You can format a text annotation by adding formatting to the text box either before or after you actually enter the text. As is always the case when you format text, you can use the buttons on the Formatting toolbar or the commands on the Format or shortcut menu to format the text in a text box. As you know by now, before you can format existing text, you must select it. To select part of the text in a text box, drag across it with the mouse. To select the entire text box, click the border of the text box. Unless you select specific characters to format, all text in the text box is reformatted.

IV

Modifying the Presentation

In addition to changing the appearance of the text in a text box, you can also change its position within the text box by choosing Text Box from the Format menu or double-clicking the border of the text box. Then click the Text Box tab, and select the appropriate options in the Format Text Box dialog box shown in Figure 12-2. These options let you set the text anchor point (position of the text within the box), change the box internal margins (distance from the box to the text inside), fit the boundaries of the text box to the text, turn word wrap on or off, and even rotate the text by 90 degrees.

FIGURE 12-2.
The Text Box tab of the Format Text Box dialog box.

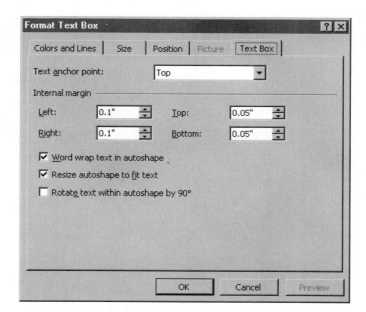

Moving, Resizing, and Formatting a Text Box

PowerPoint is very flexible when it comes to moving, resizing, and formatting text boxes. For example, you can move a text box to any location on a slide, even if it obscures other text or objects. You can also increase or decrease the size of the text box to accommodate more or less text. And if you're interested in changing the text box border or fill, PowerPoint offers a variety of options. To move a text box, follow the steps on the next page.

1 Position the mouse pointer on the border of the text box between two handles.

2 Drag the box to a new location on the slide.

To resize a text box, simply drag one of its handles.

TIP

When you finish typing text in a text box, you can press Esc and then press the arrow keys to adjust the position of the text box incrementally.

Whether you present an electronic slide show, create printed output or 35-mm slides, the default settings display only the text of a text box. The box itself does not appear because its fill and border are not formatted. To format the fill and border, you can select the text box, and then click the Fill Color button and the Line Color button on the Drawing toolbar. You can also click the Shadow On/Off button to add a shadow and give the box some depth or click the 3-D button to give the box perspective and light-source shading. And you can use the Line Style and Dashed Lines buttons to change the style of the text box border. To change the color of the text, you can click the Font Color button on the Drawing toolbar.

The Colors And Lines command on the Format menu (and the shortcut menu) opens the Format Text Box dialog box and displays the Colors And Lines tab so that you can select the Fill Color and Line Color options you want to use. On the Colors And Lines tab of the Format Text Box dialog box, shown in Figure 12-3, use the Color drop-down list in the Fill section to select a fill color or effect (Gradient, Texture, Pattern, or Picture). Use the Color drop-down list in the Line section to select a line color or pattern, and then use the Style, Dashed and Weight drop-down lists to change the appearance of the surrounding line. To format any new text boxes you create (in the current presentation) with the options you specify on the Colors And Lines tab, click the Default for New Objects check box.

TIP

How to Use a Shape Other than a Box

To create a text annotation with a more interesting shape, you can place an autoshape on a slide, and then enter text in the autoshape. To add text, click the autoshape with the right mouse button and choose Add Text from the shortcut menu. To get really fancy, you can also add a text annotation to a clip art selection. For more information about autoshapes, see "AutoShapes," page 332. For more information about using clip art, see Chapter 14, "Adding Multimedia," page 357.

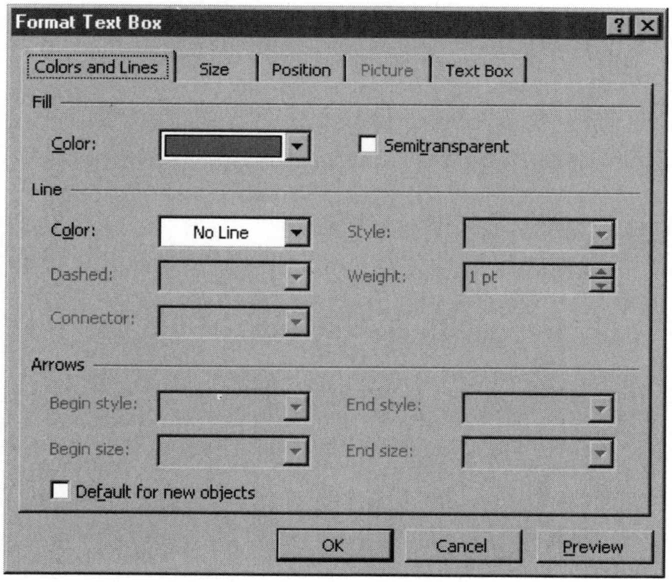

FIGURE 12-3.

The Colors And Lines dialog box.

Duplicating a Text Box

Duplicating a text box creates a second text box with the same formatting as the original. First format both the original text box and its text, and then select the original text box and choose Duplicate from the Edit menu or press Ctrl+D. After the duplicate text box appears on top of the original text box, you can drag the duplicate to a new position, select the text inside by dragging across it, and type replacement text. Another option is to hold down the Ctrl key and drag the text box to create a duplicate.

Adding Text as a Comment

Rather than add a text box annotation, which becomes visible on the slide, you may choose to add a comment, instead. Comments are useful when everyone in a workgroup is checking a presentation on the network before it is released for delivery. The comments appear like yellow sticky notes on slides. When each comment is created, PowerPoint adds the name of the person creating the comment automatically. Comments can be easily hidden from view so they do not appear when the presentation is given.

To add a comment, choose Comment from the Insert menu. Type your comment after your name, which appears within the comment box. You can also record a spoken comment by choosing Movies And Sounds from the Insert menu after starting a comment.

Adding Speaker Notes

Every slide in the presentation can have a special type of output called speaker notes or *notes pages*. On a notes page, you see two objects: the slide on the top part of the page and a text placeholder on the bottom part. The notes page for each slide is an integral part of the presentation, and is stored in the same file. To switch to Notes Page view, click the Notes Page View button in the lower left corner of the presentation window or choose Notes Page from the View menu. When you switch to Notes Page view, you see the notes page of the current slide, as shown in Figure 12-4.

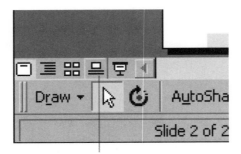

Notes Pages View button.

The notes page text, or any indication that notes page text exists, appears only in Notes Page view. But when you print the presentation, you can choose to print the notes pages.

Your initial view of the notes page is reduced so that you can see the entire page, but you may want to zoom in to see the text you type in the text placeholder below the slide image. To zoom in, change the zoom percentage in the Zoom Control box on the Standard toolbar or use the Zoom command on the View menu. A zoom percentage greater than 50% should allow you to read the notes page text.

FIGURE 12-4.

The current slide shown on a notes page in Notes Page view.

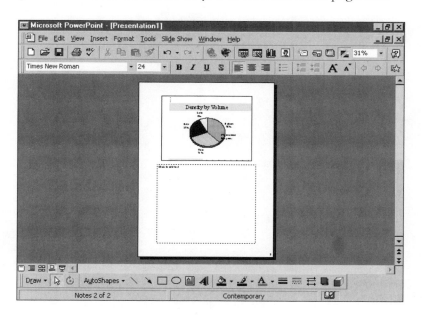

To enter a note, click the *Click to add text* placeholder below the slide image. Then begin typing in the placeholder as if you were typing text in a word processing program. The text will automatically wrap at the right edge of the text box. To start a new paragraph on the notes page, press Enter.

As with text annotations, you can use the buttons on the Formatting toolbar or the commands on the Format menu or the shortcut menu to format the notes page text before or after you type it. Again, if you want to format existing text, you must select the text first. You can also use the Line Spacing command on the Format menu to add line spacing within paragraphs or to add space before or after each paragraph. Figure 12-5 shows an enlarged view of a completed notes page where the notes text was formatted using bullets.

> **NOTE**
>
> Spell checking a presentation also checks the spelling of notes.

FIGURE 12-5.

A completed notes page formatted using bullets.

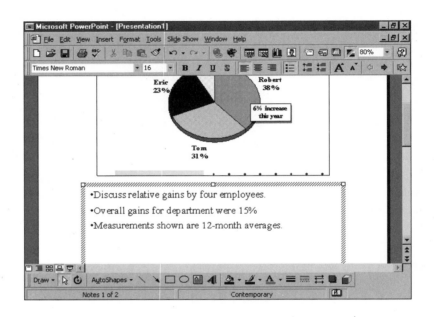

SEE ALSO

For information about printing notes pages, see Chapter 15, "Creating Printed Output, Web Pages and 35-mm Slides," page 377.

To enter speaker notes for the next slide in the presentation, click the Next Slide button or press the PgDn key. To return to the previous slide, click the Previous Slide button or press PgUp.

To open a Speaker Notes window that you can use in Slide, Outline or Slide Sorter view, choose Speaker Notes from the View menu.

After you enter text on the notes pages of a presentation, you should resave the presentation to be sure the text is stored as part of the presentation file.

In this chapter, you learned how to add text that can enhance the slides of a presentation. In the following two chapters, you'll learn how to draw graphic shapes and add ready-made images to slides.

CHAPTER 13

Drawing Graphic Objects

You don't have to be an artist to create professional-looking graphics in PowerPoint. No matter what your artistic ability, you can use the program's drawing tools to add simple graphic shapes to slides. You can enclose an area within a rectangle, for example, or add a sunburst shape that contains a message like "Special!" or "New!" You can even combine individual shapes to create a more elaborate diagram or map. PowerPoint's commands for editing shapes are also easy to use. You can resize, rotate, and flip graphic objects, combine individual objects into a grouped object, and even create three-dimensional objects with perspective.

In this chapter, you'll learn how to use the drawing tools on the Drawing toolbar to add graphic objects to a slide, and how to modify individual objects or groups of objects. In the next chapter, you'll learn how to add ready-made images to your presentation.

Setting Up the Drawing Area

In Slide view, you can turn on two built-in PowerPoint features that help you position items with accuracy. PowerPoint's rulers, which run along the top and down the side of the presentation window, measure distances from the horizontal and vertical centers of the slide. Two movable guides—dashed lines that cross the slide horizontally and vertically—allow you to line up objects with great precision against measurements on the rulers or against each other. Figure 13-1 shows both the rulers and the guides.

FIGURE 13-1.

The rulers and the guides.

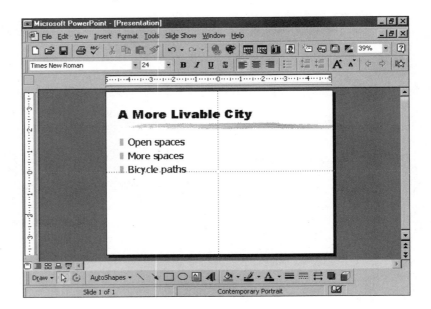

To turn on the rulers, choose Ruler from the View menu. To turn on the guides, choose Guides, also from the View menu. You can also choose both Ruler and Guides from the shortcut menu that appears when you position the mouse pointer on the slide background and click the right mouse button.

Dashed markers on the rulers track the movement of mouse pointer to help you "eyeball" the position of the pointer as you draw and edit objects. The fixed, unchangeable zero point of the rulers is the exact center of the slide. To more accurately position objects on a slide, move the guides by dragging them. As you drag a guide, an indicator

IV

Annotations and Graphics

on the guide shows the guide's horizontal or vertical distance from the ruler's zero point. For example, to precisely place an object that must extend one inch (1.00) to the left of the slide's center and two inches to the right, you can drag the vertical guide one inch to the left of the slide's center, as measured by the ruler. Next, you can draw the object from the guide to approximately two inches to the right of the slide's center, and then drag the guide to the exact two-inch mark. Finally, you can adjust the right edge of the object to align with the guide.

Perhaps a better way to precisely position objects is to use PowerPoint's new Position options on the Format AutoShape dialog box. You will learn about these options later in the chapter.

The Drawing Toolbar

The basic set of drawing and editing tools is located on the Drawing toolbar that runs along the bottom of the PowerPoint window in Slide view. When you click the Draw button at the left end of the Drawing toolbar, the pop-up Draw menu appears with a set of options for editing shapes. A third set of drawing options is located on the AutoShapes pop-up menu that you can display by clicking the AutoShapes button on the Drawing toolbar. Figure 13-2 shows the Drawing toolbar.

FIGURE 13-2.

The drawing toolbar.

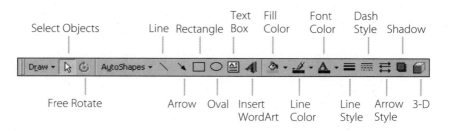

TIP

How to Create More Guides

If two guides are not sufficient, you can replicate a guide by holding down the Ctrl key and dragging a copy of the guide off the original guide. You can then use the new guide just as you would use the original.

Drawing and Formatting the Basic Shapes

On the Drawing toolbar, you'll find a button for each of the basic shapes you can add to a slide. Shapes have an outline and a fill area whose default colors are determined by the current color scheme. The color scheme's Text and Lines color sets the outline color, and the Fill color governs the interior color. Because the color scheme controls these colors, any change to the color scheme also changes the colors in shapes you've drawn. However, if you have individually formatted the line or fill color of an object, the object retains its unique colors no matter what the color scheme dictates.

Lines and Arrows

A line or arrow is the easiest drawing you can create. A straight line simply connects two end points.

To add a straight line or arrow to a slide, follow these steps:

1 Click the Line or Arrow button on the Drawing toolbar.

2 Position the mouse pointer where you want the line to start.

3 Hold down the left mouse button, and drag to the end point.

4 Release the mouse button. A line appears between the first and second end points. If you've drawn an arrow, the arrowhead points in the direction you drew.

TIP

Drawing Straight
Hold down the Shift key if you want to constrain the line to exactly horizontal, vertical, or diagonal.

When you hold down the Ctrl key as you drag, the first end point becomes the center of the line, and the line grows in opposite directions from the first end point as you drag.

To change the appearance of the line, select the line and then click one of the formatting buttons on the Drawing toolbar. These buttons, shown in Figure 13-3, allow you to make changes to the appearance of lines, arrows, and other objects you've drawn.

FIGURE 13-3.

The formatting buttons on the Drawing toolbar.

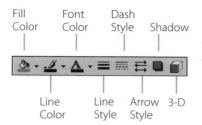

Fill Color   Font Color   Dash Style   Shadow

Line Color   Line Style   Arrow Style   3-D

The Line Color button displays the currently selected color. To choose a different color, click the down arrow at the right side of the button. You can choose one of the eight basic colors of the color scheme, or click More Line Colors to choose other colors in the Color dialog box.

To change the thickness of the line, click the Line Style button and then choose one of the displayed line styles. To set the line weight in quarter-point increments, choose More Lines from the Line Style pop-up list, and then change the Line Weight setting on the Colors And Lines tab of the Format AutoShape dialog box.

The Arrow Style button works similarly to the Line Style button. Choose an arrow style or click More Arrows for more choices in the Format AutoShape dialog box.

The Shadow and 3D buttons will apply a shadow and 3D effect to a line, but these effects are more suited to shapes like rectangles and squares. They will be covered later in the chapter, in "Adding a 3D Effect," page 345.

SEE ALSO

For information about creating custom colors, see "Creating a Custom Color Scheme," page 223.

For more options while changing the appearance of a line, you can double-click the line and then make selections on the Colors And Lines tab of the Format AutoShape dialog box, shown in Figure 13-4 on the next page. On the Colors And Lines tab, select a line color from the Color drop-down list and a line style from the Style drop-down list. When you open the Color drop-down list, you see the eight colors of the color scheme at the top, and any other colors you have applied to the objects in the presentation. If you don't like any of the eight colors, you can select one of the other standard colors on the palette, or click More Colors to choose or create one of your own.

IV

Annotations and Graphics

FIGURE 13-4.
The Colors and Lines tab of the Format AutoShape dialog box.

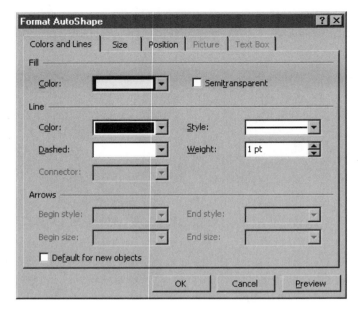

In the Style drop-down list, you can select from more than a dozen preset line weights or double- and triple-line combinations. In the Dashed drop-down list, you can leave the first option, a solid line, or select one of the dashed or dotted lines displayed. In the Begin Style and End Style drop-down lists, you can leave the current arrow style settings, or you can select one of the other options to change the arrowhead appearance at one or both ends of the line. After you select the changes, click OK to return to the slide.

If you want every line you create to look the same, click the Default For New Objects option at the bottom of the Colors And Lines tab after you make your selections.

TIP

How to Copy Formatting from One Object to Another
To copy the formatting of an existing object to a new object, click the object with the formatting you want to copy, click the Format Painter button on the Standard toolbar, and then click the new object.

Rectangles and Squares

You can use the Rectangle button on the Drawing toolbar to draw a rectangle or a square in PowerPoint. As you'll see, drawing a rectangle is almost as easy as drawing a line.

To draw a rectangle or a square, follow these steps:

1   Click the Rectangle button on the Drawing toolbar.

2   Position the mouse pointer at the location for one corner of the rectangle or square.

3   Hold down the left mouse button, and drag diagonally to the opposite corner of the rectangle or square.

4   Release the mouse button. A rectangle or square appears, displaying the line and fill colors of the current color scheme.

TIP

Drawing Perfect Squares
To draw a perfect square rather than a rectangle, hold down the Shift key.

To have a rectangle grow outward from the first point you click, hold down the Ctrl key as you drag. To have a square grow outward from the first point you click, hold down both the Shift and Ctrl keys as you drag.

To change the colors and border style of the rectangle or square, select the rectangle or square, and use the Fill Color, Line Color, and Line Style buttons on the Drawing toolbar. As with lines, you can also double-click the rectangle and change options in the Format AutoShape dialog box.

To add a more interesting fill to the rectangle or square, you can select Fill Effects from the Fill Color pop-up list. These special fills, which allow you to add shading, a texture, a pattern, or a picture, are covered in "Applying Special Fills to Objects," page 340.

You can also add a shadow or 3D effect to a rectangle or square. These two special effects are covered in "Adding a Shadow," page 344 and "Adding a 3D Effect," page 345.

Ovals and Circles

Like the Rectangle button, which lets you draw rectangles or squares, the Oval button on the Drawing toolbar lets you draw ovals or circles.

To draw an oval or a circle, follow these steps:

1 Click the Oval button on the Drawing toolbar.

2 Position the mouse pointer at the location of one corner of an imaginary rectangle that would enclose the oval or circle.

3 Hold down the left mouse button, and drag to the opposite corner of the imaginary rectangle.

4 Release the mouse button. An oval or circle appears, displaying the line and fill colors of the current color scheme.

TIP

> **Drawing a Perfect Circle**
> To draw a perfect circle rather than an oval, hold down the Shift key.

To have an oval grow outward from the first point you click, hold down the Ctrl key as you drag. To have a circle grow outward from the first point you click, hold down both the Shift and Ctrl keys as you drag.

To change the colors and border style of the oval or circle, select the shape, and then click the corresponding buttons on the Drawing toolbar. You can also double-click the shape and make changes in the Format AutoShape dialog box.

As with rectangles, ovals and circles can also have shadows and 3D effects. These two special effects are covered in "Adding a Shadow," page 344 and "Adding a 3-D Effect," page 345.

AutoShapes

PowerPoint's autoshapes are familiar shapes that you are likely to use frequently, such as arrows and stars. They are generally more complex than those on the Drawing toolbar, and many of them have an *adjustment handle*, which allows you to adjust their most characteristic feature. For example, a cube autoshape has an adjustment handle that you can drag to adjust the depth of the cube. An arrow autoshape's adjustment handle changes the shape of the arrowhead.

To draw an autoshape, follow these steps:

1   Click the AutoShapes button on the Drawing toolbar.

2   Point to an autoshape category from the autoshape menu.

3   Click an autoshape on the pop-out display of autoshapes.

4   On the slide, position the mouse pointer where you want the autoshape to begin, hold down the left mouse button, and then drag the autoshape into place.

5   If the autoshape has an adjustment handle, as shown below, drag the adjustment handle to adjust the autoshape.

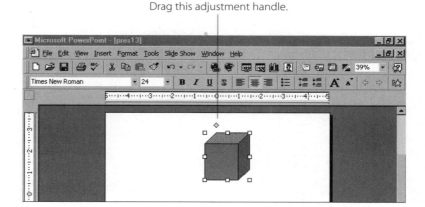

Drag this adjustment handle.

An autoshape can be filled and outlined, just like any other object you draw. You can also move, resize, copy and paste, and duplicate an autoshape.

TIP

How to Resize an AutoShape without Stretching It
To resize an autoshape without stretching it out of shape, hold down the Shift key as you drag one of the shape's corner handles.

Curves and Freeforms

You're not confined to drawing only lines, rectangles, and circles in PowerPoint. Options in the Lines category of autoshapes give you the freedom to draw curved and straight lines—even combinations of the two—along with some fairly complex objects.

To draw a curve, follow these steps:

1 Click the AutoShapes button on the Drawing toolbar.

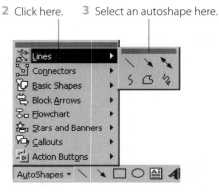

2 Click here.   **3** Select an autoshape here.

4 Position the mouse pointer on the slide, where you want the beginning of the shape.

5 Click the first point of the curve.

6 Move the pointer to the next point for the curve and click again.

7 Repeat moving the pointer and clicking until you have completed the entire shape.

8 Click once near the starting point of the shape to close the shape or double-click at any point to end the shape as it is and leave it open.

To force a straight line between two points, hold down the Ctrl key when you click the second point. To constrain a straight line segment to exactly horizontal, vertical, or diagonal, hold down the Shift key as you move the pointer.

Drawing Freeforms is just like drawing curves, except that the lines between points are straight rather than curved, unless you hold down the mouse button so that the pointer changes to a pencil shape so that lines are curved as though you are writing.

TIP

How to Back Up While Drawing a Shape
As you draw a curve or freeform shape, you can remove previous points you've added by pressing the Backspace key.

NOTE

You can re-shape a curve or freeform by editing its points. You'll learn to edit points in "Reshaping a Line by Editing Its Points," page 346.

Scribbles

Adding a scribble lets you draw anything you want on a page. It's just like doodling on a piece of paper. To add a scribble, choose scribble from the Line category of autoshapes, place the pointer on the slide, hold down the mouse button, and just draw. You can edit the points of a scribble just as you can edit the points of a curve. You'll learn to edit points in "Reshaping a Line by Editing Its Points," page 346.

Connectors

Connectors are lines and curves whose ends attach to other drawn objects. After you've added a connector between two objects, you can move the objects and they will remain connected. Connectors are very helpful when you draw flow charts and schematics, for example.

To add a connector, choose Connectors from the AutoShapes menu on the Drawing toolbar. Then choose one of the nine connector styles on the Connectors menu, as shown on the next page.

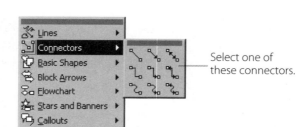

Select one of these connectors.

As you pass the mouse pointer over drawn objects on the current slide, you will see connection points appear at the edges of the objects. Click one point on each object to connect, as shown in Figure 13-5. You can add more than one connector between two objects, and you can move the end of a connector to a different connection point on an object just by dragging it there.

FIGURE 13-5.
Click connection points on two objects to add a connector.

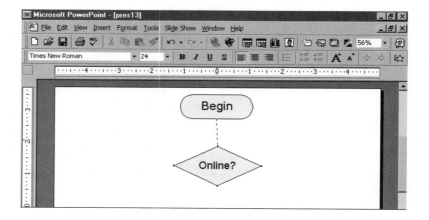

PowerPoint supplies three types of connectors: straight, elbow, and curved. To change connector types, right-click a connector and then choose a different type on the shortcut menu. Elbow and curved connectors show yellow diamonds along their paths. You can drag these diamonds to reshape the connectors. You may want to reshape a connector after you've moved one of the objects to which it is attached, for example. You can also reshape the connector automatically, joining the two closest points on the objects. To reroute a connector automatically, select the connector, click the right mouse button, and choose Reroute Connectors from the shortcut menu.

Adding Text to an Object

You can add text to the interior of any drawn object, except the Line shapes, by clicking on the object and then typing. Because the text becomes an integral part of the object, when you move the object, the text moves too.

If you try to enter more than a few words, however, the text may overrun the borders of the object, as shown in Figure 13-6. To wrap the text within the object, follow these steps:

1   Choose AutoShape from the Format menu.

2   Click the Text Box tab in the Format AutoShape dialog box.

3   Select the Word Wrap Text In AutoShape option.

4   Click OK.

Be sure not to select the Resize AutoShape To Fit Text option, because the object will adjust to the text rather than the other way around. After you turn on word wrap and click OK, you'll see the newly wrapped text, which fits within the left and right borders of the object, as shown in Figure 13-7 on the next page.

FIGURE 13-6.

The text in this object has overrun the object's borders.

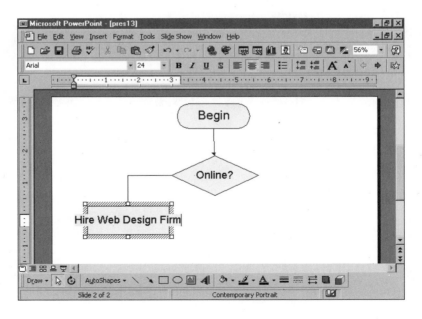

To keep the text from overrunning the top and bottom borders of the object, you can either return to the Text Box options and select the Resize Object To Fit Text option or reduce the text size. To make minor adjustments to the size of the text in the object, select the text, and then click the Increase Font Size button or the Decrease Font Size button on the Formatting toolbar. You can also press Ctrl+Shift+> to increase the font size or Ctrl+Shift+< to decrease the font size.

FIGURE 13-7.
The text in this object wraps neatly within the object.

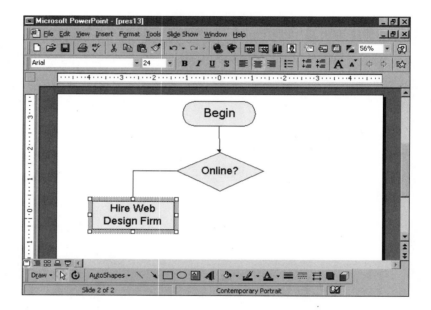

Switching Shapes

A special command on the Draw pop-up menu, Change AutoShape, lets you replace a shape you've drawn with a different shape. You simply select the shape you want to replace, choose Change AutoShape from the Draw menu, select an autoshape group, and then select a new shape from the Change AutoShape palette, shown in figure 13-8. You can convert a star to a sunburst, for example, or a thin arrow to a thick arrow.

FIGURE 13-8.
The Change
AutoShapes
menu.

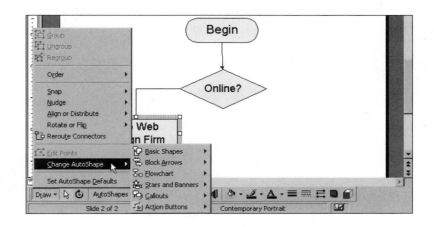

The new shape occupies the same positioning and has the same size of the original shape and retains all of the original shape's formatting.

Editing Objects

Up to this point, you've learned how to change the fill and border color and the border style of objects. PowerPoint provides other editing options as well, such as adding a shadow or 3-D effect to an object. These are discussed in the following section. But first you must learn how to select single objects and multiple objects.

Selecting Objects

Before you can make changes to a graphic object in PowerPoint, you must select the object. If you want to make changes to more than one object, you can select multiple objects.

To select a single object, simply click the object. To select more than one object, do one of the following:

- Hold down the Shift key as you click each object. (To deselect one of the selected objects, click the object again while holding down the Shift key.)

- Click the Select Objects button on the Drawing toolbar, and drag a selection box around the objects. Only objects that are completely enclosed by the selection box are selected. For example,

Figure 13-9 shows a selection box that will select two of the four objects on a slide.

To select all the objects on a slide, choose the Select All command from the Edit menu or press Ctrl+A. All objects, including titles, bulleted text, and graphs, are selected.

After you select multiple objects, any changes you make will affect all the objects in the selection.

Applying Special Fills to Objects

When you learned how to add basic shapes earlier in this chapter, you also learned how to use options on the Drawing toolbar to change the fill and line colors and styles of a selected object. Special options also let you create objects filled with a color shading, objects filled with a pattern or texture, or objects filled with a picture.

Filling an Object with Shading

Shadings in objects add richness and depth and can give the appearance that the objects have been illuminated from the side, top, or corner. Combined with shadows, shadings can create an impressive three-dimensional effect.

To add shading to an object, follow these steps:

1 Select the object.

2 Click the down arrow button just beside the Fill Color button on the Drawing toolbar.

3 Select Fill Effects to display the dialog box shown here:

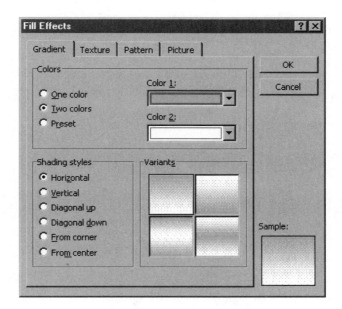

4 On the Gradient tab of the dialog box, select a Shading Style and one of the four Variants, which depict how the shading progresses from light color to dark color, dark color to light color, and so on.

5 To change the color of the shading, select one of the color options at the top of the dialog box, and then fine-tune the color by selecting options in the corresponding drop-down list(s). If you select the One Color option, you can also use the scroll bar in the Colors section to make the shading darker or lighter. To use one of PowerPoint's ready-made color schemes, click the Preset option, and then select a scheme from the Preset Colors drop-down list.

Filling an Object with a Texture, Pattern, or Picture

Adding texture to an object can give the object a whole new feel. PowerPoint provides many different textures to choose from, including oak, green marble, cork, recycled paper, and even sand.

To fill an object with a texture, follow these steps:

1 Select the object.

2 Click the down arrow button just beside the Fill Color button on the Drawing toolbar.

3 Select Fill Effects.

4 Click the Texture tab in the Fill Effects dialog box.

The Texture tab is shown in Figure 13-10. Select any of the textures shown, or click Other Texture to select a different texture stored in a file on disk.

FIGURE 13-10.

The Texture tab of the Fill Effects dialog box.

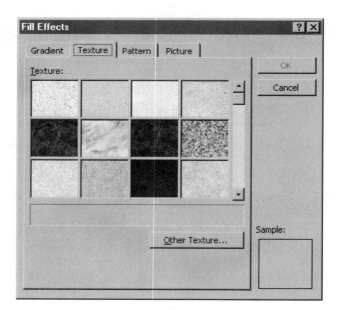

Rather than fill an object with a solid or shaded color, you can fill it with a pattern made up of two colors. PowerPoint offers a number of patterns and a wide variety of foreground and background colors to choose from.

To fill an object with a pattern, click the Pattern tab in the Fill Effects dialog box. On the Pattern tab, shown in Figure 13-11, the patterns are composed of the foreground and background colors displayed in the Foreground and Background boxes. You can select a different pattern and different foreground and background colors to create the combination you want.

FIGURE 13-11.
The Pattern tab of the Fill Effects dialog box.

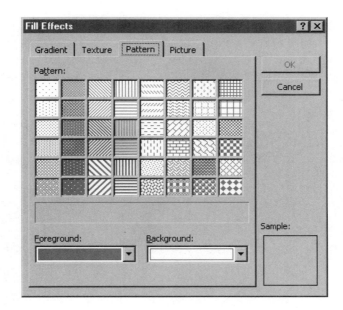

The Picture tab of the Fill Effects dialog box lets you select a picture file to place within an AutoShape. You may need to resize the autoshape to see the entire picture because you cannot resize the picture.

Filling an Object with a Semitransparent Color or the Background

The Semitransparent option on the Colors And Lines tab of the Format AutoShape dialog box allows you to set the fill color as translucent rather than fully opaque so you can see other objects through the autoshape. To fill the object with the same color used in the slide background, choose Background on the color palette.

Adding a Shadow

PowerPoint lets you add a shadow behind objects and determine the shadow's color, direction, and size. You can add a shadow to any object you've drawn and to any text you've added to a slide.

To add a shadow, select the object, and click the Shadow button on the Drawing toolbar. From the display of shadow presets, shown in Figure 13-12, choose a shadow style. To alter the color, direction, and size of the shadow, choose Shadow Settings, and then click one of the buttons on the new Shadow Settings toolbar, shown in Figure 13-13. These buttons let you turn the shadow on or off, nudge the shadow in any of four directions, and change the shadow color.

FIGURE 13-12.
The Shadow presets.

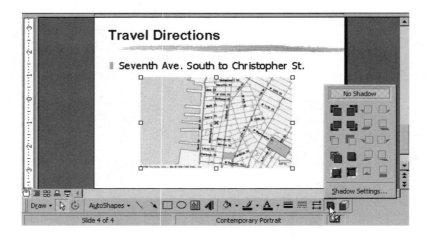

FIGURE 13-13.
The Shadow
Settings toolbar.

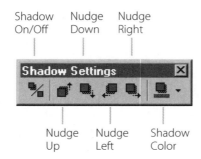

The Semitransparent Shadow option on the Shadow Color palette causes the shadow to be translucent.

TIP

Creating Consistent Graphics
To create a slide that makes visual sense, apply the same shadow to every object on the slide, even the title of the slide.

Adding a 3-D Effect

Certain autoshapes, such as the basic shapes, block arrows, and callouts, can gain a full, three-dimensional effect to give them the appearance of depth. To add or vary the 3-D effect for these objects, select the object and click the 3-D button on the Drawing toolbar. From the palette of preset 3-D styles, select a preset to display the object at a certain tilt and depth.

For more control over the 3-D effect, choose 3-D Settings after you click the 3-D button on the Drawing toolbar. This displays the 3-D Settings toolbar shown in Figure 13-14. The 3-D Settings toolbar offers fine-tuning options for the 3-D effect.

FIGURE 13-14.
The 3-D Settings toolbar.

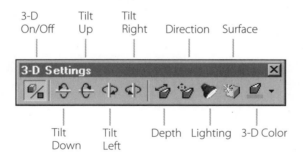

The first button turns the 3-D effect on or off. The next four buttons tilt the object in 3-D space. The Depth and Direction buttons allow you to increase the apparent depth of the object and the direction the object faces. Clicking the Lighting button lets you choose the side from which the light shines. Choose the white cube in the center to have the light appear to come directly from in front of the slide. You can also choose three light intensities: Bright, Normal, and Dim. Clicking the Surface button allows you to change the surface texture of the object, which affects how much light is reflected off the object.

Adding a 3-D effect to an autoshape removes any shadow the autoshape already has.

Reshaping a Line by Editing Its Points

Line, curve, arrow, and freeform autoshapes can be stretched, rotated, moved and copied, but to change their shape, you'll need to edit their points. You can think of all these objects as multiple segments joined end to end. The points where pairs of segments join can be moved. Moving these points reshapes the object. Figure 13-15 shows two autoshapes. The autoshape on the left is selected. The shape on the right is having its points edited.

FIGURE 13-15.
A selected figure (left) and a figure as its points are edited (right).

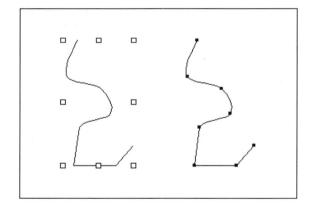

To see the points of an object, select the object, click the right mouse button, and choose Edit Points from the shortcut menu. You can drag any of these points, and add new points by pressing the Ctrl key and clicking between existing points. You can also add a point by clicking between two points and dragging. To delete a point, click the point with the right mouse button and choose Delete Point from the shortcut menu. The Close Curve option on the shortcut menu connects the first and last points of the object with a straight line.

A point can also be one of four styles. The style affects how the ends of the segments join the point. To change the point style, right-click the point and then choose an option on the shortcut menu. The default point, the Auto Point, has segments on either side whose direction and length cannot be changed manually except by dragging the point. On the other hand, the segments on either side of a Smooth Point can be modified by dragging either of the handles which appear adjacent to the point, as shown in Figure 13-16. Dragging either handle changes the segments equally, but in opposite directions. When you change a point to a Straight Point, you'll find that you can drag either handle independently to re-shape the segment on one side of a point only. Finally, choosing Corner Point creates a corner whose angle can be changed when you drag either handle.

You can also toggle the segments between points between straight and curved lines. To change a segment, right-click it and then choose Straight Segment or Curved Segment from the shortcut menu.

FIGURE 13-16.
Drag either handle to reshape a Smooth Point.

Drag either handle.

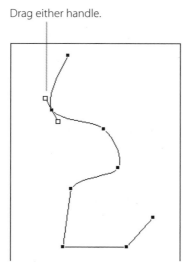

After you finish editing points, click elsewhere on the slide or choose Exit Edit Points from the shortcut menu.

Transferring Object Formats

After you finish modifying the appearance of an object, you can transfer the object's format to another object by using the Format Painter button on the Standard toolbar. Simply select the object whose format you want to transfer, click the Format Painter button, and then select the object to which you want to transfer the format. If you double-click the Format Painter button, the format will be copied to all subsequent objects you select until you press Esc or click the Format Painter button again to turn it off.

 TIP

Setting an Object Format as a Default
After you've formatted an object, you can save it as the default for autoshapes of that type by selecting the object and then choosing Set AutoShape Defaults from the Draw pop-up menu on the Drawing toolbar.

Arranging Objects

In addition to providing tools and commands that change the look of one or more objects, PowerPoint provides several features that allow you to arrange objects on slides.

Grouping Objects

If you frequently make changes to more than one object at a time, you might want to combine the objects into a group. The objects are then treated as a unit, and any changes you make affect the entire group. For example, you can select the group and then move all the objects as a unit or modify the fill color so that all the objects in the group change simultaneously.

To group objects, select the objects, click Draw on the Drawing toolbar, and then click the Group button. When the objects are grouped, one set of handles surrounds the group, as shown in Figure 13-17.

FIGURE 13-17.
A group of objects
has one set of
handles.

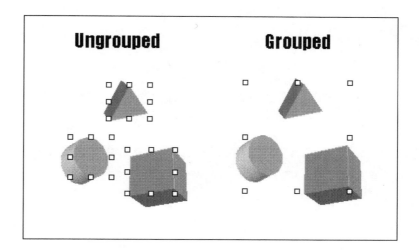

After you group objects, you can ungroup them by clicking the
Ungroup button on the Draw pop-up menu. The Regroup button
puts a group back together after it's been ungrouped.

Cutting, Copying, and Duplicating Objects

You can cut, copy, and paste graphic objects as you would any object
on a PowerPoint slide by using the Cut, Copy, and Paste buttons on
the Standard toolbar; the Cut, Copy, and Paste commands on the Edit
menu or the shortcut menu; or the keyboard equivalents (shown on
the Edit menu). Not only can you cut and copy objects from one slide
to another, but you can cut and copy objects from one presentation to
another. The easiest way is to open two presentations side by side in
Slide view, then cut or copy an object in one presentation and paste
it in another.

The fastest way to duplicate an object and simultaneously position the
duplicate is to hold down the Ctrl key and drag a copy of the object
into position. But you can also select the object, and choose Duplicate from the Edit menu or press Ctrl+D. You will still need to drag
the object into position.

How to Undo Drawing Actions
Remember, you can undo most of the commands discussed in this chapter by clicking the Undo button on the Standard toolbar or by choosing Undo from the Edit menu.

Moving, Resizing, and Scaling Objects

To move an object, place the mouse pointer on the object, hold down the left mouse button, and then drag the object to a new location. To move an object horizontally or vertically, hold down the Shift key while you drag. To resize an object, drag one of the object's handles in the desired direction. If you want to maintain the proportions of the object, hold down the Shift key while you drag a corner handle. If you want the object to grow out from its center, hold down the Ctrl key while you drag a corner handle.

How to Move an Object with the Keyboard
To use the keyboard to move an object, press Tab until the object you want to move is selected, and then press the Left, Right, Up, or Down arrow key to move the object in small increments.

To help you position an object, you can choose Snap To Grid or Snap To Shape from the Draw menu on the Drawing toolbar. Then, as you drag the object, it will automatically jump to the nearest horizontal and vertical ruler marking, or align with the nearest edge of an adjacent object, if one is near. To temporarily turn off Snap To Grid and drag an object freely on a slide, hold down the Alt key as you drag. The object will move smoothly without little jerks as it jumps from ruler marking to ruler marking.

Rather than drag objects into position, you can set object placements and sizing very precisely on the Size and Position tabs of the Format AutoShape dialog box, which appears when you double-click an object. On the Size tab, you can enter an exact height and width. You can also resize an object with the Scale Height and Scale Width settings. To double the size of an object, you'd enter 200% as the Scale Height and Scale Width. Keep in mind that objects can be scaled no larger than the size of the slide. When you also click Lock Aspect Ratio, the Width setting changes to equal the new Height setting, and vice versa. The Position tab offers you the chance to position the top left corner of the object relative to the top left corner or the center of the screen.

Rotating and Flipping Objects

You can rotate a single object or a group of objects around its center, and you can rotate multiple selected objects, each around its own center.

To rotate a single object or group of objects, follow these steps:

1   Select the object or group, as shown below.

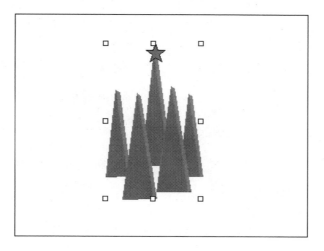

2   Click the Free Rotate button on the Drawing toolbar.

3   Place the mouse pointer on a corner handle of the object or group, and then drag the handle left or right around the center of the object or group.

⭐ **TIP**

How to Rotate Objects with More Precision
For more precision while rotating, click a handle and drag the pointer away from the object before dragging in a circle around the object.

If you select multiple objects, each object rotates around its center when you rotate any one of the objects. In Figure 13-18, the objects were not grouped before being rotated, and each object has rotated around its own center.

On the Draw menu of the Drawing toolbar, you'll find two options that rotate objects exactly 90 degrees to the left or right. Select the object and choose Rotate Or Flip from the Draw menu on the Drawing toolbar. Choose either Rotate Left or Rotate Right.

FIGURE 13-18.
Ungrouped objects rotate around their own centers.

To create a mirror image of one or more objects, use the Flip buttons or the Flip commands by following these steps:

1 Select the object or objects you want to flip, as shown here:

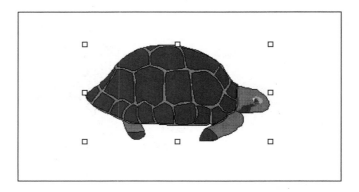

2 Select Rotate Or Flip from the Draw menu on the Drawing toolbar.

3 Click Flip Horizontal or Flip Vertical. The object shown below was flipped horizontally:

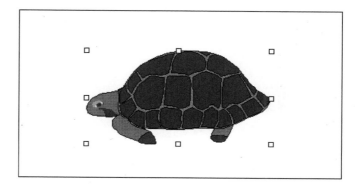

Ordering Objects

When objects overlap, you can change their order in the stack. You can move an object one level higher or lower in the stack, or send an object to the top or bottom of the stack.

To move an object one level higher or lower in a stack, select the object, and then choose Order from the Draw menu on the Drawing toolbar. Click Bring Forward or Send Backward. If you want to move an object to the top or bottom of a stack, choose Bring To Front or Send To Back, instead.

Figure 13-19 on the next page shows two versions of a simple scene. On the left, the man in the center is in the back. On the right, he has been moved to the front using the Bring To Front command.

FIGURE 13-19.
The center man in the right group has been moved forward one level using the Bring To Front command.

Aligning Objects

To line up objects on a slide, select the objects and then choose Align Or Distribute from the Draw menu on the Drawing toolbar. The six alignment commands on the submenu allow you to left-align, right-align, top-align, or bottom-align objects, as well as center objects vertically or horizontally. The objects align with the object that is farthest out. In other words, right-aligned objects align with the object that is farthest to the right. Figure 13-20 shows three objects before and after the Left Align command was chosen.

FIGURE 13-20.
Three objects before and after being left-aligned.

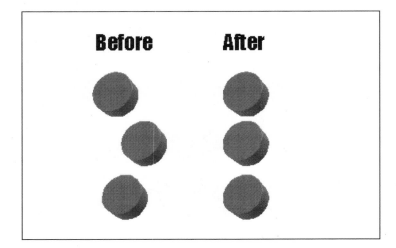

TIP

Adding Align Commands to a Toolbar
The commands on the Align Or Distribute submenu are available as toolbar buttons that you can drag to any toolbar. For information about customizing a toolbar, see "Customizing Toolbars," page 491.

Distributing Objects

To evenly space objects, select the objects and then choose Align Or Distribute from the Draw menu on the Drawing toolbar. Choose Distribute Horizontally or Distribute Vertically depending on whether you want the objects spread out across the slide, or down the slide as shown in Figure 13-21. If Relative To Slide is selected on the Align Or Distribute submenu, the slides will also be evenly spaced across or down the entire slide.

FIGURE 13-21.
Objects before and after being distributed.

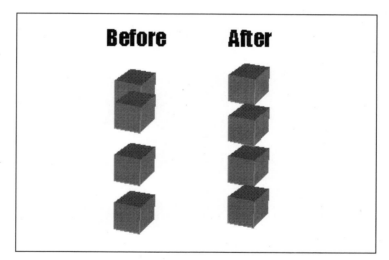

Nudging Objects

To move objects just a little, try the Nudge commands on the Draw menu from the Drawing toolbar. Sometimes a little nudge is all that you need.

Saving a Drawing for Use in Another Presentation

One method you can use to save your most valuable drawings, such as logos, is to copy and paste the drawings into a special presentation. When you need a particular drawing, you can open the presentation, copy the drawing, and then paste it into a new presentation.

? SEE ALSO

For more information about importing files into the Clip Gallery, see Chapter 14, "Adding Multimedia," page 357.

Another method is to add the drawing to PowerPoint's Clip Gallery. Unfortunately, the Clip Gallery doesn't offer an easy way to transfer graphic objects from a slide to the Gallery. Instead, you must copy and paste the objects into a drawing application such as CorelDRAW! so that you can export the objects into a file. Then, you can import the file into the Clip Gallery, where you'll always have access to the objects from within PowerPoint.

In this chapter, you learned how to create pictures by drawing them. In the next chapter, you'll learn how to import pictures that have already been created and stored in files or in PowerPoint's Clip Gallery.

Adding Multimedia

Words and graphs can tickle the brain and invoke powerful mental images, but a picture, sound, or video clip settles deep in long-term memory, where it has an effect far into the future. If you're not an artist, musician, or videographer, where do you get the multimedia files you need? PowerPoint's Clip Gallery can suggest an appropriate file from its gallery of clip art, pictures, sounds, and video. It can also store pictures, sounds, and video you've gotten on disk or from the Internet.

The Clip Gallery contains more than a thousand pictures drawn by professional artists. You can easily place any of the pictures on your presentation slides. If none of the clip art images is right, you can import an image from another program. Drawings and paintings from other Windows-based applications are especially easy to transfer over to a presentation. And if the image you need is a photo, you can insert a scanned picture into PowerPoint just as easily.

In this chapter, you'll learn how to add clip art pictures, scanned photos, sounds, music, and video clips to your presentations. You'll also learn how to transfer your favorite and most frequently used files to the Clip Gallery, so that you can use them in future presentations.

Using the Clip Gallery

The Clip Gallery is one of PowerPoint's optional components. If you installed the Gallery when you initially ran PowerPoint Setup, it is always available from within Slide view or Notes Pages view to dress up your pages with pictures. If, as you follow the instructions in this chapter, you find that the Clip Gallery was not installed, you can install it by running PowerPoint Setup and clicking the Add/Remove button. (The Gallery is shared with other Microsoft Office applications, so if you have an application such as Microsoft Word on your computer, you may already have access to the Clip Gallery.)

Adding Clip Art with AutoClipArt

PowerPoint can help you select an appropriate piece of art for your slides by looking at key words in your presentation and trying to find pictures to match.

In Slide view, choose AutoClipArt from the Tools menu. PowerPoint displays the AutoClipArt dialog box, shown in Figure 14-1.

FIGURE 14-1.

The AutoClipArt dialog box.

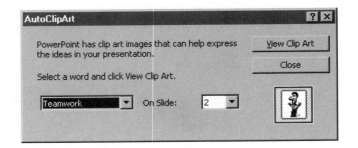

To go to a slide for which AutoClipArt suggests an image, first select a word in the drop-down list, then select a slide from the On Slide drop-down list and click the View Clip Art button. The Microsoft Clip Gallery dialog box opens with the suggested picture selected. You can click Insert to add this picture to your slide, or select any other picture from the Gallery and click Insert.

Adding Clip Art Manually

You can manually add clip art to any existing slide while in Slide view, or you can select one of the four autolayouts that come with clip art or clip media placeholders when you start a new slide. Figure 14-2 shows the four autolayouts that have clip art or clip media placeholders. When you select an autolayout that has one of these placeholders, you can double-click the placeholder to open the Clip Gallery for browsing.

> **NOTE**
>
> The first time you open the Clip Gallery, you may have to let the Gallery build its library of files by clicking Yes when you're asked if you want to add clips now. If you don't see this prompt, the Gallery has already built its library and is ready for use.

FIGURE 14-2.

The autolayouts with clip art and clip media placeholders.

Autolayouts with clip art placeholders.

Autolayouts with media clip placeholders.

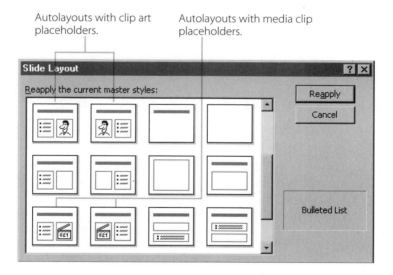

To manually add clip art to an existing slide that does not have a clip art placeholder, display the slide in Slide view and then do one of the following:

The Insert Clip Art button

- Click the Insert Clip Art button on the Standard toolbar.

- Choose the Picture command from the Insert menu, and then choose Clip Art from the Picture submenu.

The Microsoft Clip Gallery dialog box appears, as shown in Figure 14-3.

FIGURE 14-3.

The Microsoft Clip Gallery dialog box.

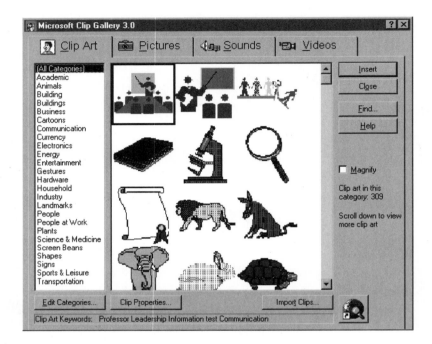

An alphabetized list of clip art categories appears on the left side of the dialog box, and clip art pictures from the currently selected category appear to the right of the list. By default, All Categories is selected in the category list so that you can scroll through all the pictures in the Gallery. If you want to see only the clip art in a specific category, click the category name and then scroll through the pictures.

Select the clip art image you want by clicking it. A dark border surrounds your clip art selection. To zoom in on the image, click the Magnify checkbox. To add the clip art selection to a slide, click Insert. You can also double-click a clip art picture in the dialog box to add it to a slide.

When you add a clip art image to a slide, the image appears in the placeholder you double-clicked to open the Clip Gallery, or it appears centered on a slide without a clip art placeholder.

After a clip art picture appears on a slide, you can drag the picture to move it. Figure 14-4 shows a clip art image that has been moved to the bottom of the slide. If you want to resize a clip art picture, drag a corner handle to maintain the clip art's proportions while you resize it, or hold down the Ctrl key and drag a corner handle to stretch or shrink the clip art picture from the center out.

FIGURE 14-4.

A clip art picture on a slide.

Adding Clip Art to the Background of a Presentation

To add a clip art picture to the background of every slide in a presentation, you can add the picture to the Slide Master background. First choose Master from the View menu and then Slide Master from the submenu. Then open the Clip Gallery, select the image you want, and click Insert. After the clip art picture has been added to the background of the presentation, you can place the picture behind the text of the presentation by selecting the clip art object and choosing Send To Back from the Draw menu's Order submenu.

Finding Clip Art with the Find Clip Dialog Box

Each picture in the Clip Gallery has a text description you can use to search for a particular image. To search for a picture, first click the Find button in the Microsoft Clip Gallery dialog box. The Find Clip dialog box appears, as shown in Figure 14-5 on the next page.

FIGURE 14-5.
The Find Clip
dialog box.

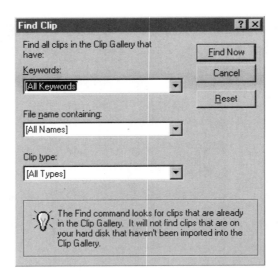

The Find Clip dialog box allows you to narrow down the list of images displayed in the Clip Gallery by selecting one of three search methods: by keyword, by filename, or by clip type.

To search for a keyword in the clip art picture's description, type the keyword in the Keywords edit box. To search for a picture filename that contains specific characters, type the characters in the File Name Containing edit box. To search by picture type, select one of the picture types from the Clip Type drop-down list.

For example, to find a clip art image that represents leadership, you can type *leadership* in the Keywords edit box and click Find Now to find all the images with the word *leadership* in their description. Figure 14-6 shows the results of the search in the Clip Gallery.

Replacing a Clip Art Selection on a Slide

After you add a picture from the Clip Gallery to a slide, you can replace the picture by first double-clicking it. (Or you can also select the picture, click the right mouse button, and choose Replace Clip Object from the shortcut menu.) Then, when the Microsoft Clip Gallery dialog box reopens, you can select a replacement picture.

FIGURE 14-6.
The Microsoft Clip Gallery dialog box after a search for descriptions containing the word *leadership*.

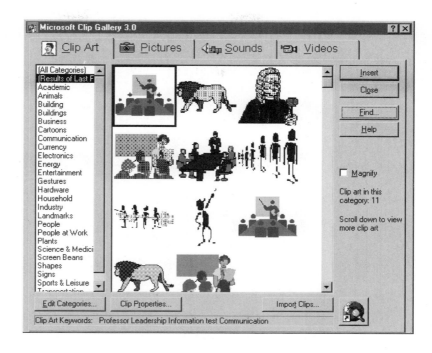

IV

Annotations and Graphics

Recoloring Clip Art to Match the Current Color Scheme

The clip art from the Clip Gallery has a preset combination of colors that may clash with the color scheme of your presentation. To recolor a clip art picture so that it displays colors from the current color scheme, select the clip art, click the right mouse button, and then choose Show Picture Toolbar from the shortcut menu. Although using the Picture toolbar is quick and convenient, you can find dialog box equivalents for the toolbar buttons by choosing Picture from the Format menu. Figure 14-7 shows the Picture Toolbar and its buttons.

FIGURE 14-7.
The Picture toolbar.

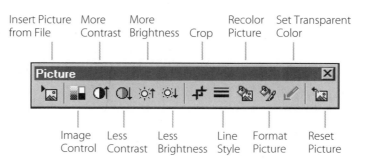

After you've summoned the Picture toolbar, click the Recolor Picture button. In the Recolor Picture dialog box, shown in Figure 14-8, find the original color that you want to change in the picture, and select a new color from the adjacent drop-down list of colors. To change only the background and fill colors in the picture without changing the colors of the lines, select the Fills option before changing colors.

FIGURE 14-8.

The Recolor Picture dialog box.

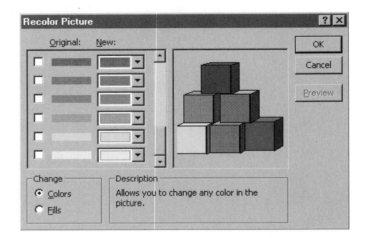

When you open a color drop-down list, you can select one of the eight color scheme colors, or you can select More Colors to make the full palette of colors available. Keep in mind that when you select a color scheme color, you gain two advantages: The colors in the picture match the colors used throughout the presentation, and the color scheme attached to the presentation controls the colors in the picture, so if you change color schemes, the picture will recolor accordingly. If you select a color from the More Colors dialog box instead, the color remains fixed even when you change the color scheme. As a result, the color might clash with the new color scheme's colors.

You can recolor as many of the colors in the picture as necessary. Then click Preview to see the results. When the new colors of the picture are satisfactory, click OK.

Using the Image Controls

The Picture toolbar offers still more controls for adjusting clip art images and other pictures. The Image Control button allows you to choose three other settings besides the standard setting, Automatic. Grayscale produces a version of the clip art that is composed entirely of shades of gray. A grayscale image will print well on a grayscale output device like a laser printer. Black & White converts the colors in the art to either black or white. Use this setting only if your output device cannot print shades of gray. Watermark produces a faint version of the clip art that is well-suited for the background of a slide. You can find examples of these settings in Figure 14-12 on page 373.

The Picture toolbar also provides quick and easy buttons for modifying the brightness and contrast of the image.

Cropping an Image

Cropping a picture is like using scissors to cut away the parts of a clip art image or photo you want to remove, but you can only make straight cuts across or down the image. To use the crop tool, select the clip art and click Crop on the Picture toolbar. Then place the mouse pointer, which looks like the cropping icon shown in Figure 14-9 on the next page, on one of the handles surrounding the image, and drag the handle toward the center of the picture. To display only the left half of a picture, for example, drag the right side handle halfway across the image to the left. You can drag other handles to close in on the part of the picture you want to display. When you're finished, click anywhere outside the image.

You can restore parts of a bitmap that have been cropped by using the Crop tool again to drag the handles back out to the edges of the image.

FIGURE 14-9.

Cropping a photo.

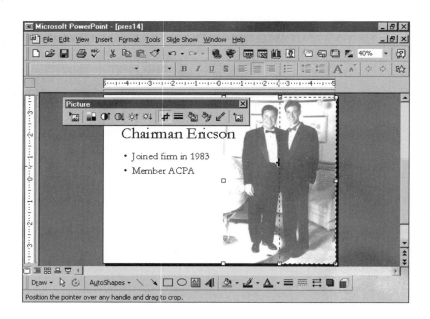

Changing the Frame Around an Image

The Line Style button on the Picture toolbar lets you select from any of the standard black, single, double, or triple borders. To design your own border, and even choose a different color, choose More Lines from the bottom of the Line Style display, which takes you to the Colors And Lines tab of the Format Picture dialog box. Choose a color for the line and then a style and weight.

Adding Clip Art to the Gallery

The Clip Gallery comes with a substantial number of images, but you may have additional clip art pictures on your system that were installed as part of other software or were purchased separately. Many word processing applications come with small libraries of clip art, for example. By adding the clip art that is already on your system to PowerPoint's Clip Gallery, you can view and gain access to all your clip art in one central place.

To add a clip art image to the Gallery, click Import Clips in the Microsoft Clip Gallery dialog box. Then in the Add Clip Art To Clip

Gallery dialog box shown in Figure 14-10, find and select the clip file to add, and click Open. In the Clip Properties dialog box, shown in Figure 14-11 on the next page, enter keywords for the new picture and click the checkboxes next to the categories in which the picture belongs. You can even click New Category to create your own categories. When you're done, click OK. The clip art is added to the Gallery in the category you specified.

FIGURE 14-10.
The Add Clip to the Clip Gallery dialog box.

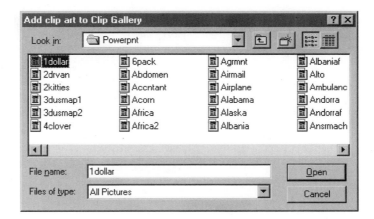

TIP

How to Change Categories and Clips Quickly
You can change the description of a picture, move it to another category in the Clip Gallery, or create a new category to put it in by pointing to the picture in the Clip Gallery and clicking the right mouse button. Choose Clip Properties from the shortcut menu to make changes, or choose Delete Clip to remove the picture from the Clip Gallery. You can also delete, rename, or create a category by pointing to the category name in the Categories list, clicking the right mouse button, and choosing the appropriate command from the shortcut menu.

The Clip Properties and Edit Categories buttons, found at the bottom of the Gallery window, allow you to edit the description of a picture and create, delete, or rename a category of clip art, respectively.

FIGURE 14-11.

The Clip Properties dialog box.

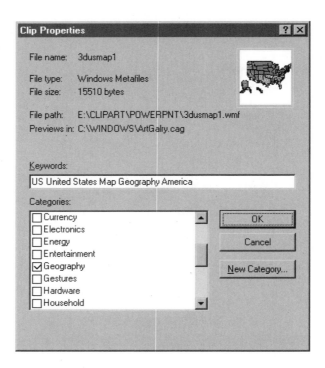

Periodically, you should update the previews shown in the Clip Gallery. Any changes to the original pictures on disk will be reflected in the Clip Gallery. To update the Clip Gallery, select any preview image in the Gallery, click the right mouse button, and choose Update Clip Previews from the shortcut menu. Click Update All on the Update dialog box to refresh all the clip previews.

Importing a Picture from Another Application

You may want to add a particular graphic to a presentation but not maintain it in the Clip Gallery. Perhaps the graphic is customized for a special presentation and will never be used again. To directly import a graphic from a graphic file, follow these steps:

1　In Slide view, choose Picture from the Insert menu.

2　Choose From File from the Picture submenu.

3 Select a graphic file in the Insert Picture dialog box. You can search for a picture by entering a file name or property into the appropriate text boxes near the bottom of the dialog box and clicking Find Now.

4 Click Insert to place the graphic on the current slide.

PowerPoint can import graphic files of two types: vector and bitmap. Vector files are produced by drawing and graphing programs, and contain an arrangement of individual objects—circles, rectangles, lines, filled areas, and text characters, for example. Bitmapped files contain a picture that is composed of a pattern of dots, much as newspaper photos are composed of tiny dots.

Because vector files contain objects, they can be easily edited. You can ungroup a vector file and then remove or resize an individual object to change the picture and leave other objects that are underneath untouched. Most clip art is provided in vector format so that it can be easily edited and resized to fit any need. Bitmapped files can be edited, too, but not as easily as vector files. To erase part of a bitmap, you must erase the dots, leaving a hole in the picture. Parts of objects that appeared to be behind the object you've erased are erased, too. But with their many dots, bitmaps can represent a photographic picture accurately, which is why software that you use with a scanner generates a bitmapped version of a photograph rather than a vector file. Therefore, if you intend to place a scanned image in a presentation—a photograph of a person or a scanned logo, for example—you must always import a bitmapped file.

Table 14-1 identifies the graphic file types you can import.

TABLE 14-1. The graphic file types you can import.

File Format	Type
Windows Bitmap (.BMP)	Bitmap
Windows Metafile (.WMF)	Vector
Windows Enhanced Metafile (.EMF)	Vector
Computer Graphics Metafile (.CGM)	Vector
Encapsulated PostScript (.EPS)	Vector
Tagged Image File Format (.TIF)	Bitmap
PC Paintbrush (.PCX)	Bitmap
Macintosh PICT (.PCT)	Bitmap
Micrografx Designer/Draw (.DRW)	Vector
CompuServe GIF (.GIF)	Bitmap
AutoCAD Format 2-D (.DXF)	Vector
CorelDRAW! 3.0 (.CDR)	Vector
DrawPerfect (.WPG)	Vector
Kodak Photo CD (.PCD)	Bitmap
Lotus 1-2-3 Graphics (.PIC)	Vector
True Vision Targa (.TGA)	Bitmap
Windows DIB (.DIB)	Bitmap
HP Graphics Language (.HGL)	Vector
Portable Network Graphics (.PMG)	Bitmap
JPEG	Bitmap

> **NOTE**

You can only import file types for which you've installed a graphic filter. The Microsoft Office applications share the same graphic filters, so if you installed a graphic filter when you installed Word or Excel, for example, you can use the same graphic filter in PowerPoint.

Adding a Photo to a Slide

To add a photo to a slide, you can select the photo from the Pictures tab of the Clip Gallery. The imported photo appears on the current slide, ready to be moved and resized to suit your needs. To move the photo, drag it to a new location on the slide. To resize the photo, drag one of its handles in the desired direction. To maintain the photo's proportions, drag a corner handle. To stretch the photo, drag a handle in the middle of one of the bitmap's sides.

> **NOTE**

If you added a photo file to the Clip Gallery, you can borrow the photo from the Gallery by following the instructions in "Using the Clip Gallery," page 358. You'll find photos on the Pictures tab of the Clip Gallery dialog box.

After you stretch a photo out of shape, you can return the photo to its original proportions by choosing Picture from the Format menu, and then clicking the Size tab of the Format Picture dialog box. Make sure Lock Aspect Ratio is turned off, click the Reset button, and click OK. Then you can resize the picture with its proper proportions by dragging a corner handle or by entering a Scale Height and Width percentage in the Size tab of Format Picture dialog box. Select Best Scale For Slide Show to let PowerPoint scale the picture for you.

> **TIP**

How to Stop Waiting for Photos to Show Up Onscreen
Photos take somewhat longer to draw than other objects on a slide. Therefore, you might want to draw a box on the slide to use as a temporary placeholder for a photo while you create and format other elements of the presentation. When the presentation is otherwise complete, you can import the photo.

Placing a Photo on the Background

By switching to the Slide Master before you insert a photo, you can place the photo on the background of every slide in a presentation except the title slide. First, choose Master from the View menu and then choose Slide Master from the submenu. Then use the Insert Picture dialog box to place the photo on the Slide Master. If you want to place the photo behind the presentation text, select the photo, and choose Send To Back from the Draw menu's Order submenu. The figure below shows a photo on presentation slides 1 through 4. To place a photo on the background of the title slide, choose Master and then Title Master from the View menu and follow the same procedure.

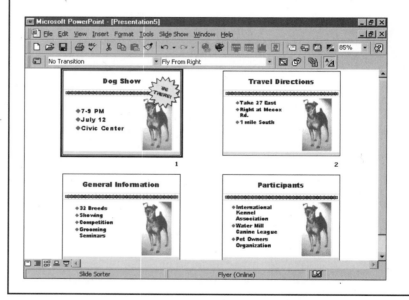

? **SEE ALSO**

For more information about adjusting a photo, see "Using the Image Controls," page 365.

Adjusting a Picture

You can convert a color picture to a grayscale or black and white image with the image controls on the Picture toolbar. You can even convert a photo to a watermark version, a very pale and low contrast version that works well behind text. To make these changes and adjust the brightness and contrast of the picture, use the image controls on the Picture toolbar the same way you used the Picture toolbar to adjust clip art images. Figure 14-12 shows the effects of the various image control options available on the Picture toolbar.

FIGURE 14-12.
The Image Control options.

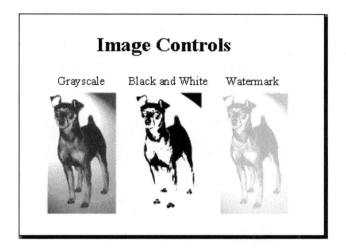

Scanning a Photo

If you have a scanner (a hardware device that captures photos and converts them to files), you can add a photo to a slide by choosing Picture from the Insert menu and then selecting From Scanner. If you installed Microsoft Photo Editor when you installed Office 97, Photo Editor starts the scanning software that came with your scanner. After the photo is scanned, you can make adjustments to it in Photo Editor before bringing it into PowerPoint.

Adding Sounds, CD Audio Music, and Movies

You can add an audio or video clip to a slide the same way you add clip art and photos, either by selecting them from the Clip Gallery or by importing them from disk. Adding sound or music places an icon on a slide. Double-clicking the icon plays the sound or music track. Adding a movie (a video clip) displays the first frame of the movie. Double-clicking the first frame starts the video playing.

Because you will most often use sound and movie clips when you are preparing a slide show, I'll save the details of working with multimedia files to Chapter 16, Creating Slide Shows, page 387.

But PowerPoint does offer some simple options you can use in Slide view to determine how and when multimedia files will be played. To see these options, select the icon or media clip in slide view and then choose Sound Object or Movie Object from the bottom of the Edit menu. In the Play Options dialog box, shown in Figure 14-13, you can choose to loop the current sound or movie so it plays continuously until you stop it. Or you can choose to rewind a movie when it's done playing. The Play CD Audio Track options allow you to play a specific music clip on a CD by specifying the track number and start and end times.

FIGURE 14-13.
The Play Options dialog box.

The Play Options dialog box also displays the current duration of the selected media clip.

In this part of the book, you learned how to apply the finishing touches to a presentation by adding text, drawings, and pictures. In the next section, you'll learn how to turn your work into something tangible: a printed page, a 35-mm slide, or an electronic presentation called a slide show.

PART V

Performing with PowerPoint

Creating Printed Output, Web Pages, and 35-mm Slides

Somehow, printing always seems to be the most difficult part of working with a computer. You work so hard to create a look on the screen, but when you print, the darks are too dark or the lights are too light. And once you print overhead transparencies in landscape orientation, you can't get audience handouts in portrait orientation without murmuring incantations over the system.

Well, PowerPoint solves these problems, as you knew it would. It takes care of all the portrait-to-landscape, overhead-to-slide, and screen-to-paper conversions behind the scenes so that you can concentrate on expressing yourself.

In this chapter, you'll learn how to tell PowerPoint exactly what type of output you want to generate. You can print overheads from your slides, or you can print audience handouts with up to six slide miniatures on each page. You can also print the speaker notes you created in Notes Pages view, or print the presentation to a PostScript file to give to a service bureau that will produce your 35-mm slides. You can even output HTML files for a Web site.

Setting Up the Pages

The first step in creating printed output or 35-mm slides is to check the current page setup. The page setup determines the size and orientation of the slides you've created. You may be wondering why you don't have to change the page setup before starting a presentation. The answer is that you can, but you don't have to. You can leave the default setting, which displays the presentation properly in a slide show and on landscape overheads printed on 8½-by-11-inch pages, and change the page setup only if you need to print 35-mm slides or custom pages with odd heights and widths.

When you change the page setup, PowerPoint does all the work to resize and reorient the material on your slides to fit the new page size and orientation. For example, you can create landscape slides, which have a horizontal orientation, and then switch to portrait slides if you need a vertical orientation. In most cases, PowerPoint adjusts everything on your slides so well that you'll think you've been creating portrait slides all along.

To check the page setup, choose Page Setup from the File menu. In the Page Setup dialog box, shown in Figure 15-1, you see options for setting the slide width and height, the slide number, and the slide or notes, handouts, and outline orientation.

FIGURE 15-1.

The Page Setup dialog box.

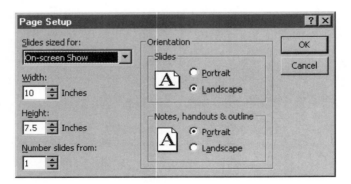

Slide Size

From the Slides Sized For drop-down list in the Page Setup dialog box, select one of the six preset slide sizes (On-screen Show, Letter Paper, A4 Paper, 35mm Slides, Overhead, or Banner), or select Custom and then set a custom width and height in the Width and Height edit boxes.

> When you select the Custom option, the default settings for the Width and Height are set to the printable area of the page for the current printer.

Slide Numbering

SEE ALSO
For more information about numbering slides, see "Inserting the Slide Number, Date, or Time on Selected Slides," page 238.

In the Page Setup dialog box, the number shown in the Number Slides From edit box sets the slide numbering that appears both on the slides and in the slide number indicator at the bottom of the PowerPoint window. Keep in mind that before the number is actually displayed on a slide, you must enter the page number symbol on the slide, by choosing the Slide Number command from the Insert menu.

You can start slide numbering at any number. For example, to number the first slide of the current presentation as 10, type *10* directly in the Number Slides From edit box or click the up arrow at the right end of the edit box to increase the setting to 10.

Slide Orientation

You can set two different orientations: one for slides and one for notes, handouts, and outline pages. With these settings, you can print speaker notes and audience handouts in portrait orientation even when you print slides in landscape orientation.

V

Performing with PowerPoint

TIP

Adding Master Embellishments

Slides, outlines, handouts, and speaker notes have masters that you can embellish with headers and footers, text, slide numbers, and graphics. To open one of the masters, hold down the Shift key as you click the corresponding view button. For example, to open the handout master, hold down the Shift key and click the Slide Sorter View button. To return to one of the standard views, click a view button without pressing the Shift key.

Printing Pages

To begin the printing process, make sure the presentation you want to print is displayed in the active presentation window in PowerPoint, and then choose Print from the File menu or press Ctrl+P. The Print dialog box opens, as shown in Figure 15-2.

FIGURE 15-2.

The Print dialog box.

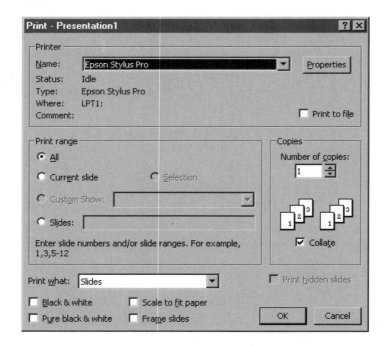

NOTE

To bypass the Print dialog box, click the Print button on the Standard toolbar. PowerPoint prints the entire presentation using the current print settings.

The name of the currently selected printer is displayed at the top of the Print dialog box. To print the presentation on a different printer, select a printer from the Name drop-down list. If you want to transport a presentation file to another system for printing, select the Print To File option, which prints the presentation to an output file on disk.

NOTE

To access additional options for the currently selected printer, click the Properties button at the top of the Print dialog box.

The Print Range options let you print all or selected slides of the presentation. To print the entire presentation, click the All option. To print only the slide shown in Slide view, click the Current Slide option. To print selected slides, click the Slides option and enter the corresponding slide numbers in the Slides edit box. You can separate nonconsecutive slides with commas and separate the first and last number of a range of slides with a hyphen. You can even combine nonconsecutive slides and ranges of slides by using both commas and hyphens. For example, to print slide 3 and also slides 6 through 8, you can enter *3,6-8* in the Slides edit box.

You can increase the number in the Number Of Copies edit box to print multiple copies of the slides. If you print more than one copy, you can also select the Collate option to print multiple, properly sequenced sets of slides rather than multiple copies of the first page followed by multiple copies of the next page, and so on. Printing collated copies can take considerably longer, because the computer must resend each page to the printer several times rather than send the page once and have the printer churn out multiple copies.

The default setting for the Print What option is Slides, or Slides (Without Animations) if the slides have custom animations, but you can also select various formats of Handouts, Notes Pages, or Outline View from the drop-down list.

V

Performing with PowerPoint

Another way to select the slides to print is to switch to Slide Sorter or Outline view, and hold down the Shift key as you click each slide or slide icon. When you open the Print dialog box, click the Selection option in the Print Range section to print only the selected slides.

 NOTE

If the presentation contains slides with custom animations, you can select either Slides (With Animations) or Slides (Without Animations) from the Print What drop-down list. When you select Slides (Without Animations), only the completely built version of each slide is printed. For more information about custom animations, see "Animating Text and Graphics," page 392.

The Special Print Options

The options in the Print dialog box let you make important changes to the way the presentation prints, although the defaults work well in most cases. Each of these special options is described here:

- The Print Hidden Slides option prints slides that you have hidden using the Hide Slide command on the Slide Show menu. If your presentation contains no hidden slides, the option is unavailable.

- The Black & White option prints color slides properly on a black and white printer, such as a black and white laser printer. Black & White replaces fills in objects with gray shades, and it replaces color patterns with patterns of black, gray, and white. This option also adds a thin black outline to objects (except text objects) that do not otherwise have borders. If you select the Black & White option to print your presentation, some objects may not appear the way you'd like them to. For example, a dark object may no longer be visible against a dark background. You can adjust the color of an individual object by selecting the object and using the Colors And Lines command on the Format or shortcut menu. If you want to change the color of a text selection, use the Font command on the Format menu.

- The Pure Black & White option converts all colors in the presentation to either black or white. Use this option when you need to print to a printer that cannot print gray shades.

- The Scale To Fit Paper option properly scales the slides to fit the printed page even if the slides have been set up for a different page size. For example, to print a slide that you sized for 35-mm slides (in the Slide Setup dialog box) on an 8½-by-11-inch page, you can use the Scale To Fit Paper option.

- The Frame Slides option prints a narrow frame around each slide. This option is useful if you want to display your slides as overheads.

Figure 15-3 shows versions of a color slide printed on a laser printer. The left page was printed with the default print options, and the right page was printed with the Black & White option.

Printing Handouts and Speaker Notes

To print audience handouts, choose Print from the File menu or press Ctrl+P, and then select one of the three Handouts options from the Print What drop-down list in the Print dialog box. These options allow you to print two, three, or six slides per page. The orientation of the handouts is determined by the Orientation setting in the Page Setup dialog box shown earlier. Figure 15-4, on the next page, shows a handout page with three slides per page, leaving the audience members plenty of room to jot down notes about each slide.

FIGURE 15-3.

A page printed with two different print options: default (left) and Black & White (right).

Local Merchants

- Hampton Coffee Company
- International Deli
- Fragrant Flower Shop

Local Merchants

- Hampton Coffee Company
- International Deli
- Fragrant Flower Shop

To print speaker notes, select Notes Pages from the Print What drop-down list. As with handouts, the orientation of the notes pages is determined by the Orientation setting in the Page Setup dialog box.

FIGURE 15-4.

A handout page with three slides on the page.

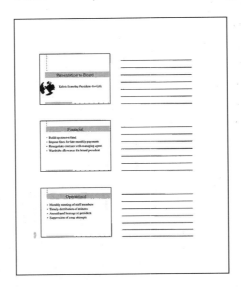

Printing the Outline

To print the presentation outline just as it appears in Outline view, select Outline View from the Print What drop-down list box in the Print dialog box. The outline prints with as much detail as is currently displayed in Outline view. Collapsed entries do not print.

The size of the text on the printed page is affected by the zoom percentage in Outline view. If the zoom percentage is at 50%, for example, text formatted to appear as 40-point in Outline view prints as 20-point text on the page.

Creating 35-mm Slides

If you're lucky enough to have a film recorder attached to your system and the Windows printer driver for the film recorder, you can select the film recorder as your printer and then print to the film recorder as if you were printing to any other printer. The film recorder creates an image of each slide on 35-mm slide film. You can then develop the film to produce 35-mm slides. You may need to refer to the documentation for the device for special instructions on using it with a Windows-based application such as PowerPoint.

Most people do not have expensive film recorders at their disposal, however. Instead, they rely on a service bureau that takes a PostScript file generated from PowerPoint and feeds it into a film recorder. Many service bureaus provide overnight service, returning the developed 35-mm slides by next-day delivery. A local service bureau may even provide same-day service.

PowerPoint comes with software that makes it especially easy to use the Genigraphics Service Center as your service bureau. When you install PowerPoint, you can also install the Genigraphics Wizard, which automatically creates a PostScript file that Genigraphics can accept. When you install the Genigraphics Wizard, a communications program called GraphicsLink is also installed so that you can transmit the PostScript file to the Genigraphics Service Center by modem.

To create a PostScript file to send to Genigraphics, choose the Send To command from the File menu and then choose Genigraphics to activate the Genigraphics Wizard. The Genigraphics Wizard prompts you for the type of products or electronic services you need in addition to your mailing and billing information. You can use the wizard to send your request electronically or save it to a file to send later either by disk or modem.

If you have a modem, you can launch the GraphicsLink software to send any files saved earlier by the Genigraphics Wizard to Genigraphics over the telephone line.

Saving a Presentation as Web Pages

The Save As HTML command on the File menu saves a presentation as a series of Web pages that you can make available on the company network or on the Internet. The Save As HTML Wizard leads you through six screens that control both content and formatting options for the Web pages you will produce.

The first screen, Layout Selection, lets you choose from a list of saved layouts or create a new layout. If you choose New, the next screen lets you select either a Standard layout or a Browser Frames layout that creates more informative, but also more complex, HTML pages.

The next screen, Graphic Type, asks you to choose a file type for the presentation's graphics. GIF files are a good choice because they are small and offer high fidelity image reproduction. If you choose PowerPoint Animation, your presentation will be saved in a format that can be displayed within the Internet Explorer window using the PowerPoint Animation Player, an ActiveX control that is available in the ValuPack folder on the Office 97 CD-ROM.

On the next screen of the wizard, you choose the size of the images on the HTML pages. Large images may not fit all monitors, so you should stick to one of the lower resolutions. 640 x 480 is the standard for the Internet.

The Information Page options on the next screen specify text for the opening page. Here you can also choose to provide buttons viewers can click to download the presentation file in standard PowerPoint format and the latest version of Microsoft Internet Explorer.

The Colors And Buttons screens let you change the color of many items on the Web pages and select a button style. Use Browser Colors, the default color selection, leaves color decisions to the viewer's browser.

The next-to-the-last screen, Layout Options, holds controls to position the navigation buttons on pages and include notes from Notes Pages.

When you click Finish to reach the last screen, the wizard asks for a folder in which it can create a new folder to store the HTML files. The new folder will get the same name as the presentation file. The main page of the presentation is an HTML file named Index. The wizard also asks whether to save your selections as a layout you can choose the next time you use the Save As HTML Wizard.

In the following chapter, you'll learn about an another alternative method of presenting with PowerPoint that avoids printing. The electronic presentation displays your work in a slide show on the computer screen. However, even if you display a slide show, you may still want to print audience handouts so that your viewers can take home pages for future reference.

Creating Slide Shows

The payoff for all your hard work in PowerPoint comes at presentation time, when your slides go on display. Traditionally, 35-mm slides have been the medium with the most professional look, but electronic slide shows, which display the presentation right on the computer screen, are rapidly surpassing 35-mm slides in popularity.

If your monitor is large enough, you can use it in a conference room. But for a sizable gathering, you'll want to use a computer projector or LCD projection panel to display a PowerPoint slide show on a large screen. The most obvious advantage of a slide show is the fancy transitions you can include between slides. Fades, wipes, dissolves, and other effects give your show the "wow" power of a Hollywood production. But these aren't the only advantages slide shows can offer.

Bulleted text slides can incorporate automatic animations, also called *progressive disclosures*, that reveal each bulleted item as the speaker refers to it. Graphs can animate, too. The columns of a column slide can grow to their full height as you speak about each one. Slides also can include video, sound, animation, and music. By embedding information from another application, you can integrate a drill-down document in a slide—perhaps a Microsoft Word letter or a Microsoft Excel spreadsheet—that you can open to reveal supporting information, such as the figures behind a confident projection. And with PowerPoint's special mark-up mode, you can mark up slides during a show, sportscaster-style.

In this chapter, you'll learn how to build and run a slide show. You'll also learn about advanced slide show techniques, timing a presentation, adding multimedia objects and creating interactive shows that can branch off at the presenter's discretion.

Developing a Slide Show

Just by creating a basic sequence of slides, you've already created a simple slide show in PowerPoint. To see the slide show, move to the first slide, and then click the Slide Show button at the bottom of the presentation window or choose Slide Show from the View menu. The first slide fills the entire screen and remains there until you advance the show to the next slide. Initially, each slide simply replaces the previous slide, like an actual slide show with 35-mm slides and a projector. But as you'll find out in this section, you can add transition and animation effects to create a presentation that will really wake up your audience.

 TIP

How to Create a Graceful Ending
To create a graceful ending to a slide show, you can add a black slide to the end of each presentation by choosing Options from the Tools menu and selecting the End With Black Slide option on the View tab of the Options dialog box. Take heed, however—if you don't include the black slide, PowerPoint will reappear after the last slide, and you'll be faced with the sudden glare of menus, buttons, and toolbars.

Assigning Slide Transitions

Transitions are special effects that you can include between slides. During a presentation, as you progress from one slide to another, a transition "draws" the next slide on the screen using one of a variety of techniques. You can also assign a sound to be played when you change slides.

The best place to assign a transition effect is in Slide Sorter view, where you can see a number of slides at once and preview the transition effects. To switch to Slide Sorter view, click the Slide Sorter View button or select Slide Sorter from the View menu. You can then use the Slide Transition Effects list box on the Slide Sorter toolbar, shown in Figure 16-1, to specify a transition effect for any or all slides.

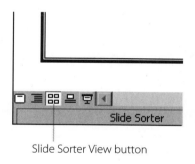

Slide Sorter View button

FIGURE 16-1.
The Slide
Sorter toolbar.

Slide Transition   Slide Transition Effects

To assign a basic transition effect to a slide, click the slide and then select an item from the Slide Transition Effects drop-down list. Watch the slide carefully in Slide Sorter view, and you'll see that it previews the transition. To see it again, click the small transition effect icon that has appeared just below the slide. Figure 16-2, on the next page, shows these icons.

FIGURE 16-2.

Click a Transition Effect icon to preview the transition effect applied to the slide.

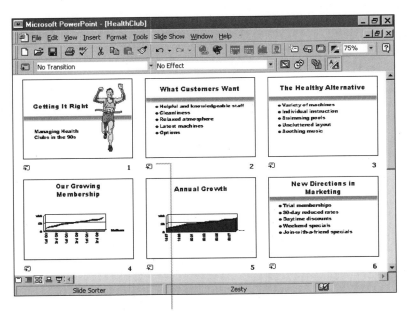

Transition Effect icon

To apply the same transition effect to slides in a sequence, select multiple slides and then select an effect from the Slide Transition Effects drop-down list. Remember, you can select more than one slide by holding down the Shift key as you click each slide or by drawing a selection box around a group of slides using the mouse pointer. To apply a single effect to all the slides, choose Select All from the Edit menu or press Ctrl+A, and then select an effect.

TIP

If you select the same transition effect for all the slides in a slide show, you might consider using a different effect for the title slides of each segment of your presentation. Simply select the title slides, and then select a different effect from the Slide Transition Effects drop-down list.

The Slide Transition button

By clicking the Slide Transition button to the left of the Slide Transition Effects box on the Slide Sorter toolbar, you can open the Slide Transition dialog box shown in Figure 16-3. (Another way to access this dialog box is to select one or more slides and choose Slide Transition from the Slide Show menu, or click the right mouse button and choose Slide Transition from the shortcut menu.) In the Slide

Transition dialog box, you can select not only a transition effect, but also a speed for the effect and the amount of time you want the slide to remain on the screen. The default Advance option, On Mouse Click, requires you to click the left mouse button or press the keys listed in Table 16-1 on page 405 during the slide show to advance to the next slide. If you have a Windows–compatible sound card installed, you can also add sound transitions to your slide show by selecting sounds from the Sound drop-down list. If you want the sound(s) to run continuously during a slide show, select the Loop Until Next Sound option. After you've made selections in this dialog box, click Apply to apply them to the selected slides, or Apply To All to apply them to the entire slide show.

FIGURE 16-3.

The Slide Transition dialog box.

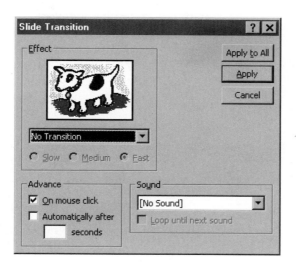

Performing with PowerPoint

TIP

Don't Overdo It
Transition effects are undoubtedly snazzy, but don't let them detract from the content of your presentation by using too many different effects during a slide show, or by setting them all to Slow to heighten the drama. Instead, use Fast for the transition speed whenever possible, and use one effect repeatedly, changing effects only for new presentation segments.

Animating Text and Graphic Objects

The bulleted text on text slides and the graphic objects you've added can appear either all at once or sequentially during a slide show. To have the items "build" on a slide, you must assign animations to them.

In Slide Show view, you can quickly assign basic, preset animations to text slides to have the title and individual bulleted items appear in sequence with a fancy, animated effect. To do so, select one or more text slides with bulleted items and then choose an animation from the Text Preset Animation drop-down list on the Slide Sorter toolbar or from the Preset Text Animation selections on the shortcut menu.

For more control over the animations on a slide, and to animate the graphic objects on a slide as well, you must double-click the slide to return to Slide view, and set the animations there.

In Slide view, deselect all objects on the slide by clicking the background of the slide. Then choose Custom Animation from the Slide Show menu. The Custom Animation dialog box appears, as shown in Figure 16-4.

FIGURE 16-4.

The Custom Animation dialog box.

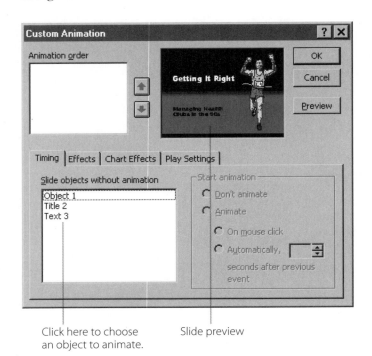

Click here to choose an object to animate.

Slide preview

On the Timing tab of the Custom Animation dialog box, you'll see a list of the slide objects that have not yet been animated. You can select an object to animate and then click Animate in the Start Animation section of the Timing tab. The default is to animate the object when you click the mouse (On Mouse Click), but you can also animate the object a certain number of seconds after the previous event or after the appearance of the slide if no previous animations have been set up.

As you select objects to animate, you establish an animation order, which appears as the Animation Order list in the dialog box, as shown in Figure 16-5. To re-order the list, select an item and click the up or down arrow buttons next to the list.

FIGURE 16-5.

Animated objects appear on the Animation order list.

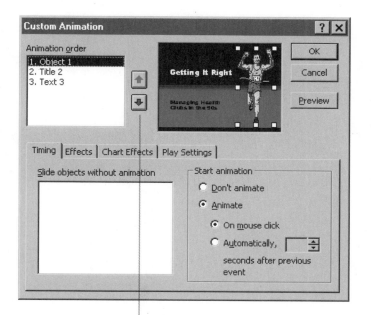

Select items on the list and re-order them by clicking the arrow buttons.

Next, you will want to choose an animation effect for each object. Click the Effects tab in the Custom Animation dialog box. You will see that the object you select on the Animation Order list appears selected in the slide preview, as shown in Figure 16-6 on the next page. You can choose an entry animation for the object, a sound to play when

Performing with PowerPoint

V

the object appears, and a color with which to dim the item once it has been revealed and discussed. (The dimmed items remain readable on the screen.) You can also hide items rather than dim them.

The object you choose on the Animation Order list appears selected here.

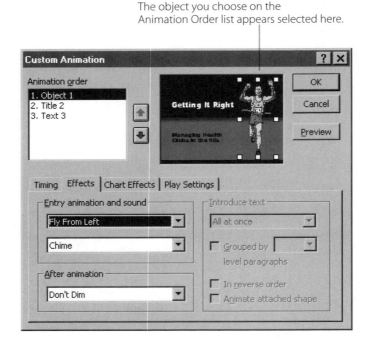

If the object is text, you can also make selections in the Introduce Text section of the Effects tab. The text can appear All At Once, By Word, or By Letter. The best way to see these options is to select each one and then click Preview in the Custom Animation window. In the preview, you won't be able to see the Grouped By Paragraph Level options, though. If you turn on grouping by clicking the checkbox next to Grouped By, you can determine how much text will appear when you advance the slide show. Grouping text by the 1st level paragraphs, for example, brings in the first level bullet point and all the text underneath it at lower levels. Grouping by the 2nd level would bring in the 1st level text and the first bullet of the second level. You would have to click again to bring in the next second level text item.

The last two options in the Introduce Text section let you bring in text items in reverse order and, if the text is within an autoshape, choose whether the autoshape should animate with the text or whether the shape should already be visible when the text arrives in animation.

TIP

Previewing a Slide's Animations
To preview a slide's animations, turn to the slide in Slide view, and choose Animation Preview from the Slide Show menu. A small, color window appears to demonstrate the animation

TIP

Quickly Changing the Animation Settings of an Object
By clicking an object in Slide view before selecting Custom Animation from the Slide Show menu, you'll find that the object has already been selected in the Custom Animation dialog box. You can immediately make changes on the Effects tab.

Using the Animation Effects Toolbar

Animation
Effects button

You can display the Animation Effects toolbar, shown in Figure 16-7, by clicking the Animation Effects button on the Formatting toolbar. (Or choose Toolbars from the View menu, and select the Animation Effects option.) You can then use the toolbar buttons to animate individual objects. Keep in mind, however, that in order to use most of the buttons on the Animation Effects toolbar, you must be in Slide view and you must first select an object on the current slide, such as a title or bulleted text. When you have time, explore these buttons further. You'll have a blast sending bullets flying and dropping in titles out of thin air.

FIGURE 16-7.
The Animation
Effects toolbar.

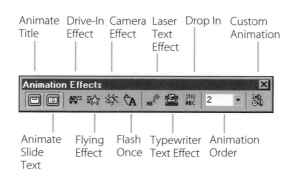

Animating Charts

When a chart resides on a slide, you can animate some of the elements within a chart. For example, you can have the bars of a bar chart appear one after another. To set the animation effects for a chart, select the chart on the Animation Order list in the Custom Animation dialog box and then click the Chart Effects tab.

On the Chart Effects tab, shown in Figure 16-8, choose a setting for Introduce Chart Elements, and make sure Animate Grid And Legend is turned on if you also want the chart's background elements to animate. Chart elements have fewer entry animation effects available, but you can still choose from a number of effects on the Chart Effects tab, and also choose a sound to play when the chart element appears. The After Animation setting goes into effect only after the entire chart has displayed.

FIGURE 16-8.
The Chart Effects tab of the Custom Animation dialog box.

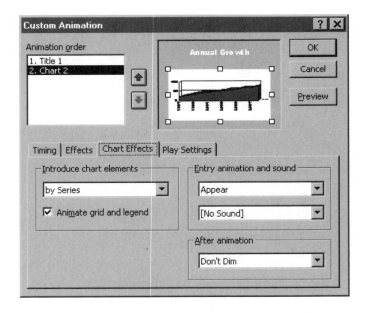

Playing Multimedia Elements

Multimedia elements on slides, such as sound and movie clips, appear on the Animation Order list as Media items.

You can change the way a media item plays by selecting the media item on the Animation Order list and then clicking the Play Settings tab of the Custom Animation dialog box, shown in Figure 16-9. You can have the slide show pause until the media clip has completed (this option is particularly useful for playing a video clip) or keep the slide show running while the music or narration continues. If you select Continue Slide Show, you can designate whether the clip should stop at the end of the current slide or after a specified number of slides have been shown. By clicking More Options, you can get to options that let you loop a media clip, rewind a movie clip after it is played, or play a CD audio track or segment.

To prevent the clip's icon from displaying on screen during a slide show, click Hide While Not Playing. The clip or its icon still appears in Slide view, but it is not visible during the actual slide show.

FIGURE 16-9.

The Play Settings tab of the Custom Animation dialog box.

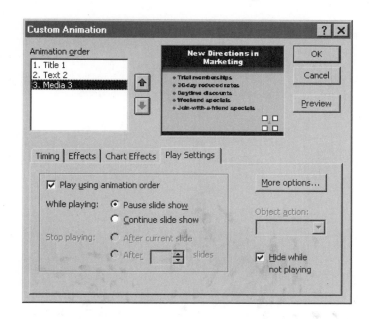

Hiding Slides

Hide Slide
button

To hide one or more slides during a slide show, select the slides in Slide Sorter view, and click the Hide Slide button on the Slide Sorter toolbar or choose Hide Slide from the shortcut or Slide Show menu. A slash appears through the slide number in Slide Sorter view to indicate that the slide is hidden. Although the hidden slide continues to display in Slide Sorter view, it does not appear during a slide show unless you call it up.

SEE ALSO

For more information about the slide show pop-up menu, see "Controlling the Slide Show with the Mouse," page 404.

To show a hidden slide during a slide show, move the mouse pointer over the current slide, and when the Pop-up button shown in Figure 16-10 appears in the lower left corner of the slide, click the button to display the pop-up menu, also shown in Figure 16-10. Next choose Go from the pop-up menu. If a hidden slide follows the current slide, the Hidden Slide command becomes available on the Go submenu. Choose this command to show the hidden slide. To display a hidden slide without opening the pop-up menu, press the H key.

FIGURE 16-10.
The slide show pop-up menu and button.

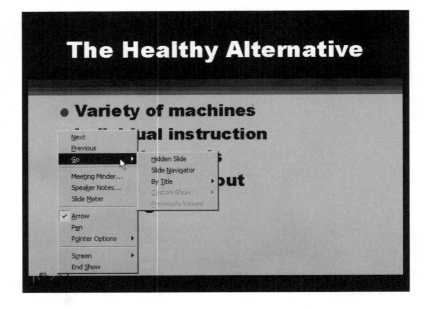

To unhide a hidden slide, select the slide in Slide Sorter view and click the Hide Slide button again or choose Hide Slide again from the shortcut or Slide Show menu.

Making a Slide Show Interactive

What could be better than a slide show with fancy transitions and animation effects? A slide show that lets viewers control what they see and when they see it! PowerPoint's new Action buttons and Action settings let you add buttons to your slides that viewers can click to jump to any slide in the slide show, play a video, play a sound, jump to an Internet web page or even start another software application. Of course, you can use Action Buttons to control the slide show when you are the presenter, but the command's real power lies in its ability to let your viewers move through a slide show at their own pace and in their own order.

To add an Action button to a slide, switch to Slide view, choose Action Buttons from the Slide Show menu, and then choose a button from the menu of buttons shown in Figure 16-11. Next, draw the button onto the slide. When the button appears, you'll see the Action Settings dialog box shown in Figure 16-12 on the next page.

FIGURE 16-11.

The Action Buttons menu.

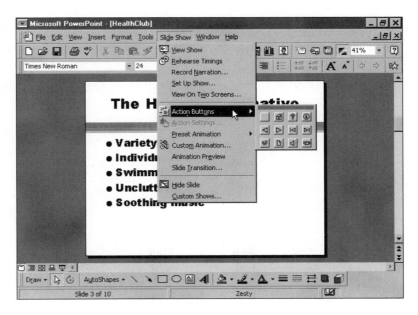

FIGURE 16-12.

The Action Settings dialog box.

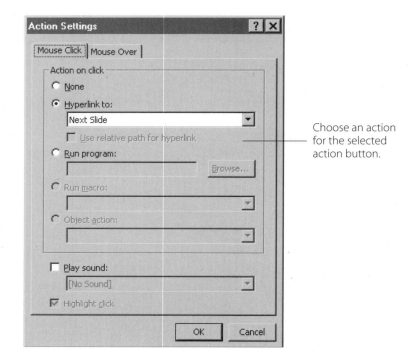

Choose an action for the selected action button.

You can also give any object on the screen, such as a text block or autoshape, its own action settings. Simply select the image or graphic object in Slide view, and choose the Action Settings command from the Slide Show menu. Next, select one of the Mouse Click options: Hyperlink To, which allows viewers to move to a specific slide, custom show, Internet URL (web page address), or to another PowerPoint program or a file from a different program; Run Program, which allows viewers to open a different application when they click the button; Run Macro, which lets viewers run a Visual Basic for Applications macro; Object Action, which allows viewers to play, edit, or open a media clip or underlying application when they click the button; or Play Sound, which allows viewers to click a button to play a sound.

A second tab in the Actions Settings dialog box, labeled Mouse Over, allows you to assign actions to buttons when the viewer moves the mouse pointer over them. You might want to have a voice tell someone to "Go ahead and click here" when he or she moves the mouse over a button, for example.

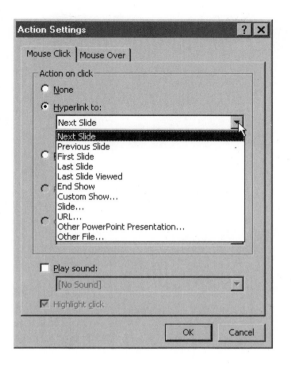

When you select the Hyperlink To option, shown above, you must also specify the destination you want viewers to move to by selecting one of the options from the Hyperlink To drop-down list. If you select the Slide... option on the list, the Hyperlink To Slide dialog box appears. You can then select a specific slide, even if it's hidden. If you select URL..., you must enter a full internet address, such as http://www.microsoft.com. When you select the Play Sound option, you must also select a sound to be played from the drop-down list. When you select the Run Program option, you must enter the full pathname for the application you want viewers to open. For example, enter the pathname for a Word document that you want viewers to read or print. When you select the Object Action option, you must also select an action from the Object Action drop-down list. For example, select Edit to allow viewers to edit the underlying data for an Excel chart.

TIP

Adding Supplemental Information on Hidden Slides
You can supply your viewers with additional information that they only see if they want to by creating a slide with the information, hiding the slide, and then making the slide the target of an interactive object on another slide.

Running a Slide Show

As you know, when you develop a slide show in Slide Sorter view, you can preview the transition effects for individual slides. But to see the transitions full-screen and to see animated, bulleted text slides, you must show the presentation as a slide show.

Starting the Slide Show

Before you actually start a slide show, you can designate the slide at which you want the show to begin, even if the slide is hidden. Simply select the slide in Slide Sorter view or display the slide in Slide view. Then, when you click the Slide Show button at the bottom of the presentation window, the slide show starts at the currently selected slide. To advance to the next slide, click the left mouse button or press N. To return to the previous slide, press P or the Backspace key. To discontinue the slide show and return to the previous view, press Esc, Ctrl+Break, or the minus key on the numeric keypad.

For more options before running a show, choose Set Up Show from the Slide Show menu. The Set Up Show dialog box appears, as shown in Figure 16-13 on the facing page.

To run the entire show, select All in the Slides section of the dialog box. You can also enter a starting and ending slide in the From and To edit boxes. To run a slide show as an unattended demonstration (in a store window or building lobby, for example), click Loop Continuously Until 'Esc' in the Show Type section of the Set Up Show dialog box. The show will run as an ever-repeating loop that can only be interrupted when someone presses the Esc key. To make the Esc key unavailable, you can remove the keyboard and the mouse after you start the show and leave only the monitor and system unit.

FIGURE 16-13.
The Set Up Show
dialog box.

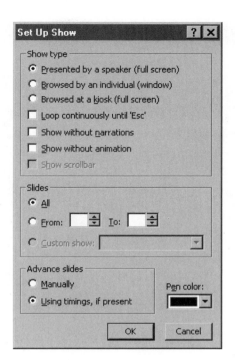

In the Set Up Show dialog box, you can also choose to run the show without narrations and/or animations, and whether to advance the show manually or with the timings you established when you rehearsed the slide show timings. You will learn about rehearsing a slide show in "Rehearsing Automatic Slide Show Timings," page 405.

Special Show Types

PowerPoint offers three new, special slide show types, available on the Set Up Show dialog box. The first, Presented By A Speaker, is the traditional, full-screen slide show. The second, Browsed By An Individual, displays the show in an Internet Explorer-like window that displays navigation controls that make it easy for the viewer to move through the show. The third option, Browsed At A Kiosk, displays the show full-screen, but it also restarts the show after five minutes of inactivity and prevents the viewer from modifying the show. When you choose this option, Loop Continuously Until 'Esc' is selected automatically.

V

Performing with PowerPoint

Controlling the Slide Show with the Mouse

We all like to control the show, but it's usually not as easy as Power-Point makes it. During a slide show, you can use the popup menu button and popup menu, shown in Figure 16-10 on page 398, to control various aspects of the show. As mentioned earlier, the button appears in the lower left corner of the current slide as soon as you move the mouse pointer. You can then click the button to display the slide show popup menu.

⭐ TIP

> **How to Hide the Popup Menu Button During a Slide Show**
> To hide the popup menu button during a slide show, choose Options from the Tools menu, and deselect the Show Popup Menu Button option on the View tab of the Options dialog box. You can still access the popup menu by clicking the right mouse button during a slide show (unless you also deselect the Popup Menu On Right Mouse Click option in the Options dialog box).

The Next and Previous commands on the popup menu let you move forward or backward through the slides in your slide show. To move to a specific slide, choose Go and then Slide Navigator from the menu, and when the Slide Navigator dialog box appears, select a slide and click Go To. As discussed on page 398, you can use the Hidden Slide command on the Go To submenu to move to hidden slides that follow the active slide in your slide show. To display a hidden slide from any slide in the presentation, you have to use the Slide Navigator. Hidden slide numbers appear in parentheses. To stop a slide show at any time during your presentation, simply choose End Show from the popup menu.

❓ SEE ALSO

For more information about the Meeting Minder, see "Managing the Meeting," page 426.

The remaining commands on the slide show popup menu let you access the Meeting Minder for note taking, turn on the Slide Meter to gauge your progress during a slide show, and change the arrow pointer to a pen so that you can mark up slides (you can even change the color of the pen's "ink"). You can also pause an automatic slide show or replace the current slide with a black screen (say, during an interruption in the proceedings). With the exception of Meeting Minder, you'll learn more about these commands in this chapter.

Controlling the Slide Show with the Keyboard

In addition to the slide show pop-up menu, you can use the keys listed in Table 16-1 to control various aspects of the show.

TABLE 16-1.   The Slide Show keyboard controls.

Press This	To Perform This Action
Spacebar, Right arrow, Down arrow, PgDn, or N	Advance to next slide
Backspace, Left arrow, Up arrow, PgUp, or P	Return to previous slide
Slide number+Enter	Go to slide number
B or period	Black screen/resume
W or comma	White screen/resume
Ctrl+A	Show mouse pointer as arrow
Ctrl+P	Show mouse pointer as pen
S or + (numeric keypad)	Pause/resume automatic show
H	Show/hide hidden slide
Ctrl+H	Hide pointer now
Ctrl+L	Hide pointer always
Esc	End show

Rehearsing Automatic Slide Show Timings

To create a slide show that proceeds on its own from slide to slide while you speak, you can simply enter the amount of time you want each slide to remain on the screen in the Slide Transition dialog box. A better method, however, is to practice giving the presentation first and have PowerPoint record the length of time you keep each slide on the screen. You can then use PowerPoint's findings to determine the amount of time you need to display each slide. You can also ascertain the overall length of the show.

V

Performing with PowerPoint

To enter the display time manually for each slide, first select the slide in Slide Sorter view and click the Slide Transition button on the Slide Sorter toolbar, or move to the slide in Slide view and choose Slide Transition from the Slide Show menu or the shortcut menu. In the Slide Transition dialog box, enter the number of seconds in the Advance section's Automatically After edit box.

To record the slide durations during a rehearsal of the slide show, click the Rehearse Timings button on the Slide Sorter toolbar; or choose Rehearse Timings from the Slide Show menu. When the slide show begins, the Rehearsal dialog box shown in Figure 16-14 is displayed in the lower right corner of the slide.

FIGURE 16-14.

The Rehearsal dialog box.

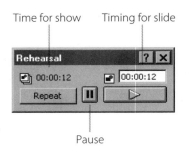

Practice giving the presentation, advancing the slides manually when needed. As you speak, the elapsed time for the slide show is displayed on the left in the Rehearsal dialog box, and the elapsed time for the current slide is displayed on the right. To advance to the next slide, click the left mouse button as you normally would, press P, or click the arrow button in the Rehearsal dialog box. You can also pause the slide show by clicking the button with the double vertical line, or you can click Repeat to repeat the current slide if you want to re-record the time for that slide.

After you complete the last slide, a dialog box shows the total length of the show and gives you the option to place the new timings in Slide Sorter view. If you click Yes, the timing for each slide appears under the slide in Slide Sorter view. To run the show with the timings, choose Slide Show from the View menu, select the Use Timings If Present option in the Set Up Show dialog box, and then show the presentation again.

To remove slide timings, select one or more slides in Slide Sorter view, click the Slide Transition button on the Slide Sorter toolbar, and then clear the Automatically After option in the Advance section of the Slide Transition dialog box.

Using Slide Meter

If you want to manually run a slide show that has rehearsed timings (to allow for interruptions, questions, ad-libbing, and so forth), you can use PowerPoint's Slide Meter to gauge your progress against the rehearsed times. To display Slide Meter (see Figure 16-15) during a show, right-click during a slide show and select Slide Meter from the pop-up menu.

FIGURE 16-15.

The Slide Meter dialog box.

The clock at the top of the Slide Meter dialog box records your time for the current slide, and the clock at the bottom of the dialog box records your cumulative time for the slide show. In addition, the progress bar in the middle of the dialog box measures how you are doing against the original rehearsed time. If you are within the time, the progress bar displays green boxes. As you get closer to the end of the rehearsed time, yellow boxes appear. And when you exceed the time, red boxes are displayed. At the bottom of the Slide Meter dialog box, a second bar indicates, on the basis of the rehearsed timings, whether you are going too slow or too fast for the entire presentation.

Marking Up Slides

To call special attention to a slide, or if you just don't know what to do with your hands during a slide show, you can use the mouse pointer to draw directly on slides. You can circle items, draw arrows, or add written comments, much as sportscasters do when drawing football plays on TV during a game.

To draw on a slide, click the pop-up menu button and choose Pen, or press Ctrl+P to activate the pen pointer. Next press the left mouse button while moving the pointer on the slide to express yourself dramatically with scribblings. To clear everything you've drawn on a slide, choose Screen and then Erase Pen from the pop-up menu or press the E key (for erase). Figure 16-16 shows annotations drawn during a slide show.

FIGURE 16-16.

Annotations drawn on a slide.

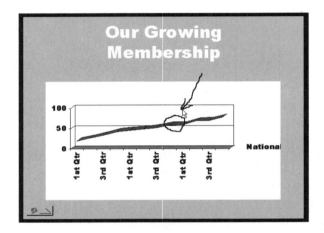

You can also change the color of the pen pointer's "ink" by choosing Pointer Options and then Pen Color from the slide show pop-up menu. When you're finished marking up your slides, choose Arrow from the pop-up menu or press Ctrl+A to return to the normal mouse pointer.

TIP

How to Hide the Mouse Pointer

If you want to hide the mouse pointer, whether it's an arrow or a pen, choose Hide Now (Ctrl+H) or Hide Always (Ctrl+L) from the Pointer Options submenu on the slide show pop-up menu. To make the pointer reappear, press Ctrl+A.

Special Slide Show Features

Special slide show features let you record a narration, create basic multimedia presentations, add backup documents, and create interactive shows that can branch to other presentations. You can even instruct PowerPoint to run a series of slide shows sequentially.

Adding a Summary Slide

Summary Slide button

To add a slide that summarizes a series of slides, select the slides in Slide Sorter view and then click the Summary Slide button on the Slide Sorter toolbar. A new slide appears, which contains the titles of the selected slides as bulleted text items. You will probably want to revise the summary slide title and add more information to the slide. Simply edit it in Slide view as you would any slide.

Recording a Narration

To record a spoken sound track that can accompany a slide show, choose Record Narration from the Slide Show menu. The Record Narration dialog box, shown in Figure 16-17 on the next page, allows you to change the recording quality, if you wish, by clicking the Settings button. Higher recording qualities sound better but they also use more disk space.

The Setting button brings up the Sound Selection dialog box. The number at the right end of the Attributes setting indicates the disk space used by each second of recorded sound. The sounds you record will be stored in the presentation file. If the recorded narration is long, you may want to link to a narration file stored in a separate file on disk. To link a narration, click the checkbox next to Link Narrations In. Then you can select the narration location by clicking Browse. Click OK to return to the Record Narration dialog box.

To begin recording, click OK back in the Record Narration dialog box. Speak into your system's microphone as you view the presentation. To finish, end the presentation as you normally would. Dialog boxes will ask whether you want to save the new timings and review the timings in Slide Sorter view. While you are recording a narration, you will not hear the standard sounds in the presentation.

FIGURE 16-17.
The Record
Narration
dialog box.

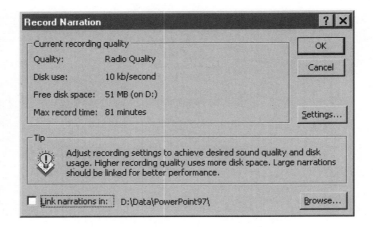

FIGURE 16-17.
The Record
Narration
dialog box.

Adding Video, Sound, and Music

Nothing brings a presentation to life like adding multimedia objects—video, sound, and music—to a slide show. As long as you have the objects available on your system, adding multimedia objects to a presentation is straightforward, and the effect is truly dramatic.

On any slide, you can embed one or more objects—perhaps a short music clip as the slide fades into view, followed by a video quote from someone involved with the project. These clips can play automatically when the slide appears, or after a set interval. A presenter can also double-click on a slide's video, sound, or music icon to start playing a particular object.

TIP

> ### Cropping and Recoloring Media Clip Icons
> You can use the Crop Picture and Recolor options on the shortcut menu to change the appearance of the media clip's icon on the slide.

When you add a slide to a presentation, you can select either of the two Text and Media Clip autolayouts that has a *Double click to add media clip* placeholder. Double-clicking this placeholder leads to the Insert Movie dialog box displaying the available movie clip files. After you select a file, the first frame of the video appears on your slide.

To add sound, music or a movie clip from the Clip Gallery to any slide, move to the slide in Slide view and click the Insert Clip Art button on the Standard toolbar. The Sounds and Videos tabs of the Microsoft Clip Gallery dialog box offers any files available in the Gallery. If you have the Microsoft Office 97 CD-ROM in the CD drive, the Clip Gallery will even find the additional sounds, photos, and video clips available in the Valuepak folder of the CD-ROM.

The three most popular multimedia file types are AVI (movie files), MID (MIDI music files), and WAV (sound files).

TIP

Adding a Multimedia Object in Slide View
You can also add a multimedia object to a slide by moving to the slide in Slide view, choosing the Object command from the Insert menu, and selecting the object type in the Insert Object dialog box.

You can have the sound play automatically by using Custom Animation settings for the slide, as you learned earlier in this chapter. You can also simply double-click the icon to play the sound during the presentation.

Adding a Custom Soundtrack

New to PowerPoint 97, the Custom Soundtrack add-in, available on the Microsoft Office 97 CD-ROM, can generate a musical score for your presentation in many different styles. Custom Soundtrack uses the synthesizer in your computer to generate new music, so your computer must be equipped with a sound card that offers a MIDI synthesizer. The best-sounding cards offer "wavetable" synthesizers. If your sound card does not offer a "wavetable" synthesizer, you may prefer to play music recorded in WAV files.

To install the Custom Soundtrack add-in, open the ValuPack folder on the CD-ROM, and then open the MusicTrk subfolder. Double-click the Setup icon to install Custom Soundtrack. If PowerPoint is open when you install Custom SoundTrack, you must close and restart PowerPoint.

To add a soundtrack to any slide, display the slide in Slide view and choose Custom Soundtrack from the Slide Show menu.

V

Performing with PowerPoint

FIGURE 16-18.

The Custom
Soundtrack dialog
box.

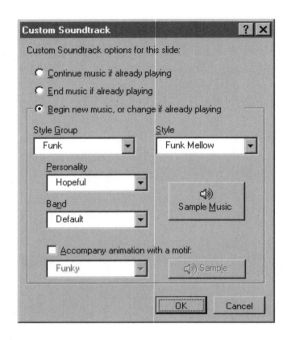

In the Custom Soundrack dialog box, shown in Figure 16-18, choose a Style Group, Style, Personality, and Band from the drop-down lists. To enhance the soundtrack, you can even click the Accompany Animation With A Motif checkbox, and choose a motif from the accompanying drop-down list. To hear the music you are about to add, click the large, Sample Music button in the Custom Soundtrack dialog box. Click OK to return to the slide when you are satisfyied with your musical selection. The music you have chosen will play when the slide appears. If music is still playing from the previous slide, the new musical selection will replace it.

The Custom Soundtrack dialog box offers two additional options for how the soundtrack will be played. Continue Music If Already Playing will continue to play the music that is playing from a previous slide rather than change to the new music. End Music If Already Playing will end the music from the previous slide. This might be the appropriate option for a slide at the end of a presentation segment.

Adding Drill-Down Documents

If you have data in another Windows application that can support an assertion you've made in a presentation or provide additional information, you can embed the data as an object on a slide so that it appears as an icon. During the slide show, you can then double-click the icon to "drill down" to the information and display the data in its original form. For example, you can embed a Microsoft Word document or a Microsoft Excel spreadsheet as a drill-down document. In fact, you can embed any file created by a Windows application that can act as an OLE server or an OLE object application. Most Windows applications can provide OLE objects for use in PowerPoint.

To embed an existing object, first choose Object from the Insert menu, and when the Insert Object dialog box appears, select Create From File and click the Browse button. In the Browse dialog box, select the file you want and then click OK. When you return to the Insert Object dialog box, select the Display As Icon option and click OK. The object appears on the current slide as an icon that you can open by double-clicking. You can move and size this icon as needed.

When you double-click the object, the application opens in its own window. Certain applications let you drag and drop files from the Windows Explorer to a PowerPoint slide. You'll have to test your application to see if it supports this feature.

Creating a Slide Show with Branching

By embedding one PowerPoint presentation as a drill-down object in another PowerPoint presentation, you can branch to that presentation from within another slide show. The embedded presentation can provide detailed information on a topic covered by the main presentation. To embed a PowerPoint presentation, follow the procedure described in "Adding Drill-Down Documents" on the previous page, but select a PowerPoint presentation as the object you want to embed.

You can also break off sections of a slide show to use as custom slide shows. Each section can contain slides that pertain to a certain audience. As you run the main slide show, you can choose to continue at any point with a custom show. You can even use custom shows to provide additional slides based on questions or feedback from your audience.

To create a custom show, choose Custom Shows from the Slide Show menu. In the Custom Shows dialog box, click New. In the Define Custom Show dialog box, shown in Figure 16-19 on the next page, enter a name for the custom show. Then select the slides you want in the custom show and click Add. When all slides are added, click OK and then choose Close to close the Custom Show dialog box.

To branch to a custom show during a slide show, click the button at the lower left corner of the current slide and choose Go from the pop-up menu. Choose Custom Show and then select the show name. You can also choose to display a custom show by choosing its name on the Set Up Show dialog box.

FIGURE 16-19.

The Define Custom Show dialog box.

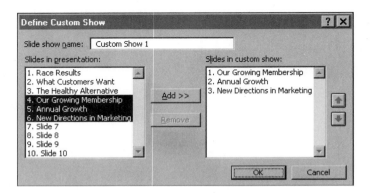

Playing a Series of Slide Shows

To play a series of slide shows automatically, you can create a batch file with a command line that contains the following: the command to start PowerPoint, the /s switch to activate Slide Show view, and the full pathname for each presentation you want to show.

For example, using a text editor like Microsoft Word or WordPad, you can create a batch file called Nextyear.bat to run the sales and project presentations stored in the slideshow folder on your system. In this case, your batch file would consist of the following command line:

    Start PowerPnt /s c:\slideshow\sales.ppt c:\slideshow\project.ppt

When you run this batch file, the slide shows play in the order in which they appear in the file.

Displaying slide shows can be the ultimate thrill in using PowerPoint, but you'll also appreciate some of the advanced topics covered next, in the final section of this book.

CHAPTER 17

Giving Your Presentation at Home, Online, or On the Road

P owerPoint includes a number of features designed to make giving an electronic slide show more efficient and foolproof. For example, do you really need to find a conference room, schedule it, set up a computer, projector, and screen, and make sure the coffee pot is full before you can present a slide show to your coworkers and superiors? Not anymore! With Presentation Conferencing, you can use your computer network to give your presentation to as many people as you want, and they don't have to leave their offices! Presentation Conferencing allows you to schedule a time for a "virtual" meeting, designate which computers on the network will receive the presentation, and then orchestrate the slide show from your desktop while you use the telephone to talk with the "meeting's" attendees.

Have you ever left a meeting without a list of the tasks everyone agreed to perform, and then had a hard time following up to see that things got done? Whether you are on the road, in a conference room down the hall, or at your desktop, you can ensure more productive meetings by using Meeting Minder to make notes to yourself, create a list of action items, and take meeting minutes. When the meeting is done, clicking a button sends the minutes and action list to Microsoft Word, where you can edit and check spelling, and then sends them to meeting attendees via electronic mail, using Microsoft Exchange or Microsoft Outlook.

No matter how professional your slide show, if you show up at a meeting without the Microsoft Excel spreadsheet you embedded in slide 15, the meeting will not go well. Before you take a presentation on the road, you can use PowerPoint's Pack And Go Wizard to assemble all of the files you need to run your slide show and put them on a floppy disk or anywhere else you designate. No more mad scrambles to air express a missing file before tomorrow's meeting! And, as with the earlier version of PowerPoint, if you know you won't be changing your presentation after you leave the office, you can pop the PowerPoint Viewer on your laptop so that you can give your slide show without taking up a lot of hard disk space with the complete PowerPoint program.

Giving a Slide Show Across the Internet or an Office Network

? SEE ALSO
For information about creating an HTML version of a presentation that you can post on a Web site, see "Saving a Presentation as Web Pages," page 385.

When you need to make a presentation but don't need everyone to be physically present in a conference room, you can host a presentation conference across your company's network, or even across the Internet. Everyone whom the presenter connects to the conference will be able to view the slide show on his or her computer, and make annotations on slides for everyone else to see. The presenter controls the flow of the show and switches from slide to slide as needed.

Unfortunately, there are some serious limitations to presentation conferencing. Objects that are embedded on slides will not be seen by audience members. These include charts, org charts, tables, sound clips, and movies. Audience members will see all the text, graphics, and backgrounds in the presentation, though, as well as hear the transition sound effects in the presentation.

As the host, you prepare for the conference by scheduling a time for the conference, gathering the computer names or Internet addresses of all the computers that will participate in the conference (as you'll learn, PowerPoint makes it easy for people to determine their Internet address), and telling PowerPoint which computers on the network or the Internet will participate in the conference. Each audience member must also start PowerPoint and go into Presentation Conferencing, as you'll learn next.

Attending a Presentation Conference

To participate in a presentation conference, you must provide the presenter with either your computer name (if you're on a local area network or office network) or your Internet IP address. Don't worry, when you are ready to join a presentation conference, you'll use the Presentation Conference Wizard, which provides your computer name or Internet address.

At the designated time that you've been told the presentation conference will start, launch PowerPoint and follow these steps:

1 Choose Presentation Conference from the Tools menu of PowerPoint. On the first screen of the Presentation Conference Wizard, click Next. You will see the Presenter or Audience screen, as shown below:

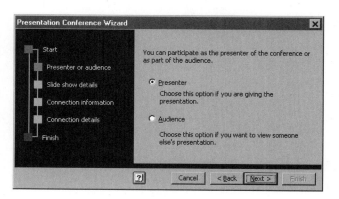

2 Click Audience and then click Next.

3 On the Connection Type screen of the wizard choose either Local Area Network or Dial-in To Internet and click Next.

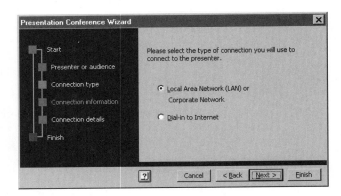

4 On the Connection Details screen, you see your computer name or Internet address (labeled "IP address"). This is the name or address that the presenter needs to know in order to connect you to the conference. Click Next to get to the final screen.

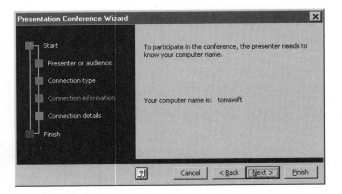

5 Click Finish to begin waiting for the conference to start. Your computer will wait for the presenter to connect you to the conference. When your computer has connected to the conference successfully, you will see the first slide of the presentation.

Delivering a Presentation Conference

The first step in setting up a presentation conference is gathering the names or Internet addresses of the computers that will participate in the conference. Have the people you are inviting to the presentation conference let you know their computer's name or their Internet IP address (perhaps by e-mail), and then make a list.

How to Use a Conference Address List

If you frequently invite the same group to your presentation conferences on an office network, make a Conference Address List file and save yourself from having to reenter the same list of computer names over and over. A Conference Address List file is a text file listing the computer names, with one name on each line. You can create the list in Notepad, WordPad, or Microsoft Word. If you use Word or WordPad, be sure to save the file as text only.

Each computer that will participate in a presentation conference must have TCP/IP installed as a network protocol and an IP address. If the network does not assign IP addresses automatically, you must assign one manually.

With the list of names in hand, follow these steps:

1 Open the presentation you want to show. If you want to show only a segment of the presentation, you must select Set Up Show from the Slide Show menu, and enter the From and To slide numbers into the Set Up Show dialog box.

2 Choose Presentation Conference from the Tools menu. The first screen of the Presentation Conference Wizard appears. Click Next to get going.

3 On the Presenter Or Audience screen of the wizard select Presenter, and then click Next.

4 On the Slide Show Details screen of the wizard, you will see the current range of slides to be shown in the presentation. If you need to change the starting and ending slide numbers, cancel out of the wizard and choose Show Setup from the Slide Show menu. Otherwise, click Next.

V

Performing with PowerPoint

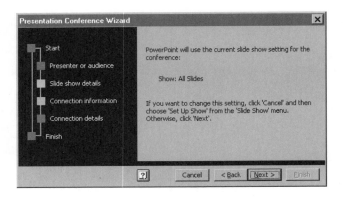

5 The Connection Information screen of the wizard reminds you to establish an Internet connection, if necessary, and then click Next. You can just click Next if you are using an office network.

6 On the Connection Details screen of the wizard, enter the name or Internet IP address of each computer that will join the conference and click Add. Each name is added to the list box underneath. Keep adding names until all the computers are listed.

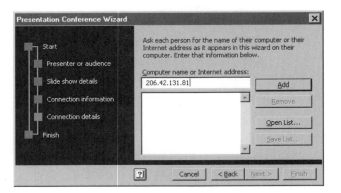

If you add a name by mistake or later need to remove the computer name of someone who cannot "attend" the conference, select the name in the list in this dialog box, and click Remove. If this particular list of computer names is one you will use again, you can click Save List and assign a filename to create a Conference Address List file. If you have already created a Conference Address List file, you can open it rather than typing each computer name, by clicking Open List and selecting the file in the Open Conference Address List dialog box.

7 When the list of computer names is complete, click Next to display the last screen of the Presentation Conference Wizard. As soon as all audience members have used their Presentation Conference Wizards to join the conference, click Finish to start the conference.

The invited computers must join the conference and be waiting for you to use the Presentation Wizard to host the conference. Your computer will then connect to the computers you've invited to the conference. This might take a couple of minutes. PowerPoint must find the computers, download a copy of your presentation to each computer, and create a temporary copy of the presentation on the host computer.

If a computer is missing, you will see a message that says the computer is not available or cannot be found. When you click OK to close this message box, you return to the wizard's third dialog box to check the spelling of the computer's name and reenter it if necessary, or to remove it from the list. At least one computer must be connected to the conference for it to proceed.

Conducting a Conference

When you host a presentation conference, you have several tools to help ensure that the meeting is productive. When you attend a presentation conference, you can participate, but your role is limited.

When a conference begins—with one host and at least one attendee connected—all the attendees see a full-screen slide show on their computer screens. The host computer's screen displays the slide show as the attendees see it, along with the Stage Manager for controlling the slide show, the Slide Navigator for moving quickly among slides, the Meeting Minder for making notes during the presentation, and the Speaker Notes for the current slide. Your screen might look something like the one in Figure 17-1 on the next page. Only the host can see Meeting Minder, so it's a great place to keep your notes to yourself.

Cleaning Your Screen

During a presentation conference, it's a good idea to minimize PowerPoint so that your screen is less cluttered, as shown in Figure 17-1.

FIGURE 17-1.

The host computer's screen, showing a slide, Slide Navigator, Stage Manager, and Meeting Minder.

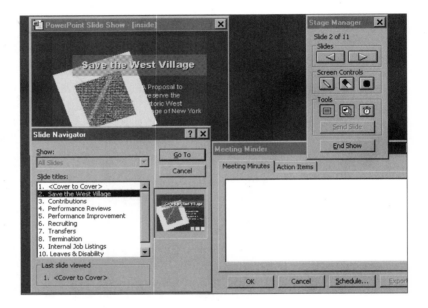

Controlling the Slide Show with Stage Manager

When you host a presentation conference, you use Stage Manager to control your presentation. If you close Stage Manager, your conference ends.

You can use the Previous and Next Slide buttons to move from slide to slide; or you can click the slide window to move to the next slide.

The Screen Controls section allows you to change the mouse pointer to a pen by clicking the Pen button. You use the pen to mark up slides—for example, you can underline an important word to emphasize a point. Audience members see any marks you make on a slide. To erase any marks you've made, click the Erase Marks button. The third control in the Screen Controls section simply displays a black screen while you pause the presentation.

TIP

SEE ALSO
For details on rehearsing a slide show and using Slide Meter, see "Using Slide Meter," page 407.

Practice Makes Perfect
Using the mouse to move the pen on a slide isn't easy! Practice before you do it for a crowd, especially if you want to write words rather than making marks such as underlines and circles.

The three buttons in the Tools section of the Stage Manager let you turn on or off the display of the Meeting Minder, the Slide Navigator, and the Slide Meter.

If the ideas are flowing fast and furious and you want to make sure everyone gets a copy of a slide they might need later, you can click Send Slide to copy the currently displayed slide, complete with any marks you've added, to the hard disk of each attendee. Clicking Stage Manager's End Show button ends the presentation conference.

Switching Slides with Slide Navigator

Suppose the reaction of your audience to your presentation indicates that you can skip some details and move on to a new point. Or suppose the conference is running long and you want to speed things up by not showing some of the slides. Slide Navigator lets you select any slide in your slide show, preview its contents, and then either show it to your audience or skip it.

The Last Slide Viewed box at the bottom of the Slide Navigator dialog box displays the title and number of the slide you are currently showing your audience. If you want to skip over slides, you can scroll through the list of slides in the Slides box to find the one you want. Selecting a slide displays a preview in the box on the right. To display this slide to conference attendees, click Go To.

Keeping Track of the Time with Slide Meter

Slide Meter keeps track of the elapsed time of your presentation, and if you rehearsed your slide show before presenting it, Slide Meter lets you know if you are going slower or faster than you planned. Figure 17-2 on the next page shows how the host computer's screen might look when the Slide Meter window is open and the Meeting Minder is closed.

FIGURE 17-2.
The Slide Meter
loaded during a
slide show.

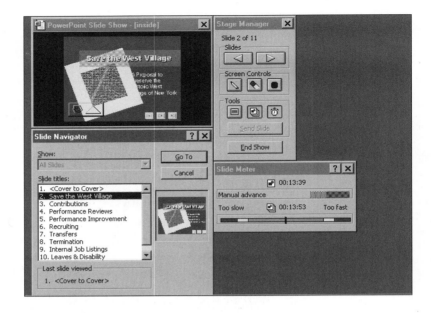

FIGURE 17-2.
The Slide Meter
loaded during a
slide show.

Participating in a Conference

You may be running the show when you host a presentation conference, but don't expect your audience to sit on their hands and watch.
As participants, they can comment on your ideas or correct your facts
and figures by picking up the pen (their mouse) and marking the
current slide. (The pen is activated when the conference starts.)
Pressing Ctrl+P deactivates the pen; so does choosing the Pen command from the slide show shortcut menu. When an attendee marks
up a slide, everyone else sees the marks. Careful, though: too many
marks from too many opinion-holders can make a slide unreadable.

SEE ALSO
For more
information
about using the
pen, see
"Marking Up
Slides," page 407.

Conference attendees cannot control the flow of the slide show; only
the host can switch the slide on everyone's screen. Attendees can
control the pen color they use to mark up slides. (You can assign a
different pen color to each attendee at the beginning of a conference
to differentiate the many marks that may accumulate on a slide.)

To leave the conference, attendees can choose End Show from the
shortcut menu. When a conference is over, the presentation's slides
remain in each attendee's computer memory as a new presentation.
The presentation can be saved for future use, or when each attendee
exits PowerPoint, he or she can click No to discard the presentation.

Viewing a Presentation on Two Screens

The ideal setup for an in-person presentation is to have two machines hooked together with which to deliver a presentation. The audience views the output of one machine while the presenter controls the show using the other. The presenter can then use the Stage Manager, Slide Navigator, and Slide Meter on the controlling machine.

To use two-screen slide shows, you must connect a "null-modem" cable between the serial or COM ports of two computers. Then choose View On Two Screens from the Slide Show menu of PowerPoint on both computers. You'll see the View On Two Screens dialog box shown in Figure 17-3.

FIGURE 17-3.

The View on Two Screens dialog box.

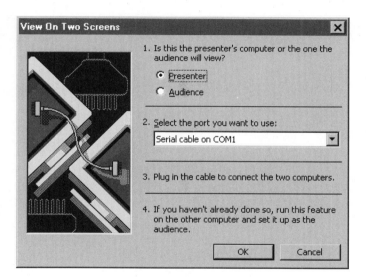

On the host computer, select Presenter in the View On Two Screens dialog box. On the other computer, choose Audience in the View On Two Screens dialog box. Make sure you choose the correct port from the list on both computers and then click OK on both computers. Now you can start the slide show on the host computer and use the Stage Manager, Slide Navigator, and Slide Meter controls to guide you while giving the presentation. Remember, the viewers will see only the slides on the second computer.

V

Performing with PowerPoint

Managing the Meeting

Meetings are more productive when someone keeps accurate minutes of what is decided and who is assigned to which follow-up tasks. You can use PowerPoint's Meeting Minder during a meeting or presentation to jot down these minutes or to refer to notes you made before the meeting.

Meeting Minder, shown in Figure 17-4, opens as soon as you start hosting a presentation conference, but you can also use it when you are displaying a slide show on a single machine by choosing Meeting Minder from the Tools menu.

FIGURE 17-4.

The Meeting Minder dialog box.

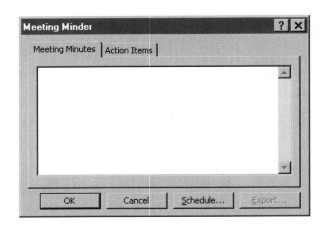

TIP

If you are displaying a slide show on your computer or projecting it on a screen or a large monitor, your audience sees Meeting Minder when you open it. You can probably interrupt the slide show to record minutes and action items without distracting your audience too much, but this method doesn't work very well as a way of making notes to yourself. You are better off creating your notes in Notes Pages view and printing them out. If you are giving a presentation conference or viewing a presentation using two computers, only you can see Meeting Minder when you open it, so you can check your notes without distracting other conference participants.

After you have opened Meeting Minder, you can type notes about the meeting on the Meeting Minutes tab. You can also enter action items for meeting attendees or others on the second tab of the Meeting Minutes dialog box. You can close Meeting Minder and continue the presentation, and then open it again as necessary to record notes, minutes, and action items for other slides.

Another way to view minutes and action items is to export them to Microsoft Outlook or Microsoft Word. Exporting the minutes gives you a chance to polish them before distributing them to the meeting's attendees. Exporting action items puts them right into your group's shared information store. To export items, click the Export button in the Meeting Minder dialog box when the meeting is over. A second Meeting Minder dialog box appears, as shown in Figure 17-5, offering you two export options. If you select Post Action Items To Microsoft Outlook, the actions items for the presentation will be sent to Outlook. If you select the second option, Post Meeting Minutes and Action Items To Microsoft Word, PowerPoint exports your notes to a Word document and opens Word so you can edit your notes. Select the export option you want, and then click the Export Now button.

FIGURE 17-5.

The Meeting Minder export dialog box.

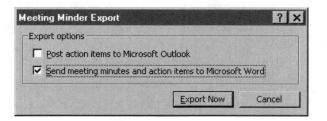

If you enter any tasks on the Action Items tab during the meeting, PowerPoint displays a list of all the task assignments as the last slide in your slide show or presentation conference. You can then check the list's accuracy and remind everyone of their individual tasks before they leave the meeting. Later, after you've had a chance to refine the list of action items in Word, you can send it to everyone as electronic mail or as a fax.

Packing Up Your Slide Show

Suppose you are going to deliver your presentation to clients in their offices on their equipment, or you need to send a presentation on disk to a colleague who is not on your computer network. Or suppose you have designed a sales presentation that will be offered to prospective customers at a trade show or will be mailed to people responding to an advertisement. In all of these situations, it is critical that you include all of the pieces required to show the presentation on the disk. The Pack And Go Wizard is designed to ensure that you do exactly that.

To use the Pack And Go Wizard, first open the presentation you want to pack, and then choose Pack And Go from the File menu to display the first Pack And Go Wizard screen introducing you to the wizard. Click Next to move to the second screen, shown in Figure 17-6.

FIGURE 17-6.

The second Pack And Go Wizard screen.

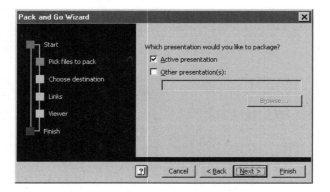

On this screen, the wizard asks which presentation you want to pack and selects the current presentation by default. To select a presentation other than the current one, select the Other Presentation(s) option, click the Browse button, and select the presentation(s) you want in the Select A Presentation To Package dialog box. When you have answered the wizard's question, click Next to display the third screen, shown in Figure 17-7 on the facing page.

FIGURE 17-7.

The Choose Destination screen of the Pack And Go Wizard.

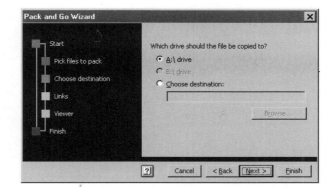

You now need to tell the wizard where to put the packed presentation. The wizard selects a default drive, usually drive A. To specify a different drive, select the Choose Destination option, click the Browse button, and select a destination in the Specify Directory dialog box. Then click Next to display the fourth screen, shown in Figure 17-8.

FIGURE 17-8.

The fourth Pack And Go Wizard screen.

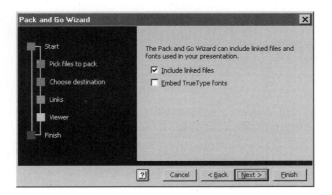

If your presentation includes linked files, be sure to select the Include Linked Files option. If you want the Wizard to pack the fonts used in the presentation, select the Embed TrueType Fonts option. (You need to use this option if your presentation includes any fonts that might not be installed on the computer that will run the presentation.)

When you click Next, the screen shown in Figure 17-9, on the next page, asks whether you want to include the PowerPoint Viewer on the disk. If you are not sure whether PowerPoint will be installed on the computer that will run the presentation, be sure to include the Viewer. Otherwise, click the check box to deselect it.

Performing with PowerPoint

FIGURE 17-9.

The Viewer screen of the Pack And Go Wizard .

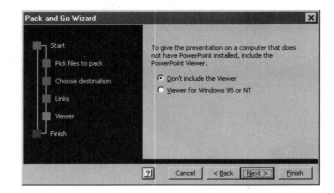

Clicking Next displays the last dialog box, which summarizes the options you selected with the wizard and reminds you to run the Pack And Go Wizard again if you make any changes to the presentation. After verifying the options, click Finish. The Pack And Go Wizard then swings into action, packing up everything you need to run the presentation.

Creating a File That Always Runs as a Slide Show

A new feature in PowerPoint gives you the ability to save a presentation as a file that always runs as a slide show. When you double-click the file in Windows Explorer, the show starts. When the show ends, PowerPoint also ends. You must have PowerPoint installed on the machine on which you'd like to run a PowerPoint show file.

To create a show file, choose Save As from the File menu. In the Save As dialog box, choose PowerPoint Show from the Save As Type drop-down list. PowerPoint show files have the file name extension PPS.

To run a show on a machine that does not have PowerPoint installed, you can use the PowerPoint Viewer, described next.

Using the PowerPoint Viewer

You don't need to have the entire PowerPoint program installed on a system to run a slide show. You can install only the PowerPoint Viewer, which displays your presentations just as if you were running the slide show in Slide Show view. The PowerPoint Viewer allows you to display PowerPoint slide shows on a portable computer where hard-disk space is too limited to install the entire PowerPoint application. It can also display slide shows created in PowerPoint for the Macintosh.

Before you can use the PowerPoint Viewer to display a slide show, you must add the transition effects, builds, and timings you want for the show; make sure the Use Timings, If Present option is selected in the Set Up Show dialog box; and save the presentation in a file.

To prepare a slide show that can be viewed on a system not equipped with PowerPoint, first copy the PPVIEW32 program onto a diskette and then copy the presentation file to a diskette. The presentation file must then be copied from the diskette to the local hard disk because a presentation cannot be read and displayed fast enough from floppy disk.

Once the presentation file and Viewer are installed, start the Viewer program. (If you don't see a Start menu item for the PowerPoint Viewer, you can download the viewer from the Microsoft web site, www.microsoft.com, or copy it from the ValuPack folder of the Microsoft Office 97 CD-ROM. It's a file named PPVIEW32.EXE) The Microsoft PowerPoint Viewer dialog box appears, as shown in Figure 17-10 on the next page.

In the Microsoft PowerPoint Viewer dialog box, select the presentation file you want to display, and click Show or press Enter to run the slide show. You also have a few options to select in the PowerPoint Viewer dialog box, such as whether to end the show with a black slide or run the show in a window. The PowerPoint viewer also lets you print a show, so it can be a handy utility to have in case you want to print a presentation on a client's computer at a remote site. When the slide show starts, you have all the mouse and keyboard control capabilities that you have in PowerPoint's Slide Show view. After the show, click Exit to exit the PowerPoint Viewer.

Performing with PowerPoint

FIGURE 17-10.

The Microsoft PowerPoint Viewer dialog box.

You may freely copy and distribute the PowerPoint Viewer with as many presentations as you want.

NOTE

> You cannot open embedded documents while using the PowerPoint Viewer to run a slide show. Nor can you branch to other presentations. For more information about drilling down to embedded documents, see "Adding Drill-Down Documents," page 412. For more information about branching to other presentations, see "Creating a Slide Show with Branching," page 413.

The Presentation Conference Wizard, Meeting Minder, the Pack And Go Wizard, and the PowerPoint Viewer are designed to help you present your slide shows efficiently. As you've seen in this chapter, using them can take a lot of the hassle out of setting up, delivering, and following up on your electronic presentations.

PART VI

Advanced PowerPoint

Using PowerPoint with Other Applications

A lthough PowerPoint certainly stands on its own, it becomes even more powerful when combined with its partners in Microsoft Office 97: Microsoft Word 97 and Microsoft Excel 97. PowerPoint is the public voice of Office, telling the stories you write in Word and the numbers you crunch in Excel with professionally and consistently designed images.

Many of the common attributes shared by the Microsoft Office applications are perfectly obvious after you've used them a little. You'll notice the common menus, dialog boxes, toolbars, and even procedures that make switching from one application to another easy. You'll also find that the applications share spelling dictionaries, AutoCorrect word lists, drawing tools and the Clip Gallery. And using the Office Binder, you can bundle pieces from different applications into one unit for even easier access.

But below the surface of Office, a powerful technology called OLE (pronouced olé) gives the Office suite the capability to gracefully share information. For example, you can move objects such as text or numbers from one application to another just by dragging them from one window into another. And when you move an object between applications and then decide to edit the object, a featured called *in-place editing* summons the menus, dialog boxes, toolbars, and procedures you used to create the object so you can make changes as though you were working in the original program. You can move a worksheet from Excel to PowerPoint, for example, and then choose to edit the object. Suddenly, Excel's menus and toolbars appear within PowerPoint's window. When you finish editing, PowerPoint's menus and toolbars reclaim the screen.

The drag-and-drop method is the key to transferring information among the Office applications. You can almost always select an item in one application and drag it to another application's window. And if you want a copy of the information to remain in the original application, all you have to do is hold down the Ctrl key as you drag. In this chapter, you'll learn how to select objects and drag them between applications. You'll also learn about a few considerations to keep in mind as you exchange information between the Office applications, and you'll learn about menu alternatives that you can use with other Windows applications that do not support drag-and-drop procedures.

Using PowerPoint with Microsoft Word

In Chapter 4, you learned how to exchange outlines between Microsoft Word and PowerPoint, and in Chapter 17, you learned how to export meeting minutes and action item lists from PowerPoint to Word. But you can also exchange one paragraph or one picture with similar ease. Best of all, you can embed an entire PowerPoint slide show in a Word document, transforming a drab report into a lively, stimulating presentation complete with special effects, sound, music, and perhaps even video.

Of course, you can embed individual multimedia elements in a Word document without using PowerPoint, but embedding them in a PowerPoint presentation and then embedding the presentation in Word allows the multimedia objects and the presentation to be played together in a slide show.

Dragging Text from Word to PowerPoint

You'll appreciate dragging and dropping when you need to enter text in PowerPoint that you've already typed in Word. Rather than retype the text, you can simply drag it from Word to PowerPoint as easily as you drag it from place to place within a Word document.

To drag text from Word to PowerPoint, start by opening the Word and PowerPoint windows, and then arrange them so they share the screen, even if one window overlaps the other. Make sure the slide in which you want to embed the Word text is displayed in the PowerPoint window and that Slide view is active. Figure 18-1 shows how you might arrange the windows. Then, select the text in Word—a word, a paragraph, or anything else you've created in Word, including a Word table. Place the mouse pointer on the selection, and drag the selection to the current PowerPoint slide. To copy the text to PowerPoint rather than move it, hold down the Ctrl key as you drag.

FIGURE 18-1.

The PowerPoint window overlapping a Word document.

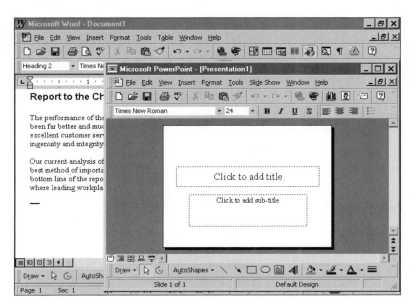

VI

Advanced PowerPoint

If you drag text from Word directly into a text placeholder on a slide, the text acts as if you had typed it directly into the placeholder in PowerPoint. In this case, all of the rules for working with text objects on slides will apply. If, on the other hand, you drag text from Word and drop it anywhere on a slide, but not in a text placeholder, it appears as a picture of the text, with all of its Word formatting intact. It is important to note that in this case the rules for working with text will not apply. When you stretch or compress the picture by dragging its handles, the text becomes distorted.

By contrast, text that you've entered in a PowerPoint text box (using the Text Tool button on the Drawing toolbar) maintains its size and shape when you stretch or compress its text box, but the word wrapping changes. Figure 18-2 illustrates the difference between text that has been dragged from Word and text that has been entered in a PowerPoint text box.

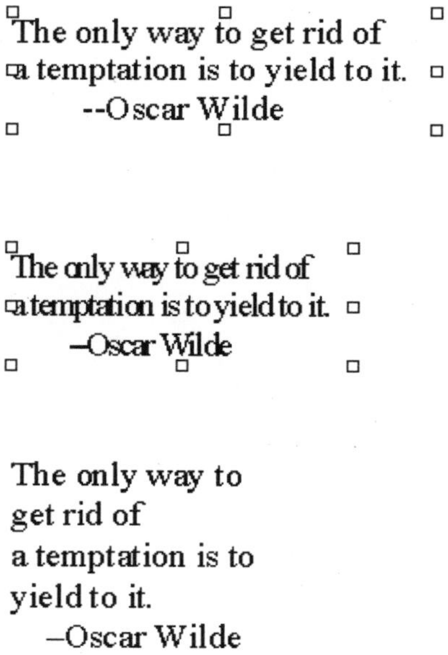

FIGURE 18-2.
When embedded text from Word (top) is compressed, it becomes distorted (center). When a PowerPoint text box is compressed, its text rewraps (bottom).

The only way to get rid of
a temptation is to yield to it.
--Oscar Wilde

The only way to get rid of
a temptation is to yield to it.
--Oscar Wilde

The only way to
get rid of
a temptation is to
yield to it.
--Oscar Wilde

Because the object is a picture of the text from Word, you cannot edit the text with PowerPoint's text editing tools. Instead, you do the editing in Word by double-clicking the text picture. Word's menus and toolbars replace those of PowerPoint, and a frame that represents a small Word editing window, complete with its own rulers, appears around the text. Without leaving PowerPoint, you can work within this frame and use all of Word's commands and controls as if you were actually in Word. When you finish editing the text, click the PowerPoint slide outside the frame. The frame disappears, but the revised text picture remains, and all of PowerPoint's menus and toolbars reappear within the PowerPoint window.

You can also edit the text using Word's menus and toolbars by clicking it with the right mouse button and choosing Edit Document Object from the shortcut menu. When you have finished your edits, simply click outside the text picture to save your edits and return to the PowerPoint slide.

If you would be more comfortable editing the text in a separate Word window, you can use the right mouse button to click the Word text picture within PowerPoint, and then choose Open Document Object from the shortcut menu. After you edit the text, you must choose the Update command from Word's File menu, and then choose Close And Return To *<Presentation>* from the File menu.

? SEE ALSO

For more information about the Paste Special dialog box, see "Linking a PowerPoint Slide to Word," page 443.

The alternative to using drag and drop is to select the text in Word, copy the text using the Copy command on the Edit menu (or using one of the shortcuts for copying items, such as clicking the Copy button on the Standard toolbar), switch to PowerPoint, and then choose Paste from the Edit menu (or use one of the shortcuts for pasting items, such as clicking the Paste button on the Standard toolbar). This procedure always copies selected text from another application to PowerPoint, but it does not always tie the text in PowerPoint to Word. Therefore, when you double-click the text, you might not return to the application from which the text originated. To embed the Word text in PowerPoint, choose Paste Special rather than Paste from PowerPoint's Edit menu, make sure the Paste option (not Paste Link) is selected in the Paste Special dialog box, and then select the description of the text that includes the word "object," in this case Microsoft Word Document Object, from the list in the dialog box.

VI

Advanced PowerPoint

Only when the text is embedded as an object can you double-click the object to return to the original application and revise the text.

> To place a Word icon that represents embedded text in a PowerPoint presentation, select the Display As Icon option in the Paste Special dialog box.

Embedding a Slide in a Word Document

By using the Insert Object command in Word, you can access Microsoft Graph as easily as you can from within PowerPoint, so you don't need PowerPoint to create a graph for a Word document. WordArt is also available in Word, so you can have fancy headings in memos as well as in a slide show. In addition, PowerPoint gets its tables from Word, so you don't need PowerPoint's help there. But by dragging a PowerPoint slide to Word, you can place an image of the slide in a document, complete with a background design and a combination of foreground and background text and graphical objects. You can also copy and paste individual objects from a PowerPoint slide into a Word document using the Copy and Paste commands.

To drag a slide from PowerPoint to Word, arrange the PowerPoint and Word windows on the screen, and make sure the slide you want to drag is visible in PowerPoint's Slide Sorter view. Then drag the slide from PowerPoint to Word, holding down the Ctrl key if you want to copy the slide rather than move it.

After the slide appears in Word, you can drag and drop it within the Word window as you would a block of text. You can also drag a corner handle to resize the slide proportionally. By clicking the slide with the right mouse button, you can bring up a Word shortcut menu with commands that apply to the slide. For example, you can add a border, shading, and caption to the slide, or frame the slide so that you can wrap text around it and use other techniques that apply only to framed elements. Figure 18-3, on the facing page, shows the shortcut menu that appears in Word.

Also on the shortcut menu, you'll see a command called Slide Object. When you choose this command and then choose Edit from the submenu, the menus and toolbars change to those for PowerPoint, even though the Microsoft Word title bar remains. Edit your slide just as you would if you had opened PowerPoint yourself. After you finish, move the insertion point to anywhere in your Word document; the menus and toolbars change back to Word's, and you can continue editing the rest of your Word document.

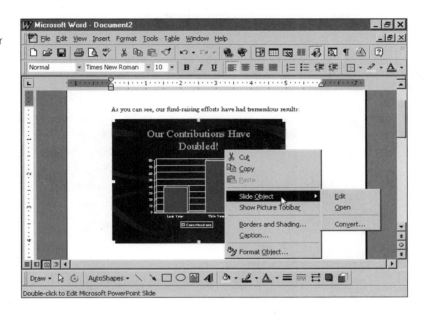

You can try dragging and dropping a slide into any other Windows application in the same way, but if it won't budge, you must use the Cut or Copy command in PowerPoint's Slide Sorter view, switch to the other application's window, and then use the Paste command.

Transferring a Graphic to Word

To transfer a graphic from a PowerPoint slide to a Word document, position Word and PowerPoint side-by-side as you would to transfer text, and then drag the graphic from one to the other. You can then edit the graphic directly in Word by double-clicking it to display Word's drawing tools, which work just like PowerPoint's drawing tools. Since Word and PowerPoint share the same Clip Gallery, you can also open the Gallery to get a duplicate of a picture you used in PowerPoint.

VI

Advanced PowerPoint

TIP

> To copy the entire text of your presentation to Word (but without the graphics), choose Send To from PowerPoint's File menu. Then choose Microsoft Word from the Send To submenu. In the Write Up dialog box, choose Outline Only. PowerPoint copies the text to Word, creating a new document.

Embedding a PowerPoint Presentation in Word

To embed an entire PowerPoint presentation in a Word document, you can drag the file icon from a folder or the desktop into Word, or you can open the presentation and then select the entire presentation in Slide Sorter view by choosing Select All from the Edit menu or by pressing Ctrl+A. Drag any one of the selected slides to Word while holding down the Ctrl key. The first slide of the presentation appears in Word, and when you double-click the slide, the presentation displays as a full-screen slide show. To edit the presentation, click the slide displayed in Word once with the right mouse button, and choose Presentation Object from the shortcut menu and Edit from the submenu. After you make changes to the presentation, click anywhere else in the Word document to leave the presentation. Remember that the changes you make in Word exist only in Word. The original presentation is not changed. You can also create a brand-new slide show for your Word document without ever leaving Word.

To create a new PowerPoint presentation or a single slide from within Word, follow these steps:

1 From the Word Insert menu, choose Object to open the Object dialog box.

2 In the Object Type list, select Microsoft PowerPoint Presentation or Microsoft PowerPoint Slide. If you want to display only the PowerPoint icon in the Word document and not a slide, select Display As Icon.

3 Click OK.

The object is inserted in your Word document, and the Word toolbar and commands are changed to the PowerPoint toolbar and commands. If you selected Display As Icon, Word will open PowerPoint for you to create your slide. When you have finished creating your slide, first choose the Update command from the File menu, and then, also from the File menu, choose Close And Return To *<Document>*. You can then edit your slide or presentation just as if you had opened PowerPoint without being in Word. However, you will not be able to open this slide show from within PowerPoint; an embedded slide show exists only within the document in which it is embedded.

Linking a PowerPoint Slide to Word

If you want to show a slide from within Word but also make sure that it resides in PowerPoint and reflects any changes you make to it in PowerPoint, you can link to it from Word. The slide's data is stored in a PowerPoint presentation rather than in a Word document, and only a representation is displayed in Word. When you double-click the representation in Word, the slide appears, just as if you had embedded it. Because you have linked the slide, any changes you make to it in PowerPoint are reflected in the representation in Word. The advantage is that you don't have to update the slide twice—once in PowerPoint and again in Word. The disadvantage is that you can't move the Word document to another computer without also moving the PowerPoint file. If you move the Word document without moving the PowerPoint file to the same destination, Word cannot access the PowerPoint data when you call for it. Only when you drag and drop a slide or use Paste Special to paste the slide in Word as an embedded object can you transport the document and simultaneously transport the data.

You can link an existing PowerPoint slide to a Word document in one of two ways: by using the Insert Object command or by using the Paste Special command.

To link a PowerPoint presentation using the Object command:

1 From Word's Insert menu, choose Object.

2 Click the Create From File tab of the Object dialog box.

3 In the File Name edit box, type the name of the presentation you want to link, or click the Browse button to locate it, and click OK to return to the Object dialog box.

4 Select the Link To File option, and then click OK.

The Paste Special command allows you to link individual slides of a presentation to a Word document. To link a slide from a PowerPoint presentation using Paste Special:

1 Open the presentation containing the slide you want to link and switch to Slide Sorter view.

2 Select the slide you want to link and choose Copy from the Edit menu.

3 Switch to Word and place an insertion point where you want the slide to appear.

4 Choose Paste Special from Word's Edit menu.

5 In the Paste Special dialog box, shown in Figure 18-4, select the Paste Link option, and then click OK.

FIGURE 18-4.

The Paste Special dialog box in Word.

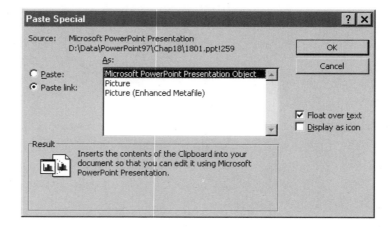

To edit a slide, double-click the slide in Word or click the slide once with the right mouse button and choose Linked Slide Object from the shortcut menu, then Edit Link from the submenu. You could also select the slide, choose Linked Slide Object from Word's Edit menu, and then choose Edit Link from the submenu. After you make changes to the slide in the PowerPoint window, save the file again. As soon as you save the file, the linked copy of the slide in Word is updated with the changes.

Modifying the Link

When you save a PowerPoint slide in a file, link it to Word, and then modify it in PowerPoint, the changes flow through to Word as soon as you save the modifications in the PowerPoint file. If Word is closed, the changes appear the next time you open the Word document that contains the linked slide.

To prevent changes to a linked slide from flowing through to Word, select the presentation's slide in Word, and choose Links from the Edit menu. In the Links dialog box, shown in Figure 18-5, select Manual rather than Automatic as the Update option. The linked slide will be updated only when you click Update Now in the Links dialog box, or when you select the slide and then choose either Update Link from the shortcut menu or press F9. To prevent the slide from being updated even when you use the Update Now command, select the Locked option in the Links dialog box.

FIGURE 18-5.

The Links dialog box in Word.

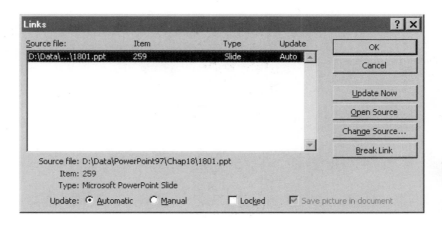

Other options in the Links dialog box are: Open Source, which opens the presentation in PowerPoint for editing; Change Source, which allows you to link a different object from another application; and Break Link, which severs the link and leaves a static slide in Word that cannot be edited or updated in PowerPoint.

VI

Advanced PowerPoint

Hyperlinking to a Presentation in Word

In addition to placing a PowerPoint slide in Word, you can create a hyperlink in Word to a PowerPoint presentation. The title of the first slide appears as a hyperlink in the Word document. When you click this hyperlink, the PowerPoint slide show opens with the Web toolbar visible.

To create a hyperlink, select the slides of a presentation in PowerPoint and choose Copy. In Word, move the pointer to the destination for the hyperlink and choose Paste As Hyperlink from the Edit menu. The hyperlink will appear in the Word document.

Using Word to Format and Print Notes Pages and Handouts

PowerPoint lets you print handouts that have blank lines for audience notes, but it does not let you print handout sheets based on your notes pages, and it does not let you print notes pages with blank lines. It also provides no easy way to include the handouts for a slide show in a report or training manual that contains other material written in Word. At times like these, choose the Send To command from the PowerPoint File menu, and then select Microsoft Word from the Send To submenu.

Choose one of the five layout options in the Write-Up dialog box, shown in Figure 18-6—you can always change the formatting and layout once you have the information in Word. You can also choose whether to link the slides and notes to Word, so that any changes you make in the original slide show are also made in the Word document. Click OK to begin the write-up.

If you select the Blank Lines Next To Slides option, for example, you will get the layout shown in Figure 18-7. The first column contains the slides. The second column contains blank lines for hand-written notes about the slide.

FIGURE 18-6.

The Write-Up dialog box.

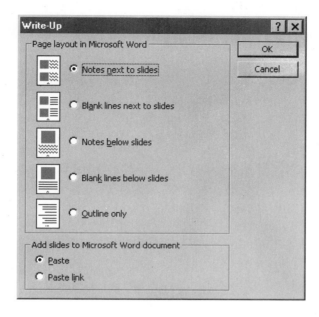

FIGURE 18-7.

The layout for these handouts is Blank Lines Next To Slides.

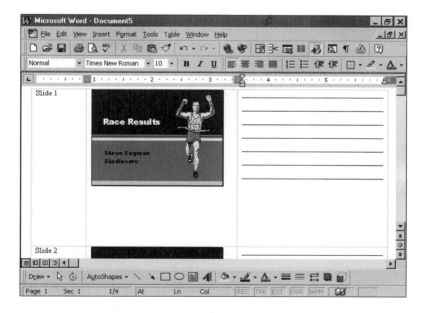

Using PowerPoint with Microsoft Excel

The vast majority of presentations relate information using words rather than numbers, but if you have numeric data, you are likely to accumulate it, calculate it, and analyze it in a spreadsheet program such as Microsoft Excel. You'll be glad to know that you can communicate between PowerPoint and Excel as easily as you can between PowerPoint and Word. In fact, you can create an Excel worksheet from within PowerPoint, drag a worksheet from Excel to PowerPoint, or drag a PowerPoint slide or presentation to an Excel worksheet using the same techniques you use with Word.

Embedding an Excel Worksheet in PowerPoint

By clicking the Insert Microsoft Excel Worksheet button on PowerPoint's Standard toolbar, and higlighting the number of columns and rows your worksheet should contain, you can embed a new Excel worksheet on a PowerPoint slide. This has the same effect as choosing Object from the Insert menu and then selecting Excel Worksheet as the object type. While you are creating the worksheet, Excel's menus and toolbars appear in PowerPoint, and a framed worksheet window overlaps the PowerPoint slide. When you finish the worksheet and click outside of it, PowerPoint's menus and toolbars reappear, and a picture of the Excel worksheet is displayed on the slide.

 NOTE

> It's best to format the worksheet while Excel's menus and toolbars are available so that the worksheet picture looks just right when it appears in PowerPoint.

When you first click the Insert Microsoft Excel Worksheet button, a grid of empty cells appears. Drag across as many as 11 columns and up to 6 rows of cells, and then release the mouse button. A worksheet frame opens on the current slide, displaying the number of columns and rows you specified. Using the Excel menus, toolbars, and procedures, create the worksheet within the worksheet frame. When the worksheet is complete, be sure all the cells that you want included in it are visible in the worksheet frame, and then click outside the frame to place a picture of the worksheet on the PowerPoint slide. You can move and stretch the picture by dragging its handles.

As in Word, you can embed an entire Excel worksheet in PowerPoint by dragging the worksheet icon from a folder or the desktop onto a slide. A picture of the worksheet will appear on the current PowerPoint slide. You can also drag any part of an existing worksheet to a slide. Arrange the Excel and PowerPoint windows on the screen (and be sure Slide view is active), and then select the worksheet range that you want to move or copy. Drag the border of the range to move the worksheet from Excel to the current PowerPoint slide. If you want to copy rather than move the worksheet, hold down the Ctrl key as you drag. Figure 18-8 shows a range of numbers in Excel and the same range copied to PowerPoint using drag and drop.

FIGURE 18-8.

An Excel worksheet that has been copied to PowerPoint using drag and drop.

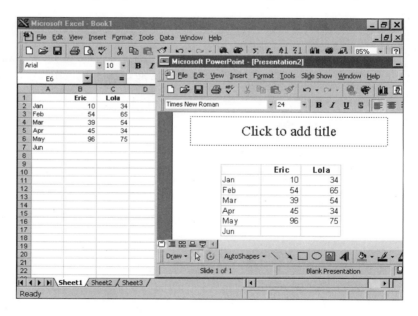

Once again, because the Excel worksheet appears in PowerPoint as a picture, you can move and stretch the worksheet by dragging its handles.

TIP

> If you want to accentuate a worksheet on a slide, use the Shadow option on PowerPoint's Drawing toolbar. Adding a shadow gives the worksheet a slightly raised look.

Modifying an Embedded Worksheet

To edit the worksheet, double-click it, or click it with the right mouse button and select Edit Worksheet Object from the shortcut menu. Excel's menus and toolbars appear in place of PowerPoint's, and the worksheet is surrounded by a frame. After you finish editing the worksheet, click outside the frame. To reopen the worksheet in a separate Excel window, select the worksheet, click the right mouse button, and choose Open Worksheet Object. When you finish editing from within Excel, choose the Update command from Excel's File menu, and then choose Close And Return To *<Presentation>*, also from the File menu.

TIP

> You can crop a worksheet that has been placed on a PowerPoint slide by clicking the worksheet's picture with the right mouse button, choosing Crop Picture from the shortcut menu, and placing the cropping icon on one of the worksheet picture's side handles. Then drag the handle inward to reduce the width or height of the picture.

Linking an Excel Worksheet to PowerPoint

You use either the Object command on the Insert menu or Paste Special on the Edit menu to link an Excel worksheet to PowerPoint.

To link an Excel worksheet using the Object command:

1 From the PowerPoint Insert menu, choose Object.

2 Select the Create From File option.

3 In the File edit box, type the name of the Excel worksheet you want to link, or click the Browse button to locate it.

4 Select the Link option, and then click OK.

To link an Excel worksheet using Paste Special:

1   Open the worksheet, select the data you want in the slide, and copy it using the Copy command on Excel's Edit menu (or use one of the shortcuts for copying items, such as clicking the Copy button on the Standard toolbar).

2   Switch to PowerPoint's Slide view, and choose Paste Special from the Edit menu.

3   Select the Paste Link option in the Paste Special dialog box, and then click OK.

The worksheet appears in PowerPoint. If you make subsequent editing changes to the worksheet in Excel, the changes will flow through to the linked PowerPoint presentation when you resave the Excel file. If you make changes to the Excel file when the linked presentation is closed, the changes will appear the next time you open the presentation.

Remember, when you link an Excel worksheet to a PowerPoint presentation and you move the presentation to another system, you must also move the Excel worksheet.

Displaying a PowerPoint Slide or Slide Show in Excel

To display a PowerPoint slide or slide show in an Excel worksheet, follow the same procedures you use to display a slide or slide show in Word. Simply drag a single slide from PowerPoint's Slide Sorter view to Excel, select all the slides in PowerPoint's Slide Sorter view and then drag the entire presentation to Excel, or drag a presentation icon from a folder or the desktop to the worksheet.

VI

Advanced PowerPoint

⭐ **TIP**

After you drag a slide to Excel, you can resize the slide's width and height proportionally by dragging one of its corner handles.

If you've dragged a single slide to Excel, double-click the slide to place it in the PowerPoint window for editing. If you've dragged an entire presentation to Excel, double-click its representative slide to start the slide show. You can control the slide show as if you were displaying it in PowerPoint's Slide Show view. To edit an entire presentation, select its representative slide in Excel, click the right mouse button, and choose Presentation Object and then Edit from the submenu.

Sending a Presentation to Microsoft Exchange

If Microsoft Exchange is installed on your computer, you can use it to send or receive a presentation as electronic mail or as a fax message, or you can post it to a public folder that is accessible to everyone on your network, by choosing the Send To Exchange Folder command from the File menu. Exchange allows you to set up multiple "profiles" for different kinds of electronic communication services, including Microsoft Mail, The Microsoft Network, and Internet mail. When you choose the command, you see a dialog box that allows you to select the profile or service to which you want to post the presentation.

CHAPTER 19

Automating PowerPoint with Visual Basic for Applications

To make many tasks easier, you can program PowerPoint to do them for you by using its built-in programming language, Visual Basic for Applications (VBA). Simple VBA programs in PowerPoint can automate frequent tasks and handle chores that would otherwise require multiple steps.

All the applications in Microsoft Office 97 share the VBA programming tools, which let you build automated business solutions with the Office applications. In fact, instead of buying customized applications, many companies are using Office and VBA to fulfill their needs. For example, instead of buying a dedicated forms-generator, the Philip Morris human resources department programmed a business application in Word that automates and simplifies the process of filling in personnel review and evaluation forms. Companies can now use VBA in PowerPoint to create toolbar and menu commands that help employees create standard presentations.

This chapter provides an introduction to programming automated solutions with PowerPoint.

What is Visual Basic for Applications?

A computer program is a cyborg version of a Miss Manners guide instructing the computer how to behave. For example, you can program a computer to display "Hello" on startup or "Bye" on exit. Computer programs are nothing more than a series of instructions (referred to as code) that control the computer.

VBA, which you use to create "code," is a modern version of the BASIC programming language, which was invented to teach programming to beginners. BASIC commands are essentially English commands, so you will find them easy to understand.

To create simple VBA programs, you should understand a number of procedures, which are the basis of this chapter. You should know how to:

- Use the macro recorder

- Run a recorded macro

- View (and eventually edit) a VBA macro

- Read VBA

- Use variables

- Get information from users

- Add your macros to custom toolbars and menus so that you can find them and run them easily

- Get your macro to make its own decisions.

Recording Basic Macros

The first PC macros, a shortened version of the term "macroinstructions," simply recorded a sequence of keystrokes, assigned them to a single keystroke, and then played them back. Microsoft redeveloped and extended this early concept of macros to create a fully programmable macro language for its Office suite. Microsoft later merged the idea of programmable macro languages with a bona fide programming language – BASIC – and VBA was born.

A macro language is a programming language built into an application that lets you automate a series of tasks by combining them into a single command. Macro recorders allow you to record the code necessary to automate such a series of tasks while you perform the task. You can then replay the macro when you want to perform that task again. Microsoft Excel, Microsoft Word, and Microsoft PowerPoint provide macro recorders.

How to Use the Macro Recorder

Although you have to be careful when using macro-recorded code wholesale, the code you get while recording a macro is a great starting point from which to expand.

How to Record a PowerPoint Macro

To use PowerPoint's macro recorder, follow these steps:

1   In PowerPoint, choose Macro from the Tools menu, then select Record New Macro. This opens the Record Macro dialog box, shown in Figure 19-1, on the next page.

2   In the Record Macro dialog box, you can:

- Change the name the macro to something more descriptive.

- Select the template or presentation in which to store the macro. PowerPoint defaults to storing the macro in the current presentation.

- Enter a brief description of the macro.

FIGURE 19-1.
The Record Macro dialog box lets you name and store the macro you're about to record.

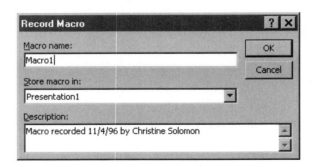

3 When you click OK in the Record Macro dialog box, PowerPoint displays the Stop Recording toolbar, which has one button: Stop Recording.

4 Perform the task in PowerPoint that you want to record.

5 After you finish recording the macro, click the Stop Recording button.

How to Run a Macro

When you run a macro, whatever you did when you recorded the macro happens again. In some cases you may get an error message indicating that the macro can't perform the task it's trying to do. Often such errors occur because you're trying to redo something that's already been done. For example, you're trying to open a file that's already open or close a file that's no longer open. In such cases, make the necessary adjustment and then try running the macro again.

To run a macro that you have recorded:

1 Choose Macro from the Tools menu, then select Macros. This opens the Macro dialog box, as shown in Figure 19-2.

FIGURE 19-2.

The Macro dialog box lets you run, edit, create, and delete macros.

2 Select the macro you recorded from the list, then click Run.

How to View (and Eventually Edit) a PowerPoint Macro

After you record a macro, you might want to look at it and eventually edit it. To look at (and change) a recorded macro:

1 Choose Macro from the Tools menu, then select Macros. This opens the Macro dialog box.

2 Select the macro from the list, then click the Edit button.

When you edit a macro, you're actually opening an application separate from PowerPoint called the Visual Basic Editor. (You may have noticed that Visual Basic Editor appears as on option on the Tools Macro submenu.) When you first edit a macro, the Visual Basic Editor is arranged into two windows:

■ The macro itself appears in the large window on the right. To edit a macro, simply type in the macro window.

■ The Project Explorer, which lets you manage the elements of your VBA project including such things as code and dialog boxes, appears at the left. If you don't see the Project Explorer, you can open it from the View menu.

Because you can rearrange these windows, resize them, or close them, your Visual Basic Editor may not look exactly like the one pictured in Figure 19-3. To close the Project Explorer window, click the Close button in the upper right corner of the window.

FIGURE 19-3.

The Visual Basic Editor.

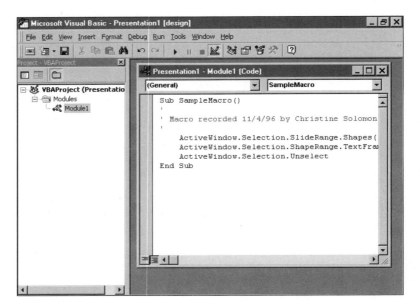

To close the Visual Basic Editor choose Close And Return To PowerPoint from the File menu.

How to Read VBA

The best way to learn about VBA is to try recording some sample macros and then take a guided look at them to see what they mean. Later, you will learn to write some code from scratch. These code samples are short so you can duplicate them easily and run them on your own computer.

First, try recording the following macro, named FirstExample, which opens a PowerPoint presentation. Before you record the macro, name any presentation *Example One* and save it in the C:\My Documents folder. Then close the presentation and start a new presentation.

To record the macro, follow these steps:

1   Start the macro recorder by choosing Macro from the Tools menu and choosing Record New Macro from the Macro submenu.

2   In the Record Macro dialog box, change the macro name to *OpenExampleOne* (without spaces between the words) and click OK.

3   From the File menu, choose Open.

4   Switch to the C:\My Documents folder, if necessary.

5   Select the presentation named "Example One", and click Open.

6   Click the Stop Recording button on the Stop Recording toolbar.

To see the macro you've just recorded, choose Macro from the Tools menu, and then choose Macros. In the Macro dialog box, select *OpenExampleOne* and click Edit.

The macro should look something like this:

```
Sub FirstExample()
'
' Macro recorded 11/4/96 by Christine Solomon
'
    Presentations.Open FileName:="C:\My Documents_
    \Example One.ppt", ReadOnly:=msoFalse
End Sub
```

NOTE

In these code samples, the underscore (_) means that the current line of code continues.

To read the VBA code in the macro shown above, you need to understand a few things about macros. First, every macro you record is a subroutine. Subroutines are defined as instructions that perform specific tasks. Subroutines start with the keyword "Sub" followed by the name of the subroutine, in this case, the macro name, and a set of

VI

Advanced PowerPoint

parentheses, and all subroutines end with the phrase "End Sub," as shown below.

```
Sub NameOfThisSubroutine()
    Code
End Sub
```

Second, VBA code consists largely of objects – essentially, bundles of functionality – that you can manipulate in two ways:

- By setting or retrieving an object's properties (or characteristics)

- By using an object's methods (or procedures)

For example, PowerPoint presentations are objects. When you get a presentation's name through code, you get its Name property. When you open it through code, you use the Open method. The general syntax for manipulating objects is:

```
object.property or object.method
```

In any given line of code, you can either set a property or perform a method – you can't do both at once.

The sample code shown in the previous section (and repeated below) uses the Open method of the Presentations object (shown in bold). In this code, the first object is Presentation and the first action is a method, Open, as shown below:

```
Presentations.Open FileName:="C:\My Documents_
    \Example One.ppt", ReadOnly:=msoFalse
```

The code following the Open method consists of the arguments (or additional information) that the method requires in order to do anything. In the sample code shown above, the first argument is FileName and the second is ReadOnly. Each argument is followed by a colon plus an equal sign (:=) and then the information the argument is to use. The information each argument uses is shown in bold.

```
Presentations.Open FileName:="C:\My Documents_
    \Example One.ppt", ReadOnly:=msoFalse
```

The information that the FileName argument uses is fairly straightforward: It's the path and the filename of the presentation you want to open, enclosed in quotes. In VBA, all plain text must be enclosed in quotes so that VBA knows it's plain text rather than a misspelled object, property, method, etc. The information that the ReadOnly argument uses is quite a bit more obscure: It's a value (called an intrinsic constant) that's built into VBA and equals False. The meaning of **ReadOnly:=msoFalse** amounts to this: Don't open this presentation in read-only mode.

About VBA Syntax

Here are two other things you need to know to read (and write) VBA:

- Each use of a VBA property or method and each VBA statement or function (programming terms for "command") is a single line of code (even though it may wrap onto more than one line for display purposes) that ends with a carriage return. For example, in the sample macro **Presentations.Open FileName:="C:\My Documents\Example One.ppt", ReadOnly:=msoFalse** is a single line of code that ends with a carriage return.

- Text that starts with an apostrophe (') indicates a comment line. (A comment is a note to yourself, which the macro ignores.) The default color for comments is green. The comment from the sample macro would be:

```
' Macro recorded 11/4/96 by Christine Solomon
```

Remember that the comment is considered to be a single line of code even though it wraps for display purposes. The comment ends with a carriage return after the word "Solomon."

NOTE

> Do not break the use of a VBA property, method, statement, function, or comment onto multiple lines by pressing Enter.

How to Extend the Useful Life of Your Macros

The problem with macro-recorded code is that it's hard-coded – in other words, it performs only the specific actions that you record. For example, the macro you recorded in the previous section can open only one file (Example One), and it can open this file only when it's located in C:\My Documents. To turn hard-coded code into code

VI

Advanced PowerPoint

that's more widely usable requires two programming techniques: the use of variables and a way to get information from the people who run your macro.

How to Use Variables

Suppose television sets were hardwired to receive a single channel. You'd have to own three TVs just to watch the major networks. (Don't even think about cable.) Code that doesn't use variables is as inefficient as a TV that gets only one channel.

Variables are single-word names that store a particular type of data. The data might come from users or from another macro. Every programming language enables you to work with two general types of data – string data (text) and numeric data (integers). Some languages, such as VBA, support a variety of other types of data as well.

It's generally a good practice to declare variables – in other words, to list at the start of the program the variables used and the type of data each variable represents. You declare variables using the keyword "Dim" followed by the single-word name for the variable (such as FileToOpen) plus the data type (such as string).

For example, the following code specifies that the variable MyName is a string, sets the variable equal to "Christine," and then displays that variable in a message box. The word "MsgBox" is a VBA function that opens a message box; the information that immediately follows the word MsgBox appears in the message box. Note that because MyName is a variable, the word "MyName" itself doesn't appear in the message box. Instead, the message box displays whatever MyName equals – in this case, "Christine." (Note that variable names are not enclosed in quotation marks.)

```
Sub MyName()
    Dim MyName As String
    MyName = "Christine"
    MsgBox Prompt:=MyName
End Sub
```

You can create a new macro and type the preceding code to test how variables work (and to see how to write code from scratch) by following the steps on the next page.

1   Choose Macro from the Tools menu, and then select Macros.

2   In the Macro dialog box, type a single-word name for your new macro in the Macro Name box, such as MyName.

3   Click Create. This opens the Visual Basic Editor.

If the macro you just created is the first macro in the PowerPoint presentation that you're currently working in, the subroutine MyName will appear at the top of the macro window. Otherwise, it will probably appear below the other macros stored in the presentation. At this point, the subroutine consists of the following two lines of code:

```
Sub MyName()
End Sub
```

NOTE

To adjust the macro window so that it displays only one macro at a time no matter how many macros are stored in a particular PowerPoint presentation, click the Procedure View button in the lower left corner of the macro window.

To add code to this subroutine, follow these steps:

1   Position the cursor after the parentheses in the first line of code, and press Enter.

2   Type the second line of code, which declares that the variable MyName contains a string (a.k.a. plain text).

```
Dim MyName As String
```

Notice that as you type, the Visual Basic Editor displays tips listing the options (alphabetically, of course) that might be correct in this context. For example, when you start to type the keyword "string," the Visual Basic Editor displays a list box (see Figure 19-4 on the next page) that lists options that start with "s." After you type "str" the word "String" appears highlighted at the top of the listbox. Press Enter to insert "String" at your cursor.

VI

Advanced PowerPoint

FIGURE 19-4.

As you type, the Visual Basic Editor displays programming tips.

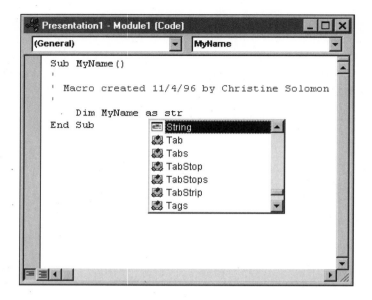

3 Press Enter at the end of the second line of code, and then add the third line, which sets the variable MyName equal to "Christine."

```
MyName = "Christine"
```

4 Press Enter at the end of the third line of code, and then add the fourth line, which displays a message box with the name "Christine."

```
MsgBox Prompt:=MyName
```

When you press the Spacebar after you finish typing "MsgBox," the Visual Basic Editor displays another tip with the complete syntax of the MsgBox function, as shown in Figure 19-5. Although it can take some time before you're comfortable reading tips such as this, one thing to remember is that boldface arguments are required; non-boldface arguments are optional. So the tip means this: The MsgBox function requires a single argument called Prompt, which tells it what to display. In this case it will display the text that the variable MyName contains.

FIGURE 19-5.

When you type the keyword "MsgBox," the Visual Basic Editor displays the complete syntax for the MsgBox function.

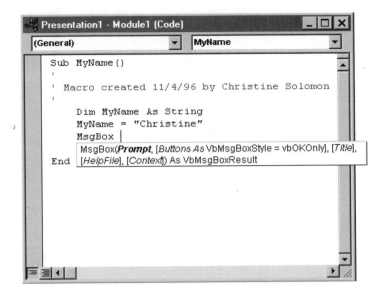

5 Save your work by clicking the Visual Basic Editor's Save toolbar button or by selecting the Save command from the File menu.

At this point, you can run the macro in one of two ways:

■ Return to PowerPoint and run it from the Macro dialog box.

■ In the Visual Basic Editor, make sure the cursor is somewhere in the MyName subroutine, and then click the Run Sub/UserForm button on the Standard toolbar (see Figure 19-6).

FIGURE 19-6.

The Standard toolbar of the Visual Basic Editor.

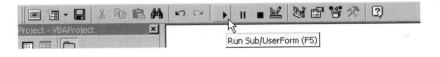

When you run the macro, you should see the message box shown in Figure 19-7.

FIGURE 19-7.

The macro MyName displays a message box with the value of the variable MyName.

VI

Advanced PowerPoint

To change this macro so that it displays another name, simply type the name to display in the message box in the third line of code. For example, this line of code displays "Chuck" in the message box.

```
MyName = "Chuck"
```

This line of code displays "George Washington, first president of the United States" in the message box.

```
MyName = "George Washington, first president of the
United States"
```

To close the Visual Basic Editor, choose Close And Return To Microsoft PowerPoint from the File menu.

How to Get Information from People Who Run Your Macro

Although variables clearly make it easier to change the information that your macro uses, the subroutine presented above is still hard-coded. In other words, the only way to specify the name to display in the message box is for the programmer (that's you) to type as part of the code itself a new value for the MyName variable. However, it makes sense for the user (not the programmer) to indicate the name that the message box displays.

The simplest way to allow users to provide information to your macros is with an input box – a one-line dialog box in which people type text that your macro then uses. The InputBox function is similar to the MsgBox function in that it requires a single argument – Prompt – which, in this case, is used to tell users what information you need from them. The following macro asks users their name and then displays their answer in a message box.

```
Sub YourName()
    Dim YourName As String
    YourName = InputBox(Prompt:="What is your _
    name?")
    MsgBox Prompt:=YourName
End Sub
```

Notice that in this subroutine, the variable YourName is not set equal to plain text such as "Christine" or "Chuck." Rather, it's set equal to the result of the InputBox function. In other words, it's set equal to whatever users type in the input box. And this is the significance of the parentheses around the argument *Prompt:* These parentheses indicate that the function will return information to the program. If users type "Devra" or "Ezmarelda" or whatever, the InputBox will return that information and store it in the variable YourName, which the MsgBox function can then display. Figure 19-8 shows the input box that this subroutine displays and the message box that results when the user types "Steve."

FIGURE 19-8.
Whatever users type in the input box (left) is displayed in the message box (right).

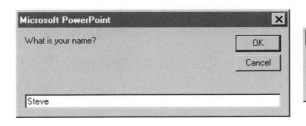

Of course, the input box is the simplest way to get information from users. The more flexible and complex way to do this is to use a dialog box, which you create with the UserForms feature in the Visual Basic Editor. You can find instructions on how to use this feature in the Help file that comes with the Visual Basic Editor.

How to Create an Interface that Makes it Easy to Run Your Macros

Although you can run macros with the Run command in the Macro dialog box (see "How to Run a Macro," page 456), it's easier to run them from toolbars and menus, just as you would run any other PowerPoint command. This section explains how to add macros to custom toolbars and menus so that they're easy to use.

When you create a custom toolbar or add a custom menu to the menu bar, you're essentially doing the same thing: you're customizing Microsoft's toolbars. Toolbars can contain buttons, menus, or a combination of both.

How to Add a Macro to a Custom Toolbar

To create a custom toolbar and add a macro to it:

1 Choose Toolbars from the View menu, and then select Customize.

FIGURE 19-9.

Use the Toolbars tab in the Customize dialog box to create a custom toolbar.

2 Choose the Toolbars tab in the Customize dialog box.

3 Click New.

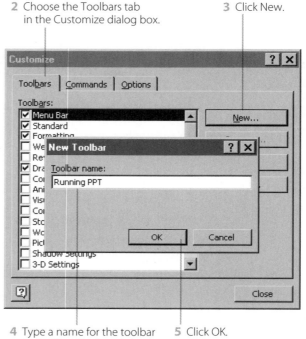

4 Type a name for the toolbar in the New Toolbar dialog box.

5 Click OK.

A new, blank toolbar appears. Move this toolbar away from the Customize dialog box so that it doesn't disappear behind it.

6 Choose the Commands tab in the Customize dialog box, and then select Macros from the Categories list box. The available macros appear in the Commands list, shown in Figure 19-10.

FIGURE 19-10.
When you select Macros from the Categories list on the left, the available macros appear in the Commands list on the right.

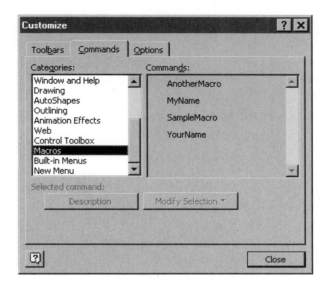

7 Drag the macros to add to the custom toolbar and drop them on the toolbar one-at-a-time. The Figure below shows a custom toolbar with macros displayed as text buttons.

8 When you first add your macros to a toolbar, the macro's name appears on the toolbar. To swap the name for a graphic, click the toolbar button with the macro's name, and then click the Modify Selection button in the Customize dialog box.

9 Select Default Style from the bottom third of the Modify Selection menu, and then select Change Button Image.

10 From the Change Button Image palette, click the graphic to use for your macro.

11 Click Close to close the Customize dialog box. Figure 19-12, on the next page, shows a finished toolbar with graphic buttons representing your macros.

FIGURE 19-12.
A custom toolbar with macros displayed as graphic buttons.

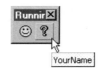

How to Add a Macro to a Custom Menu on the Menu Bar

To add a custom menu to the menu bar, follow these steps:

1 Choose Toolbars from the View menu, and then select Customize.

2 Click the Toolbars tab in the Customize dialog box, then select Menu Bar, which is the first item in the Toolbars list.

3 Click the Commands tab, and then select New Menu from the bottom of the Categories list box. When you do this, "New Menu" appears in the Commands list as well.

4 Drag "New Menu" from the Commands list to the PowerPoint's menu bar. You can gauge the position of the new menu by the oversized cursor that appears as you point with your mouse to various menu bar positions. In Windows, it's standard practice to add custom menus to the left of the Window menu.

5 Drop "New Menu" onto the menu bar, and then click on it with the right mouse button.

6 Give the custom menu a new name, such as "Running PPT" by typing it into the Name text box, as shown below.

7 To add a macro to your custom menu, select Macros from the Categories list box on the Command tab of the Customize dialog box.

8 Open your custom menu by clicking on it. When it's open, a short, blank stub appears beneath it, as shown below. Drag a macro from the Commands list to the open menu.

9 Click Close to close the Customize dialog box. The image below shows a finished menu bar with a custom menu for your macros.

Creating Advanced Macros that Make Their Own Decisions

In order to create more sophisticated macros – for example, macros that make their own decisions – you need to understand how to use control structures. Control structures determine the order in which code executes. Generally, macros run one line at a time, from beginning to end, unless this sequential flow is altered by events or control structures that cause the program either to execute code repeatedly or to execute code out of sequence. (Events are "outside" elements that affect the computer program, such as a given amount of time passing, the user clicking a certain button, or the user opening a certain file. Control structures are techniques for processing "decisions" within the computer program itself.) The most basic VBA control structure is If.. Then... Else.

VI

Advanced PowerPoint

If... Then...Else

If... Then...Else is not only the most basic control structure, it's also the most intuitive because it means exactly what it says. The simplest form of this control structure executes code based on whether a certain condition exists. Here's the syntax:

```
If Condition1 Then
       Code1
End If
```

SEE ALSO

For more information, see "How to Use Variables" page 462.

When a program executes this control structure, it first evaluates Condition1. If Condition1 is True, program execution continues with the first line of code in Code1. If Condition1 is False, Code1 is skipped and execution continues with the first statement following End If. For example, the code shown below works as follows: If x = 1, then the computer beeps; if x doesn't equal 1, nothing happens. Create this macro as described in the previous section titled What is a Variable? using the following code. Use different values for x, and hear what happens.

```
Sub ExampleI()
     Dim x As Integer
     x = 1
     If x = 1 Then
             Beep
     End If
End Sub
```

NOTE

"Beep" is one of the simplest VBA statements: It does just what it says.

Two clauses, ElseIf and Else, allow you to add additional tests to your If... Then...Else control structures. Use these optional clauses to enable your code to take different actions depending on current conditions or user input. You see the syntax on the next page (the square brackets enclose optional parts of the control structure).

```
If Condition1 Then
       Code1
```

```
[ElseIf Condition2 Then
     Code2]
[ElseIf Condition3 Then
     Code3]
     .
     .
     .
[ElseIf ConditionN Then
     CodeN]
[Else
     CodeElse]
End If
```

When a program executes this control structure, it evaluates Condition1 first. If Condition1 is True, Code1 executes. When Code1 finishes, the program skips to the first statement following End If. If Condition1 is False, however, the program skips to the next ElseIf clause and evaluates Condition2. If Condition2 is True, Code2 executes and the program continues with the first statement following End If. If Condition2 is False, the program skips to the next ElseIf clause. The same process continues until one of three things happens:

- An ElseIf condition is True (in which case its block of code executes).

- The program reaches the end of the control structure before a condition evaluates to True (in which case none of the code inside the control structure executes).

- The program encounters an Else clause.

An If...Then...Else control structure can have only one Else, which always appears as the last clause. Else clauses don't have conditions; they execute when all of the other conditions fail.

? SEE ALSO
For more information, see "How to Use Variables" page 462.

Here's a more complicated example using If...Then...Else. The code shown below works as follows: If x = – 1 and y = – 1, then the computer beeps; else if y = 0, then the computer does nothing; else if x or y equals any other number, the computer displays a message box with the word "Hi!" Again, create this macro as described in the previous section titled "How to Use Variables," use different values for x and y, and watch the results.

```
Sub ExampleII()
    Dim x As Integer
    Dim y As Integer
    x = -1
    y = 0
    If x = -1 And y = -1 Then
        Beep
    ElseIf y = 0 Then
    Else
        MsgBox Prompt:="Hi!"
    End If
End Sub
```

Concatenation

Concatenation is a very big word for a simple and disproportionately powerful programming technique. Concatenation lets you combine a variable with plain text or one variable with another. To do this, put an ampersand (&) between the items to concatenate. For example, the following line of code concatenates the words "Your name is " with the information stored in the variable *YourName*. Note that the space after the words "Your name is " separates these words and the information in the variable with a single blank space.

```
"Your name is " & YourName
```

As you can see from this example, one thing that concatenation lets you do is provide more detailed feedback to users. The following VBA code provides an example of this. It uses the Date function to get the current date; assigns that date to the variable Today; concatenates it with two bits of plain text, "Today is " and a period (.); and displays the result in a message box. Instead of just displaying the date to users, you tell them what date you're displaying – i.e., today's. "Date" is another of the simplest VBA functions.

```
Sub SampleConcatenation()
    Dim Today As String
    Today = Date
    MsgBox Prompt:="Today is " & Today & "."
End Sub
```

Comparison Operators

Comparison operators are symbols that allow you to compare expressions. The simplest comparison operator is the equal sign (=). Common comparison operators are listed below.

=   equal to

< >   not equal to

<   less than

>   greater than

< =   less than or equal to

> =   greater than or equal to

The following example uses an If... Then...Else control structure to check whether users have entered a valid number in the input box. If the number is valid, the program concatenates it with explanatory text and displays a message box. Otherwise, the program beeps and displays a message box informing users that they entered an invalid number. Since the InputBox function returns a string and the "greater than or equal to" operator requires a number, you must use the Val function to turn that string into a number.

> **NOTE**
>
> To use the Val() function, put the text value or string variable to convert into a number in parentheses after the keyword Val. For example, Val("10") = 10.

```
Sub ShowAnswer()
    Dim Answer As String
    Answer = InputBox("Enter a number_
    from 1 through 99:")
    If Val(Answer) <= 99 And Val(Answer) >= 1 _
        Then MsgBox Prompt:="You entered: " _
        & Answer & "."
    Else
        Beep
        MsgBox Prompt:="You entered an invalid _
        number."
    End If
End Sub
```

VI

Advanced PowerPoint

Using VBA to Automate Office Applications

In addition to automating routine tasks that you perform within PowerPoint, you can also automate the interaction of the Microsoft Office applications with VBA. For example, you can create a PowerPoint macro that will bring in numbers from Excel or enclose a PowerPoint presentation in a Word document.

To see how you can perform office automation with VBA, try following the procedure below to record a PowerPoint macro that will embed an Excel workbook into a presentation, add code to size the embedded object correctly, and allow users to type into an input box the path of the file to embed. Before continuing, make sure you have an Excel workbook with a short table suitable for displaying in a PowerPoint slideshow.

1 In PowerPoint, move to a blank slide formatted in a way that's appropriate for displaying an Excel table—for example, use the Bulleted List format or the Title Only format. Don't select anything on the slide.

2 Choose Macro from the Tools menu, then select Record New Macro. Name the macro *InsertWorkbook*.

3 Record the following: Choose Object from the Insert menu. This opens the Insert Object dialog box.

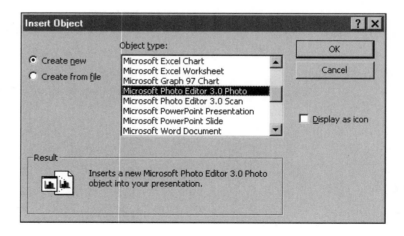

4 In the Insert Object dialog box, select the Create From File option.

5 Click Browse to open the Browse dialog box, which lets you select a file to embed into the active PowerPoint presentation.

6 After selecting an Excel workbook, click OK in the Browse dialog box. This returns you to the original Insert Object dialog box.

7 Click OK to close the Insert Object dialog box and insert the selected file into the PowerPoint presentation.

8 Click the Stop Recording button.

After recording the macro, view it. Naturally, your macro will include the path information for the workbook you embedded rather than C:\My Documents\Sales Data.xls. The values indicating height, width, etc. may also differ. However, the basic structure of your macro will be the same as the one shown below.

```
Sub InsertWorkbook()
'
' Macro recorded 11/4/96 by Christine Solomon
'

ActiveWindow.Selection.SlideRange.Shapes._
AddOLEObject(Left:=120, Top:=110, Width:=480,_
Height:=320, FileName:="C:\My Documents\Sales _
Data.xls", Link:=msoFalse).Select
    With ActiveWindow.Selection.ShapeRange
        .Left = 201.875
        .Top = 218.375
        .Width = 316.125
        .Height = 103.25
    End With
End Sub
```

Unfortunately, this macro is unnecessarily verbose. To cut it back to a more manageable size, delete the following code:

```
With ActiveWindow.Selection.ShapeRange
        .Left = 201.875
        .Top = 218.375
        .Width = 316.125
        .Height = 103.25
    End With
```

Your macro should now look (more or less) like the following:

```
Sub InsertWorkbook()
    '
    ' Macro recorded 11/4/96 by Christine Solomon
    '
    ActiveWindow.Selection.SlideRange.Shapes._
    AddOLEObject(Left:=120, Top:=110, Width:=480, _
    Height:=320, FileName:="C:\My Documents\Sales _
    Data.xls", Link:=msoFalse).Select
End Sub
```

The arguments Width and Height in the above code set the workbook's size (in points). To resize the workbook manually, select it, then choose Worksheet Object from the Edit menu and select Edit. Resize the embedded object by dragging its edges, then click anywhere *off* the object to stop editing it. To automatically display a greater portion of the embedded object when you insert it, increase the Height and Width values in the macro. Remember, however, that if you're running in VGA mode, the maximum width is 640 and the maximum height is 480.

If you move to another slide and run the macro you just recorded, it will insert the same Excel workbook into the *active slide*, which is referred to in code as the *ActiveWindow*. In some cases, the embedded workbook will appear misshapen. The following four lines of code—which you should insert immediately before the last line of code, End Sub—corrects this problem by scaling the object to 100% of its original size.

```
        With ActiveWindow.Selection.ShapeRange
             .ScaleHeight 1, msoCTrue
             .ScaleWidth 1, msoCTrue
        End With
```

Your macro should now look (more or less) like the following:

```
Sub InsertWorkbook()
    '
    ' Macro recorded 11/4/96 by Christine Solomon
    '
    ActiveWindow.Selection.SlideRange.Shapes._
    AddOLEObject(Left:=120, Top:=110, Width:=480, _
    Height:=320, FileName:="C:\My Documents\Sales _
    Data.xls", Link:=msoFalse).Select
        With ActiveWindow.Selection.ShapeRange
             .ScaleHeight 1, msoCTrue
             .ScaleWidth 1, msoCTrue
        End With
End Sub
```

To display an input box where users can type the path of the Excel workbook to embed, add the following lines of code at the top of the macro after the comments:

```
Dim WhichWorkbook as String
WhichWorkbook = InputBox(Prompt:="Type the full _
path of the Excel workbook to insert into this _
presentation.")
```

Locate the hard-coded path for the Excel workbook and replace it with the variable WhichWorkbook. The FileName argument should now be as follows:

```
FileName:=WhichWorkbook
```

Your macro should now look (more or less) like the following:

```
Sub InsertWorkbook()
'
' Macro recorded 9/28/96 by Christine Solomon for
Running PowerPoint
'
    Dim WhichWorkbook As String
    WhichWorkbook = InputBox(Prompt:="Type the _
    full path of the Excel workbook to insert _
    into this presentation.")
    ActiveWindow.Selection.SlideRange.Shapes._
    AddOLEObject(Left:=120, Top:=110, Width:=480, _
    Height:=320, FileName:=WhichWorkbook, _
    Link:=msoFalse).Select
    With ActiveWindow.Selection.ShapeRange
        .ScaleHeight 1, msoCTrue
        .ScaleWidth 1, msoCTrue
    End With
End Sub
```

Choose Close And Return To PowerPoint from the File menu.

Move to another slide and run the InsertWorkbook macro. This time it displays an input box where you can type the path of the Excel workbook to embed.

TIP

For more information on creating automated solutions with PowerPoint, see:
- The Help file that comes with the Visual Basic Editor
- *The Office Developer's Kit*, published by Microsoft Press
- *Developing Business Applications with Microsoft Office 97* by Christine Solomon, published by Microsoft Press

CHAPTER 20

Customizing PowerPoint

F ortunately, you have plenty of control over how PowerPoint works. You can customize the way PowerPoint looks, change the default choices it makes, and even circumvent some of the steps that it would otherwise have you follow in its quest to guide you through the process unharmed.

In this chapter, you'll learn how to customize PowerPoint from top to bottom, changing the defaults for everything from the blank presentation to the composition of the toolbars. Only when you've demonstrated your total domination over the program can you truly be considered a Power-Point master.

Creating a Default Presentation

When you select Blank Presentation from the PowerPoint dialog box or on the General tab of the New Presentation dialog box, PowerPoint loads a default presentation. You can replace the default presentation with a customized presentation so that the customized presentation appears when you select Blank Presentation.

You might want to change the default presentation when you've taken the time to customize a presentation with your corporate colors, a corporate standard background design, your corporate logo, and special text. You can then start each new presentation with your customized look already in place.

First you'll need to customize a presentation. Start a new presentation, or open an existing presentation, and then change any or all of the following elements, as needed:

- The template attached to the presentation

- Any graphic objects on the slide background, such as logos

- Special text on the slide background, such as the date, time, and slide number

- The color scheme

- The formatting of the slide master

- The Set Up Show dialog box options

> **NOTE**
>
> You only need to format the slide master of the presentation. Special formatting that you apply to particular slide layouts is not applied to the default presentation.

When you have finished customizing the presentation, save it as a PowerPoint Presentation Template with the name *Blank Presentation* in the Templates folder that holds the templates for all the Microsoft Office applications (the Templates subfolder of the MSOffice folder—unless you specified a different folder as you installed PowerPoint).

Instead of overwriting the default presentation that comes with PowerPoint, you should rename the Blank Presentation file—to Old Blank, for example— before creating a new Blank Presentation file. Then, you can always retrieve the original blank default presentation.

When you next select Blank Presentation on the General tab of the New Presentation dialog box, all the formatting of the sample presentation appears in the new presentation.

Adding Templates to the General Tab

To add presentations to the General tab of the New Presentation dialog box, simply place copies of the presentations in the Templates folder, which resides within the MSOffice folder. Do *not* place them in any of the folders that are within the Templates folder, though, such as Presentations Designs or Presentations, because then they will not appear on the General tab.

Changing the Start-Up Defaults

The basic operating defaults for PowerPoint are stored and set in the Options dialog box, available from the Tools menu (choose Options). The Options dialog box contains seven tabs, each of which is reviewed here.

The View Options

The options on the View tab, shown in Figure 20-1 on the next page, let you change what you see as you work in PowerPoint and what you see during Slide Shows, as follows:

- The Startup Dialog settings lets you skip the PowerPoint dialog box that appears whenever you start the program. When you opt to skip this dialog box, PowerPoint loads the default presentation and displays the New Slide dialog box, where you can select an autolayout whose placeholders you'll fill with text, charts, and graphics. When you skip the PowerPoint dialog box, you do not see the option to use the AutoContent Wizard to start a presentation, and you get whatever formatting is applied to the default presentation. But you can always use the AutoContent Wizard later by selecting it on the Presentations tab of the New Presentation dialog box. You can also select a template by choosing Apply Design from the Format menu or the Common Tasks toolbar. You might find it handy to skip the PowerPoint dialog box if you almost always use the same presentation design or when you have the presentation's content worked out, such as when you use PowerPoint to prepare presentations that vary only slightly.

- The New Slide Dialog setting lets you skip the New Slide dialog box that normally appears when you choose to add a new slide and jump right to a new Bulleted List autolayout. To select a different layout, you can always choose Slide Layout from the Format button or hold down the Shift key as you click the New Slide button. This might be the ideal setup if you frequently create presentations that consist of series of text slides. The first slide of a new presentation is a title slide, and successive slides are bulleted list slides, unless you choose otherwise when you add each slide.

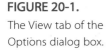

FIGURE 20-1.

The View tab of the Options dialog box.

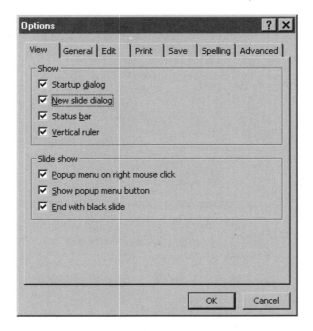

- The Status Bar and Vertical Ruler options turn on or off the Status bar along the bottom of the PowerPoint window and the vertical ruler along the left side of the screen. Deselecting the Vertical Ruler option lets you see more of the presentation window. If you've selected the Vertical Ruler option but still do not see the ruler, choose Ruler from the View menu.

- The Slide Show options let you show the popup menu during slide shows (Show Popup Menu button) and also, for convenience, click the right mouse button during a slide show to bring up the popup menu. The last option, End With Black Slide, adds a black screen to the end of a slide show to give you a graceful ending.

The General Options

The options on the General tab let you change how you interact with PowerPoint.

- The Provide Feedback With Sound To Screen Elements option on the General tab of the Options dialog box allows you to add sound to events that occur while you are working in PowerPoint, such as selecting menu options and closing dialog boxes. This option has nothing to do with the sounds you add to slide shows. To change the feedback sounds, use the Sounds option in the Windows Control Panel.

- The Recently Used File List setting determines the number of presentation names that appear on the File menu. You can choose up to nine entries; that is, nine presentations to which you can quickly return. Remember, another way to return to recent presentations is to select them from the Documents submenu that one of the options on the Windows Start menu.

- Macro Virus Protection is not as effective as it sounds. This option simply warns you when you are about to open a presentation containing macros, which in turn might contain viruses. It then gives you the option to not open the presentation to avoid possibly infecting your computer. Unfortunately, Macro Virus Protection doesn't really protect your computer from viruses.

VI

Advanced PowerPoint

- The Link Sounds With File Size Greater Than setting keeps the presentation file from becoming excessively large when you add sounds for slide shows. Sounds with file sizes over the size you designate with this option are linked to the presentation but stored in separate files. If you move the presentation to another computer, you also need to copy these files.

- User Information contains the name that will appear on comments you add to the presentation with the Insert Comment command.

The Edit Options

The options on the Edit tab let you change how text is handled.

- Replace Straight Quotes With Smart Quotes enters typographically correct quotation marks (opening and closing) when you type a passage of text enclosed in quotation marks.

- Automatic Word Selection selects the entire first and last words of a text passage even if you don't drag the mouse pointer across the beginning of the first word and the end of the last word.

- Use Smart Cut And Paste ensures that spaces are adjusted when you cut and paste text so that only one space appears before and after the text.

- Drag-And-Drop Text Editing lets you use your mouse to select text and then move and copy text by dragging it to a new location.

- New Charts Take On PowerPoint Font, in the Inserting section of the Edit tab, forces the fonts in charts that are inserted from another presentation to 18-point Arial. Clear this option to let the charts keep their existing font settings.

- Maximum Number Of Undos determines how many actions you can reverse. Clicking the Undo button on the Standard toolbar reverses your most recent action. (You can also choose Undo from the Edit menu or press Ctrl+Z.) To undo the action before that one, you can click the Undo button again, and so on. When you have clicked the Undo button the maximum number of times, PowerPoint will not reverse any more actions.

The Print Options

The settings on the Print tab of the Options dialog box let you change settings for printing presentations.

- If the Background Printing option is selected, you can continue to work on a presentation while another presentation is printing. Otherwise, the Print Status dialog box appears each time you print, tying up your computer until the printer has finished.

- Print TrueType Fonts As Graphics sends TrueType fonts to your printer as graphic images rather than downloading the actual font. Select this option to try to resolve the problem if you have found text missing from printed slides.

- Print Inserted Objects At Printer Resolution prints objects at the printer's resolution rather than the resolution you have selected for them to display in a slide show.

- The Options For Current Document Only determine the print settings that will be used if you click the Print button on the Standard toolbar or choose to print a presentation from the Microsoft Office Binder.

The Save Options

The settings on the Save tab of the Options dialog box change what happens when you save a presentation.

- Allow Fast Saves re-saves any changes to slides at the end of the existing file, rather than resaving the entire presentation. The result is faster saves, but larger file sizes. After you complete a presentation, you should deselect Allow Fast Saves and save the presentation again to reduce the size of the file on disk.

- Select the Prompt For File Properties option to force the Properties dialog box to appear whenever you save a presentation.

- Select the Full Text Search Information option to create a search index PowerPoint can use when you select Full Text Search from the File Open dialog box.

- The Save AutoRecover Info Every X Minutes saves an autorecover file on the disk at the interval you select in case your computer stops working or the power fails as you create a presentation. If disaster strikes, you will be prompted to recover the presentation the next time you start PowerPoint.

- Save PowerPoint Files As gives you the option to save the current presentation in a file that is compatible with an earlier version of PowerPoint. Use this option if you are in a workgroup that has computers with older versions of PowerPoint installed.

The Spelling Options

The settings on the Spelling tab of the Options dialog box affect PowerPoint's built-in spelling checker.

- Clearing the Spelling setting will keep PowerPoint from checking the spelling of text as you type it. With Hide Spelling Errors selected, PowerPoint still checks the spelling, but does not display the wavy red lines under text that indicate misspelled words.

- Always Suggest in the Spelling section determines whether the spelling checker suggests alternatives to a misspelled word. If you select this option, the spelling checker functions more slowly than if it simply has to point out spelling errors.

- The two Ignore options let you avoid checking the spelling of words that are in uppercase or that contain numbers.

The Advanced Options

The last tab in the Options dialog box provides three specialized options:

- Render 24-bit Bitmaps At Highest Quality controls the display quality of pictures. Turn this option on if you are using a high-quality video system in your computer.

- Export Pictures determines whether pictures are rendered to look their best when they are printed or when they are viewed on screen.

- Default File Location allows you to specify where files are stored by default when you save them. (You can override this default by specifying a different location in the File Save dialog box.)

Customizing the Default Chart Type and Datasheet Settings

When you start a graph, Microsoft Graph always chooses a default chart type, but you can modify this style to obtain a standard chart design more suited to your needs.

To modify the default chart type, follow these steps:

1 Load Graph by clicking the Insert Graph button on the Standard toolbar, choosing Microsoft Graph from the Insert menu, or by double-clicking a *Double click to add graph* placeholder.

2 From the Chart menu, choose Chart Type.

3 In the Chart Type dialog box, select a Chart Type and Chart Sub-Type.

4 Click the Set as Default Chart button.

5 Click OK.

The next time you start a chart, the revised chart type will plot the data in the datasheet.

VI

Advanced PowerPoint

To customize some of the default settings for working with charts, start Microsoft Graph and choose Options from the Tools menu.

The Datasheet Options tab of the Graph Options dialog box provides two options that you can use to control the datasheet. The first option, Move Selection After Enter, determines whether the cell pointer moves to the next cell of the datasheet after you press Enter or whether it remains in the current cell. The second option, Cell Drag And Drop, turns drag and drop on or off within the datasheet window.

On the Chart tab of the dialog box, you can also specify whether empty cells of the datasheet should be omitted from the graph or plotted as zero. When empty cells are omitted, gaps may occur in the graph. The Chart Tips options determine whether Graph displays the name of a chart element and the value of a marker when you pass the mouse pointer over it.

NOTE

The Color tab of the Graph Options dialog box displays the colors used to fill the markers (Chart Fills) and the colors used for the lines and outlines (Chart Lines) of the graph. These colors are set by the current color scheme. You can override the colors of a graph by formatting its markers and lines directly, so you should not need to modify the colors on the Color tab.

Setting the Drawing Defaults

To change the default fill color, line style, text style, shadow and other effects of objects you draw using PowerPoint's drawing tools, follow this procedure:

1 Draw an object and apply settings for the fill color, line style, text style, and other attributes.

2 Select the object.

3 Choose Set AutoShape Defaults from the Draw menu on the Drawing toolbar.

Now when you draw any object, the new default settings are applied.

Customizing Toolbars

As you've seen, PowerPoint's toolbars give you easy access to the most popular menu commands. But you may not find a toolbar button for every command you use frequently. Fortunately, you can customize the toolbars. You can add and remove buttons, move buttons from one toolbar to another, and create a custom toolbar with your favorite toolbar buttons.

Displaying a Toolbar

The easiest way to display a toolbar is to click any visible toolbar with the right mouse button. On the shortcut menu that appears, the toolbars accompanied by check marks are already displayed. To bring any other toolbar to the screen, click its name on the shortcut menu. Figure 20-2 shows the shortcut menu for toolbars. You can also choose Toolbars from the View menu to open the Toolbars submenu.

FIGURE 20-2.

The shortcut menu for toolbars.

Adding and Removing Buttons

To add a button to a toolbar, make sure the toolbar you want to customize is visible, and then click it with the right mouse button. From the shortcut menu, choose Customize. You can also choose Toolbars from the View menu, and click Customize in the Toolbars dialog box. Either way, the Customize dialog box appears.

VI

Advanced PowerPoint

FIGURE 20-3.

The Commands tab of the Customize dialog box.

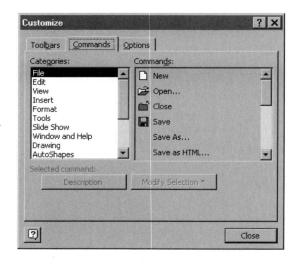

On the Commands tab of the Customize dialog box, shown above in Figure 20-3, you see a list of categories that corresponds to the PowerPoint menus and toolbars, and a set of buttons that represents the commands in the selected category. Simply select a category, and then drag the command you want to any toolbar. You can drag as many commands from as many categories as you want, and you can drop the buttons in exact positions on the toolbars. For a description of any command, click the Description button. When you're finished adding buttons, click Close to close the dialog box.

Removing a toolbar button is even easier. With the Customize dialog box open, simply drag the button off its toolbar. The button is always available in the Customize dialog box if you need it again.

You don't have to open the Customize dialog box to remove a button from a toolbar. Simply hold down the Alt key, and drag the button off its toolbar.

Moving Buttons
Within and Between Toolbars

If you don't like the order of buttons on a toolbar or if you want to move a button to another toolbar, you can drag buttons within toolbars and between toolbars. You can drag a button up two positions in a vertical toolbar, for example, or drag a button from one toolbar to another. You can even choose to display the Custom toolbar, which starts with no buttons, and then drag your favorite buttons to it.

To move a button from one toolbar to another, hold down the Alt key and drag the button. To copy a button from one toolbar to another, hold down both the Alt key and the Ctrl key as you drag the button. As always, a small plus sign appears next to the mouse pointer to indicate that you are copying rather than moving an object.

Creating a New Toolbar

To create a custom toolbar, first choose Customize from the toolbar's shortcut menu or choose Toolbars from the View menu, and then choose Customize from the submenu. Click New on the Toolbars tab of the Customize dialog box. When the New Toolbar dialog box appears, type a name in the Toolbar Name edit box, and click OK. A small, empty toolbar appears floating on your screen, as shown in Figure 20-4.

FIGURE 20-4.

The Custom toolbar floating on the Customize dialog box.

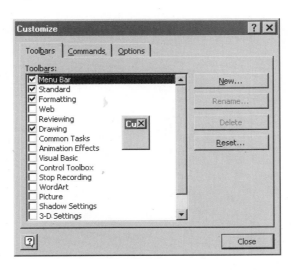

VI

Advanced PowerPoint

Now all you have to do is drag copies of your favorite buttons or commands from the toolbars displayed on your screen or from the Customize dialog box to the custom toolbar. Then you can reposition the toolbar by dragging it to one side of the PowerPoint window.

With that final bit of customization, you've done it. You've achieved the coveted status of PowerPoint guru. You're now ready to go out and present to the world!

Index

Colophon

The manuscript for this book was prepared in Microsoft Word 7.0 for Windows and submitted to Microsoft Press in electronic form. Pages were composed by Studioserv, using Adobe PageMaker 6.01 for Windows, Adobe Illustrator 4.1, and Adobe PhotoShop 3.05, with text type in Garamond and display type in Myriad Black. Composed pages were delivered to the printer as electronic prepress files.

Cover Art Direction
Gregory J. Erickson

Cover Illustration
Landor and Associates

Composition and Layout
Studioserv
www.studioserv.com

Cover Graphic Design
Tim Girvin Design

Interior Graphic Design
designLab
www.dzynlab.com

Get quick, easy answers— anywhere!

Microsoft® Excel 97 Field Guide
Stephen L. Nelson
U.S.A. $9.95   ($12.95 Canada)
ISBN: 1-57231-326-9

Microsoft® Word 97 Field Guide
Stephen L. Nelson
U.S.A. $9.95   ($12.95 Canada)
ISBN: 1-57231-325-0

Microsoft® PowerPoint® 97 Field Guide
Stephen L. Nelson
U.S.A. $9.95   ($12.95 Canada)
ISBN: 1-57231-327-7

Microsoft® Outlook™ 97 Field Guide
Stephen L. Nelson
U.S.A. $9.99   ($12.99 Canada)
ISBN: 1-57231-383-8

Microsoft® Access 97 Field Guide
Stephen L. Nelson
U.S.A. $9.95   ($12.95 Canada)
ISBN: 1-57231-328-5

Microsoft Press® Field Guides are a quick, accurate source of information about Microsoft® Office 97 applications. In no time, you'll have the lay of the land, identify toolbar buttons and commands, stay safely out of danger, and have all the tools you need for survival!

Microsoft Press® products are available worldwide wherever quality computer books are sold. For more information, contact your book retailer, computer reseller, or local Microsoft Sales Office.

To locate your nearest source for Microsoft Press products, reach us at www.microsoft.com/mspress/, or call 1-800-MSPRESS in the U.S. (in Canada: 1-800-667-1115 or 416-293-8464).

To order Microsoft Press products, call 1-800-MSPRESS in the U.S. (in Canada: 1-800-667-1115 or 416-293-8464).

Prices and availability dates are subject to change.

Microsoft Press

Keep things **running** smoothly around the **Office.**

These are *the* answer books for business users of Microsoft® Office 97 applications. They are packed with everything from quick, clear instructions for new users to comprehensive answers for power users. The Microsoft Press® *Running* series features authoritative handbooks you'll keep by your computer and use every day.

Running Microsoft® Excel 97
Mark Dodge, Chris Kinata, and Craig Stinson
U.S.A. $39.95   ($53.95 Canada)
ISBN 1-57231-321-8

Running Microsoft® Office 97
Michael Halvorson and Michael Young
U.S.A. $39.95   ($53.95 Canada)
ISBN 1-57231-322-6

Running Microsoft® Word 97
Russell Borland
U.S.A. $39.95   ($53.95 Canada)
ISBN 1-57231-320-X

Running Microsoft® PowerPoint® 97
Stephen W. Sagman
U.S.A. $29.95   ($39.95 Canada)
ISBN 1-57231-324-2

Running Microsoft® Access 97
John L. Viescas
U.S.A. $39.95   ($53.95 Canada)
ISBN 1-57231-323-4

Microsoft Press® products are available worldwide wherever quality computer books are sold. For more information, contact your book retailer, computer reseller, or local Microsoft Sales Office.

To locate your nearest source for Microsoft Press products, reach us at www.microsoft.com/mspress/, or call 1-800-MSPRESS in the U.S. (in Canada: 1-800-667-1115 or 416-293-8464).

To order Microsoft Press products, call 1-800-MSPRESS in the U.S. (in Canada: 1-800-667-1115 or 416-293-8464).

Prices and availability dates are subject to change.

Microsoft *Press*

Take productivity in **stride.**

Microsoft Press® *Step by Step* books provide quick and easy self-paced training that will help you learn to use the powerful word processor, spreadsheet, database, desktop information manager and presentation applications of Microsoft Office 97, both individually and together. Prepared by the professional trainers at Catapult, Inc., and Perspection, Inc., these books present easy-to-follow lessons with clear objectives, real-world business examples, and numerous screen shots and illustrations. Each book contains approximately eight hours of instruction. Put Microsoft's Office 97 applications to work today, *Step by Step*.

Microsoft® Excel 97 Step by Step
U.S.A. $29.95 ($39.95 Canada)
ISBN 1-57231-314-5

Microsoft® Word 97 Step by Step
U.S.A. $29.95 ($39.95 Canada)
ISBN 1-57231-313-7

Microsoft® PowerPoint® 97
Step by Step
U.S.A. $29.95 ($39.95 Canada)
ISBN 1-57231-315-3

Microsoft® Outlook™ 97 Step by Step
U.S.A. $29.99 ($39.99 Canada)
ISBN 1-57231-382-X

Microsoft® Access 97 Step by Step
U.S.A. $29.95 ($39.95 Canada)
ISBN 1-57231-316-1

Microsoft® Office 97 Integration
Step by Step
U.S.A. $29.95 ($39.95 Canada)
ISBN 1-57231-317-X

Microsoft Press® products are available worldwide wherever quality computer books are sold. For more information, contact your book retailer, computer reseller, or local Microsoft Sales Office.

To locate your nearest source for Microsoft Press products, reach us at www.microsoft.com/mspress/, or call 1-800-MSPRESS in the U.S. (in Canada: 1-800-667-1115 or 416-293-8464).

To order Microsoft Press products, call 1-800-MSPRESS in the U.S. (in Canada: 1-800-667-1115 or 416-293-8464).

Prices and availability dates are subject to change.

Microsoft® *Press*

About the CD-ROM

Bound into the back of this book is the companion CD-ROM for this book, containing *Running Microsoft PowerPoint 97 Online,* an HTML (Web format) version of this book.

Although you can use most Web browsers to view the online version, installing the included version of Internet Explorer 3.0 gives you access to additional features you can use on the Internet, such as NetMeeting, Comic Chat, Microsoft Internet Mail & News, and ActiveMovie.

To install Internet Explorer from the CD, choose Run from the Start menu, and in the Run dialog box, type *d:\IE30\setup.exe* (where *d* is the drive letter of your CD-ROM.) Then follow the onscreen instructions.

Although you do *not* have to be connected to the Internet to use the files on the CD, the Internet Connection Wizard, which appears the first time you start Internet Explorer, can help you set up a new account with an Internet service provider, or establish a connection to your current service provider.

Viewing the Online Version of the Book

To view the home page of *Running Microsoft PowerPoint 97 Online,* select Run from the Start menu and enter *d:\contents.htm* in the Run dialog box (where *d* is the drive letter of your CD-ROM drive).

Additional Information

The CD's home page offers access to the Microsoft Knowledge Base, the Microsoft Press home page, the author's home page, and an email link to the author.

If you have comments, questions, or ideas regarding this book or the companion disc, please write to Microsoft Press at the following address:

Microsoft Press
Attn: Running Series Editor
One Microsoft Way
Redmond, WA 98052-6399

You can also send feedback to Microsoft Press via electronic mail at mspinput@microsoft.com. Please note that product support is not offered through this e-mail address.

Managing a Slide Show

Using the Keyboard

N, ENTER, SPACEBAR	Next Slide
P, BACKSPACE	Previous Slide
<Number>+ENTER	Go to slide <number>
S	Stop/restart automatic show
Esc	End show
H	Advance to hidden slide
Ctrl+P	Change pointer to pen
Ctrl+A or Esc	Change pen to pointer
Ctrl+H	Hide pointer and button temporarily
Ctrl+L	Hide pointer and button always
Shift+F10	Display the shortcut menu
B	Display a black screen, or return to the slide show from a black screen
W	Display a white screen, or return to the slide show from a white screen
E	Erase on-screen annotations
Shift+F10	Shortcut menu

Using the Mouse

Click	Next Slide
Press both mouse buttons for 2 seconds	First Slide
Right-click	Shortcut menu
Move the mouse pointer	Pop-up menu button
Click the pop-up menu button	Pop-up menu

Rehearsing

T	Set new timings
O	Use original timings
M	Use mouse click to advance

Running Microsoft PowerPoint 97 quick reference card

Quick Procedures	
To Do These Common Things:	**_Do This:_**
Open a new presentation	Click ▯.
Create a new slide	Click ▮, and choose an autolayout.
Change a slide layout	Click ▮, and choose a new autolayout.
Change the design template	Click ▮, and choose a presentation design.
View the slides in black and white	Click ◪.
Change to Slide View	Click ▯.
Change to Outline View	Click ▤.
Change to Slide Sorter View	Click ▦.
Change to Notes Page View	Click ▣.
Run a slide show	Click ▼.
Change the color scheme	From the Format menu, choose Slide Color Scheme, and select a standard or custom color scheme.
Change the background	From the Format menu, choose Background, and then select a background.
Edit the Title Master	Show the Title slide, press SHIFT, and click ▯.
Edit the Slide Master	Show any slide other than a title slide, press SHIFT, and click ▯.

Quick Procedures

To Do These Common Things:	Do This:
Edit the Notes Page Master	Press SHIFT, and click 💻.
Edit the Handout Master	Press SHIFT, and click 🔲.
Finish editing the Title or Slide Master	Click 🔲.
Finish editing other Masters	Click any View button.
Insert a HyperLink	Click to place an insertion point in a text block, and click 🌐.
Add a Picture, Sound, or Movie Clip	Click 🖼, and choose a clip from the Clip Gallery.
Draw an object	Click an object on the Drawing toolbar, and then drag across the slide.
Animate a Slide	Click 🌟, and select options on the Animation Effects toolbar.
Display/remove the Web toolbar	Click 🌐.
Insert a Microsoft Word table	Click 📋, and drag out the table size.
Insert a Microsoft Excel worksheet	Click 📊, and drag out a spreadsheet size.
Add a Chart to an existing slide	Click 📊.
Get Help from the Office Assistant	Click ❓.

Running Microsoft PowerPoint 97 quick reference card

Keyboard Shortcuts

To Create and Edit Presentations

CTRL+N	Open a new presentation
CTRL+O	Open an existing presentation
CTRL+W or CTRL+F4	Close a presentation
CTRL+S or SHIFT+F12	Save a presentation
CTRL+P or CTRL+SHIFT+F12	Print a presentation
CTRL+F	Find a word or a phrase
CTRL+M	Create a new slide
F7	Check spelling
F1	Display help topics
CTRL+Q or ALT+F4	Exit/Quit

To Move Around

LEFT ARROW	One character left
RIGHT ARROW	One character right
UP ARROW	One line up
DOWN ARROW	One line down
END	End of line
HOME	Beginning of line
CTRL+SHIFT+F6	To previous presentation window
CTRL+F6 or CTRL+TAB	To next presentation window

To Select Text and Objects

Select a word	Double-click the word
Select a paragraph	Triple-click within the paragraph
Select all	CTRL+A

To Delete and Copy

CTRL+X	Cut
CTRL+C	Copy
CTRL+V	Paste
CTRL+select	Drag and drop a copy
CTRL+Z	Undo
BACKSPACE	Delete character to the left
DELETE	Delete character to the right

To Work in an Outline

ALT+SHIFT+LEFT ARROW	Promote paragraph
ALT+SHIFT+RIGHT ARROW	Demote paragraph
ALT+SHIFT+UP ARROW	Move selected paragraphs up
ALT+SHIFT+DOWN ARROW	Move selected paragraphs down
ALT+SHIFT+PLUS	Expand text under a heading
ALT+SHIFT+MINUS	Collapse text under a heading
ALT+SHIFT+A	Show all text and headings

Register Today!

Return this
Running Microsoft® PowerPoint® 97
registration card for
a Microsoft Press® catalog

U.S. and Canada addresses only. Fill in information below and mail postage-free. Please mail only the bottom half of this page.

1-57231-324-2A   *RUNNING MICROSOFT® POWERPOINT® 97*   *Owner Registration Card*

_____

NAME

_____

INSTITUTION OR COMPANY NAME

_____

ADDRESS

_____

CITY   STATE   ZIP

Microsoft®Press
Quality Computer Books

**For a free catalog of
Microsoft Press® products, call
1-800-MSPRESS**